JESUS AND THE DEAD SEA SCROLLS

THE ANCHOR BIBLE REFERENCE LIBRARY is designed to be a third major component of the Anchor Bible group, which includes the Anchor Bible commentaries on the books of the Old Testament, the New Testament, and the Apocrypha, and the Anchor Bible Dictionary. While the Anchor Bible commentaries and the Anchor Bible Dictionary are structurally defined by their subject matter, the Anchor Bible Reference Library will serve as a supplement on the cutting edge of the most recent scholarship. The series is open-ended; its scope and reach are nothing less than the biblical world in its totality, and its methods and techniques the most up-to-date available or devisable. Separate volumes will deal with one or more of the following topics relating to the Bible: anthropology, archaeology, ecology, economy, geography, history, languages and literatures, philosophy, religion(s), theology.

As with the Anchor Bible commentaries and the Anchor Bible Dictionary, the philosophy underlying the Anchor Bible Reference Library finds expression in the following: the approach is scholarly, the perspective is balanced and fair-minded, the methods are scientific, and the goal is to inform and enlighten. Contributors are chosen on the basis of their scholarly skills and achievements, and they come from a variety of religious backgrounds and communities. The books in the Anchor Bible Reference Library are intended for the broadest possible readership, ranging from world-class scholars, whose qualifications match those of the authors, to general readers, who may not have special training or skill in studying the Bible but are as enthusiastic as any dedicated professional in expanding their knowledge of the Bible and its world.

David Noel Freedman
GENERAL EDITOR

THE ANCHOR BIBLE REFERENCE LIBRARY

Jesus and the
Dead Sea Scrolls

JAMES H. CHARLESWORTH

WITH INTERNATIONALLY
RENOWNED EXPERTS

ABRL

Doubleday

NEW YORK LONDON TORONTO SYDNEY AUCKLAND

THE ANCHOR BIBLE REFERENCE LIBRARY
PUBLISHED BY DOUBLEDAY
a division of Bantam Doubleday Dell Publishing Group, Inc.
1540 Broadway, New York, New York 10036

THE ANCHOR BIBLE REFERENCE LIBRARY, DOUBLEDAY, and the portrayal
of an anchor with the letters ABRL are trademarks of Doubleday,
a division of Bantam Doubleday Dell Publishing Group, Inc.

Book design by Patrice Fodero

The Library of Congress has cataloged the
Anchor Bible Reference Library hardcover edition as follows:
Charlesworth, James H.
Jesus and the Dead Sea Scrolls/James H. Charlesworth,
with internationally renowned experts.—1st ed.
p.   cm.—(The Anchor Bible reference library)
Includes bibliographical references and index.
1. Jesus Christ—Person and offices.   2. Dead Sea Scrolls—
Criticism, interpretation, etc.   I. Title.   II. Series.
BT205.C43   1992
232—dc20   92-2617
                                       CIP
ISBN 0-385-47844-5

DEDICATED TO MY MENTORS
IN QUMRAN RESEARCH

Pierre Benoit
Frank Moore Cross
David Noel Freedman
James A. Sanders
John Strugnell
Shemaryahu Talmon
Roland de Vaux

Contents

List of Maps
and Diagrams

List of Illustrations

Preface

Jesus of Nazareth and his own time are fascinating topics for many readers. The attempt to understand Jesus' place in history often excites many who usually brand such preoccupations as trivial pursuits. "Jesus and the Authors of the Dead Sea Scrolls" is uniquely entrancing; it wins attentive listeners who often seem somewhat mystified.

When Qumran experts present a lecture on "Jesus and the Dead Sea Scrolls,"[1] unusual numbers, representing a wide cultural span, attend and sit for an extended period somewhat mesmerized. For example, when I offer lectures on Christian Origins at universities in the United States or abroad the attendance may not exceed twenty devoted listeners. When the lecture is entitled "Jesus and His Place in History" about sixty may attend. But when the subject becomes "Jesus and the Dead Sea Scrolls," so many attend that the ones in charge frequently run into trouble with fire marshals.

A team of journalists in *Newsweek* (July 1, 1991) spoke about a recent macabre stimulus to many readers in the Western world. Buzzing within and popping to the surface of conversations heard in restaurants, and everywhere the public gathered, were questions about the twelfth president of the United States, Zachary Taylor. Strangers swapped opinions on whether he was poisoned with arsenic. The journalists captured the engagement with these words: "The lesson of last week was that there is nothing so irresistible as a mystery and few objects so compelling as a lead box sealed shut during the last century" (p. 64). Reading these words I thought, almost spontaneously: nothing has proved to be so irresistible as the mystery of the Dead Sea Scrolls and so compelling as desert caves concealed for the last twenty centuries.

Why are so many interested in such a limited subject? Is it because of the fascination with the unknown and the fear that some precious dimensions of Judaism and Christianity have been hidden from the public? Or is it the romantic lure of an ancient land, its lunaresque desert, and mysterious caves?

The purpose of this book is to share with all who are interested some groundbreaking discoveries. Virtually every scholar admits now that the recovery of leather and papyrus scrolls from caves west of the Dead Sea is the most momentous archaeological discovery of the twentieth century. According to the leading experts, and (of course) the specialists who have written the following chapters, these writings have revolutionized our understanding of Jesus' time, and—to a significant degree—of Jesus himself.

Specialists on the Dead Sea Scrolls are not embroiled in controversy and crises. Yet many readers of the *Jerusalem Post Magazine, Time,* the *New York Times,* the *Washington Post,* the Australian *Daily Telegraph,* and other similar publications have received the impression that something precious, perhaps something damaging to faith, is being concealed from them. The foreword in this book, however, discloses the broad consensus shared by specialists around the world.

Jesus and the Dead Sea Scrolls contains a cornucopia of fruitful research by specialists from Canada, England, Germany, Israel, Italy, and the United States. These international experts share some important insights on how the Dead Sea Scrolls open new opportunities for understanding Jesus in his own time. The scholars are Roman Catholic (Sacchi), Jewish (Flusser, Segal), and Protestant (Betz, Charlesworth, Dunn, Evans, Kee, Lichtenberger, Riesner), or transcend the customary categories (Smith, Zias). The book does not reflect a parochial bias. All successfully avoid distorting prejudices. The horn lost in a fight with Hercules has been filled with fruits that will challenge many for decades.

In preparing this work I became impressed with the quantity of publications on Jesus and the Dead Sea Scrolls. From virtually every developed country scholars have made significant contributions. Their dedication and the advance in scholarship permit the intriguing explorations carried out in the following pages; sometimes the discoveries are startling.

Chapter 1 supplies notes that provide the reader with some indication of the vast territory already covered by research experts. The "Selected Bibliography" is a guide to the most authoritative publications over the last forty years.

All areas have been explored and some deep explorations have resulted in geysers of new perspectives. Historical research is tedious, but it is the only way to clean windows that have become opaque over two thousand years.

At the end of T. S. Eliot's renowned *Waste Land,* an erudite reflection on what life is all about, a thunderous echo is heard: "*Datta. Dayadhvam. Damyata.*" From the following studies of Qumran fragments much is shored against acquiescing with skepticism that nothing can really be known about the historical Jesus. Three strains ring throughout the following pages: (1) The figure of Jesus begins to emerge out of the shadows of history. (2) The Dead Sea Scrolls are clarifying not only Jesus' time but also his own life and teachings. (3) Jesus' sayings, which have been misunderstood, ring forth with new dimensions of vitality.

I wish to thank each of the contributors for devoting impressive energy, skill, and time to this collection. I apologize to each for the inordinate delay in completing my responsibilities. The final product seems to justify the extra labor and time in attempting to publish a classic in the field.

Deep appreciations are extended to my assistants David Freedholm and Jerry Gorham. My research assistant, Loren Stuckenbruck, deserves my special thanks. He worked on this book with me for over ten months, the last three of which were full-time. I would also like to thank Michael Davis and Loren Johns for help with final proofing and indexing.

As usual, Noel Freedman has served as editor par excellence; he deserves the admiration and appreciation of the two generations who have already benefited from the Anchor Bible, and the Anchor Bible Reference Library. Future generations will praise him for these, his own original publications and the Anchor Bible Dictionary. I am honored we call each other friends.

The Foundation on Christian Origins and especially Princeton Theological Seminary have helped support this research. To each I am grateful. Once again, I am pleased to be associated with Doubleday and its distinguished list of books.

James H. Charlesworth
Princeton, New Jersey
June 1991

Notes

1. Qumran is the name of the site in which the Dead Sea Scrolls were probably copied or composed. Qumran Scrolls is synonymous with Dead Sea Scrolls, the popular name for the writings found in eleven caves west of the Dead Sea.

Abbreviations

Modern Publications

AB	Anchor Bible
ABR	*Australian Biblical Review*
ABRL	Anchor Bible Reference Library. New York, 1988–
AGAJU	Arbeiten zur Geschichte des antiken Judentums und des Urchristentums
AJBA	*Australian Journal of Biblical Archaeology*
ANRW	Haase, W., and H. Temporini (eds.), *Aufstieg und Niedergang der römischen Welt.* Berlin, New York, 1979–
ASOR	American Schools of Oriental Research
BA	*The Biblical Archaeologist*
BAGD	Bauer, W., and W. Arndt. *A Greek-English Lexicon of the New Testament and Other Early Christian Literature*, rev. F. W. Gingrich and F. W. Danker. Chicago, 1979².
BAR	*Biblical Archaeology Review*
BASOR	*Bulletin of the American Schools of Oriental Research*
BETL	*Bibliotheca Ephemeridum Theologicarum Louvaniensium.* Paris/Gembloux
BFChTh	Beiträge zur Förderung christlicher Theologie

Bib	*Biblica*
BibRev	*Bible Review*
BibToday	*The Bible Today*
BK	*Bibel und Kirche*
BJS	Brown Judaic Studies
BJRL	*Bulletin of the John Rylands Library*
BR	*Biblical Research*
BTAVO	Beihefte zum Tübinger Atlas des Vorderen Orients
BZ	*Biblische Zeitschrift*
CBQ	*Catholic Biblical Quarterly*
CEv	*Cahiers Évangile*
CNfI	*Christian News from Israel*
CRHPhR	Cahiers de la Revue d'histoire et de philosophie religieuses
CRINT	Compendia Rerum Iudaicarum ad Novum Testamentum
CSCO	Corpus scriptorum christianorum orientalium
CTM	*Concordia Theological Monthly*
*DB*Supp	Pirot, L., et al. (eds.), *Dictionnaire de la Bible, Suppléments.* Paris, 1928–
DJD	Discoveries in the Judaean Desert. Oxford, 1955–
EA	*Erbe und Auftrag*
EJ	*Encyclopaedia Judaica*, Berlin
EKK	Evangelisch-katholischer Kommentar zum Neuen Testament
EThL	*Ephemerides theologicae Louvanienses*
ETR	*Études théologiques et religieuses*
EUNSA	Ediciones Universitad da Navarra
EvQ	*Evangelical Quarterly*
EWbNT	H. Baltz and G. Schneider (eds.), *Exegetisches Wörterbuch zum Neuen Testament*
ExpT	*Expository Times*
FRLANT	Forschungen zur Religion und Literatur des Alten und Neuen Testaments
FZB	Forschungen zur Bibel
GCS	Die griechischen christlichen Schriftsteller der ersten drei Jahrhunderte
HlL	*Das Heilige Land*, Cologne
HSM	Harvard Semitic Monographs
HSS	Harvard Semitic Studies
HThK	Herders theologischer Kommentar zum Neuen Testament
HTR	*Harvard Theological Review*
HUCA	*Hebrew Union College Annual*
IEJ	*Israel Exploration Journal*
IJT	*Indian Journal of Theology*

IRT	*Issues in Religion and Theology*
JBL	*Journal of Biblical Literature*
JE	Singer, I., et al. (eds.), *The Jewish Encyclopedia*. 12 vols. New York, London, 1901–6.
JETS	*Journal of the Evangelical Theological Society*
JJS	*Journal of Jewish Studies*
JQR	*Jewish Quarterly Review*
JSJ	*Journal for the Study of Judaism*
JSNTSS	*Journal for the Study of the New Testament:* Supplement Series
JSOT	*Journal for the Study of the Old Testament*
JSOTSS	*Journal for the Study of the Old Testament:* Supplement Series
JSP	*Journal for the Study of the Pseudepigrapha*
JSPSS	*Journal for the Study of the Pseudepigrapha:* Supplement Series
JSS	*Journal of Semitic Studies*
JTS	*Journal of Theological Studies*
KlT	Kleine Texte für (theologische und philologische) Vorlesungen und Übungen
LCL	Loeb Classical Library
LD	*Lectio Divina*
LuthMonat	*Lutherische Monatshefte*
MHUC	Monographs of the Hebrew Union College
NEB	New English Bible
Neot	*Neotestamentica*
NIGTC	The New International Greek Theological Commentary
NJBC	*The New Jerome Biblical Commentary.* R. Brown, J. A. Fitzmyer, R. E. Murphy (eds.). Englewood Cliffs, 1990.
NKZ	*Neue Kirchliche Zeitschrift*
NovT	*Novum Testamentum*
NovTSup	*Novum Testamentum:* Supplements
NRSV	New Revised Standard Version
NTS	*New Testament Studies*
OTP	J. H. Charlesworth (ed.), *The Old Testament Pseudepigrapha* 2 vols. (Garden City, 1983)
PEFQS	*Palestine Exploration Fund: Quarterly Statement*
PG	Patrologiae cursus completus, accurante J. P. Minge: Series Graeca
PGM	Preisendanz, K., and A. Henrichs (eds.), *Papyri Graecae Magicae*. 2 vols. Stuttgart, 1973–74.
PS	Patrologia Syriaca
PSB	*Princeton Seminary Bulletin*
RB	*Revue biblique*
RE	*Realencyklopädie für protestantische Theologie und Kirche*
RelLife	*Religion in Life*

RHR	*Revue de l'histoire des religions*
RivB	*Rivista biblica*
RQ	*Revue de Qumran*
RScRel	*Revue des Sciences Religieuses*
RSR	*Recherches de science religieuse*
RThL	*Revue théologique de Louvain*
SANT	Studien zum Alten und Neuen Testament
SAOC	Studies in Ancient Oriental Civilizations
SBEC	Studies in Bible and Early Christianity
SBFA	Studii in biblici Franciscani analecta
SBF.CMa	Studium biblicum Franciscanum: Collectio major
SBF.CMi	Studium biblicum Franciscanum: Collectio minor
SBFLA	Studii biblici franciscani liber annuus
SBLDS	Society of Biblical Literature Dissertation Series
SBLMS	Society of Biblical Literature Monograph Series
SBLSBS	Society of Biblical Literature Sources for Biblical Study
SBS	Stuttgarter Bibelstudien
SBT	Studies in Biblical Theology
SC	Sources chrétiennes
ScEs	*Science et esprit*
ScrT	*Scripta Theologica*
SCS	*Septuagint and Cognate Studies*
SHR	*Studies in History of Religions*
SJLA	*Studies in Judaism in Late Antiquity*
SJT	*Scottish Journal of Theology*
SNTS	Studiorum Novi Testamenti Societas
SNTU	*Studien zum NT und seiner Umwelt*
SPB	Studia patristica et Byzantina
SSN	Studia Semitica Neerlandica
SSTDJ	Studies on the Texts of the Desert of Judah
ST	*Studia Theologica*
SUNT	Studien zur Umwelt des Neuen Testaments
SuppNT	Supplements to Novum Testamentum
SWJTh	*Southwestern Journal of Theology*
TD	*Textus et documenta*
TDNT	Kittel, G. (ed.), *Theological Dictionary of the New Testament*. 10 vols., trans. G. W. Bromiley. Grand Rapids, Mich., London, 1964–76.
ThBeitr	*Theologische Beiträge*
ThD	*Theology Digest*
ThGl	*Theologie und Glaube*
ThR	*Theologische Rundschau*

ThWNT	*Theologische Wörterbuch zum Neuen Testament*
ThZ	*Theologische Zeitschrift*
TLG	Berkowitz, Luci. *Thesaurus Linguae Graecae.* New York, 1986².
TQ	*Theologische Quartalschrift*
TS	*Theological Studies*
TU	Texte und Untersuchungen
TynBul	*Tyndale Bulletin*
VC	*Vigiliae christianae*
VT	*Vetus Testamentum*
VT Supp	*Vetus Testamentum:* Supplements
WUNT	Wissenschaftliche Untersuchungen zum Neuen Testament
ZDPV	*Zeitschrift des deutschen Palästina-Vereins*
ZNW	*Zeitschrift für die neutestamentliche Wissenschaft und die Kunde der älteren Kirche*
ZTK	*Zeitschrift für Theologie und Kirche*

ANCIENT DOCUMENTS

Bible and Apocrypha

Gen	Genesis	Prov	Proverbs
Ex	Exodus	Eccl (Qoh)	Ecclesiastes
Lev	Leviticus	Song	Song of Songs
Num	Numbers	Isa	Isaiah
Deut	Deuteronomy	Jer	Jeremiah
Josh	Joshua	Lam	Lamentations
Judg	Judges	Ezek	Ezekiel
Ruth	Ruth	Dan	Daniel
1Sam	1 Samuel	Hos	Hosea
2Sam	2 Samuel	Joel	Joel
1Kgs	1 Kings	Amos	Amos
2Kgs	2 Kings	Obad	Obadiah
1Chr	1 Chronicles	Jonah	Jonah
2Chr	2 Chronicles	Micah	Micah
Ezra	Ezra	Nah	Nahum
Neh	Nehemiah	Hab	Habakkuk
Esth	Esther	Zeph	Zephaniah
Job	Job	Hag	Haggai
Ps(s)	Psalms	Zech	Zechariah

Mal	Malachi	2Cor	2 Corinthians
2Ezra	2 Ezra	Gal	Galatians
Tob	Tobit	Eph	Ephesians
Jdt	Judith	Phil	Philippians
AddEsth	Additions to Esther	Col	Colossians
WisSol	Wisdom of Solomon	1Thes	1 Thessalonians
Sir	Sirach	2Thes	2 Thessalonians
1Bar	1 Baruch	1Tim	1 Timothy
LetJer	Letter of Jeremiah	2Tim	2 Timothy
PrAzar	Prayer of Azariah	Tit	Titus
Sus	Susanna	Phlm	Philemon
Bel	Bel and the Dragon	Heb	Hebrews
1Mac	1 Maccabees	Jas	James
2Mac	2 Maccabees	1Pet	1 Peter
Mt	Matthew	2Pet	2 Peter
Mk	Mark	1Jn	1 John
Lk	Luke	2Jn	2 John
Jn	John	3Jn	3 John
Acts	Acts	Jude	Jude
Rom	Romans	Rev	Revelation
1Cor	1 Corinthians		

Pseudepigrapha

ApAb	Apocalypse of Abraham
TAb	Testament of Abraham
ApAdam	Apocalypse of Adam
LAE	Life of Adam and Eve
LetAris	Letter of Aristeas
2Bar	2 (Syriac Apocalypse of) Baruch
3Bar	3 (Greek Apocalypse of) Baruch
4Bar	4 Baruch
1En	1 (Ethiopic Apocalypse of) Enoch
2En	2 (Slavonic Apocalypse of) Enoch
3En	3 (Hebrew Apocalypse of) Enoch
ApocEzek	Apocryphon of Ezekiel
EzekTrag	Ezekiel the Tragedian
4Ezra	4 Ezra
AscenIs	Ascension of Isaiah
MarIs	Martyrdom of Isaiah
LadJac	Ladder of Jacob

TJob	Testament of Job
JosAsen	Joseph and Aseneth
PrMan	Prayer of Manasseh
SyrMen	Syriac Menander
AsMos	Assumption of Moses
TMos	Testament of Moses
Ps-Philo	Pseudo-Philo
LivPro	Lives of the Prophets
HistRech	History of the Rechabites
SibOr	Sibylline Oracles
OdesSol	Odes of Solomon
PssSol	Psalms of Solomon
T12P	Testaments of the Twelve Patriarchs
TLevi	Testament of Levi
TDan	Testament of Dan
TNaph	Testament of Naphtali
ApZeph	Apocalypse of Zephaniah

Other Writings

Dead Sea Scrolls

CD	The Damascus Document
MasShirShabb	Angelic Liturgy
1Q20	Genesis Apocryphon
1QapGen	Genesis Apocryphon
1QIs^a	Large Isaiah Scroll
1QMyst=1Q27	Book of the Mysteries
1QpHab	Habakkuk Pesher
1QH	The Thanksgiving Hymns
1QJN ar=1Q32	The New Jerusalem
1QM	War Scroll
1QS	Rule of the Community
1Q28a=1QSa	Rule of the Congregation
1Q28b=1QSb	Collection of Blessings
3Q15	The Copper Scroll
4Q180=4QAgesCreat	Ages of Creation
4Q83 Mish Ba	Psalms. Unpublished Fragment
4Q181	The Wicked and Holy
4Q186=4QCryptic	Horoscopes
4Q266	Damascus Document Fragment a
4Q268	Damascus Document Fragment c

4Q272	Damascus Document Fragment g
4Q380–381	Qumran Pseudepigraphic Psalm
4Q394–399=4QMMT	Some of the Precepts of the Torah
4Q375	Moses Apocryphon
4Q376	Liturgy of 3 Tongues of Fire
4Q400–407=4QShirShabb	Angelic Liturgy
4Q502	So-Called Marriage Ritual
4Q503	Daily Prayers
4Q504–506=pap4QPrLit	Psalms
4Q512	Purification Ritual
4Q513–514	Rules
4QpIsa^{a-e}=4Q161–165	Isaiah Pesher 1
4QCD^b	Damascus Document Fragment b
4QpNah=4Q169	Nahum Pesher
4QpPs^a=4Q171–4QPs37	Psalm Pesher 2
4QpsDan	Pseudo-Daniel
4QFlor=4Q174	Florilegium
4Q491–4Q496	War Scroll
4QPBless=4QpGen49	Patriarchal Blessings
4QTestim=4Q175	Testimonies
4QTob	Tobit. Unpublished Fragment
5Q13=4QRègle	A Sectarian Rule
11QMelch	Melchizedek
11QShirShabb	Angelic Liturgy
11QtgJob	Targum on Job
11QTemple	Temple Scroll

Josephus

Ant	*Jewish Antiquities*
Apion	*Against Apion*
Life	*Life of Josephus*
War	*Jewish Wars*

New Testament Apocrypha and Pseudepigrapha

EBar	Epistle of Barnabas
1Clem	1 Clement
2Clem	2 Clement
Did	Didache
ActsJn	Acts of John
GThom	Gospel of Thomas

Early Fathers

AdvHaer	Epiphanius, *Adversus haereses*
AposCon	Apostolic Constitutions
DialTrypho	Justin, *Dialogue with Trypho*
HE	Eusebius, *Historia ecclesiastica*
Philoc	Origen, *Philocalia*
PrEv	Eusebius, *Praeparatio evangelica*
Ref	Hippolytus, *Refutation of All Heresies*
Strom	Clement of Alexandria, *Stromata*

Rabbinics

Ab	Abot
ARN	Abot de-Rabbi Nathan
b. (before a rabbinic text)	Babylonian Talmud
Ber	Berakot
BMes	Baba Meṣi'a (Talmudic tractate)
Dem	Demai
ExR	Šemot Rabbah
GenR	Bere'šit Rabbah
Hag	Ḥagigah
Ker	Keritot
Ket	Ketubot
Kid	Kiddushin
m. (before a rabbinic text)	Mishnah
Ma'asSh	Ma'aser Sheni
Mek	Mekilta
Men	Menaḥot
Nidd	Niddah
Pes	Pesaḥim
PR	Pesikta Rabbati
Sanh	Sanhedrin
Shab	Shabbat
Sheq	Sheqalim
SifDeut	Sifre Deuteronomy
SifLev	Sifre Leviticus
SifNum	Sifre Numbers
Soṭ	Soṭah
t. (before a rabbinic text)	Tosephta
Ta'an	Ta'anit
TargEzek	Targum of Ezekiel
TargIsa	Targum of Isaiah
TargJon	Targum Jonathan

TargOnk	Targum Onkelos
TargYer	Targum Yerushalmi
TargPsJ.	Targum Pseudo-Jonathan
y. (before a rabbinic text)	Jerusalem Talmud
Zeb	Zebahim

Other Ancient Documents

arab	arabic
Hev	Nahal Hever
Mird	Khirbet Mird
Mur	Murabba'at
nab	Nabatean

Contributors

Otto Betz
Professor of New Testament Emeritus
Universität Tübingen

James H. Charlesworth
George L. Collord Professor of New Testament Language and Literature
Editor, Dead Sea Scrolls Project
Princeton Theological Seminary

James D. G. Dunn
Lightfoot Professor of Divinity
Department of Theology
University of Durham

Craig A. Evans
Professor of New Testament and Chairman
Department of Religious Studies
Trinity Western University
Langley, British Columbia

David Flusser
Professor of Early Judaism and Christian Origins Emeritus
The Hebrew University of Jerusalem

Howard C. Kee
William Goodwin Aurelio Professor of Biblical Studies
Professor of New Testament Emeritus
School of Theology
Boston University

Rainer Riesner
Dr. theol. habil.
Universität Tübingen

Paolo Sacchi
Professor of Old Testament
Editor, *Apocrifi dell'Antico Testamento*
Università di Torino

Alan F. Segal
Professor of Religion
Barnard College

Morton Smith
Professor of Ancient History Emeritus
Columbia University

Joe Zias
Curator
Israel Antiquities Authority
Jerusalem

Qumran Scrolls and a Critical Consensus

JAMES H. CHARLESWORTH

Journalists have announced a crisis in the study of the Dead Sea Scrolls. They have published sensational articles in major newspapers, magazines, periodicals, and even a book.[1] Obviously journalists are trained to feature what is exceptional, controversial, and new; but have they not been unusually guilty of superficial thoughts and hurried conclusions?

Readers of these features have been arrested by the scandalous and have often wondered out loud, "What is going on?" Have the wild claims made by some research specialists and published by journalists in the media shaken the consensus among scholars, or is there any consensus?

AN INTERNATIONAL AND CRITICAL CONSENSUS

How does one isolate and focus on a consensus? The best way is to study what is shared as reliable by the best scholars. But who are the best scholars, and are they reliable in each instance?

An impressive consensus obviously does exist.[2] It is held by Qumran specialists who teach at (inter alia) the Catholic University of America, University of Chicago, Claremont Graduate School, École Biblique et Archéologique Française de Jérusalem, Edinburgh University, Duke University, Emory University, Göttingen University, Groningen University, Harvard University, Hebrew University (Jerusalem), Institut für Judaistik der Freien Universität Berlin, Institutum Judaicum Delitzschianum (Münster), Leiden University, Munich University, New York University, University of Notre Dame, Oxford University, Princeton Theological Seminary, Princeton University, Strasbourg University, Università di Torino, Universität Tübingen, Union Theological Seminary, Yale University, and in other advanced programs that feature Qumran research.[3]

The consensus is also impressively represented in the major reference works such as the forthcoming *Anchor Bible Dictionary,* Compendia Rerum Iudaicarum ad Novum Testamentum, *Encyclopaedia Judaica,* the Hebrew Encyclopedia *Mikra'it,* the new Schürer,[4] and in major scholarly publications such as the series entitled Discoveries in the Judaean Desert, in which the Dead Sea Scrolls are often first published. It has also set the agenda for the major collections of translations of the Dead Sea Scrolls into Danish, Dutch, English, French, German, Hebrew, Italian, Japanese, Polish, Russian, Spanish, and Swedish.[5]

The international extent and wide endorsement of the consensus are remarkable. They certainly extend beyond the boundaries of countries and creeds.

ARTICULATING THE CONSENSUS

Dead Sea Scrolls have been found in eleven caves in the Judean desert near a site known by the Arabic name Khirbet Qumran. These scrolls have been studied intensively by scholars around the world. There are debates on many issues, but a consensus can be said to exist. In my own words the consensus may be described as follows:[6]

1. All the scrolls were authored by Jews and none has been edited by a Christian scribe (as is the case with some Jewish Pseudepigrapha).

2. All the scrolls are in Hebrew and Aramaic (a few fragments are in Greek).[7]

3. All the scrolls (except the Copper Scroll)[8] can be dated prior to 68 or 69 C.E., by means of archaeological, historical, and paleographical criteria, as well as by Carbon 14 tests.[9] The earliest possible date for the oldest Qumran Scrolls is debated; but it would probably go back to about 250 B.C.E.—that is, about one hundred years before the establishment of the community at Qumran around 150 B.C.E.

4. Archaeologists found in the ruins at Qumran Roman arrowheads and Roman coins on top of a layer of ash and burned timbers; below this layer they found Jewish coins and clear indications of habitation. The Jewish occupation ends in 68 C.E. The archaeologists rightly point to the probability that the eleven caves are linked to a community centered at Qumran, primarily because they are geographically close to Khirbet Qumran and were in use during the same period that people worked at Qumran.

5. This unexpected discovery confirms historical studies based on Josephus, who reported that Roman soldiers burned Jericho and the regions near Qumran in 68 C.E.

6. Paleography (the study of ancient handwriting) is a science and an art; it cannot pinpoint the year, or even the decade, in which a manuscript was written, but it can indicate a date within fifty years, or a generation. An undeniable paleographical sequence can be seen in the Dead Sea Scrolls, and it concludes with the destruction of Qumran in 68 and with manuscripts found at Masada, which fell to the Roman soldiers in 73 or 74.[10]

7. Cave 4 contains the largest collection of scrolls; it is where the Qumranites deposited the community's collection of manuscripts. In that sense it was the library of the Qumran community. Cave 4, and the other ten caves, preserved documents that were probably composed at Qumran (e.g., 1QS) and others (viz., 1QIs[a]) that were brought to Qumran from diverse locations in Palestine, originally by the followers of "the Righteous Teacher" when they departed from Jerusalem, and later by other Jews who brought scrolls with them when they joined the community.

8. The Qumran community existed from the middle of the second century B.C.E, until 68 C.E.

9. Originally, the community consisted of priests who had been expelled from—or had left—the Temple in Jerusalem. These priests were led into the Judean desert by a man they called "the Righteous Teacher." We know virtually nothing certain about him, except that he was a priest

(4QpPs 37) and probably of Zadokite lineage (CD). Scholars debate whether he had formerly served in the Temple as high priest. It is conceivable that he composed some portions of the Rule of the Community, some of the Thanksgiving Hymns,[11] and possibly the not yet published legal (halakic) epistle (4QMMT).[12]

10. In the early decades of the second century B.C.E. other Jews joined the earliest members of the community. Some of the new members may well have been Pharisees or precursors of the Pharisees. The Qumran community was clearly enlarged sometime around the beginning of the first century B.C.E.

11. There is no monolithic system of Qumran theology. Since the Dead Sea Scrolls represent three centuries of work, it is obvious that some differences or development in thought would appear. There is a variety of reflections, for example, on the particular solar calendar of 364 days and its relation to the lunar calendar, marriage, messianology, dualism, anthropology, angelology, eschatology, and the vision of the future.[13]

12. Some features of Qumran theology can be pointed out on the basis of information found in the major scrolls of the community (1QS, 1QH, the Pesharim). The Qumranites tended to vilify the cult in the Jerusalem Temple and scorn the Hasmonean dynasty. The archrival at the time of the expulsion of the Qumranites from Jerusalem was called by them "the Wicked Priest," who was then the ruling high priest and one of the Maccabees, probably Jonathan (160–143) or Simon (143–135).

The Qumran covenanters called themselves "the poor," and members of "the Way." They were "the sons of light" (found in many scrolls); all others were "the sons of darkness" (found in a few scrolls). They conceived of themselves as "the holy ones," who lived in "the house of holiness," because "the Holy Spirit" dwelt with them (and no longer resided in—or hovered over—the Temple).

13. The Qumranites revered and were influenced by some Jewish pseudepigrapha (especially so-called 1 Enoch and Jubilees). They had in their library hitherto unknown pseudepigrapha attributed notably to Moses, Joshua, and David.

14. Either the Qumranites were a previously unknown group within Early Judaism (c. 250 B.C.E.–200 C.E.) that was strikingly similar to the Essenes, or they are to be identified with the strict group of the Essenes described by Josephus (37/8–100 C.E.; *War* 2; cf. Philo [c. 20 B.C.E.–c. 40s C.E.]).[14] The Roman naturalist and geographer Pliny the Elder (23/4–79 C.E.), who

died during the volcanic destruction of Pompeii, describes an Essene community on the western shore of the Dead Sea, close to where Khirbet Qumran is situated (*Natural History* 5.73).

15.   If the Qumran covenanters were the most conservative and strict Essenes, and if they were celibate, it follows that there were other groups of Essenes living throughout ancient Palestine who resided in villages (and perhaps cities) and were married. This reconstruction derives from a critical reading of the ancient sources, especially Josephus and Philo, and of the major scrolls, notably 1QS and CD.

16.   The Qumranites (and Essenes, if these groups are different) existed during the time of the ministry of Jesus of Nazareth (26–30 c.e.). But none of the Dead Sea Scrolls refer to him, and they do not mention any follower of Jesus described in the New Testament.

Notes

1.   See especially the following: *Jerusalem Post Magazine,* August 7, 1987; *New York Times,* November 21, 1989; Australian (Melbourne) *Daily Telegraph,* April 2, 1990; *News Herald,* June 30, 1990; *Biblical Archaeology Review,* July/August 1990; *New York Times,* December 11, 1990; *New York Times,* December 12, 1990; *Biblical Archaeologist,* December 1990; *Time,* January 14, 1991; *Biblical Archaeology Review,* January/February 1991; *Washington Post,* March 31, 1991; N. Golb, "The Dead Sea Scrolls: A New Perspective," *American Scholar* 58 (1989) 177–207 [N. Golb is not a journalist; he is the Ludwig Rosenberger Professor of Jewish History and Civilization at the University of Chicago]. The book in which the alleged crisis is celebrated is a popularizing of the positions of J. M. Allegro, R. Eisenman, and Golb. It is written by two men who are not scholars—M. Baigent and R. Leigh—and titled *The Dead Sea Scrolls Deception* (London, 1991).

2.   I wish to express my appreciation for counsel received from Qumran experts of the highest rank: Frank Moore Cross, John Hancock Professor Emeritus of Hebrew and Other Oriental Languages, Harvard University; David Noel Freedman, Arthur F. Thurnau Professor of Biblical Studies, University of Michigan and holder of the Endowed Chair in Hebrew Biblical Studies at University of California, San Diego; and Shemaryahu Talmon, J. L. Magnes Professor Emeritus, Hebrew University, Jerusalem.

3.   I am impressed how internationally advocated is the consensus. The broad lines of the consensus have been emphasized to me while lecturing or studying in

Australia, Austria, Canada, England, France, Germany, Ireland, Israel, Italy, Japan, the Netherlands, Norway, Scotland, Sweden, and (of course) throughout the United States.

4. E. Schürer, *The History of the Jewish People in the Age of Jesus Christ (175 B.C.– A.D. 135)*, 3 vols., new English version revised and edited by G. Vermes, F. Millar, and M. Black (Edinburgh, 1973–).

5. Danish: E. Nielsen and B. Otzen, *Dødehavs teksterne: Skrifter fra den jødiske menigheid i Qumran i oversaettelse og med noter* (Copenhagen, 1959 [2d ed.]).

Dutch: See the series *De Handschriften van de Dode Zee in Nederlands Vertaling* (Amsterdam, 1957–60), which contains translations by A. S. van der Woude and H. A. Brongers.

English: As far as I know, everyone in the Princeton Theological Seminary Dead Sea Scrolls Project would agree with this broad statement of consensus. It is basically supported by G. Vermes's publications; his translation is now used widely. See Vermes's *The Dead Sea Scrolls in English* (London, New York, 1987 [3d ed.]). A classic is Vermes's translation of A. Dupont-Sommer's excellent French edition: *The Essene Writings from Qumran* (Oxford, 1961; repr., Magnolia, Mass., 1971). See also T. H. Gaster, *The Dead Sea Scriptures: In English Translation with Introduction and Notes* (Garden City, N.Y., 1976 [3d ed.]). An important selection is translated and discussed by M. A. Knibb in *The Qumran Community* (Cambridge, New York, 1987).

French: J. Carmignac and others, *Les textes de Qumrân traduits et annotés,* 2 vols. (Paris, 1961, 1963); A. Dupont-Sommer, *Les Écrits Esséniens découverts près de la Mer Morte* (Paris, 1980 [4th ed.]); A. Dupont-Sommer and M. Philonenko, *La Bible: Écrits intertestamentaires* (Bibliothèque de la Pléiade; Paris, 1987).

German: Especially H. Bardtke, *Die Handschriftenfunde am Toten Meer: Die Sekte von Qumran* (Berlin, 1961 [2d ed.]); J. Maier, *Die Texte vom Toten Meer,* 2 vols. (Munich, Basel, 1960); E. Lohse, *Die Texte aus Qumran: Hebräisch und Deutsch, mit masoretischer Punktation. Übersetzung, Einführung and Anmerkungen* (Munich, 1981 [3d ed.]).

Hebrew: Notably A. M. Habermann, *Megilloth Midbar Yehudah* (Tel Aviv, 1959); J. Licht, *Mgylt hsrkym: Srk hyḥd, srk lkwl ʿdt yśrʾl lʾḥryt hymym, srk hbrkwt* (Jerusalem, 1961–62); Y. Yadin published modern Hebrew editions of 1QM and 11QTemple. Other Israeli scholars have published translations of one or more scrolls. The present list pertains only to collections of translations.

Italian: One of the best collections is edited by L. Moraldi and titled *I manoscritti di Qumran* (Classici delle religioni; Turin, 1971). See also F. Michelini Tocci, *I manoscritti del Mar Morto: Introduzione, traduzione e commento* (Bari, 1967).

Japanese: M. Sekine, *Shikai-bunsho* (Tokyo, 1963).

Polish: W. Tyloch, *Rekopisy z Qumran ned Morzem Martwym* (Polskie Tow. Religioznawcze, Rozprawy i Materialy 6; Warsaw, 1963).

Russian: I. D. Amusin, *Nakhodki u Mertvogo moria* (Moscow, 1964); idem, *Teksty Kumrana* (Moscow, 1971).

Spanish: A. G. Lamadrid, *Los descubrimientos del Mar Muerto: Balance de veinticinco años de hallazgos y estudio* (Biblioteca de autores cristianos 317; Madrid, 1971).

Swedish: B. Reicke, *Handskrifterna från Qumran (eller 'Ain Feshcha) I–IV* (Symbolae Biblicae Upsalienses 14; Uppsala, 1952).

6. Lists of Qumran manuscripts have been published by F. García Martínez and S. A. Reed. See F. García Martínez, "Lista de MSS procedentes de Qumran," *Henoch* 11.2–3 (1989) 149–232; and Reed, *Qumran Cave 1* (Dead Sea Scroll Inventory Project 1; Claremont, Calif., 1991). The best bibliography of Qumran Scrolls is J. A. Fitzmyer's *The Dead Sea Scrolls: Major Publications and Tools for Study* (SBL Sources for Biblical Study 20; Atlanta, 1990 [rev. ed.]). A concordance to over 220 documents and 3,500 fragments of the sectarian Dead Sea Scrolls is the *Qumran Graphic Concordance,* ed. J. H. Charlesworth (Tübingen, 1991).

7. Latin fragments have been found in other caves south of Qumran (viz., Mur 158–59 lat; Mur 160–63 lat). Nabatean script has been found on some other fragments (viz., Mur 71 nab; pap5/6HevA nab). Arabic is found on papyri from Khirbet Mird (papMird 1–100 arab). These other caves are not related to Qumran, although their manuscripts are sometimes categorized geographically as "Dead Sea Scrolls."

8. The Copper Scroll can be dated to the middle of the first century C.E. Frank Cross reminds me that, after examining each consonant, he has dated the Copper Scroll to "the second half of the Herodian era, that is, within the broad limits A.D. 25–75." See Cross, "Excursus on the Palaeographical Dating of the Copper Document," DJD 3, p. 217. It is not certain that this document is related to the Qumran covenanters.

9. These Carbon 14 tests have been announced in the media, but have not been discussed by scholars. They confirm the dates assigned to the scrolls through archaeological, historical, and paleographical methods.

10. Some paleographers have unfortunately claimed too much, sometimes allowing the critics to conclude that paleography is a notoriously imprecise science.

11. See chapter 5.

12. This important letter is discussed in chapter 1.

13. For discussions on most of these theological ideas, see chapter 1.

14. The reader deserves to know that some excellent scholars are questioning the attribution of Essene to Qumran.

CHAPTER 1

The Dead Sea Scrolls
and the Historical Jesus

JAMES H. CHARLESWORTH

CONTROVERSY

The controversy surrounding the Dead Sea Scrolls began in the early fifties, especially with Edmund Wilson's popular and widely read articles in the *New Yorker* (May 14, 1955).[1] It continues until the present, with features in most newspapers and the leading magazines. Claims and charges over these ancient manuscripts have excited many throughout the world for a variety of reasons.[2] No field of the humanities, and no aspect of biblical studies, has so fascinated contemporary readers. In the *National Geographic Magazine* of 1958, A. D. Tushingham came to the end of his article with these words: "And, for the first time, the hitherto mysterious Essenes stand revealed to us. The story of their spiritual struggle swells out of the past like a mighty hymn."[3]

CRITICAL CONSENSUS

Almost every well-read individual today knows that the Dead Sea Scrolls were first discovered in a desert cave west of the Dead Sea by an Arab shepherd boy in 1947 in Palestine just before the establishment of the state of Israel.[4] Since then scrolls and related objects (*realia*) have been found in eleven caves near ruins, called Khirbet Qumran, just west of the Dead Sea. These ruins were excavated in the fifties by Père Roland de Vaux. Scholars now recognize that the ruins are the remains of a center[5] for Jewish priests who were forced to live in the desert because they were exiled from Jerusalem and the Temple. The leader of this exiled community of priests, the Righteous Teacher, who may have once served as high priest in the Temple,[6] was apparently persecuted by "the Wicked Priest" on the Day of Atonement at his desert retreat (1QpHab 9.4–8).[7]

These priests, and other Jews who later joined the community, worked at Qumran (often living in nearby caves) from approximately the second half of the second century B.C.E. to 68 C.E., the third year of the great Jewish revolt against Rome (66–70).[8] Archaeological data and literary evidence have enabled us to determine the date 68 with considerable accuracy. The buildings at Qumran were burned by the tenth legion of the Roman army. This destruction is attested by the discovery of charred timbers, ash, and Roman arrowheads within the remaining stone walls.[9] More recent excavations at Jericho, only a few miles north of Qumran, also reveal impressive evidence of destruction by Roman soldiers. Ash, Roman iron arrowheads, and broken jars from the early first century were found in and around Herod's palace. These archaeological discoveries confirm the report of Josephus, the famous first-century Jewish historian, who described the Roman devastation of Jericho and its environs in 68 C.E. (*War* 4).[10]

The priests who left—or, better, were driven from—the Temple in Jerusalem were legitimate priests. They claimed to trace their line back to Zadok, the high priest of kings David and Solomon, and even to Aaron, the brother of Moses and the first Israelite priest who officiated in the Tabernacle in the wilderness.[11] These priests followed one powerful, articulate, and perhaps charismatic leader.[12] In the Dead Sea Scrolls he is called "the Righteous Teacher," but we do not know his name and cannot identify him with any known person in history.[13]

He and his followers composed many of the Dead Sea Scrolls, and they can be reliably identified. The Qumran covenanters are almost certainly one of the Essene groups, probably the strictest one, and are mentioned in the ancient accounts by Philo, Josephus, Pliny, a source attributed to Hippolytus,[14] and others.[15] The judgment of F. M. Cross, one of the most eminent scholars in Qumran research, is still apposite and deserves to be quoted:[16]

The scholar who would "exercise caution" in identifying the sect of Qumran with the Essenes places himself in an astonishing position: he must suggest seriously that two major parties formed communistic religious communities in the same district of the desert of the Dead Sea and lived together in effect for two centuries, holding similar bizarre views, performing similar or rather identical lustrations, ritual meals, and ceremonies. He must suppose that one, carefully described by classical authors, disappeared without leaving building remains or even potsherds behind: the other, systematically ignored by classical authors, left extensive ruins, and indeed a great library. I prefer to be reckless and flatly identify the men of Qumran with their perennial houseguests, the Essenes.[17]

As the rabbis stressed, caution or timidity is not always a virtue. I would add to Cross's statement the qualification that the Dead Sea Scrolls reflect the strict, celibate, exiled, and extremely conservative Essenes; hence, when necessary for specification, I shall refer to "the Qumran Essenes" and frequently, especially when caution seems warranted, to "the Qumran covenanters."

EXCESSIVE CLAIMS AND OVERREACTIONS

In the first decade or so after the preliminary publications of some of the Dead Sea Scrolls, self-styled critics, often masquerading as scholars, made sensational claims. These brought them momentary fame. They announced that Jesus was an Essene. Some even claimed that he had lived and worked in the buildings now called Khirbet Qumran. Others went on to proclaim that Jesus was to be identified as the Righteous Teacher.

Reactions to such excessive claims were equally emotional.[18] Some excellent scholars erroneously thought that if Jesus was influenced by the Essenes he would have had to visit Qumran. They then rightly claimed that there is no evidence to warrant the hypothesis that Jesus was in the Qumran community. They incorrectly concluded, therefore, that Jesus could not have been influenced in any way by the Essenes. Other New Testament specialists contended that the links between the Dead Sea Scrolls and Jesus were entirely, or almost completely, negative. Jesus and the authors of the Dead Sea Scrolls were exceedingly different. Virtually all similarities can be dismissed; they are insignificant and are caused by a shared origin within early "sectarian" Judaism.[19]

These conclusions are at opposite ends of the range of possibilities: Jesus was either an Essene or he was in no way influenced by this group. Authors engaged in these debates often unintentionally betrayed concerns that were not strictly historical. Their thoughts mirrored the perennial voices of either polemics or apologetics.

Those who concluded that Jesus was an Essene, or the Righteous Teacher, thought they were able to expose the essential claims of the Christian religion as fraudulent. Thus, they claimed Jesus was not the Son of God but the son of man.[20]

These claims have not lain dormant; they bubbled up in the recent charges that many of the Dead Sea Scrolls are still not published because they are being edited by Christians who despise Judaism or do not want to undermine the Christian faith.[21] In the last two years—1990 and 1991— such charges and claims have been expressed or implied in featured articles[22] in such renowned publications as the *New York Times*,[23] *Time*,[24] the *Jerusalem Post International Edition*,[25] the *Biblical Archaeologist*,[26] and *Biblical Archaeology Review*.[27]

The consensus developed among scholars over the past forty years is impressive;[28] nevertheless, one scholar specializing on the Dead Sea Scrolls contends that it is to be discarded. R. H. Eisenman concludes that these documents are to be placed in a Herodian milieu and that virtually all the passages in the Qumran Habbakuk Commentary should be seen in light of the life and teachings of James, the brother of Jesus and head of the Jerusalem Jesus Movement.[29]

Even more astounding are the claims of Barbara Thiering, an Australian.[30] She contends, with Eisenman, that the Dead Sea Scrolls have been misinterpreted. She concludes that the Righteous Teacher "worked at Qumran about 26–30 A.D." She argues that the history of the Righteous Teacher "and his rival corresponds to that of John the Baptist and Jesus."[31] The Dead Sea Scrolls, she claims, reveal that Jesus was born at Qumran and did not die on the cross but spent the remainder of his life in an Essene monastery.

Her views were highlighted in a documentary featured on Australian television (ABC). The heated debates over these claims aroused sensational discussions and reactions.[32] Father Terry Purcell condemned the showing:

"I think it is absurd for the ABC to screen a documentary on Palm Sunday that debunks the whole of Christianity and shows Christianity as a sham."[33]

Charges that the Dead Sea Scrolls remain unpublished because they will disprove the Christian faith are unfounded. Roman Catholics, Protestants, and Jews are working together to edit the unpublished material. Moreover, all extensive scrolls have been published. Remaining unpublished are thousands of fragments, many of which belong to previously unknown documents. We have no so-called jigsaw puzzle picture from which to work so that the odd pieces can be joined together. I have worked on some of the unpublished fragments, and none of the fragments known to me and others who work on them can be judged in any way to disprove the essential claims of the Christian faith.[34] The proof of this claim, like the ones to which it reacts, can only be convincing to those interested when all fragments are made available and published.

The contentions that Jesus was not influenced in any way by the Essenes have a nonhistorical, dogmatic, and apologetic ring to them. Jesus must be unique—he is divine and in no way human—appears to be an underlying presupposition of many published statements. He is thereby shorn of his historicity, and the earliest Christian heresy, combated by 2 John 7 and endorsed by the Acts of John, begins to triumph. Docetism, the doctrine that Jesus was not human but a being of celestial substance, is surreptitiously endorsed.

Is it not time to reexamine this fascinating issue? Should we not approach it primarily as historians? If we are Jewish or Christian, do we need to read these ancient writings only in light of our cherished traditions in the Mishna or the New Testament? Dare we be blinded by confessing what we have wanted to affirm from sacred texts? Is there any truth in the claim by numerous scholars that parts of the New Testament have been found among the Dead Sea Scrolls?[35] Should we not be optimistic about the possibility of discovering something new in the nineties, since we have not only the seven scrolls found in Cave 1 but now well over 223 sectarian documents which are finally in computer readable form?[36] We also have much more data to help us comprehend the geographical extent of the Essenes, thanks to archaeological discoveries on the western littoral of the Dead Sea and especially just west of the present western walls of the Old City of Jerusalem.[37]

The purpose of this introductory chapter is to explain rapidly what appears to be the relation between Jesus and the Dead Sea Scrolls. Although I do not intend to offer a report of research, some guide to scholarly publications will be provided in the notes. A rapid survey of all issues would be more helpful for the wide audience for whom *Jesus and the Dead Sea Scrolls* is written. After presenting some methodological observations I shall discuss major similarities, significant differences, and probable conclusions.

Confusion and impossible speculations have been disseminated not only among scholars but also among the impressively large interested public by improper assumptions and methods. Hence, I shall try to sharpen the view by which we might be able to make worthwhile observations.

THE ESSENE GROUPS

The Qumran covenanters, the authors of the Dead Sea Scrolls, are not an insignificant group of Jews living in isolation in the Judean desert. They are a conservative wing of a large and influential group in Early Judaism,[38] which had at least two subgroups, according to Josephus (*War* 2.160) and to many specialists who have studied the history of the Essenes and compared the Rule of the Community with the Damascus Document. Philo and Josephus reported that the Essenes living in Palestine numbered more than four thousand.[39] Since no more than two hundred men could live at Qumran, the vast majority lived elsewhere.[40] Josephus clarifies where they may be found: "They occupy no one city, but settle in large numbers in every town" (*War* 2.124). He even goes so far as to report that they are "in every city" (*War* 2.126). Philo commented that the Essenes live throughout Judea.[41]

It becomes obvious that Jesus did not have to venture into the desert to discover how the Essenes lived and what they thought. As an itinerant preacher,[42] he certainly could have encountered Essenes in Galilee, throughout Palestine, and within the environs of Jerusalem.[43]

If we uncover a possible parallel between the Essenes and Jesus, how should we access it? First, we know that all the Dead Sea Scrolls antedate 68 C.E.[44] and that thus they are almost always earlier or on rare occasions contemporaneous with Jesus who was crucified outside the western walls of Jerusalem in 30 C.E.[45] Hence, evidence of influence will be in one direction: from the Essenes to Jesus.

Second, we know that these scrolls, unlike many of the Jewish Pseudepigrapha, were not edited by Christians as they copied them over the last nearly two thousand years. They are Jewish primary sources that are unedited by Christians. They represent more than an isolated community exiled in the desert of Judah. Moreover, the theologies in the hundreds of Dead Sea Scrolls should not be forced into a system,[46] but reflect various perspectives and traditions on such major issues as anthropology, calendars, dualism, ethics, eschatology, and messianology.[47]

Third, the earliest Gospel, probably Mark, was written about two years after the burning of Qumran in 68. It was composed, in Rome or northern Palestine, sometime shortly before, or around, 70. The Gospels of Matthew, Luke, and John were written—probably in that order—sometime and somewhere between 80 and 100.

Fourth, since Jesus wrote nothing and he died in 30 we must allow for forty years in which the deeds and sayings of Jesus were transmitted to the evangelists. During this period Jesus' sayings and deeds were shaped by the needs of the Palestinian Jesus Movement.

Fifth, the Jesus traditions were edited by Jesus' followers. They composed their accounts and gospels in light of their fervent belief that God had raised Jesus from the dead and that soon he would return gloriously and triumphantly to earth. They did not intend to publish an objective biography of Jesus that could withstand the acids of modern criticism.

Sixth, some of the traditions derive authentically from Jesus. They were passed on by Jews who had amazing memories and who lived in polemical relations with many who did not believe in Jesus and rejected the claim of his followers that he was the long-awaited Messiah. Some interest in Jesus' life and career was certainly typical of his followers and those who joined his movement; otherwise, we would never be able to explain the appearance of the Gospels, especially Mark, Matthew, Luke, and John.

METHOD IN JESUS RESEARCH

It should now be clear that it is possible, profitable, and necessary to ask historical questions about Jesus and the Essenes. We should not attempt to present what Jesus said in a positivistic fashion.[48] We should not seek to isolate and elevate putative uninterpreted words of Jesus (the *ipsissima verba Jesu*). Because Jesus' sayings were meaningful they were interpreted; because they were interpreted they continue to be meaningful.

We should rather seek to discern what Jesus intended to communicate to his listeners. We shall probably come the closest to arriving at what Jesus actually said and meant if we focus primarily on his words quoted in the New Testament,[49] eliminating those that were created out of the needs and perspectives of his followers (or the "church"), and giving priority for authenticity to those that are found in more than one gospel tradition and that cohere with other reliable Jesus sayings.

COMMONALITY

At the outset it is imperative to emphasize the vast amount of commonality between Jesus and the Essenes.[50] We now know that Jesus' group and the Essene groups are examples of the diversities that existed in Judaism before 70 C.E.[51] Both Jesus and the Essenes shared the same territory, which they considered their birthright. They lived in the Land[52] promised to Abraham and his descendants and conquered by Joshua, Deborah, and David. They were of the same race. They were devout and religious Jews who observed the Torah and considered it God's gracious self-disclosure.[53] It was a cherished possession; it was God's will and hence a joyous possession.

The Essenes clearly and Jesus probably, according to the passages about the centurion and the Syrophoenician woman, were Jews who treated the Gentiles with a contempt that is disconcerting. They had common enemies within Judaism: the scribes, the Temple priests, the Sadducees, and some (but not all) of the Pharisees. Some of the latter group may have joined the Qumran Essenes during the persecutions by Alexander Janneus (103–76 B.C.E.),[54] and some, in the late twenties of the first century C.E. and shortly thereafter, clearly joined Jesus and his movement (see especially Acts 15:5).[55]

The Essenes and Jesus shared the dream that God had not forgotten his promises recorded in scripture; they affirmed that he was actually in the process of fulfilling them. They inherited and developed in similar ways an apocalyptic perspective, but neither Jesus nor the Essenes (at least the Qumran Essenes) wrote an apocalypse.

Finally, both lived in Palestine prior to the destruction of Jerusalem and the Temple, and before the revolt of 66–70 C.E.[56] Jesus in 30, the Qumran Essenes in 68, and other Essenes in the years 68 to 73/4[57] were killed by Roman soldiers.

Would it not be obviously interesting for us—as members of Western culture, and especially for those of us who are Jews or Christians—to ask how and in what ways Jesus may have been influenced, if at all, by the Essenes? Certainly many have rightly found the task not only intriguing but also imperative.

Since the early 1950s many leading New Testament experts have sought to discern what may have been the relation between Jesus and the Essenes. It would be misleading to summarize this work as if it leads to a non-debatable consensus. The following summary thus reflects my own opinions; but, of course, many of the following insights were developed and defended in lengthy monographs by international experts.

MAJOR SIMILARITIES

To summarize, Jesus and the Essenes were similar in numerous fundamental ways: they shared the same territory and race; they were devout, religious, conservative, and anti-Gentile. They struggled against common enemies (especially the Sadducees and sacerdotal aristocracy in Jerusalem), were close to some Pharisees, were animated by the belief that God was about to bring to fruition his promises, and were apocalyptically and eschatologically oriented. Jesus and most of the Essenes were put to death by Roman soldiers.

These commonalities open the way for a critical review of similarities and differences, and a critical approach is the only way to allow for the possibility of clarifying potential uniqueness within Early Judaism.[58] The twenty-four listed similarities are organized under three categories: scripture-based theology, cosmic-shaped chronology, and humility before God.

Scripture-based Theology

1. Concept of God. Jesus and the Essenes believed in one and the same God. Although they knew of the power of the Evil One, calling him either Satan (Mt, Mk, Lk, Jn)[59] or Belial (1QS, 1QM, 4QFlor, CD),[60] they affirmed monotheism through the belief in one and only one creator (Mk 13:39; 1QS 3). The Torah (Law) embodied God's will; Jesus and the Essenes endeavored to live in absolute devotion to God's Torah. Both affirmed that God was being challenged for power, but they claimed that God is the source of all power and would eventually defeat the Evil One (Mt 12:28–

37; Mk 13:19–36;[61] cf. Rom 16:20; 1QM).[62] They yearned and prayed for God's kingship, so obviously known in heaven,[63] to come on.[64] Devotion to God and monotheism were shared by Jesus and the Essenes with other Jews.[65]

2. Jesus and the Essenes inherited the same guiding source for thought and deed; it was the Hebrew Scriptures (the Old Testament).[66] As H. Stegemann argues, "the Qumran community and Jesus basically agreed with one another in their acceptance of the Torah as the central and decisive authority for their beliefs."[67]

While the Qumran community and other Essenes, along with the author of Jude, perceived prophecy in other writings (especially so-called 1 Enoch, Jubilees, Tobit, and Testaments of Levi and Naphtali),[68] Jesus apparently quoted only from—and may have deemed solely "scriptural"—what is now in the canonical scriptures (the Hebrew Scriptures or Old Testament).[69] Obviously Jesus shared these ideas with other Jews.

3. Among the scriptures Jesus maybe and the Essenes probably had special fondness for the same books, namely, Deuteronomy, Isaiah, and especially the Davidic Psalms.[70] This preference may, but does not necessarily, indicate some relation between Jesus and the Essenes. They were probably more indebted to Deuteronomy than he. This area for fruitful research will need much work, discerning what can be ascertained reliably about Jesus and whether we have now ample evidence to access Qumran preferences. Nevertheless, it is interesting to ponder why Jesus and the Essenes seemed to share a fondness for the same books of scripture.

4. Jesus and the Essenes used a similar means to interpret the scriptures. They read them under the guidance of the Spirit (that is pneumatically),[71] and affirmed that God's promises were now being fulfilled. Both Jesus and the Essenes were eschatologically oriented; that is, they believed that the present belonged to the beginning of the new age (viz., Mk 9:1; 1QH 8). Stegemann is of the opinion that Jesus developed his eschatology "to a certain extent against the background of specific ideas of the Qumran community. But, in contrast to its understanding, he offered a new way of reading the Torah."[72]

Neither Jesus' sayings nor the Essene writings can be reduced to a system;[73] neither, moreover, should be categorized as either futuristic eschatology or "realized"[74] eschatology. W. G. Kümmel's claim that only Jesus' eschatology was a mixture of present and future,[75] has been disproved by an intensive study of Qumran eschatology.[76] Both shared a similar hermeneutical principle, which resulted in an interpretation indicating that only they, and their group, really understood the meaning of the scriptures. The key word is "revelation." Jesus believed that the true meaning of scripture had been revealed to him. The Qumran Essenes believed that God "had made known" to the Righteous Teacher "all the mysteries of the words of his servants the prophets" (1QpHab 7.4–5).

The Essenes were more extreme than Jesus; they affirmed that only the Righteous Teacher understood the scriptures (1QpHab 7). They contended that the original author, specifically Habakkuk, and others never comprehended the meaning of scripture. Jesus never made such a sweeping claim; rather, he held that the scriptural promises pointed to him and his time.[77]

Jesus and the Essenes, in a uniquely shared way, did indicate that the scriptures spoke about them specifically, eschatologically, and sometimes "messianically."[78] Both contended that the prophets spoke about the end of time and that this future time was now and present in their own community. This commonality obviously results from their "sectarian" and social isolation within a larger society;[79] but similar—and somewhat unique—pneumatic, eschatological, and messianic exegesis may indicate some influence of the Essenes on Jesus. Any Essene exegetical influence on Jesus would have been reshaped creatively by his own revelatory experiences and claims and understanding of his mission.[80]

5. Jesus' followers (Mk 1:3), John the Baptizer (Mt 3:3; Jn 1:23), and the Essenes stressed the clarion call of Isaiah 40:3, "A voice cries in the wilderness, 'Prepare the way of Yahweh (or the Lord).'" It is conceivable that Jesus' followers may have inherited this concept from John the Baptizer, whom some specialists conclude was once a Qumran Essene,[81] or even maybe from some Essenes, because the Qumran Essene Isaiah scroll highlighted this verse by separating it from its context,[82] and because the Qumran Essenes believed they were acting out the prophecy, by preparing the way of Yahweh. Note this passage in one of the oldest sections of the Rule of the Community:[83] ". . . they shall separate from the midst of the dwelling of perverse men to go into the wilderness to prepare there the way of him; as it is written, 'In the wilderness prepare the way of Yahweh'"[84] (1QS 8.13–14). We are led, however, to ponder whether Jesus' followers may have been in some way influenced by the Essenes. While there is no evidence that Jesus stressed the importance of Isaiah 40:3, we must remember that it is possible that his followers developed something implicit in his

teachings or knew a saying of Jesus not know to us. Jesus' fondness for Isaiah, his association with John the Baptizer, and his eschatological claims warrant this speculation.

6. Apparently Jesus and the Essenes saw their actions as constituting a new *covenant*.[85] According to Mark 14:24 and Matthew 26:28 Jesus instituted at the Last Supper a "covenant."[86] According to Luke 22:20 Jesus said, "This cup which is poured out for you is the new covenant in my blood." The Qumran Essenes stressed the importance of "the new covenant"[87] that was established by God through the Righteous Teacher.[88] Each year the covenant was renewed, perhaps at the Day of Atonement (Yom Kippur), during a most sacred ceremony (1QS 1–2). To enter the Qumran Community was "to pass over into the covenant,"[89] or "to enter into the new covenant."[90] The Qumran Essenes thought of their community (*yahad*) as the eternal covenant.[91] Their unique theology, history, and social setting led them to talk about their community as "God's covenant."[92] In a certain sense Qumran theology is covenantal theology.

It is intriguing to ponder if Jesus may have been influenced in some ways by peculiarly Essene covenant theology. This possibility must not be excluded, but it may not be probable because of the covenant theology found in many Old Testament passages and the widespread influence of Jeremiah 31:31–34, which contains the Lord's promise of a "new covenant" that will be written on the heart.[93] This passage was well known in early Jewish theology and influenced many New Testament authors.[94]

7. Jesus and the Essenes—unlike other Jews—affirmed the continuation of prophecy.[95] Both Jesus probably and the Righteous Teacher possibly thought of themselves as prophets; both certainly saw themselves as the true heirs of the prophetic tradition.[96] According to Luke 4 Jesus claimed that Isaiah's prophecy was being fulfilled in him; the Spirit of the Lord had anointed him to preach and act. According to the Habakkuk Pesher, God made known to the Righteous Teacher alone the exact meaning of the prophets (1QpHab 7.4–5); this passage may indicate that after the death of the Righteous Teacher the Qumranites portrayed him as "a prophet." While there is no reason to posit any influence here, there is some uniqueness. A large segment of Early Judaism assumed that prophecy had ceased long ago; recall Psalm 74:9, "there is no longer any prophet; no one among us knows for how long."[97] Rabbi Akiba, for example, is famous for this claim (b. Yoma 9b).[98]

In summarizing the previous discussions, numbers 1 and 2 indicate ways Jesus was closer to other Jews than to the Essenes. Numbers 3, 4, 5, 6, and 7 indicate that there may have been some uniqueness shared between Jesus and the Essenes. These possibilities should stimulate further exploration. How and in what ways were Jesus and the Essenes related, if at all, in perceiving the cosmos and time.

Cosmic-shaped Chronology

8. Although Jesus and the Essenes did not share the same calendar (as we shall see in the discussion of differences), they did assume that there were two ages and two worlds. Both affirmed that the old age was rapidly passing away and the new one was beginning. Their eschatologies were not different in kind but in degree. For Jesus the time was closer to the end than for the Essenes, so that while the Essenes spoke about the end of time as the end of *days*,[99] Jesus referred to the *hour*.[100]

He taught his disciples to pray that God's will would be done on earth as in heaven, and the Qumranic Angelic Liturgy portrays angels in heaven worshiping the king of heaven. The Qumranic Daily Prayers (4Q503) contain numerous passages that reveal how cosmically oriented were the Qumran Essenes; they participated through prayer in the bringing of light back to earth during the twilight of the morning and prepared for the darkness by prayer during the twilight of the evening.

Jesus shared with other Jews the idea that there are two ages (see esp. 4 Ezra 8:1) and two worlds (see esp. 1 Enoch). There is no indication that Jesus shared the Essene fear of darkness and adoration of light or employed the light–darkness paradigm they developed.[101]

9. Jesus and the Essenes thought that the cosmos was full of demons and angels. Jesus' healing miracles,[102] which seem to have some ring of historicity to them, were portrayed not in modern medical terms but in terms of his power over demons. He saw his struggle as one against Satan. The Essenes affirmed that there were two warring cosmic powers, one that is evil and the other good (1QS 3–4; and 1QM). These ideas Jesus shared with many other Jews,[103] so it is unwise to seek to discern some influence from the Essenes.

10. Both Jesus and the Essenes emphasized that the promised eschatological redemption was now being offered to the poor—which was clearly a technical term for the Essenes and may have been for Jesus. According to

Matthew 5:3, in the Sermon on the Mount, Jesus blessed "the poor in spirit," and according to Luke 6:20, in the Sermon on the Plain, he blessed "the poor." To them is promised "the kingdom."

According to the Dead Sea Scrolls the terms "the poor in spirit" and "the poor" are terms which the Qumran Essenes employed as technical self-designations.[104] In the War Scroll "the poor" is synonymous with "we in the lot of your truth" (1QM 13.12–14). They are the ones who will eventually conquer, thanks to God's intervention in the final (eschatological) war. The members of the Qumran community transformed the concept of "the poor ones" from a sociological and economic term to a religious concept.[105] In view of the uniqueness of this term, "the poor ones," in the Dead Sea Scrolls, it is conceivable that Jesus may have inherited it from the Essenes,[106] with whom he could well have discussed his concept of God's kingdom.[107]

11.   Few movements in Judaism prior to the destruction of the Temple in 70 C.E. can be categorized as expecting the coming of "the Messiah."[108] The two major exceptions are Jesus and his group and the Essenes.[109] Moreover, both espoused earthly messianic beliefs. The "Messiah" will not arise out of the sea, as in 4 Ezra, or out of heaven, as in 1 Enoch. He will arise out of the chosen people.[110]

How are we to assess these similarities? The fact that only two messianic movements are clearly identifiable prior to 70 is significant. The Maccabean wars, beginning in 167 B.C.E. and the revolt of 66–70 C.E. were not messianic; they were certainly not like the revolt of 132–35, which was led by the warrior Bar Kosiba, who was considered the Messiah. He was thence titled Bar Kokhba, "Son of the Star."

It is difficult to assess the evidence. Some pre-70 Pharisees obviously believed in the coming of "the Messiah." The famous Amidah (Eighteen Benedictions), however, if it can be judged to antedate 70 C.E., does not mention "the Messiah"; and although it refers to "the royal seed of David, your justly anointed," it celebrates God, and not the Messiah, as the one who will redeem Israel and bring in peace.[111]

Jesus' messianic self-awareness, which once seemed unlikely to many scholars, is now being acknowledged by a wide spectrum of them.[112] The Essenes certainly believed in the coming of the Messiah (1QS, CD, 4QFlor, 4QpsDan),[113] but it is unlikely that they considered the Righteous Teacher the Messiah.[114]

Should we assume that Jesus was influenced by Essene messianology? Some relation seems possible. At least according to some scrolls[115] the

Essenes looked for the coming of two messiahs, one kingly and the other priestly. It is obvious that Jesus was seen as both "kingly" (Mt 1-2, Lk 1-2)[116] and priestly (see esp. Lk 1:5, 26-36). Did Jesus think of himself in such terms, and if so was he influenced by Essenes? While similarities here are obvious, there is no reason to argue for direct Essene influence on Jesus.[117]

12. Jesus[118] and the Essenes held an intriguing ambivalence toward Jerusalem,[119] revering the Temple but distressed with its cult (or at least with some of the priests who officiated over it). Both recognized that Jerusalem was "the Holy City"; they honored the Temple but despised—as did other Jews—the corruption of the cult.[120] Unlike the Samaritans, Jesus went up to Jerusalem[121] for Passover.

Jesus is never portrayed as bringing offerings to the Temple. The Qumran Essenes probably contended that worship and sacrifice were in the final days of "the present age" only to be offered to God in the "house of holiness," Qumran. Hence, it is surprising that Jesus clearly (Mt 17:24)[122] and the Essenes probably,[123] as S. Safrai perceived,[124] paid the half-shekel Temple obligatory offering.[125] This parallel is interesting; but in itself it reveals only that Jesus and the Essenes shared a similar devotion to Torah obligations and reverence for the Temple.

Is there any link between Jesus' attitude to the Temple cult and the Essenes? Were there Essenes living in Jerusalem during the time of Jesus, and did they, like Jesus, affirm that God is to be worshiped in the Temple (despite some of the officiating priests)?[126] Clearly at least one Essene frequented the Temple after the establishment of the Qumran Community: Judas the Essene (*Ant* 13.311-13); and he is depicted in the Temple with his companions and disciples.

Jesus shared with other Jews points 8 and 9. Some relation between Jesus and the Essenes is suggested by points 10, 11, and 12.

Humility before God

13. Jesus and the Essenes emphasized the sinfulness of all humans before God. Jesus' ministry was centered on the proclamation of God's good news to all Jews,[127] and it was based on the presupposition that all need God's forgiveness and acceptance. The Essenes also affirmed humanity's sinfulness and the need for God's forgiveness and acceptance. Note, in particular, 1QS 11.9-10:

And I, (I belong) to an evil humanity
And to the company of wicked flesh.
My iniquities, my transgressions, my sins . . .
(Belong) to the assembly of maggot(s)
and those who move in darkness.

Further, observe the concept of sin and unworthiness in 1QH 4.30–31:

And I, I know that righteousness is not of man,
Nor perfection of way in the son of man;
To the Most High God (are ascribed) all works of righteousness. . . .

Jesus, in the Lord's Prayer and elsewhere, affirmed the need to express to God the need for forgiveness. He shared this concept not only with the Essenes, however, but with other Jews.[128] Yom Kippur (the Day of Atonement) was a public and national event; the high priest confessed his own sins, those of his family, and then those of Israel (m.Yoma 3:8).

14. Jesus[129] and the Essenes[130] also stressed that God was a God of forgiveness who freely offered his grace, love, and mercy to all who called upon him with contrite hearts.[131] This idea was also a dimension of Judaism that Jesus shared with other Jews (see esp. Ps 51, PssSol, 18 Benedictions, PrMan).

15. Jesus and the Essenes also affirmed the certainty of receiving forgiveness from God.[132] Jesus is reputed to have said, "Truly all sins will be forgiven the sons of men, and all blasphemies they may utter; but whoever blasphemes against the Holy Spirit shall never have forgiveness" (Mk 3:28–29). The Essenes would have lauded Jesus' understanding of forgiveness. Note in particular the following thought:

But all the children of your truth
You bring with forgiveness before you,
Cleansing them of their transgressions by your great goodness,
And by the multitude of your mercies allowing them to
    stand before you for ever. (1QH 7.28–29)

In the Rule of Community this attitude of full dependence on God is also expressed: "And I, if I stumble, God's mercies are my salvation for ever . . .

and by his mercies he will bring my justification" (1QS 11.11–14). Thus both Jesus and the Essenes contended that salvation and justification are God's gift.[133] Essene influence on Jesus for the concept of God's merciful justification is an intriguing possibility, but presently—given the paucity of our knowledge of pre-rabbinic Judaism and the full range of its concepts of justification—it is difficult to assess this possibility.[134]

16.   While devout Jews ordered their daily lives (especially those living in Jerusalem around the time of prayer in the Temple[135]) and began and ended meals with prayer,[136] Jesus, the Righteous Teacher,[137] and the Essenes put an unusual emphasis on prayer. On occasion—how frequently we do not know—Jesus probably spent all night in prayer.[138] According to the Rule of the Community, the Essene is to praise God at all times—during the day and the night—and in every situation (1QS 10.9–17). With the recent publication of the Angelic Liturgy, the Pseudepigraphic Psalms, and the Daily Prayers (4Q503) the Essene preoccupation with prayer seems to stand out in Early Judaism.[139]

There is reason to conclude that Jesus may well have been favorably impressed—and perhaps influenced—by the Essene devotion to God, especially through prayer. D. Flusser even offers the opinion that Jesus knew the Thanksgiving Hymns (1QH), because he (Mt 11:25–27, Lk 10:21–22) used the Hodayot formula ("Blessed are you, O Lord, because . . ."), knew the free rhythm and content of these hymns, and shared the author's high self-awareness of mission.[140]

17.   Jesus and the Essenes certainly held contrasting views regarding purity (as we shall see),[141] but they both held a heightened concept of inward holiness.[142] Jesus[143] and the Essenes—in striking contrast to the Jerusalem cult but in line with some emphases of the prophets—affirmed that devotion to and praise of God were more important than any sacrifice. Jesus would have approved of the section of the Rule of the Community that urges initiates to comprehend[144] that far more important than sacrifice are the "offering of the lips" and "perfection (or blamelessness) of conduct" (1QS 9.4–5). Perhaps there is some still unknown link between Jesus and the Essenes on this point.

18.   Jesus and the Essenes put an unusual stress on the symbolic meaning of "water." According to an early version of the Gospel of John Jesus spent his early ministry as a baptizer (3:22; 4:1),[145] but there is insufficient evidence to conclude that Jesus inherited the concept of "baptism" from Essenes.[146] The Qumran Essenes emphasized the need for ritualistic cleansings

that were repeated (viz., 4Q514; 1QS 3.4–9, 5.13–14). The numerous cisterns and channels at Qumran provided water for drinking and washing, but—more importantly—they attest to the need for purification.

The Essenes employed the concept of "water" in numerous symbolic ways. Water symbolized life and was salvific.[147] "Water" is used symbolically five times in columns 3 and 4 of the Rule of the Community, a passage that was to be memorized by initiates. It appears six times in column 3 and eleven times in column 8 of the Thanksgiving Hymns, which was the "hymnbook" of the community. Some of the water symbolism most likely derives from the founder of the community, the Righteous Teacher.[148] He may have composed the following section of a hymn:

> And Thou, O my God, hast put in my mouth
> as it were an autumn rain for all [the sons of men]
> and a spring of living waters which shall not run dry. (1QH 8.16)[149]

If Jesus did refer to salvation as "living water,"[150] then he was clearly influenced by the Essenes at this point; but such phrases were perhaps added at a later stage in the transmission of Jesus' sayings.[151] Even though there were other baptist groups besides that of John the Baptizer,[152] it is conceivable that Jesus may have been influenced by the Essenes' symbolic use of "water."

19. Jesus and the Essenes contended that possessions are to be shared. Jesus exhorted *some* Jews to give all they possessed to the poor and follow him. Judas is said to have been in charge of the common "money box" (Jn 12:6; 13:29). Jesus and his little band of followers, unlike Paul, did not earn wages; they lived off the land—for example, plucking corn to eat—or received support from others. The author of Acts reports that the members of the Palestinian Jesus Movement held "everything in common" (Acts 2:44),[153] and this probably was not an innovation of Jesus' followers.[154]

According to the Rule of the Community, the Essene, when fully initiated, gave all his possessions to the community (1QS 6.22). There may well be some Essene influence on Jesus at this point; but it is important to observe that Jesus did not make this practice into a law or a requirement for acceptance. H. Braun is correct to suggest that Jesus independently reworked this "possible inheritance from Qumran."[155]

20. Jesus and the Essenes were appreciably different from all other known Jews in their apparent condemnation of divorce.[156] The stern

Shammaites interpreted Deut 24:1 to mean that divorce was permitted when adultery was committed. The much more conciliatory Hillelites understood the text broadly to include such absurdly trivial cases as when a wife burned her husband's supper.[157]

Jesus taught that there is no divorce (Mk 10:2–9; Mt 19:6),[158] although Matthew and his community added "except for unchastity" (Mt 5:32; 19:9).[159] A text revered by the Essenes, and at least edited by them, implies[160] that as the king should not divorce his wife neither should others (11QTemple 57).[161] It is conceivable that Jesus was influenced by the apparent prohibition of divorce by the Essenes.

21. Only Jesus (Lk 16:8) and the Essenes[162] are known to have employed the technical term "sons of light." There is every reason to think that the Qumran Essenes, perhaps the Righteous Teacher, coined this *term* and its antithesis "sons of darkness." If so, Jesus and his followers inherited the term "the sons of light" from the Essenes (see esp. 1QS 3–4).[163] D. Flusser, one of the leading experts on the Dead Sea Scrolls in Jerusalem, concludes that when "Jesus used the technical term the 'sons of light,' he was making an allusion to the Essenes."[164]

22. Jesus' group and the Essenes were shaped by the galvanizing force of one prophetic and charismatic person:[165] specifically Jesus[166] and the Righteous Teacher.[167] Both of these reformers were committed to scripture, exhibited an obsessive love of God, and were unusually dedicated to his will, as they understood it, regardless of the opinions of other Jewish leaders. Both expressed their strong egos with a sense of pride toward others but with stunning humility in relation to God. Both demanded of their followers unswerving faith in their claim of special revelation, unique teachings, and leadership.[168] Only Hillel seems comparable to these unique dimensions shared by Jesus and the Righteous Teacher, but he was not charismatic and prophetic as they were. Apparently Jesus and the Righteous Teacher developed these shared personality characteristics because of their independent experience of God and the crises they faced. There is no evidence that Jesus knew anything about the Righteous Teacher; and if he did he would have abhorred his hatred of others and refusal to associate with those deemed "impure."

23. Jesus was not married,[169] and the Qumran Essenes are the only celibate group known in Early Judaism (*War* 2.121).[170] Jews married because of the commandment to Adam ("be fruitful and multiply," Gen 1:28); as G. F. Moore stated, marriage was considered "a divine ordinance."[171] Even

polygamy was permitted (cf. m.Ket)[172] and its prohibition in Deuteronomy 17:17[173] was only apparent,[174] permitting the rabbis to allow as many as four wives for subjects and eighteen wives for kings (m.Sanh 2:4). The Temple Scroll (56.17–19)[175] and the Damascus Document indicate that polygamy was practiced by some Jews; otherwise their proscriptions cannot be explained. The Damascus Document apparently condemned the practice of having more than one wife, because Noah and his family went into the ark "two by two" (CD 4.20–5.2).[176]

Jesus and the Qumran Essenes were "married" to God and dedicated to his rule. The Essenes apparently extended to the community the most rigid rules for purity formerly designated only for priests when officiating in the Temple (cf. m.Yoma 1:1; 8:1),[177] or transferred to themselves in preparation of the eschatological battle (1QM) the abstinence demanded of Israelite warriors who were engaged in a holy duty (Dt 20:7; 24:5).

According to Matthew 19:12 Jesus praises the men who become eunuchs for the kingdom. He was not praising celibacy; but he may have been lauding the Essenes who were celibate because of their devotion to God alone.[178]

24. Jesus may have inherited from the Essenes their concept of "the Holy Spirit." The technical term "the Holy Spirit" appears frequently in the New Testament. Many of these references are comments attributed to John the Baptist or to Gabriel.[179] Many describe Jesus[180] and interpret his words.[181] A significant number in all four Gospels are in quotations attributed to Jesus.[182] The term "the Holy Spirit" in some of these sayings may not derive ultimately from Jesus, and some are clearly editorial;[183] but, a good case can be made for the possibility that the term "the Holy Spirit" was used by Jesus.[184] Perhaps authentic to Jesus is the warning that blaspheming "the Holy Spirit" is an unforgivable sin (Mk 3:29; Mt 12:32; Lk 12:10).[185] The radicalness and dissimilarity[186] of this saying of Jesus argue in favor of its authenticity.

If Jesus used the term "the Holy Spirit," then the links with the Dead Sea Scrolls must be considered. The technical term—the Holy Spirit—does not appear in the Old Testament,[187] and a discussion of it is conspicuously absent from the major volumes on Old Testament theology (viz., W. Eichrodt and G. von Rad). In the Old Testament "the holy spirit" represents God's charisma or presence.

The term "the Holy Spirit" occurs only three times in the Jewish apocryphal works.[188] It is also rare in the later Mishna (m.Soṭ 9:6, 15)[189] and in even later rabbinics the "Holy Spirit" is frequently mentioned to explain why prophecy ceased (t.Soṭ 13.2).[190]

It is abundant, however, in the Dead Sea Scrolls.[191] At Qumran "the Holy Spirit" is angelic and a separate being (hypostasis); it is not the holy spirit of God but "the Holy Spirit" from God.[192] As F. F. Bruce perceived, it "is remarkable" that a phrase or term so seldom found in the Old Testament and apocryphal writings should appear so frequently and importantly "in the New Testament and other Christian literature, and also in the Qumran texts."[193]

The Qumran Essenes in the middle of the second century B.C.E. developed the concept of "the Holy Spirit" to substantiate their claims against the Temple priests[194] and their choice to live in the desert. They claimed that "the Holy Spirit" had left the polluted Temple and accompanied them into the wilderness. There "the Holy Spirit" dwelt in "the house of holiness." The Qumran Essenes hence called themselves "the men of holiness" and "the men of most holiness." Since they perceived themselves as the true priests, and since they lived where "the Holy Spirit" dwells, they continued in their devotion to God and to truth because "the Holy Spirit" was with them, in "the house," and no longer in the Temple. "The Holy Spirit" dwells now in their community (yaḥad).

The Qumran Essenes clearly developed the concept of "the Holy Spirit" from God in contrast to "the Holy Spirit" of God in earlier and other writings.[195] If Jesus used the term "the Holy Spirit" he may well have inherited it from the Essenes. One factor, however, inhibits the conclusion that Jesus was directly dependent on the Essenes for the concept of "the Holy Spirit." Rabbinic tradition claims that Hillel spoke about "the Holy Spirit":

> They said to him (Hillel the Elder), "What will happen to the people who do not bring their knives and their Passover-offerings to the sanctuary?" He said to them, "Leave them alone. The holy spirit (rwḥ hqwdš) is upon them. If they are not prophets, they are sons of the prophets." . . . On that very day they appointed Hillel Chief (nśy') and he perpetually taught them concerning the rules (hylkwt) of Passover. (t.Pisha 4.14)[196]

This pericope raises suspicions; it does not seem to be historically accurate.[197] It is much later than the New Testament pericopes and the Dead Sea Scrolls, and contains seams that indicate a long process of transmission.

It indicates that Hillel was elevated to the office of Chief of the Great Sanhedrin in Jerusalem (*Nasi*) because of his ruling that included "the holy spirit." It looks as if the Hillelites, who compiled the rabbinic writings, sought to explain why Hillel rose to power; their claims here are dubious.[198]

The polemical character is obvious. It is conceivably directed to Jews who had converted to Christianity and claimed that they now were baptized and possessed "the Holy Spirit" (see Acts 2:1-4, 38 and 19:17).[199]

There is no evidence, as far as I know,[200] that Hillel, like the Righteous Teacher and Jesus, received special revelation or was empowered by the spirit or "the Holy Spirit."[201] One of our unexpected discoveries is that Jesus was apparently influenced by the Essenes' concept of "the Holy Spirit." He, of course, developed it in line with his proclamation of the coming of "God's rule" or "the kingdom of God."[202] Since only Jesus, his followers, and the Righteous Teacher and his group, without doubt,[203] conceived of "the Holy Spirit," it is understandable why followers of John the Baptizer were forced to admit that "we have never even heard that there is a Holy Spirit" (Acts 19:2).[204]

In summary, numbers 13 and 14 were shared by Jesus with many other Jews. Numbers 15, 16, 17, 18, and 23 raise the possibility that Jesus may have been influenced by the Essenes. Number 22 does not indicate a relationship. Numbers 19, 20, 21, and especially 24 suggest that Jesus was influenced, in some way, by the Essenes.

MAJOR DIFFERENCES

After this summary of major similarities between Jesus and the Essenes, an obvious question arises: What are the most important differences? Recognizing the need to be succinct, I have organized twenty-seven major differences under three categories. We shall begin with sociological features.

Sociological Features

1. Jesus' group was open; the Essenes' community was closed; and he and they espoused very different views of those not associated with them.[205] In terms of liminality[206] Jesus' group had a thin and porous border, the Qumranites a thick and impregnable barrier.[207] Jesus' message was

public, but the Qumran Essenes' teachings were secret.[208] The barriers were paradigmatically different. Virtually antithetical to the Qumran Essene attitude is that of Jesus: "he who is not against us is for us" (Mk 9:40).[209]

As David Noel Freedman states, the "Essenes were essentially a closed and secret society while Christianity was essentially an open one."[210] He then adds a new thought to the discussion: this contrast explains why "we cannot be sure from the Dead Sea Scrolls of the actual name of a single Essene," while we know the names of many of Jesus' followers.

Jesus fellowshiped with others virtually everywhere. The Essenes transferred the restrictive barriers of the Temple to their own community.[211] Jesus was dissimilar to the Essenes and similar to other Jews of his time on this point. It is a major difference between Jesus and the Essenes.

2. Jesus stands out in the history of Judaism with his emphasis on "love," even going so far as to exhort love of an enemy: "But I say to you, love your enemies and pray for those who persecute you" (Mt 5:44).[212] The Essenes also stand out in the history of Judaism with their teaching of hatred.[213] During the yearly renewal of the covenant, the Qumran Essenes even cursed other Jews,[214] and of course all others who were not members of their group. The Levites shall curse those who are not members of the lot of truth:

> Be cursed in all the works of your guilty wickedness.
> May God make of you an object of terror by the hand of all the avengers
>   of vengeance. . . .
> Be cursed, without mercy, according to the darkness of your works.
> Be damned[215] in the dark place of everlasting fire. (1QS 2.5–8)

Jesus' attitude to enemies, especially Roman soldiers, is placarded by his injunction to turn the other cheek and to carry the military bag one mile beyond what is required (Mt 5:39–41). This is the opposite of the militancy found in the War Scroll.[216] Some of Jesus' unique teachings are confronted in this example; but his teaching of moderation would have been shared by many Jews.

Prior to the sentence quoted from Matthew 5:44 is the following: "You have heard that it was said, 'You shall love your neighbor but hate your enemy'" (Mt 5:43). The first part of this quotation derives from Leviticus 19:18; but to what—or whom—is Jesus referring in the exhortation "to hate your enemy"? The passage cannot be found in the Hebrew Scriptures, the

Old Testament. Long ago K. Schubert, an Austrian specialist on the Dead Sea Scrolls, offered this informed insight:

> Who are these listeners, who had heard that they should hate their enemies? Nowhere in the entire Jewish tradition, and still less in the Old Testament, is there any trace of a command to hate one's enemies. Probably, however, such a concept is to be found in the writings of the Qumran sect, which is associated by the majority of investigators, and with good reason, with the Essene movement.[217]

Schubert then cites as the proof text the Rule of the Community: it is the duty of the members of the community "to love everyone whom he (God) has elected, and to hate everyone whom he has rejected" (1QS 1.4). The passage continues, ". . . to hate all sons of darkness, each one according to his sinfulness in the revenge of God" (1QS 1.10). It is important to comprehend that all "sons of darkness" are all who are not members of the community, or "sons of light."

The revered and distinguished Israeli specialist on the Dead Sea Scrolls Y. Yadin agreed with Schubert:

> There seems to be no doubt that Jesus was referring to the Essenes when he spoke scathingly of those who urged it as a duty to hate one's enemies, and it is my opinion that the people he was addressing were familiar with this Essene injunction, having perhaps been close to the Essene sect and believed in its doctrines, but who had now converted or were about to convert to the views of Jesus, and follow him.[218]

The quotations from Schubert and Yadin are right on target.[219] Jesus probably knew this aspect of Essene theology, abhorred it, and spoke out against it. He well knew what lay ahead for the people of Israel if hatred was the *modus operandi* for relating to the Romans. Unfortunately, his advice was not heeded, and the grandeur of ancient Israel went up in smoke in 70 C.E.

3. Jesus' concept of purity and impurity is reflected in his contention that impurity is not external—for example, whether one fasts[220] or washes before eating[221]—but internal: "there is nothing outside a person which when entering can defile one; but the things which come out of a person are what defiles the person" (Mk 7:16; cf. Mt 15:11). Antithetical to Essene rules for purity is Jesus' contention that all foods are clean (Mk 7:19).

In contrast to Jesus, the Essenes developed rigid and extensive rules to protect them from impurity, to punish those among them who were defiled, and to restore their momentarily lost purity.[222]

Typically Qumranic is the praise of God for purifying the faithful from impurities (4Q512). Note the following Qumran Pseudepigraphic Psalm: "[And y]ou will test all. And chosen ones, like offerings, you will declare pure (*tthr*) before you. But hated one[s] like impurity (*kndh*) you will reject" (4Q381 46 5–6).[223] As we know from an unpublished letter ("Some of the Precepts of the Torah"),[224] which the Righteous Teacher may have sent to a priest in Jerusalem, the Qumran group held to rules for purification that differed from other Jews (4QMMT).[225] The Qumranic penal code, which included the death penalty,[226] was closely aligned with the rules for purity.[227]

In terms of the concept of purity Jesus was categorically different from the Essenes.[228] G. Jeremias is correct to point to "an irreconcilable contrast."[229] For Jesus impurity was not a danger, as it was for the Essenes.[230] Jesus seems aloof from the debates over purity that were rife in first-century Palestine.[231] While he called for repentance, he did not demand it from his associates.[232] The concern for purity and protection from impurity explains the stone vessels mentioned in the New Testament (Jn 2:6) and discovered recently in the Upper City of Jerusalem.[233] Pottery transmitted impurity to the contents within: "All earthenware vessels shall be broken for they are unclean and never can be purified" (11QTemple 50.17–19).

4. Jesus associated with commoners, and even with lepers, the outcasts, and women; these actions would have been anathema to the Essenes. In contrast to the Essenes, Jesus visited in the house of a leper (Mk 14:3 and parallels). The Essenes were afraid of lepers, developed strict rules for dealing with such dangers (1QS, 1QM, 11QTemple), and placed lepers as outcasts in a section to the east of Jerusalem (11QTemple 46), precisely where Jesus is said to have entered a leper's home. Jesus' attitude to lepers and outcasts was unusual.

Jesus even associated with whores. As Vermes points out, "Jesus the Galilean holy man, who addressed not the learned or the seekers of perfection, but the simple country people, including publicans, sinners and whores" contrasts with "the austere figure of the Teacher of Righteousness. . . ."[234]

Jesus and the Essenes were on opposite ends of the spectrum with regard to women. Jesus included women in his group, considered them his friends, taught them scripture (Lk 10:38–42), and even broke Jewish taboos by conversing with a Gentile woman from Syrophoenicia and a woman of Samaria. As R. Hamerton-Kelly has shown, "Jesus broke the forms of the patriarchal family in the name of God the Father, and recognized the natural right of women to equal humanity with men."[235] This perspective is developed by numerous scholars, including B. Witherington and E. Schüssler Fiorenza.[236]

The Essenes, in bold contrast to Jesus, considered women unreliable and faithless and strove to separate themselves from a woman's natural wantonness (Josephus, *War* 2.121). The authors (and editors) of the Damascus Document explain that the corruption in the Temple cult resulted from impure association with women (CD 4-5), and they stipulate that those Essenes who marry must obey not only the scriptures (Torah) but also the Essene statutes and binding oaths they have sworn (CD 7). One of the statutes prohibited intercourse with one's wife in Jerusalem (CD 12).[237] A wisdom poem from Qumran Cave 4 (4Q184)[238] depicts the dangers of false interpretations of scripture as a woman whose heart is "a snare," who is the "cause of all wickedness," and whose paths are "ways of death." The Rule of the Community does not mention or include a "woman" ('*iššâ*).[239] These perspectives are not to be equated with the attitudes to women found among most Jews, probably reflected in Mishna *Nashim*, which *inter alia* requires that a woman *and a man* when married are equally responsible in consenting to sexual intercourse (m.Ket 5:7; cf. 1Cor 7:3-4, which was composed by the Pharisaic-Christian Paul).

5. Jesus is reputed to love a good party (Jn 2) and to socialize with leading Pharisees. He even admitted to having a reputation for enjoying wine, and his opponents labeled him "a glutton and a drunkard" (Mt 11:19; Lk 7:34). Jesus was certainly no ascetic as were the Essenes.[240]

6. Jesus called people to follow him; many rejected him. He was in this respect impressively dissimilar to the Essenes. In fact, there is no missionary document among the Qumran Essenes.[241] At least during the early phase of the community, the Qumran Essenes accepted only volunteers who were priests; many were rejected by them. Jesus' appeal to the masses was very different from the Essenes';[242] and it marks him off from most other Jewish religious leaders of his day.[243] In fact Jesus' missionary zeal contrasts with Judaism, which was a religion with little missionary zeal.[244]

7. Jesus' chose to speak simply and preferred clear pictorial language. The Gospels are easy to comprehend, but the Dead Sea Scrolls are sometimes obtuse.[245] The Qumran Essenes sometimes wrote in codes so as to

hide their message from the uninitiated (4QCryptic).[246] They sometimes wrote a mirror image of the text and used different alphabets and symbols known only to a few. In contrast, Jesus' message was not only pellucidly clear but also for the masses:[247] "if any would be first, he must be last of all and servant of all" (Mk 9:35). The Essenes wrote only for the learned and initiated into their closed group: "They are the sons of Zadok who [seek their own] counsel and follow [their own inclination] apart from the Council of the Community" (4Q174).[248] Jesus' simple language categorizes him with the authors of many of the rabbinic traditions; his use of language was frequently unlike that of the Essenes. For example, Jesus' famous golden rule (Mt 7:12; Lk 6:31) is reputedly[249] shared by his near contemporary Hillel, who said, "Do not unto others what you would not have them do unto you" (b.Shab 31a).[250]

8. In the eyes of many pious Jews, Jesus was polluted by his association with the needy, outcast, and impure. The Qumran Essenes dissociated themselves from the impure, stating that the unclean shall never enter "the sanctuary" (11QTemple 45; 4Q174). Jesus crossed the boundaries of purity; the Essenes withdrew behind protective boundaries.[251] Jesus moved about the countryside, crossed the Sea of Galilee, and traversed the land from Caesarea Philippi in the north to Jerusalem in the south. The Qumran Essenes lived in guaranteed isolation in the desert; the other Essenes lived in self-imposed ghettoes on the fringes of the cities and villages (Josephus and Philo). Jesus conversed with a Syrophoenician woman (Mk) and a Samaritan woman (Jn). He discussed religious matters with many Romans and commended the "faith" of a centurion (Mt 8:5–13; Lk 7:1–10). The Qumran Essenes developed strict rules which prohibited any commerce or association with Gentiles (1QS; Josephus). While Jesus' conciliatory attitude is similar to that of the Hillelites, he seems to be unique in his cavalier attitude to the taboos and mores of his Jewish culture.

These observations reflect major differences between Jesus and the Essenes.[252] Boundaries reflect self-identifications.[253] Many of the new legislations in the Rule of the Community[254] devised by the Qumran covenanters illustrate how antithetical the Qumran group was to Jesus and his group; they also fit Douglas's insight that "when rituals express anxiety about the body's orifices the sociological counterpart of this anxiety is a care to protect the political and cultural unity of a minority group. The Israelites were always in their history a hard-pressed minority. . . . The anxiety about bodily margins expresses danger to group survival."[255] Not only were Palestinian Jews a minority in the Roman Empire, but the Qumranites were marginal within Judaism (and perhaps also within the larger Essene group).

9. Jesus was famous for his healing miracles. That some of these are historical seems assured by their wide attestation in numerous sources, including the Talmud, and the claims of his opponents that he performed them because he was in league with Beelzebul: "And the scribes who had come down from Jerusalem said, 'He is possessed by Beelzebul, and by the ruler of demons he casts out the demons'" (Mk 3:22). Although Josephus reports that the Essenes were interested in treating diseases and medical cures (*War* 2.136),[256] there is only meager evidence in the Dead Sea Scrolls that the Essenes were interested in medical issues.[257]

Jesus performed healings like those attributed to Apollonius of Tyana, but he was a Pythagorean philosopher and not an Essene.[258] Jesus' healing miracles are similar to those claimed for his contemporary Ḥanina ben Dosa,[259] but the latter was a pupil of Johanan ben Zakkai (b.Ber. 34b).[260] There may be some link between Jesus and the Essenes,[261] but he—and not they—was famous for performing healing miracles.[262]

10. Jesus and the Essenes were very different in terms of their concept of initiation. For Jesus "initiation" was not prolonged; rapidly one could leave all behind and "follow him," by repenting and perhaps by being baptized. To join the *ḥaberim* required at least one month (t.Dem 2.10–12); but to join the Essene group took at least two years of preparation and examination, after which all personal items were irretrievably given to the community (1QS 6.13–23).[263] Full initiation involved study and devotion to the Essene rules, hatred of others, shifting to a solar calendar, devotion to the Righteous Teacher, acceptance of the claim that the Teacher had received a special revelation, following the Teacher's means of interpreting scripture (see 1QS, 1QpHab), and severe testing.[264] Jesus' call to follow him marks him out as different within first-century Judaism.[265]

11. Although Jesus elevated twelve disciples,[266] among whom were three special leaders (Peter, James, and John),[267] he did not establish a strong hierarchy and rules for advancement. Rather, he stressed not so much egalitarianism as being a servant: "whoever would be first among you must be slave of all" (Mk 10:44; cf. 9:35).[268] Jesus constituted new communities that were structured in nonpatriarchal familial terms.[269]

Jesus contrasts markedly with the Qumran Essenes, who had set strata within the community, rules for advancement and demotion, and even severe punishments (1QS).[270] The Qumran community was rigidly structured.[271] Josephus reported that the "four grades" were so separate that if "a senior" was "touched by a junior" he must cleanse himself, as if contacted by one impure (*War* 2.150).

Jesus' apparent lack of concern for strict organization links him with many other groups of his time. But it would be patently absurd to classify him on that ground alone with others who lacked organization or were disorganized, like the false messiahs, zealous ones or Zealots, or the bandits. As R. B. Y. Scott pointed out long ago, some of Jesus' sayings "seem to be deliberately critical of the Essene position. . . . He warned his disciples against consciousness of rank, in contrast to the marked emphasis on order and precedence in the regulations of the Qumran Covenanters."[272]

12. Jesus and the Essenes would be sharply divided on the veneration shown the Righteous Teacher.[273] Like most Jews, Jesus would have vehemently rejected the Essenes' devotion to the Righteous Teacher and their claims that only he knew the meaning of Torah (1QpHab 7).[274]

13. Some excellent scholars have attempted to forge some link between Jesus and the Essene solar calendar,[275] but there is no strong evidence to support this hypothesis. If the Gospels of Mark and John can be trusted, then it seems self-evident that Jesus followed the lunar calendar with other Jews. Different calendars cause major theological and sociological problems; it is imperative to know on which day to celebrate the Sabbath and the great festivals, such as Passover. The requirement is also cosmological, since according to many of the apocalyptic writings the angels observe the Sabbath (see the Angelic Liturgy).[276]

The Qumran Scrolls disclose that a solar calendar,[277] divergent from the lunar calendar of the Temple, was not fiction or some distant ideal, as many had suspected on the basis of 1 Enoch and Jubilees; it was actually followed by the Essenes.[278] By following a unique and divergent calendar, the Essenes deliberately set themselves up as a separate "self-contained socioreligious entity cut off from the mother community."[279] Jesus did not follow a special calendar and so separate himself from the mainstream community of Jews.

14. Jesus wrote nothing.[280] The Essenes were the writing group in Early Judaism.[281] Jesus focused his energies on oral proclamations; the Qumran Essenes (including probably the Righteous Teacher) were preoccupied with writing and copying. Jesus left no book; the Essenes left a library of books.

15. Jesus possessed no formal training. The Essenes were dedicated to

studying the scriptures and their own writings.[282] Their way was "the study of Torah" (1QS 8.15). In his lack of scholarly credentials and methods, Jesus stands out as unique among the other Jewish leaders of his day:

> And many who heard him were astonished, saying, "Where did this (man get) these (teachings)? What is the wisdom given to him? What mighty works are wrought by his hands! Is not this the carpenter, the son of Mary and brother of James and Joses and Judas and Simon, and are not his sisters here with us?" (Mk 6:2–3).[283]

Jesus' authority was not derivative from others;[284] in Jerusalem the chief priests and scribes ostensibly asked him, "By what authority are you doing these things, or who gave you this authority to do them?" (Mk 11:28). Unlike Hillel, who studied under Shemaiah and Abtalion,[285] Jesus did not study in an academy. Jesus' training was also unlike the Qumran Essenes, who were drilled by an "Instructor," who taught "all understanding" and the proper calendar (1QS 9.12–14).

16. Jesus was vulnerable; he was opposed by religious lawyers and even his own followers. The Essenes benefited by a private support group, especially the community into which they entered after initiation. Philo notes that the Essenes "dwell together in communities" and that "the door is open to others (Essenes) from elsewhere who share their convictions."[286] Josephus claimed that the Essenes "show a greater attachment to each other than do the other" Jewish groups (*War* 2.119); and, in line with Philo, he added that when Essenes traveled they entered the houses of other Essenes "whom they have never formerly seen as though they were the most intimate friends" (*War* 2.125).

Jesus is portrayed as being intermittently reclusive. He often retires alone to the mountains. His life was one of rejection, as H. Boers states, "Those who knew him well historically, rejected him."[287] Finally his disciples, perpetually confused, abandon him at the end of his life. As an isolated, misunderstood leader of a religious group, Jesus was rather unusual in first-century Palestine.

Sociologically there were vast differences between Jesus and the Essenes. He was frequently more similar to other Jews of his day than to the Essenes (numbers 1, 2, 5, 7, 11, 12, 13, 14). In many ways Jesus was also different from other Jews, including the Essenes (numbers 3, 4, 6, 8, 9, 10, 15, 16). One example discloses that Jesus may well have spoken against an Essene teaching (number 2).

Concepts and Interpretations of Scripture

Obviously some of what has already been said applies also to the following conceptions. Jesus' teaching on love and prohibition of hate evolved out of his interpretation of scriptures and observations of his contemporaries, which certainly included the Essenes.

17.   As a deeply religious Jew, Jesus was often liberally critical of sacred scripture. The Jesus tradition was highlighted by the author of Matthew, who quoted the famous antitheses of the Sermon on the Mount, for example, "Again you have heard that it was said to the men of old, 'You shall not swear falsely. . . .' But I say to you, Do not swear (or take an oath)[288] at all . . ." (Mt 5:33–34).[289]

This teaching may well have been directed against the Essenes,[290] who institutionalized the swearing of a solemn and binding oath when entering into the community (1QS 5.7–20; cf. 1QH 14.17; CD 16.10–12).[291] Moreover, the Levites ceremonially were to "curse"—swear against—all those in the lot of Belial, and this was to be performed before the gathering of the community during the yearly renewal of the covenant (1QS 2.4–10). Jesus' prohibition of swearing an oath may well have been directed against the Essenes, perhaps those living in villages and cities in Galilee and Judea.

Along with Hillel, Jesus could summarize the Torah by quoting the first two commandments in the Decalogue of Exodus 20 (and Dt 5).[292] Such a perspective and method would have been abhorrent to the Essenes. The Dead Sea Scrolls clarify the rules and statutes added to Torah as part of the essential teaching.[293] The Righteous Teacher and his followers were far more strict in interpreting the scriptures. As J. Milgrom has pointed out from his impressive knowledge of Jewish exegesis, the Qumranites, following the basic axiom of fundamentalism, held one exegetical technique that "made all the difference" among their contemporaries. "It is exemplified by their respective use of the exegetical technique of homogenization/*binyan 'ab*."[294] That means that for the Qumranites "divergent opinions are intolerable. . . ." Unlike Jesus and Hillel, the Essenes, like the Shammaites, could not summarize the Torah "while standing on one foot."

Jesus was very different from the Essenes. While he was liberally critical of Torah, they were conservative and added regulations. Yet he was devout in ways that, as E. Käsemann said, contrast him with other devout Jews of his time, raising the key question, "not whether the 'liberal' man was devout, but, in so far as there ever was anything here to discuss, whether and why the devout man was 'liberal.'"[295]

18.   Jesus admired the great prophets and quoted them to substantiate a point. The Essenes tended to think that the prophets were ignorant of the meaning of their prophecies (see 1QpHab 7). Jesus was more attuned to the reverence of the sages found in such famous passages as Sirach 44–50.[296]

19.   For both Jesus and the Essenes "the Lord" (*Yhwh*) was a God who had a story (*Heilsgeschichte*). Jesus laced his teachings with stories, while the Essenes developed binding rules. Jesus taught other Jews to be free from legalistic religion; the Essenes originated as a separate group because of their interpretation of legal issues (4QMMT). Many of the Dead Sea Scrolls are legalistic (1QS, CD, 5Q13, 4Q513–514).

While Jesus was interested in rules (halakot), his message was shaped by parables. While the Dead Sea Scrolls do contain some stories (1QapGen) and some allegories (1QH 8), they do not contain parables as we find in the Jesus tradition, within early rabbinics,[297] in the Apocryphon of Ezekiel, and in 4 Ezra.

20.   No saying that can be traced back to the historical Jesus is clearly predestinarian or deterministic.[298] Predestination or determinism, however, is a hallmark[299] of the Essenes.[300] As the Curator of the Shrine of the Book, M. Broshi, stated, "Perhaps the most important theological point differentiating the sectarians [=Essenes] from the rest of Judaism was their belief in predestination, coupled with a dualistic view of the world (*praedestinatio duplex*)."[301] Jesus did not teach that one was a "son of light" or a "son of darkness" because of the scoops of light or darkness given to one at creation.

21.   Like many other Jews of his time, especially the Pharisees, Jesus believed in the resurrection of the dead at the endtime (see Mk 12:18–27). There is no clear evidence that the Essenes believed in bodily resurrection, as we know, for example, from 2 Maccabees 14.[302] The passages that have been interpreted to imply a belief in the resurrection of the dead are ambiguous and probably metaphorical.[303]

22.   Jesus affirmed the beauty of nature in a natural, realistic, and pictorial way. He illustrated his teachings, for example, by describing animals and the lilies of the field (Mt 6). The Qumran Essenes tended to refer to nature in a quasi-allegorical fashion (1QH 8).

23.   Jesus never mentioned Michael, Gabriel, Raphael, and Sariel.[304] The Essenes, however, developed an extensive angelology; and these names

appear, for example, in the War Scroll (1QM 9.15–16). Jesus developed no angelology as we find in the numerous apocalyptic writings (especially 1 Enoch). Josephus was right, therefore, to single out the Essenes for their careful attention to "the names of the angels" (*War* 2.142).

24. Jesus apparently knew that his way of life and challenging teachings could well lead to martyrdom.[305] He probably knew how Honi, an earlier Galilean miracle worker who talked about being God's son[306] had been stoned outside the walls of Jerusalem.[307] He probably knew also about the traditions concerning the deaths and martyrdoms suffered by the great prophets, like Isaiah and Jeremiah.[308] He probably knew the traditions about suffering and martyrdom in early Jewish sources.[309] He certainly knew about the beheading of his former colleague, John the Baptizer. Some of his premonitions about facing martyrdom appear to be authentic and not created later by his followers.[310]

J. M. Allegro continued to claim that the Righteous Teacher was martyred; he even suggested that he had been crucified by Alexander Janneus.[311] This suggestion is forced onto the texts; it derives from contorted historiography and exegesis. There is also insufficient reason to conclude that the Qumran Essenes were "a pre-Christian martyr-cult."[312] There is no parallel here between Jesus and the Essenes. Moreover, in contrast to Jesus and his followers, there is no evidence that the Righteous Teacher, or his followers, claimed he was the Messiah.[313] As R. E. Brown, P. Perkins, and A. J. Saldarini conclude, "The claims that he [the Righteous Teacher] was a messiah, that he was crucified, that he came back to life, or that he was the forerunner of Jesus Christ are totally unfounded."[314]

25. Jesus had a liberal attitude to the laws governing the Sabbath. He stressed that the Sabbath was made for the human and not the human for the Sabbath. His teachings were here antithetical to the Essenes, who were strict Sabbatarians. Josephus reported that the Essenes "of all Jews were most strict in abstaining from work on the seventh day" (*War* 2.147).[315] This judgment harmonizes with exegetical studies on the Damascus Document (CD 10–11).[316]

One of Jesus' Sabbath teachings may well have been directed against the Essenes. According to Mt 12:11 Jesus asked, "Which man[317] of you, if he has one sheep and it falls into a pit on the Sabbath, will not lay hold of it and lift it out?"[318] Jesus was clearly directing this charge to Jews who would have assumed that absolutely no such work should be performed on the Sabbath. Who could they be? They may well have been Jews who revered the book of Jubilees, but there is no such ruling in this pseudepigraphon. The link is found in a stunning way in the Damascus Document, which was revered at Qumran and probably edited by the Essenes. Note the following passage: "Let no man help a beast to give birth[319] on the Sabbath day; and if it fall into a cistern or into a pit, let it not be lifted out on the Sabbath" (CD 11.13). The link between Jesus' teaching and the Essene injunction is at once impressive and astounding. Again we see that Jesus was liberal and the Essenes extremely conservative in interpreting Torah. He may well have directed his attack against an Essene teaching on the Sabbath. This possibility becomes even more probable if the Damascus Document, as seems likely, contained the rules for Essenes not living in exile at Qumran. To celebrate the Sabbath incorrectly is disorienting[320] and has not only liturgical but cosmic ramifications (Angelic Liturgy, ApAdam, AsMos).

26. Jesus' self-understanding is hotly debated among scholars, but it seems reasonable to conclude that he thought of himself as God's son,[321] and in a special way that is not now possible to discern.[322] Flusser is convinced that Jesus knew the Thanksgiving Hymns[323] and "used their form in order to express his own place in the divine economy, though he introduced into his own hymn[324] the motif of his divine sonship, which is naturally absent from the Thanksgiving Scroll.[325]

It can be reported that Jesus shared this self-perception of being God's son with Honi, if the tradition is reliable. But he certainly did not share it with the Righteous Teacher.

27. As is well known, Jesus' essential message is the proclamation that God's rule, "the kingdom of God," is now beginning to dawn around him.[326] This technical term was shared by Jesus with other Jews, especially such diverse Jews as the authors of Wisdom 10:10 ("She [Wisdom] showed him the kingdom of God") and Psalms of Solomon 17:4 ("the kingdom of our God").[327] It is paralleled by pronouns referring to God, "your kingdom" (Dan 3:54), "his kingdom" (Tob 13:2 [1]; WisSol 6:4), and synonymous with the circumlocutions for the divine, ineffable name, in the Testaments of the Twelve Patriarchs 9:1 ("the kingdom of the Lord"), Matthew ("the kingdom of heaven"), and early rabbinics.[328] The term "kingdom of God" has not been found among the Dead Sea Scrolls. The closest links are the following: "And the kingdom shall be to the God of Israel" (1QM 6.6); "And you are an awe[some] God in the glory of your kingdom" (1QM 12.7). The recently published Qumranic Angelic Liturgy refers more to God as "king" and to "his kingdom" than any other early Jewish text,[329] but it does not contain

the technical term so familiar in the teachings of Jesus. Here Jesus' message is a major development of terms and concepts found in early Jewish theology. Jesus, and not the Essenes, explained the meaning of God's rule, "the kingdom of God."[330]

In summary, Jesus was closely linked with many other Jews as they differed from the Essenes (numbers 18, 19, 20, 21, 22). He was dissimilar in many ways to most, and sometimes all, Jews including the Essenes (numbers 23, 24, 26, 27). In at least two ways he seems to have directly opposed the Essenes (17, 25).

In the discussion above an attempt has been made to present a balanced and inclusiveness perspective. Moderation was aimed at, since a similarity when stressed can become a dissimilarity. The most important aspects of this exploration are surely the questions raised, the possibilities assessed, and the perspectives obtained. Unintentionally, it becomes apparent both how dependent Jesus was upon early Jewish theology and how creative he was within Early Judaism. The following summary clarifies these points.

Summary The following list repeats the similarities and differences discussed with clarifying notations. "C" (for common) at the end of a parallel denotes that a similarity is shared with many other early Jews.

Use of italics signifies that in some ways Jesus may have been influenced by the Essenes. When it is followed by an asterisk the influence may be direct. An asterisk followed by a plus (+) or minus (–) sign suggests that Jesus could have been positively or negatively reacting to an Essene thought or life-style. An asterisk followed by a question mark (?) implies that the issue points to a new insight that requires additional research. Regarding differences, MSO indicates that Jesus was more similar to other Jews than to Essenes, DFO points out that Jesus was different from other Jews, including Essenes (but does not prove uniqueness).

MAJOR SIMILARITIES
Scripture-based Theology
1. Concept of God C
2. Hebrew Scriptures for guiding source C
3. *Possible fondness for same scriptural books* * ?
4. *Pneumatic, eschatological, and messianic exegesis* * ?
5. *Isaiah 40:3*

6. *The new covenant*
7. *The continuation of prophecy*

Cosmic-shaped Chronology
8. Two ages and two worlds C
9. Cosmos full of demons and angels C
10. *Eschatological redemption for "the poor" * +*
11. *Messianology*
12. *Attitude toward Jerusalem, Temple, and cult*

Humility before God
13. Sinfulness of all humans C
14. God of forgiveness and grace C
15. Salvation and justification are God's gift
16. *An unusual stress on prayer*
17. *Heightened concept of inward holiness*
18. *Symbolic use of water*
19. *Shared possessions * +*
20. *Condemnation of divorce * +*
21. *The technical term "sons of light" * +*
22. One prophetic and charismatic person
23. *Celibacy as being "married" to God*
24. *The concept of the Holy Spirit * +*

MAJOR DIFFERENCES
Sociological Features
1. Open versus closed concept of group MSO
2. *Concept of love and hatred * – MSO*
3. Concept of purity and impurity DFO
4. Attitude to lepers and outcasts DFO
5. Socializing MSO
6. Missionary zeal DFO
7. Simple, pictorial language MSO

8. Boundaries of purity DFO
9. Healing miracles DFO
10. Initiation DFO
11. Hierarchy and rules MSO
12. Veneration of the Righteous Teacher MSO
13. Calendar MSO
14. Writing MSO
15. Nonderivative authority DFO
16. Vulnerability and intermittent reclusiveness DFO

Concepts and Interpretations of Scripture
17. Liberally critical (*Swearing* * –) DFO
18. Prophets were not ignorant of meaning MSO
19. Parables MSO
20. Predestination or determination MSO
21. Belief in the resurrection of the dead MSO
22. The natural beauty of nature in discourse MSO
23. Angelology DFO
24. Martyrdom DFO
25. *Sabbath* * – DFO
26. Concept of sonship DFO
27. God's rule or "kingdom of God" DFO

CONCLUSION

The study of the possible relation of Jesus to the Essenes has been profitable. Most importantly, we have been able to free ourselves from the stresses of our own day and ponder what life was like back then and over there. Of course, I mean before the end of the history of ancient Israel in 70, with the burning of the Temple by Titus's troops, and in a land called the "Holy Land" by Jews and Christians.[331]

Five conclusions are apparent. First, Jesus was certainly not an Essene,[332] as some authors have claimed.[333] He was also not taught by or significantly influenced by the Essenes, despite the attempts of many scholars from Bahrdt in the eighteenth century until today at the close of the twentieth century.

Second, Jesus was probably influenced in minor ways by the Essenes.[334] He could have shared their fondness for the same scriptural books (3), and been influenced by their pneumatic, eschatological, and messianic exegesis (4). He may have inherited from Essenes the ideas of redemption eschatologically for "the Poor" (10), sharing of possessions (19), and condemnation of divorce (20); the technical term "sons of light"; and the concept of "the Holy Spirit."

Jesus could have been attracted to the Essenes' dedication to Torah. He referred to Essenes appreciatively—if the saying about the eunuchs in Matthew derives ultimately from him and he had the Essenes in mind. Perhaps with the publication of more of the Dead Sea Scrolls we may be able to shed some light on this still-unresolved problem. Presently, we can only be intrigued by the possibility that Jesus referred to the Essenes with admiration when he praised those who became eunuchs for the kingdom (Mt 19:10–12).

Even so, it is clear that Jesus would have rejected the Essenes' calendar (13), strict conservatism (17), concept of purity (3, 4, 8), and rigid binding rules (11). He would have abhorred—and may well have castigated—their rules for hating (2), their swearing (17) and their dehumanizing understanding of the Sabbath (25).

Yadin concluded that Jesus knew the Essenes' teachings and was "anti-Essene."[335] This assessment is only partly true; some of Jesus' sayings indicate that he may have been fond of some Essene life-styles and a few dimensions of their theology.

Third, the Dead Sea Scrolls are an invaluable source for helping us understand the life and teaching of Jesus. They provide some ideological context for his thought, and they illumine the social setting and context of pre-70 Jewish life in the Land. These scrolls transport us to the scribes who wrote upon, and even helped prepare, the leather and papyrus for writing. We are not left sequestered, either in the academic halls of the early church councils or in the communities—or schools—that shaped the canonical Gospels. We begin to appreciate more fully the wise counsel of Sandmel, one of the great Jewish scholars of the last generation; he urged us to comprehend that Jesus was not only a Jew, "but a figure such as he could not have arisen in any other tradition or culture but Judaism."[336]

Fourth Jesus was influenced by many groups within Judaism. He was obviously influenced by John the Baptizer and his group, since he was baptized by him, and may well have initially led a similar baptist movement and inherited some of John the Baptist's disciples. The latter possibilities depend on the historical validity of the early chapters of the Gospel of John.

Jesus may well have been directly influenced by Hillel, who died sometime before his public ministry began around 26 C.E. He was certainly influenced by the Jewish apocalyptic groups; but although some excellent scholars entertain the possibility that he was influenced by the authors of the Apocalypses of Enoch (1 Enoch), there is no compelling evidence that he was directly influenced by any extant apocalypse. Unlike the Righteous Teacher, Hillel, and even Paul, Jesus was not a member of any Jewish group. The recent attempts to define him as a Pharisee have not convinced many scholars.[337]

Jesus was influenced by numerous groups and currents of thought within Judaism of his time, which was very diverse and creative. Worth contemplating is L. Schiffman's overview: "Contrary to what was previously assumed, the Houses of Hillel and Shammai did not exert as much influence upon Christianity as the various sects and groups whose literature survives in the Dead Sea Scrolls and in the Apocrypha and Pseudepigrapha."[338] Schiffman is speaking about "Christianity." I have been focusing on Jesus[339] and the setting before the emergence of "Christianity" after 70 C.E.[340] Personally, I tend to agree with Schiffman, without closing the door on strong influences from Hillel on Jesus.

Fifth, the attempts to revive E. Renan's claim that Christianity is Essenism that has survived have failed. Christianity is not a form of Essenism. Yet, as research on the Dead Sea Scrolls continues especially with the publication of additional fragments, and with the elucidation of the social world and thought of the evangelists, it has become more obvious that Essene influence is greater in the second and third generations of Jesus' followers than in Jesus' times and among his earliest followers. Hence, there is more evidence of Essene influence in the post-Pauline epistles (especially Ephesians) than in the undisputed letters of Paul (notably Galatians and Romans).[341] There is more evidence of Essene influence in Matthew and John, than in Mark, which antedates them.[342]

The Dead Sea Scrolls are now internationally recognized as essential reading in the attempt to understand Jesus as a human being in his own time. They are illuminating as we attempt to comprehend how and in what ways Jesus was similar and dissimilar to the Essenes. We have much to ponder; for example, I am convinced that Jesus was closer to the non-Qumran Essenes than to the strict and withdrawn Essenes living in the desert of Judea.

Out of the gray shadows of history a unique figure begins to emerge. He moves and begins to call Jews to follow him and restore the covenant loyalty of Israel. He is obsessed with doing God's will. He announces that God's rule, "the kingdom of God," is becoming powerfully present in his healing miracles and parables. Surely the rise of Christianity can be explained only in light of the creative genius of Jesus of Nazareth.[343]

That mysterious historical figure, Jesus, stirs imagination. The chasm between the first century and now vanishes only momentarily. For Christians who struggle to understand their commitment to God through Jesus, he is, of course, much more. To them, he is the one who challenges and forms commitments and dreams.

By examining Jewish documents, like the Dead Sea Scrolls that are contemporaneous with Jesus, we find many terms, phrases, and concepts once considered unique to Jesus. This discovery may disappoint those who wish a Jesus who is unique and in no way similar to his Jewish contemporaries or influenced by their thoughts and writings. Christian theologians for over nineteen hundred years have warned that this line of reasoning is dangerous and denies the truth encapsulated in John 1:14, "And the Word became flesh and dwelt among us. . . ."

As we comprehend Jesus within his Jewish culture we are learning to confront a real person in a specific time and place. This endeavor safeguards Christians from the greatest of Christian heresies — Docetism. This doctrine denies that Jesus became human and suffered. It affirms that he was only a heavenly being. We are now, thanks to the discovery of the Dead Sea Scrolls, more realistically confronted with the dynamics of human life empowered by the awesome presence of God. After historical inquiries such as this one, Christians will feel a kinship with Jews; they will also seek to ponder the christological truths embodied in such confessions as Jesus' prayer to God that they may be "one even as we are one" (Jn 17:22).

These explorations raise far more questions than they answer. Perhaps such curiosity will help readers comprehend the creative reflections in the following chapters.

Notes

1. E. Wilson (1895–1972) was not just a journalist; he was a famous author and critic. He was opinionated, controversial, and at times brilliantly insightful. His articles in the *New Yorker* succeeded in making the "Dead Sea Scrolls" popular, and a household world. His books are assembled together in *Israel and the Dead Sea Scrolls* (New York, 1978).

2. See the Foreword at the beginning of this book.

3. A. D. Tushingham, "The Men Who Hid the Dead Sea Scrolls," *National Geographic Magazine* 94.6 (1958) 785–808; quotation from p. 808. Tushingham was the head of the Division of Art and Archaeology, Royal Ontario Museum.

4. For example, read the exciting account of Professor E. L. Sukenik's risky trip to see the first discovered scrolls, his conversations with Arabs through barbed wire barriers in Jerusalem, and his eventual success. These are described by his son, Y. Yadin, in *The Message of the Scrolls* (New York, 1957, 1962 [to be reprinted by Crossroad]).

5. Often the buildings are called a "monastery," but this term seems to transport Christian ideas into pre-70 Judaism.

6. This hypothesis was advanced by H. Stegemann in *Die Entstehung der Qumrangemeinde* (Bonn, 1971). It was questioned by me in "The Origin and Subsequent History of the Authors of the Dead Sea Scrolls: Four Transitional Phases Among the Quman Essenes," *RQ* 10 (1979–80) 213–33 and more recently by J. J. Collins in "The Origin of the Qumran Community: A Review of the Evidence," in *To Touch the Text: Biblical and Related Studies in Honor of Joseph A. Fitzmyer, S.J.*, ed. M. P. Horgan and P. J. Kobelski (New York, 1989) pp. 159–78. P. R. Callaway has warned against too much speculation in reconstructing the history of the Qumran community; see his *The History of the Qumran Community: An Investigation* (JSPS 3; Sheffield, 1988).

7. J. Strugnell, on the basis of reflections on 4Q375 and 4Q376, with penetrating historical imagination, suggests that the Righteous Teacher may have carried "off with him on his flight to Qumran" the high-priestly garments. Why did the Wicked Priest go to Qumran on the Day of Atonement? Strugnell asks, ". . . was this not more precisely an attempt to regain possession of those bejewelled high-priestly vestments which, on that day if any, his opponent would have to be wearing?" (p. 247) In fairness to Strugnell it is important to note that this is presented as a question to ponder. See Strugnell, "Moses-Pseudepigrapha at Qumran: 4Q375, 4Q376, and Similar Works," in *Archaeology and History in the Dead Sea Scrolls: The New York University Conference in Memory of Yigael Yadin*, ed. L. H. Schiffman (JSPS; JSOT/ASOR 2; Sheffield, 1990) pp. 221–56.

8. G. W. Buchanan disputes the date for the destruction of Qumran. See his "Some Unfinished Business with the Dead Sea Scrolls," *RQ* 13 (1988) 411–20.

9. See R. de Vaux, *Archaeology and the Dead Sea Scrolls,* trans. D. Bourke (London, 1973).

10. Some of these discoveries near Herod's palace at Jericho, especially the numerous ritual baths (*mikvaoth*) to the west of the gigantic swimming pool, have not yet been adequately published or discussed.

11. F. M. Cross has rightly shown that Zadok was a descendant of Aaron. Hence, the Zadokites—descendants of Zadok—are also Aaronites.

12. See chapter 5 in this book, which focuses on the Righteous Teacher.

13. One of the most famous attempts is by J. Carmignac, who claimed in numerous publications that he is to be identified with Judas the Essene (Josephus, *War* 1.78-80; *Ant* 13.311-13). See J. Carmignac, "Qui etait le docteur de Justice?" *RQ* 10 (1980) 235-46; however, consult the critique by J. Murphy-O'Connor, "Judah the Essene and the Teacher of Righteousness," *RQ* 10 (1981) 579-85. Also consult H. Burgmann, *Zwei lösbare Qumranprobleme: Die Person des Lügenmannes: Die Interkalation im Kalender* (Frankfurt am Main, New York, 1986), who concludes that the name of the Righteous Teacher is unknown (pp. 254-55).

14. M. Smith argues that the account of the Essenes in the Philosophumena (ed. E. Miller, *Origenis Philosophumena*) and in Josephus's *War* 2 are related; they are two independent copies and translations of another document. Smith, "The Description of the Essenes in Josephus and the Philosophumena," *HUCA* 29 (1958) 273-313.

15. See J. C. Vanderkam, "The People of the Dead Sea Scrolls: Essenes or Sadducees?" *BibRev* 7 (1991) 42-47. A convenient collection of ancient references to the Essenes was published by A. Adam in *Antike Berichte über die Essener,* new edition by C. Burchard (KlT 182; Berlin, 1972).

16. S. Talmon rightly warns me that the identification of the Qumran covenanters with the Essenes is *sub judice,* especially since the work on 4QMMT. I have reread the ancient accounts of the Essenes and am more impressed than formerly of the Essene nature of the Dead Sea Scrolls. Surely what became Sadducean halakot may have been shared by the Essenes in the second century B.C.E. The links between Josephus' Essenes and the Qumran Scrolls are too numerous and striking to ignore. Obviously the Essenes of Josephus cannot be simply equated with the Qumranites; the history of the Qumranites is long, covering three centuries, and there is considerable development at Qumran. Likewise the life-style of the "Qumran Essenes" would be more strict than those living, for example, in Jerusalem. There were at least two distinct types of Essenes in Palestine.

17. F. M. Cross, *Canaanite Myth and Hebrew Epic: Essays in the History of the Religion of Israel* (Cambridge, Mass., 1973) pp. 331-32.

18. For a discussion of the sensational claims and the excessive reactions, see J. H. Charlesworth, "Jesus and the Dead Sea Scrolls," *Jesus Within Judaism: New Light from Exciting Archaeological Discoveries* (ABRL 1; New York, 1988) pp. 54-76.

19. See especially the conclusions by the excellent scholar W. S. LaSor in *The Dead Sea Scrolls and the New Testament* (Grand Rapids, 1972).

20. In using these terms the authors exposed their ignorance of the history of christological titles. "Son of Man" was not used by the earliest followers of Jesus to explain his humanity; it was a title that denoted heavenly, cosmic, and eschatological powers. See the classic by F. H. Borsch titled *The Son of Man in Myth and History* (New Testament Library; Philadelphia, 1967); A. J. B. Higgins, *The Son of Man in the Teaching of Jesus* (SNTS Monograph Series 39; Cambridge, 1980); B. Lindars, *Jesus Son of Man* (Grand Rapids, 1983); D. R. A. Hare, *The Son of Man Tradition* (Minneapolis, 1990).

21. See now the judicious comments by H. Shanks in *The Dead Sea Scrolls After Forty Years (Symposium at the Smithsonian Institution October 27, 1990)* (Washington, 1991) p. 75.

22. See the Foreword for the consensus shared by most leading scholars.

23. "Sea Scrolls Editor Removed," *New York Times,* December 11, 1990. "Dead Sea Scrolls Editor's Exit Tied to Anti-Jewish Remarks," *New York Times,* December 12, 1990.

24. "Ouster of an 'Anti-Judaist,' " *Time,* January 14, 1991, p. 63.

25. "Scrolls and the Strugnell Antisemitic Mindset," February 23, 1991.

26. See notably the editorial "Qumran Update," *BA* (December 1990) 235.

27. This leading periodical on biblical archaeology has run for years a feature on the publication of the Dead Sea Scrolls, which the editor, H. Shanks, judges to be scandalous. See, e.g., "Chief Dead Sea Scrolls Editor Denounces Judaism, Israel; Claims He's Seen Four More Scrolls Found by Bedouin," *BAR* 17 (1991) 64–72.

28. See "Qumran Scrolls and a Critical Consensus" at the beginning of this book.

29. R. H. Eisenman, *Maccabees, Zadokites, Christians and Qumran* (Studia Post-Biblica 34; Leiden, 1983); *James the Just in the Habakkuk Pesher* (Studia Post-Biblica 35; Leiden, 1986); "The Historical Provenance of the 'Three Nets of Belial': Allusion in the Zadokite Document and *Balla'/Bela'* in the Temple Scroll," *Folia Orientalia* 25 (1988) 51–66.

30. See B. E. Thiering's *The Gospels and Qumran: A New Hypothesis* (Australian and New Zealand Studies in Theology and Religion 2; Sydney, 1981) and *The Qumran Origins of the Christian Church* (Australian and New Zealand Studies in Theology and Religion; Sydney, 1983).

31. Thiering, *Gospels and Qumran,* p. 11. See also her *Redating the Teacher of Righteousness* (Australian and New Zealand Studies in Theology and Religion 1; Sydney, 1979).

32. "Scrolls are Laying Bible Secrets Bare," *Daily Telegraph,* April 2, 1990.

33. "Scrolls are Laying Bible Secrets Bare," *Daily Telegraph,* April 2, 1990.

34. Assuming that the consensus among the most prestigious Qumran specialists is correct, I trust the reader will join me in asking this question: How can an

ancient Jewish fragment—which in no way could refer to the life, crucifixion, and proclaimed resurrection of Jesus of Nazareth—undermine, let alone disprove, the Christian faith?

35. See the following: J. O'Callaghan, "New Testament Papyri in Qumran Cave 7?" *Supplement to JBL 91 (1972) No. 2*; P. Benoit, "Note sur les fragments grecs de la grotte 7 de Qumrân," *RB* 79 (1972) 321–24; Benoit, "Nouvelle note sur les fragments grecs de la grotte 7 de Qumrân," *RB* 80 (1973) 5–12 [conclusion: "Father O'Callaghan has not proved his thesis" (p. 12)]; D. Estrada and W. White, *The First New Testament* (New York, 1978); C. P. Thiede, *Die älteste Evangelien-Handschrift?: Das Markus-Fragment von Qumran und die Anfänge der Schriftlichen Überlieferung des Neuen Testaments* (Wuppertal, 1986); S. R. Pickering and R. R. E. Cook, *Has a Fragment of the Gospel of Mark Been Found at Qumran?* (Papyrology and Historical Perspectives 1; Sydney, 1989 [see p. 4: ". . . none of the fragments is from the New Testament. . . ."]).

36. The Princeton Theological Seminary Dead Sea Scrolls Project has completed a Hebrew and Aramaic concordance to this corpus of 223 texts and over 3,500 fragments. The *Graphic Concordance to the Dead Sea Scrolls* is being published by Mohr (Siebeck) in Tübingen.

37. See chapter 7, by Rainer Riesner, and the bibliography cited there. See also see M. Tanislaw, "Le camp des Esséniens de Jérusalem à la lumière des récentes recherches archéologiques," *Folia Orientalia* 25 (1988) 67–74.

38. This is the technical term for the various types of Judaisms that existed from approximately 250 B.C.E. to about 200 C.E.

39. Philo, *Every Good Man Is Free* 75. Josephus, *Ant.* 18.21.

40. I wish to acknowledge benefiting from discussions on this subject with Professors Cross, Stegemann, and Strugnell.

41. In *Every Good Man Is Free* 76 Philo reports that the Essenes live in villages and avoid cities; in *Hypothetica* 11.1 he states that they are in many cities of Judea "and in many villages." Why Philo contradicts himself is not our present concern.

42. Even though G. Theissen focuses on the Palestinian Jesus Movement of 30 to 70 C.E., he has demonstrated, from sociologically inspired historical research, why Jesus was probably a wandering charismatic. See his *Sociology of Early Palestinian Christianity*, trans. J. Bowden (Philadelphia, 1978).

43. I agree with M. Hengel, who contends that the "Essenes actually had settlements in Jerusalem itself. . . ." (*The Pre-Christian Paul*, trans. J. Bowden [London, Philadelphia, 1991]; quotation from p. 49).

44. The Copper Scroll is a possible exception. We cannot be sure that it belonged to the Qumran covenanters. See the discussion by B. Pixner, "Unraveling the Copper Scroll Code: A Study on the Topography of 3Q15," *RQ* 43 (1983) 323–61.

45. I have studied some fragments that may postdate Jesus, but in each case they are portions of a much earlier document.

46. As, for example, in the popular and attractive *Jesus and His Times* (Reader's Digest; New York, Montreal, 1987) pp. 216–21.

47. On anthropology, see H. Lichtenberger, *Studien zum Menschenbild in Texten der Qumrangemeinde* (SUNT 15; Göttingen, 1980). On calendars, see S. Talmon, *The World of Qumran from Within* (Jerusalem, Leiden, 1989). On dualism, see J. Duhaime, "Dualistic Reworking in the Scrolls from Qumran," *CBQ* 49 (1987) 32–56. On ethics, see S. T. Kimbrough, "The Ethic of the Qumran Community," *RQ* 6 (1969) 483–98. On eschatology, see J. J. Collins, "Patterns of Eschatology at Qumran," in *Traditions in Transformation,* ed. J. D. Levenson and B. Halpern (Winona Lake, Ind., 1981) 351–75. In addition to the so-called futuristic eschatology of Qumran, the Qumranites believed they could enjoy in the present the glories of paradise. See C. Rowland, *Christian Origins: From Messianic Movement to Christian Religion* (Minneapolis, 1985) pp. 106–7. On messianology, see A. S. van der Woude, *Die messianischen Vorstellungen der Gemeinde von Qumran* (SSN 3; Assen, 1957); M. de Jonge, "The Role of Intermediaries in God's Final Intervention in the Future According to the Dead Sea Scrolls," in *Studies on the Jewish Background of the New Testament,* ed. O. Michel et al. (Assen, 1969) pp. 44–63. See L. Schiffman in *The Messiah,* ed. J. H. Charlesworth et al. (Minneapolis, in press).

48. One of the best assessments of criteria for discerning authentic sayings of Jesus is C. A. Evans's "Authenticity Criteria in Life of Jesus Research," *Christian Scholar's Review* 19 (1989) 6–31.

49. Numerous extracanonical gospels have been recovered over the last two centuries. Most of the sayings of Jesus found in them are tainted by doctrinal issues and the desire to attribute attractive sayings to him. The lone exceptions are some sayings preserved in the Gospel of Thomas. I attempt to evaluate some of these issues in "Jesus, the Nag Hammadi Codices, and Josephus," in *Jesus Within Judaism,* pp. 77–102.

50. See the authoritative comments in L. Moraldi, ed., *I manoscritti di Qumrān* (Classici delle religioni; Turin, 1971, 1974), in *Supplément au dictionnaire de la Bible* 51 (1978) cols. 737–1014; M. Delcor and F. García Martínez, *Introducción a la literatura esenia de Qumran* (Madrid, 1982); J. Maier and K. Schubert, *Die Qumran-Essener* (Munich, Basel, 1982); and E. Schürer, *The History of the Jewish People in the Age of Jesus Christ (175 B.C.–A.D. 135),* ed. G. Vermes et al. (Edinburgh, 1986) vol. 3.1, pp. 380–469.

51. In 1958 R. Bultmann admitted in his preface to the third edition of his monumental *Theology of the New Testament,* that the Dead Sea Scrolls prove that the picture of Judaism during the time of Jesus was not so unified as we would expect from rabbinics. Bultmann, *Theologie des Neuen Testaments* (Tübingen, 1984 [9th ed.]) p. vii.

52. The "Land" was promised to Israel (Genesis 12; 15; 17) but it nevertheless rightly belongs only to Yahweh (Lev 25:23). See W. D. Davies, *The Gospel and the Land* (Berkeley, 1974) and D. A. Fiensy, *The Social History of Palestine in the*

Herodian Period: The Land is Mine (SBEC 20; Lewiston, N.Y., 1991). See also H. Stegemann, "'Das Land' in der Tempelrolle und in anderen Texten aus den Qumranfunden," in *Das Land Israel in biblischer Zeit (Jerusalem Symposium 1981),* ed. G. Strecker (Göttingen, 1983) pp. 154–71.

53. Jesus' own self-understanding was shaped by his struggle with Torah. See V. Fusco, "Gesù e la Legge," *Rassegna di teologia* 30 (1989) 528–38.

54. See Charlesworth, "The Origin and Subsequent History of the Authors of the Dead Sea Scrolls: Four Transitional Phases Among the Qumran Essenes," *RQ* 10 (1980) 213–33.

55. Acts 15:5: "But some believers who belonged to the party of the Pharisees rose up, and. . . ."

56. For a succinct summary, see M. Avi-Yonah, *The Jews Under Roman and Byzantine Rule* (Jerusalem, 1984) pp. 1–14.

57. It is not clear when Masada fell. Some unpublished fragments in the files of the late Y. Yadin suggest that it may have fallen in 73.

58. Long ago R. E. Murphy compiled a list of parallels between the New Testament writings and the Qumran scrolls. Murphy, "The Dead Sea Scrolls and New Testament Comparisons," *CBQ* 18 (1956) 263–72. It is interesting to observe the contacts in each Gospel: Mt (25), Mk (5), Lk (14), and Jn (18).

59. The documents listed are not intended to be exhaustive.

60. Belial never appears in the New Testament. Beliar appears only once: 2Cor 6:15, which some scholars have evaluated as perhaps part of an Essene-type writing inserted within 2 Corinthians. J. Gnilka concluded that it was inserted into 2 Corinthians by the compiler of Paul's Corinthians letters along with this "Christian exhortation in the Essene tradition, whose author is not Paul, but some unknown Christian." See Gnilka's arguments in *Paul and the Dead Sea Scrolls,* ed. J. Murphy-O'Connor and J. H. Charlesworth (New York, 1990); quotation from p. 66.

61. No passage can be found that clearly goes back to Jesus and pellucidly contains the claim that God will defeat Satan. This thought is implied in Jesus' sayings but explicit in the Dead Sea Scrolls.

62. According to Luke Jesus affirmed the defeat of the devil and claimed to have seen Satan fall from heaven.

63. As in the Angelic Liturgy (4QShirShabb, 11QShirShabb, MasShirShabb) and Lord's Prayer (Mt, Lk).

64. See 1QH 8 (which portrays God's kingdom [a term that does not appear in this column] as an eternal planting here on earth) and the Lord's Prayer (Mt and Lk). J. A. Fitzmyer points out that Jesus' praise of God the Father as "Lord of heaven and earth" (Mt 11:25; Lk 10:21) now receives a Palestinian setting "previously unsuspected." It appears in the Genesis Apocryphon 22.16, 21. See Fitzmyer, "The Qumran Scrolls and the New Testament after Forty Years," *RQ* 13 (1988) 609–20, esp. 617–18.

65.   Monotheism—if not explicit as in modern creeds—is found in Second Isaiah (Isa 44:6–8) and in a variety of early Jewish texts, most notably LetJer 6:16, 23, 29, 44, 52, 56, 65, 69; Pseudo-Hecataeus (according to Clement of Alexandria, *Strom.* 5.113 [*OTP* vol. 2, p. 912]); LetAris 132–41; Pseudo-Phocylides 54 ["The only God is wise and . . ."]; SibOr 3.8–45; cf. Sir 39:16, 27; 51:22; Orphica 16 (the short version in *OTP* 2.800). Condemnation of idolatry is not to be confused with explicit monotheism (see esp. Pseudo-Philo 2.358–62; SibOr 1.426–27; ApAb 1–8; WisSol 12–17). Thoroughgoing and explicit monotheism is often conspicuously absent in many Early Jewish texts; sometimes God is "a god" (LadJac 2:22) or "the God of gods" (LadJac 6:13). Jewish thinkers inadvertently influenced by enthusiasm for Moses (EzekTrag) or Enoch (3En 6–16) so elevated these figures that monotheism was sometimes compromised.

66.   L. Goppelt argued that "no less than the Teacher of Righteousness at Qumran, Jesus too developed a direct, unique relationship to the Old Testament throughout his involvement with Jewish tradition." Goppelt, *Theology of the New Testament,* trans. J. E. Alsup (Grand Rapids, 1975, 1985); quotation from vol. 1, p. 31.

67.   H. Stegemann, "Some Aspects of Eschatology in Texts from the Qumran Community and in the Teachings of Jesus," in *Biblical Archaeology Today: Proceedings of the International Congress on Biblical Archaeology (Jerusalem, April 1984),* ed. J. Amitai (Jerusalem, 1985) pp. 408–26; quotation from p. 418.

68.   This suggestion does not mean that the Qumran Essenes accepted 1 Enoch and other so-called extracanonical writings into a "canon," even though I am convinced that the canon at Qumran was not closed. Three concepts need to be distinguished: scripture (=the canon), inspired writings, and authoritative documents. For the Essenes of Jesus' time, 1 Enoch may well have been not "scripture" but an "inspired writing" that contained revelation.

69.   I am convinced that Jesus may well have been influenced by many of the so-called apocrypha and pseudepigrapha, and he may have assumed something like an open canon. But he apparently did not accept such documents as equal to Isaiah, Jeremiah, the Davidic Psalms, or other writings that later in the first and second centuries C.E. were accepted by Jews into the "canon."

70.   I am indebted to Professor S. Talmon for many fruitful conversations on the Qumran covenanters' preference for Deuteronomy, Isaiah, and especially the Davidic Psalter.

71.   See especially Mk 12:36 and the Pesharim. F. M. Cross stressed that Essene exegesis has no parallel in rabbinic or Philonic Judaism; "it falls precisely into the pattern of the New Testament's use of the Old Testament. In both, exegesis is 'historical' (i.e. eschatological), and pneumatic." Cross, *The Ancient Library of Qumran and Modern Biblical Studies* (Garden City, N.Y., 1961) p. 218. I am of the opinion that this exegetical method was developed by Jesus' followers from Jesus and that he was clearly shaped by his culture and his isolation within it. It is

conceivable that Jesus may have been influenced by Essene exegesis, but if so he reshaped it in light of his own claims to direct revelation. F. F. Bruce rightly saw that "here is one of the most important points of resemblance between the Teacher of Righteousness and Jesus, in that each imparted to the community which he founded its distinctive features of biblical interpretation." Bruce, "The Dead Sea Scrolls and Early Christianity," *BJRL* 49 (1966) 69–90; quotation from p. 76.

72.   Stegemann in *Biblical Archaeology Today*, ed. Amitai, p. 420.

73.   For further discussion, see S. Lowry, "Some Aspects of Normative and Sectarian Interpretation of the Scriptures (The Contribution of the Judaean Scrolls Towards Systematization)," in *The Annual of Leeds University Oriental Society*, ed. J. MacDonald (Leiden, 1969) pp. 98–163; M. Fishbane, "The Qumran Pesher and Traits of Ancient Hermeneutics," in *Proceedings of the Sixth World Congress of Jewish Studies*, ed. A. Shinan (Jerusalem, 1977) pp. 97–114; W. H. Brownlee, "The Background of Biblical Interpretation at Qumran," in *Qumrân: Sa piété, sa théologie et son milieu*, ed. M. Delcor (BETL 46; Paris, Leuven, 1978) pp. 183–93; idem, *The Midrash Pesher of Habakkuk* (SBL Monograph Series 24; Missoula, Mont., 1979); M. P. Horgan, *Pesharim: Qumran Interpretations of Biblical Books* (CBQ Monograph Series 8; Washington, 1979); G. J. Brooke, *Exegesis at Qumran: 4QFlorilegium in its Jewish Context* (JSOTSS 29; Sheffield, 1985); B. Nitzan, *Pesher Habakkuk: A Scroll from the Wilderness of Judaea* (Jerusalem, 1986 [in Hebrew]); H. Feltes, *Die Gattung des Habakukkommentars von Qumran (1QpHab): Eine Studie zum frühen jüdischen Midrash* (FZB 58; Würzburg, 1986); and B. D. Chilton, "Commenting on the Old Testament (with particular reference to the Pesharim, Philo, and the Mekilta)," in *It Is Written: Scripture Citing Scripture: Essays in Honour of Barnabas Lindars*, ed. D. A. Carson and H. G. M. Williamson (Cambridge, 1988) pp. 122–40.

74.   This adjective is unfortunately still used in scholarly publications. When combined with eschatology it violates the essential meaning of that noun, which denotes that which is about to happen at the end of time.

75.   W. G. Kümmel, *Promise and Fulfilment: The Eschatological Message of Jesus*, trans. D. M. Barton (SBT 23; London, 1961 [2d ed.]).

76.   H.-W. Kuhn, *Enderwartung und gegenwärtiges Heil: Untersuchungen zu den Gemeindeliedern von Qumran* (SUNT 4; Göttingen, 1966).

77.   I do not think that this claim was created by his followers and can be dismissed as a creation by the "church."

78.   See D. Juel's attempt to show that 2 Samuel 7 was interpreted messianically by the Qumran Essenes and Jesus' followers. While Juel sees Nathan's oracle as "one of the foundational christological texts" (p. 88), he wisely does not argue that 4QFlorilegium, which interprets 2 Samuel / eschatologically and messianically, shaped Jesus' concept of being God's son. See Juel, *Messianic Exegesis: Christological Interpretation of the Old Testament in Early Christianity* (Philadelphia, 1988) pp. 59–88.

79. G. Vermes, "The Qumran Interpretation of Scripture in its Historical Setting," *Post-Biblical Jewish Studies* (SJLA 8; Leiden, 1975) pp. 37–49.

80. See especially Mark 1:9–11, which, though shaped by Mark's own christology, probably is built upon a revelation experience of Jesus when he was baptized by John. Luke 4:16–22, though altered by Luke's concept of "the spirit," preserves an early tradition indicating that Jesus did think the promises of Isaiah 61 were being fulfilled. His contemporaries did not doubt that he preached God's good news to the poor and gave sight to some who were blind.

81. See W. H. Brownlee's discussion in *John and the Dead Sea Scrolls*, ed. J. H. Charlesworth (New York, 1990).

82. See the color photograph opposite the title page in *Scrolls from Qumran Cave I*, ed. F. M. Cross, D. N. Freedman, and J. A. Sanders (Jerusalem, 1972).

83. See the judicious and insightful comments on the Qumran Essene literal interpretation of Isaiah 40:3 by P. R. Davies in *Qumran* (Grand Rapids, 1982) p. 88.

84. The ineffable Tetragrammaton (Yahweh) is written with four dots.

85. See A. Dupont-Sommer, *Trente années de recherches sur les manuscrits de la mer morte (1947–1977)* (Paris, 1977) p. 15. P. Fredriksen struggles with the possibility of a pre-resurrection tradition in which Jesus mentioned a new covenant. Fredriksen, *From Jesus to Christ: The Origins of the New Testament Images of Jesus* (New Haven, London, 1988) pp. 101, 115.

86. According to some Greek, Syriac, Coptic, and Latin manuscripts of Mark and Matthew, Jesus instituted a "new covenant"; but this reading looks like an accommodation to Luke's reading.

87. See esp. CD 6.19; 8.21 = 19.33b–34a; 20.12. For significant scholarly discussion, see A. Jaubert, *La notion d'alliance dans le judaïsme aux abords de l'ère chrétienne* (PS 6; Paris, 1963) and A. Segal, "Covenant in Rabbinic Writings," *The Other Judaisms of Late Antiquity* (BJS 127; Atlanta, 1987) pp. 147–65.

88. Consult N. Ilg, "Überlegungen zum Verständnis von *bryt* in den Qumrantexten," in *Qumrân: Sa piété, sa théologie et son milieu*, ed. M. Delcor (BETL 46; Paris, Leuven, 1978) 257–63.

89. See esp. 1QS 1.16, 18, 20, 24; 2.10; note "to enter" in 2.12, 18.

90. See esp. CD 6.19; 8.21 = 19.33b–34a.

91. See esp. 1QS 3.11; 4.22; 5.5.

92. See esp. 1QpHab 2.4; 1QS 5.8; 10.10; cf. 1QS 1.16.

93. See the related reflections by J. Murphy-O'Connor, who contends that the concept of the new covenant "belongs to the prehistory of the Qumran community" and that "the concept of a new covenant was fundamentally alien to Paul's theology." Murphy-O'Connor, "The New Covenant in the Letters of Paul and the Essene Documents," in *To Touch the Text: Biblical and Related Studies in Honor of Joseph A. Fitzmyer. S.J.*, ed. M. P. Horgan and P. J. Kobelski (New York, 1989) pp. 194–204.

94. See esp. Mt 26:28; Mk 14:24; Heb 8:8–12; cf. Rom 2:15.

95. Strugnell offers the opinion that "if 4Q375 and 4Q376 were both composed at Qumran, they would imply the presence of prophecy there (which is quite possible in any case, as in similar groups, and certainly attested for the Essenes). . . ." Strugnell, "Moses-Pseudepigrapha," in *Archaeology and History*, ed. Schiffman, p. 247.

96. D. Hill points out that the Qumran covenanters never called the Righteous Teacher a "prophet," and he never clearly claimed to be a prophet; yet there are "prophetic features in his self-understanding." Hill, *New Testament Prophecy* (Atlanta, 1979) p. 40. D. E. Aune thinks that the Righteous Teacher was probably considered a prophet by the members of the community. Aune, *Prophecy in Early Christianity and the Ancient Mediterranean World* (Grand Rapids, 1983) pp. 132–33. G. Jeremias has examined 1QH and refined our understanding of the composition of the hymns that reflect a strong personality. He concludes, and I tend to agree, that these were composed by the Righteous Teacher. Such research enables Jeremias to conclude that "the Righteous Teacher is a prophet of God." Jeremias, *Der Lehrer der Gerechtigkeit* (SUNT 2; Göttingen, 1963) p. 141. Most scholars rightly conclude that Jesus thought of himself as a prophet or in the tradition of the great prophets; he may have had a prophetic self-understanding. M. Borg concludes that Jesus identified himself with the prophets. Borg, *Jesus: A New Vision: Spirit, Culture, and the Life of Discipleship* (New York, London, 1987) p. 48.

97. *TANAKH: A New Translation of the HOLY SCRIPTURES According to the Traditional Hebrew Text* (Philadelphia, New York, Jerusalem, 5746=1985).

98. See G. Jeremias, "Der Lehrer der Gerechtigkeit und der historische Jesus," *Der Lehrer der Gerechtigkeit*, pp. 319–53, esp. pp. 334–35.

99. See esp. 1QpHab 2.5–6; 9.6; 1QSa 1.1; 4QpIsa[a]; 4QpIsa[b]; 4QpIsa[c]; 4QFlor 1.2, 12, 15, 19; CD 4.4; 6.11.

100. See esp. Mt 24:44; 26:45; Mk 13:32; Lk 12:40; Jn 4:23; 5:25, 28. This distinction is perhaps only heuristic; it should not be exaggerated. As M. Weinfeld reminds us "day," "time," and "hour" are sometimes synonymous. Weinfeld, "The Day of the Lord: Aspirations for the Kingdom of God in the Bible and Jewish Liturgy," *Scripta Hierosolymitana* 31 (1986) 341–72.

101. See Charlesworth, in *John and the Dead Sea Scrolls*, ed. Charlesworth, pp. 76–96.

102. See below "Major Differences" number 9.

103. See esp. 1 Enoch, 2 Enoch, Apocalypse of Abraham, and numerous other apocalypses in which Gabriel or Michael (or another archangel) is opposed by Satan.

104. See esp. 1QpHab 12.3, 6, 10; 1QM 11.9, 13; 13.14; 1QH 2.32; 3.25; 5.16, 18, 22; 4QpPs 37 1.9; 2.10; CD 6.21; 14.14.

105. See the discussion by M. Hengel in *Property and Riches in the Early Church: Aspects of a Social History of Early Christianity*, trans. J. Bowden (Philadelphia, 1974) pp. 18–19.

106. See Hengel's discussion in Maier and Schubert, *Die Qumran-Essener*, p. 120.

107. "Kingdom" or "reign" (*mlkwt*) is a major term in the Dead Sea Scrolls; note esp. 1QM 12:7; 19.7; 1QSb 5.21; 4QPBless 2 and 4. Noteworthy is the reference to God as "king," and his "kingdom" in the Angelic Liturgy (see esp. 4Q400 l.i; 4Q401 i; MasShirShabb 17–19; 4Q403 l; 4Q403 l.ii; 4Q405 23.ii, lines 10–11). No other document in Early Judaism so frequently refers to God as "king" and his "kingdom" as the Angelic Liturgy. See also the discussion of God's rule, or "kingdom of God," under dissimilarities.

108. See the discussions of this point by many experts in *The Messiah*, ed. Charlesworth et al.

109. Even so we must be careful not to equate either with phenomena associated with Bar Kokhba and Sabbatai Sevi. Jesus never discusses messianism and developed no messianology. His disciples are never portrayed as asking him about "the Messiah." Similarly, the references to the Messiah are rare in the Dead Sea Scrolls, and sometimes the priest is seen as the anointed one. Note, for example, the reference to "[the] anointed priest" (*[h]kwhn hmšyh*) in 4Q375. Regarding Bar Kokhba, see P. Schäfer, *Der Bar Kokhba-Aufstand* (TSAJ 1; Tübingen, 1981); for Sabbatai Sevi, see G. Scholem, *Sabbatai Sevi: The Mystical Messiah (1626–1676)*, trans. R. J. Zwi Werblowsky (Bollingen Series 93; Princeton, 1973).

110. See also PssSol 17 and 18. How widespread were the ideas reflected in the Psalms of Solomon and what kind of community do these psalms represent? Jesus and the Essenes would have much to discuss with the community that is behind the Psalms of Solomon. This issue warrants examination.

111. See the translation and discussion in J. Heinemann, *Prayer in the Talmud: Forms and Patterns*, trans. R. S. Sarason (Studia Judaica 9; Berlin, New York, 1977) pp. 26–29. The Hebrew text was published by S. Schechter: "Genizah Specimens," *Jewish Quarterly Review* o.s. 10 (1898) 654–59.

112. Working on the Melchizedek traditions at Qumran, D. E. Aune comes to the conclusion that Jesus may have thought of himself as the Messiah. Aune, "A Note on Jesus' Messianic Consciousness and 11QMelchizedek," *EvQ* 45 (1973) 161–65. B. F. Meyer can talk about "Jesus' self-understanding as messianic builder of the house of God." See Meyer, *The Aims of Jesus* (London, 1979) p. 221. M. Hengel concludes that the unique way Jesus called others "to follow" him was "an expression of his underivable 'messianic' authority." Hengel, *The Charismatic Leader and His Followers*, trans. J. C. G. Greig (Edinburgh, 1981) p. 87. R. Leivestad comes to the conclusion "that Jesus understood himself as Messiah." Leivestad, "Jesus—Messias—Menschensohn: Die jüdischen Heilandserwartungen zur Zeit der ersten römischen Kaiser und die Frage nach dem messianischen Selbstbewusstsein Jesu," *ANRW* II.25.1 (1982) 220–64; quotation from p. 255. Hengel lists numerous New Testament passages that "can only be explained on the basis of the

eschatological 'enthusiasm' of Jesus, i.e. his unique messianic assurance of God, his awareness that with his activity the kingdom of God was itself dawning." See Hengel, *Between Jesus and Paul* (London, 1983) p. xii. E. P. Sanders concludes that it is "highly probable" that Jesus "accepted the role" of king, "either implicitly or explicitly." See Sanders, *Jesus and Judaism* (Philadelphia, 1985) p. 326. H. Boers concludes that the Romans crucified Jesus as a messianic pretender, that at least some of his followers "considered him a political messiah," and that some passages, especially the account of Jesus' triumphal entry into Jerusalem, raise the issue that he may have (at times) held some messianic self-understandings. Boers cannot decide if Jesus held some messianic conceptions, because "almost everything else we know about Jesus tends to contradict an understanding of him as a messianic pretender." See Boers, *Who Was Jesus? The Historical Jesus and the Synoptic Gospels* (New York, 1989) p. 89. D. R. A. Hare considers it probable that Jesus "regarded himself as Messiah." See Hare, *The Son of Man Tradition* (Minneapolis, 1990) p. 278. J. D. G. Dunn and M. J. Borg both stress that in terms of the understanding and use of "son" in Early Judaism Jesus could have thought of himself as God's son. See Dunn, *The Evidence for Jesus* (Philadelphia, 1985) pp. 47–50; and Borg, *Jesus: A New Vision,* esp. p. 50: "Jesus was aware of both 'sonship' and being anointed by the Spirit, as we have seen. Thus the phrases 'anointed by God,' 'son of God,' and the term 'Messiah' are all closely related." Finally, see the judicious insights of H. Merklein, "Zum Selbstverständnis Jesu," in *Jesu Botschaft von der Gottesherrschaft: Eine Skizze* (SBS 111; Stuttgart, 1989 [3d. ed.]) pp. 147–67.

113.   At least five additional references to "the Messiah" appear to be found in some significant unpublished Qumranic fragments.

114.   See M. A. Knibb, "The Teacher of Righteousness—A Messianic Title?" in *A Tribute to Geza Vermes: Essays on Jewish and Christian Literature and History,* eds. P. R. Davies and R. T. White (JSOT SS 100; Sheffield, 199) pp. 51–65.

115.   Especially 1QS and CD, and these were formative writings in the Qumran community.

116.   He was traced back genealogically to David. He was called "the son of David."

117.   J. A. Fitzmyer rightly points to a striking parallel between Qumran and Lk 1:32 (Jesus "will be called Son of the Most High"). But this passage is from Luke; it is not a quotation attributed to Jesus. See Fitzmyer, *RQ* 13 (1988) 617.

118.   In one of the great books on the historical Jesus E. P. Sanders begins his attempt to reconstruct the life of Jesus with Jesus' overturning the tables of the money changers in the Temple. See Sanders, *Jesus and Judaism.*

119.   For the author and the community behind Jubilees, Jerusalem was the center of the world (*axis mundi*).

120.   Josephus describes the actions of a "Jesus, son of Ananias" who for "seven years and five months" (before the destruction of 70) stood in the Temple and

shouted "Woe to Jerusalem" (*War* 6.301–9). He was killed on the walls of Jerusalem by a stone hurled by a Roman soldier during the siege of 69–70.

121. He probably was on pilgrimage to the Temple for Passover. The importance of this fact is not appreciated by many specialists. What happens on a pilgrimage is significant: during the journey a special relationship develops with those on the way who have left home behind, and a kind of new home within the group develops. The goal becomes more and more the object of expectation and veneration, but when seen it is often disappointing and "corrupt." See the socio-logical studies on pilgrimage by V. Turner in *Process, Performance, and Pilgrimage: A Study in Comparative Symbology* (New Delhi, 1979) and in "Pilgrimages as Social Processes," *Dramas, Fields, and Metaphors: Symbolic Action in Human Society* (London, 1974). See also S. Safrai, *Pilgrimage at the Time of the Second Temple* (Tel Aviv, 1965 [in Hebrew]); but see his "Pilgrimage in the Time of Jesus," *Jerusalem Perspective* (September/October 1989) 3, 4, 12.

122. Unique to Matthew is the pericope of the payment of the Temple tax (Mt 17:24–27). I am suspicious of the authenticity of this pericope. It may be a creation by the Matthean community or by any of Jesus' followers for the following reasons: (1) It is only in Matthew, and the principle of multiple attestation is against authenticity. (2) Jesus tells Peter that a shekel will be found in a fish that can be caught with one cast and a hook (not a net). This story reflects the sensational powers attributed to Jesus after his death and is similar to the nature miracles that cannot be traced back to Jesus.

In favor of authenticity are the following: (1) The setting is typical of Jesus' time and not the post-70 community (according to 17:24 the collectors of the half-shekel tax have come to Capernaum). (2) Mt 17:24–27 has more than one layer. The authentic elements of the pericope seem to be the following: collectors come to Capernaum; they ask Peter if Jesus ("your teacher") pays the half-shekel tax; he replies in the affirmative. (3) The evidence that Jesus was in favor of paying the half-shekel tax seems in harmony with other authentic Jesus traditions and his devotion to Jerusalem and to the Jewish religion (here I appeal to the principle of coherence). Hence, we may conclude that Jesus was in favor of paying the Temple tax.

123. The exact meaning of *Ant* 19 is unclear. Josephus seems to report that Essenes do not offer sacrifices in the Temple (he is correct, according to the thoughts in the Dead Sea Scrolls); but they do send to the Temple what is dedicated to God. It seems that the Essenes did pay the Temple tax which had become obliga-tory long before the time of Jesus. It would be what was demanded of priests (by this time) and in line with their devotion to Torah, which they did not allegorize.

124. S. Safrai writes, "Thus the Essenes sent their sheqels though they offered no sacrifices in the Temple, while Jesus and his associates, though not recorded as having brought an offering with them when they came to the Temple, paid their sheqels in Capernaum." Safrai, "The Temple and the Divine Service," in *The*

Herodian Period, ed. M. Avi-Yonah and Z. Baras (World History of the Jewish People 1.7; Jerusalem, New Brunswick, 1975) pp. 284–337; quotation from p. 319.

125. One shekel equaled about two Greek drachmas or two Roman denars. See Ex 30:11; Neh 10:32; also m.Sheq 1:3.

126. The Qumran covenanters did not frequent the Temple because the cult was corrupted by the officiating priests (CD, 1QS, the Pesharim). K. Schubert incorrectly stated that the Qumran "Essenes shunned the temple cult mainly because of their calendar calculations, but Jesus went to the temple more than once." See Schubert's *The Dead Sea Community: Its Origin and Teachings,* trans. J. W. Doberstein (London, 1959) p. 142.

127. The inclusion of non-Jews in this proclamation seems to be a later addition to the Jesus tradition.

128. Philo, *Life of Moses* 2.147; JosAsen 11:18; 13:11–13; 4Ezra 7:105; 2Bar 84:10; and esp. PrMan.

129. Perhaps Jesus was influenced by John the Baptizer's preaching and call for "repentance for the forgiveness of sins" (Mk 1:4). Jesus preached about a God who was a Father who forgave; see esp. Mt 6:14–15; 12:31–32; Mk 2:5–10 and parallels. One of the charges against Jesus was that he claimed to have the power to forgive sins. Clearly that was unique to him and markedly contrasts him with the Righteous Teacher and the Essenes.

130. See esp. 1QS 11.11–14:
   And I, if I totter,
   God's mercies (are) my salvation for ever; . . .
   He has justified me by his true justice
   and by his great goodness he will forgive all my iniquities.

131. See J. H. Charlesworth, "Forgiveness (Early Judaism)," in *The Anchor Bible Dictionary* (in press).

132. H. Thyen, *Studien zur Sündenvergebung im Neuen Testament und seinen altestamentlichen und jüdischen Voraussetzungen* (FRLANT 96; Göttingen, 1970).

133. See P. Garnet, *Salvation and Atonement in the Qumran Scrolls* (WUNT, 2. Reihe, 3; Tübingen, 1977). See also J. Starcky in *Dictionnaire de la Bible,* Fascicule 51, cols. 999–1003. D. Dimant correctly reports that "salvation, if possible, depends on God too. So it is expressed in the *Hodayot* and elsewhere. Yet such salvation demands a corresponding attitude of man." Dimant, "Qumran Sectarian Literature," in *Jewish Writings of the Second Temple Period,* ed. M. E. Stone (CRINT 2.2; Assen, Philadelphia, 1984) pp. 483–550; quotation from p. 537.

134. See G. Jeremias, *Der Lehrer der Gerechtigkeit,* pp. 329–32.

135. A popular and reliable account of prayer during the time of Jesus was published by J. Jeremias; see his *The Prayers of Jesus* (SBT 6; London, 1967).

136. The Grace after Meals is very early and proto-rabbinic. See J. H. Charlesworth, "Jewish Hymns, Odes, and Prayers," in *Early Judaism and Its Modern*

Interpreters, ed. R. A. Kraft and G. W. E. Nickelsburg (Philadelphia, Atlanta, 1986) pp. 411–36.

137. G. Jeremias calls the Righteous Teacher "the greatest representative of piety" in Early Judaism. See his *Der Lehrer der Gerechtigkeit,* p. 352.

138. See esp. Lk 6:12: "But it happened in these days he went out to the mountain to pray; and throughout the night he continued in prayer to God." Presumably Jesus went "out" of the village "to the mountain" in order to spend all night in prayer to God. This tradition seems reliable in light of Mk 6:46–48 and the episode in the garden of Gethsemane (Mk 14:32–42 and parallels).

139. The comment about the Essenes by Josephus is apposite: "Before the sun rises they utter no word on mundane matters, but offer towards (*eis*) it certain prayers, which have been handed down from the forefathers, as if entreating it to rise" (*War* 2.128).

140. D. Flusser in *Jewish Writings of the Second Temple Period,* ed. Stone, p. 567; and "Jubelruf und selige Augenzeugen," *Die rabbinischen Gleichnisse und der Gleichniserzähler Jesus* (Judaica et Christiana 4; Bern, 1981) pp. 265–81.

141. See below, "Major Differences" numbers 1–8.

142. Rightly concerned with the social matrix of Jesus and the Palestinian setting of the historical Jesus, M. J. Borg points out that Jesus' concept of holiness caused conflict with Romans and other Jews. See Borg, *Conflict, Holiness & Politics in the Teachings of Jesus* (SBEC 5; New York, Toronto, 1984).

143. E.g., see Mk 11:17; 12:33.

144. The use of "knowledge" in Matthew may derive from Essene thought; the influence may be caused by Essene converts in Matthew's school or community. See W. D. Davies, " 'Knowledge' in the Dead Sea Scrolls and Matthew 11:25–30," *HTR* 46 (1953) 113–39.

145. John 4:2 was obviously added later.

146. It is misleading to label the Qumranites a "baptismal cult" or a Jewish group that "practiced baptismal rites"; contrast M. Black, *The Scrolls and Christian Origins: Studies in the Jewish Background of the New Testament* (New York, 1961; repr. BJS 48; Chico, Calif., 1983) pp. 95–97, 166, and the caption opposite p. 115. Qumranic lustrations were repeated; baptism occurs once.

147. See F. Manns, "Le symbole eau-esprit à Qumrân," *Le symbole eau-esprit dans le judaïsme ancien* (SBFA 19; Jerusalem, 1983) pp. 65–97.

148. See chapter 5, on the Righteous Teacher and Jesus of Nazareth.

149. Translated by one of the great scholars in Qumran research, A. Dupont-Sommer. See his *The Essene Writings from Qumran,* trans. G. Vermes (Oxford, 1961) p. 228. This hymn describes a leader as the gardener; long ago Dupont-Sommer correctly identified the author as the Righteous Teacher (see p. 229 n. 1).

150. In the Old Testament "living water" denotes "running water." The concept of "living water" as salvific is not found in the Jewish Apocrypha and Pseudepigrapha.

151. See A. R. C. Leaney's comments in *John and the Dead Sea Scrolls*, ed. Charlesworth, pp. 48–53.

152. See especially the traditions behind the Apocalypse of Adam and SibOr 5. Consult J. Thomas, *Le mouvement baptiste en Palestine et Syrie (150 av. J.C.–300 ap. J.C.)* (Gembloux, 1935) esp. pp. 48–49.

153. The little summaries in Acts are, of course, Luke's own; but some recollections are clearly historical. Two that seem obvious are the "attending the Temple together" and the sharing of goods. Behind Acts 5:1–11 lies some historical event that is sustained by the habit of selling one's own possessions and giving all the proceeds to the group.

154. See Hengel, *Property and Riches*.

155. H. Braun, *Jesus of Nazareth: The Man and His Time* (Philadelphia, 1979) p. 87.

156. The rabbis interpreted Lev 18:18, which prohibits marrying your wife's "sister," to explain why the Israelites had more than one wife. The Temple Scroll, however, interpreted "sister" to mean any other woman.

157. See J. J. Dougherty, "Hillel and Shammai," *The New Catholic Encyclopedia* (New York, 1967) vol. 6, p. 1119.

158. Mk 10:9: "What therefore God has joined together, let no human separate."

159. Mt 5:32: "But I say to you that every one who divorces his wife, except on the ground of unchastity, makes her an adulteress. . . ." See J. R. Mueller, "The Temple Scroll and the Gospel Divorce Texts," *RQ* 10 (1980) 247–56; J. A. Fitzmyer, "The Matthean Divorce Texts and Some New Palestinian Evidence," *To Advance the Gospel: New Testament Studies* (New York, 1981) pp. 79–111; and Vermes, *Post-Biblical Studies*, pp. 53–56.

160. Y. Yadin overstated the subtleties in the Hebrew text, but he did catch the intentionality of the passage: "The ban on bigamy and divorce is unequivocal in the scroll's command that the king's wife alone shall be with him all her life and that he can take another only when she dies." See Yadin's *The Temple Scroll: The Hidden Law of the Dead Sea Sect* (London, 1985) p. 198.

161. The text is not halakic; it says that a king's wife shall "alone be with him all the time of her life." The implication is clearly against divorce. If the text was edited during the time of Alexander Janneus, then the prohibition is grounded in his excesses. See Josephus's account of his feasting with concubines (*Ant* 13.380).

162. The term appears frequently in the Dead Sea Scrolls. It was apparently created by them—and in my judgment by the Righteous Teacher who gave definite shape to their dualism.

163. The Qumran Essenes referred to themselves as members of the Way (1QS 8.13–16; 9.16–21); the early followers of Jesus were also called members of "the Way" (Acts 19:9, 23; 22:4; 24:14, 22). Essene influence on Jesus' followers after Easter is possible; there is no evidence that Jesus called his followers members of

"the Way." S. V. McCasland rightly concludes that Jesus' followers "derived the idiom ultimately from Qumran." McCasland, "The Way," *JBL* 77 (1958) 222-30; quotation from p. 230.

164. D. Flusser, *Judaism and the Origins of Christianity* (Jerusalem, 1988) p. 157.

165. Max Weber accurately described Jesus as a charismatic individual. See M. Weber, "The Sociology of Charismatic Authority," in *From Max Weber: Essays in Sociology*, ed. H. H. Gerth and W. Wright Mills (New York, 1958) pp. 245-52; see esp. p. 248. Appropriate to both Jesus and the Righteous Teacher is Weber's following definition: "Charisma knows only inner determination and inner restraint. The holder of charisma seizes the task that is adequate for him and demands obedience and a following by virtue of his mission" (p. 246). M. Hengel brilliantly builds upon Weber's genius; see *The Charismatic Leader and His Followers*. The charismatic virtuosity of Jesus is discussed by I. M. Zeitlin in *Jesus and the Judaism of His Time* (New York, Oxford, 1988, 1989). M. Borg rightly portrays the historical Jesus "as a Spirit-filled person in the charismatic stream of Judaism. . . ." Borg, *Jesus: A New Vision*, p. 45.

166. For an assessment of the most recent research on Jesus, see the chapters by Charlesworth (a Methodist), D. Flusser (a Jew), D. J. Harrington (a Roman Catholic), J. P. Meier (a Roman Catholic), E. Rivkin (a Jew), A. E. Segal (a Jew), and G. Vermes (a Jew) in *Jesus' Jewishness: Exploring the Place of Jesus within Judaism*, ed. J. H. Charlesworth (New York, 1991).

167. On the Righteous Teacher, see especially (chronologically) F. F. Bruce, *The Teacher of Righteousness in the Qumran-Texts* (London, 1957); J. Carmignac, *Le docteur de justice et Jésus-Christ* (Paris, 1957); H. H. Rowley, "The Teacher of Righteousness and the Dead Sea Scrolls," *BJRL* 40 (1957) 114-46; G. Jeremias, *Der Lehrer der Gerechtigkeit;* H. Braun, "Jesus und der qumranische Lehrer," *Qumran und das Neue Testament* (Tübingen, 1966) vol. 2, pp. 54-74; P. Schulz, *Der Autoritätsanspruch des Lehrers der Gerechtigkeit in Qumran* (Meisenheim am Glan, 1974); C. A. Newsom, "Kenneth Burke Meets the Teacher of Righteousness: Rhetorical Strategies in the Hodayot and the Serek Ha-Yahad," in *Of Scribes and Scrolls: Studies on the Hebrew Bible, Intertestamental Judaism, and Christian Origins Presented to John Strugnell on the Occasion of His Sixtieth Birthday*, ed. H. W. Attridge, J. J. Collins, and T. H. Tobin (New York, London, 1990) pp. 121-31.

168. At the beginnings of research on the Dead Sea Scrolls M. Burrows, one of the great pioneers, pointed this out and wisely cautioned that faith in Jesus and "faith" in the Righteous Teacher are not identical: "There is no implication in the Dead Sea Scrolls that the teacher of righteousness had himself accomplished a redemptive work in any way comparable to the saving work of Christ." Burrows, *The Dead Sea Scrolls* (London, 1956) p. 335. The passage for special discussion is 1QpHab 7-8, which refers to the followers of the Righteous Teacher and their faithfulness to (or in) him (1QpHab 7.2-3).

169. Despite the suggestion of some novelists and W. E. Phipps in *Was Jesus Married?* (New York, London, 1970).

170. J. Baumgarten, one of the gifted experts on the Dead Sea Scrolls, rightly points out (especially on the basis of 4Q502, CD, 11QTemple, 1QSa) that "celibacy at Qumran was never made into a universal norm." See his "The Qumran-Essene Restraints on Marriage," in *Archaeology and History*, ed. Schiffman, pp. 13–24; quotation from p. 20. Phipps denies that the Qumranites were celibate; but he provides no exegetical support for this interpretation. Phipps, *Was Jesus Married?* pp. 31–33. See J. Coppens, "Le célibat essenién," in *Qumrân*, ed. Delcor, pp. 297–303.

171. G. F. Moore, *Judaism in the First Centuries of the Christian Era: The Age of the Tannaim* (Cambridge, Mass., 1950) vol. 2, p. 119.

172. Braun, *Jesus of Nazareth*, p. 74; Vermes, *Post-Biblical Jewish Studies*, p. 54.

173. Polygamy was not allowed according to one of the oldest law codes in the Near East, namely, the Code of Hammurabi (1700 B.C.E.), which allows for another wife only if the first is barren.

174. See R. de Vaux, "Marriage," *Ancient Israel: Its Life and Institutions*, trans. J. McHugh (London, 1965 [2d ed.]) pp. 24–38.

175. 11QTemple 56.18: *wlw' yrbh lw nšym* (exactly [except for the *matres lectionis*] as in Dt 17:17). See Y. Yadin, *The Temple Scroll* (Jerusalem, 1983) vol. 2, p. 404.

176. I am indebted to Vermes for this insight. Vermes, *Post-Biblical Jewish Studies*, pp. 50–56.

177. Meyer, *Aims of Jesus*, p. 233.

178. There is also a significant difference here. Jesus included women in his group; the Essenes, however, shunned marriage because they did not trust women (Philo, *Hypothetica* 11.14) and considered them unfaithful to their marriage vows (*War* 2.121). Such ideas may also be found in the Dead Sea Scrolls (4Q184) and related documents (T12P).

179. John the Baptist: Mk 1:8; 3:29; Mt 1:11; Lk 3:16; Jn 1:33; cf. Lk 1:67. Gabriel: Lk 1:15, 35.

180. Mt 1:18, 20; Lk 2:25, 26; 3:22; 4:1, 41.

181. See the well-attested variant in Jn 7:39.

182. Mk 12:36; 13:11; Mt 12:32; Lk 11:13; 12:10, 12; Jn 14:26.

183. See esp. Mt 28:19 and Jn 20:22.

184. Mk 12:36 (parallels in Mt 22:43 and Lk 20:42) seems to be authentic to Jesus. Mark's quotation from Jesus, "David spoke by the Holy Spirit," is changed by Matthew to "David by the spirit called" and by Luke to "David said in the Book of Psalms." Likewise, Mk 13:11 (parallels in Mt 10:20 and Jn 14:26) has all the signs of being authentic to Jesus; during trial "the Holy Spirit" will defend and speak for the faithful one. Matthew changes the technical term to "the spirit of your father"; Luke omits the end of the verse. John refers to "the Paraclete, the Holy Spirit

whom [not which] the Father shall send." E. Schweizer rightly points out that Jesus' followers showed "astonishing fidelity" to the tradition about Jesus' use of "the Holy Spirit"; Mk 13:11 "may be traced back in substance to Jesus Himself"; see Schweizer's insights in *TDNT*, vol. 6, p. 402; cf. Schweizer, *The Good News According to Mark*, trans. D. H. Madvig (Atlanta, 1970) pp. 18, 271. Mark 13 is surely a "radical early Christian reorientation" of Jewish apocalyptic tradition, and since Mark seldom mentions the term "the Holy Spirit" (3:29; 12:36; cf. 1:8, 10) it is warranted to ponder if the term does indeed derive from Jesus. See H. Anderson, *The Gospel of Mark* (London, 1976) p. 294.

185. This sin is the only one that is unforgivable. The unconditional harshness is remarkable. It is possible to think that it was "created" by Jesus' followers, who felt empowered by the Holy Spirit, as we know from the accounts in Acts (esp. Acts 2). But here we also confront the theology of Luke. See the context and meaning of this saying of Jesus in F. F. Bruce, "The Sin Against the Holy Spirit," *The Hard Sayings of Jesus* (London, Toronto, 1983) pp. 88–93. Despite the fact that Jesus seldom mentions "the Holy Spirit" (in the sayings preserved) and that Mark 3:29 may reflect some reworking, the sheer harshness of the saying seems to speak in favor of its authenticity. V. Taylor apparently thought that Jesus did use the term "the Holy Spirit," although "Mark has generalized the saying, while the compiler of Q has read it Messianically." *The Gospel According to St. Mark* (New York, 1966 [2d ed.]) p. 242.

186. It is dissimilar to early Jewish theology and also to Jesus' followers' stress on forgiveness: "the blood of Jesus . . . cleanses us from all sin" (1Jn 1:7).

187. "The Holy Spirit" does not appear in Isa 63:10, in which we hear about God's holy spirit (*rwḥ qdšw*). Also, Ps 51:13 refers to God's holy spirit (*wrwḥ qdšk*). The comments by A. Heron are incorrect; see *Encyclopedia of Early Christianity*, ed. E. Ferguson (New York, London, 1990) p. 429. While it is appropriate to state that the followers of Jesus and those earlier of the Righteous Teacher contended that their leader was inspired by "the Holy Spirit," the charismatic leaders earlier were "anointed ones" who were possessed by "the spirit of Jahweh," as G. von Rad stated. See von Rad, *Old Testament Theology*, trans. D. M. G. Stalker (New York, 1962) vol. 1, p. 323.

188. According to MartIs 5 (perhaps the second century B.C.E.) Isaiah "spoke with the Holy Spirit until he was sawn in two." According to the Psalms of Solomon (mid-first century B.C.E.), the Messiah is to be powerful "in the holy spirit" (17:37). In 4 Ezra (late first century C.E.) Ezra prays to God to send "the Holy Spirit to me" (14:22). In each of these passages the "Holy Spirit" is close to God's holy spirit of the Old Testament; it is not a hypostatic being as in the Dead Sea Scrolls. The "Holy Spirit" appears elsewhere in the Pseudepigrapha only in Christian sections or redactions.

189. The conclusion to m.Soṭ 9:15 is extended and reads like a remnant of an older apocalyptic tradition or text. See A. Saldarini's comments in *CBQ* 39 (1977)

404. In major works on the New Testament "the Holy Spirit" is mentioned frequently. It is instructive, by way of contrast, to note that E. E. Urbach mentioned "the Holy Spirit" on only three pages (399, 565, 577) in his magisterial *The Sages: Their Concepts and Beliefs*, 2 vols., trans. I. Abrahams (Jerusalem, 1979).

190. See P. Schäfer, *Die Vorstellung vom Heiligen Geist in der rabbinischen Literatur* (SANT 28; Munich, 1972). Schäfer shows that there is no system in rabbinics and that "the Holy Spirit" *inter alia* signifies the presence of God.

191. See 1QS 3.7; 4.21; 8.16; 9.3; 1QSb 2.24; CD 2.12; 1QH 7.6; 9.32; 12.12; 16.2, 3, 7, 12; 17.26; 1Q39 1.6; 4Q403 1 ii.1; 4Q404 5 i.1; 4Q405 14+ i.2; 4Q405 23 ii.8; 4Q504 1+R v.15; 4Q504 iv 1.5; 11QShirShabb 8+ i.3; possible restorations in 1QH 16.2, 7; 14.13. It is conspicuously absent from 1QM, 11QTemple, 11QtgJob, and the Pesharim.

192. See M. Delcor, "L'Esprit Saint," *Supplément au dictionnaire de la Bible*, vol. 9, cols. 972–74.

193. F. F. Bruce, "Holy Spirit in the Qumran Texts," *The Annual of Leeds University Oriental Society* 6 (1969) 49–55.

194. The Qumran Essenes were not against the Temple nor necessarily the cult per se.

195. Although (in my judgment) A. E. Sekki misunderstands 1QS 3–4, in stressing the spirits as "impersonal dispositions within men," he rightly perceives that "the Holy Spirit" is not the human spirit. He tends to confuse it, however, with "God's Spirit," when it is a separate hypostatic being *from* God. See Sekki, *The Meaning of Ruaḥ at Qumran* (SBLDS 110; Atlanta, 1989).

196. M. S. Zuckermandel, ed., *Tosephta* (Jerusalem, 1970) pp. 162–63.

197. Gamaliel allegedly was at least once empowered by the Holy Spirit; see t.Pes 1.27.

198. J. Neusner wisely offers this explanation: "The anonymity of the pericope, the clumsy joining of its composite elements into a single, unitary account, and the historical dubiety of the story that Hillel's arguments were accepted by Temple authorities and he was therefore made patriarch or *Nasi* over the Temple all point to a relatively late date for the story as a whole. I do not see how anyone could have made it up or put it together while the Temple was standing, for at that point no one could have believed it." Neusner, "The Figure of Hillel: A Counterpart to the Problem of the Historical Jesus," *Judaism in the Beginning of Christianity* (Philadelphia, 1984) p. 75.

199. I shall attempt to develop this discovery in my contribution to *Hillel and Jesus*, forthcoming.

200. Such a tradition was prohibited from developing because of the power of the rabbinic claim that scripture was written under the power of the Holy Spirit and that the Holy Spirit left Israel with the latter prophets. Hence, the theology that explained the closing of the canon also prohibited the claim that Hillel, the greatest of the rabbis, received the Holy Spirit.

201. Neusner comments, without notation, that "other sayings concerning Hillel allege that he alone of his generation was worthy of receiving the holy spirit, but the generation in which he lived was of such poor character that the holy spirit was withheld in their day even from Hillel. . . ." Neusner, *Judaism in the Beginning of Christianity,* pp. 74–75. See t.Soṭ 13.3 (Zuckermandel, pp. 318–19): "It once happened that when the Sages entered the house of Guryo in Jericho, they heard the heavenly voice (*bt qwl*) say 'There is here a man who is worthy of the Holy Spirit (*lrwḥ hqwdš*), but his generation is not worthy of it'; and they all looked at Hillel. . . ." See the discussion by Urbach in *Sages,* vol. 1, pp. 577, 948 (which cites parallel passages).

202. Obviously the Palestinian Jesus Movement stressed the presence of "the Holy Spirit" in their community (Acts 2), and the evangelists clarified how Jesus and his followers were (and would be) guided by "the Holy Spirit" (Mt 28:19; esp. Luke: Lk 2:25, 26; 3:22; 4:1; 10:21; Jn 20:22). The wide variety of independent evidence, however, indicates that Jesus probably spoke about "the Holy Spirit" (see Mk 3:29 = Mt 12:32 and Lk 12:10; Lk 11:13; 12:12; Jn 14:26).

203. See also the words of Tanna R. Nehemiah, "Whoever accepts one commandment in faith is worthy that the Holy Spirit should rest upon him" (*Mekhilta de-R. Ishmael,* Massekhta de-Wa-yehi, vi, p. 114). See Urbach, *Sages,* pp. 399, 857. The rabbinic claim that prophecy ceased (in this case with the beginning of the rule of Alexander the Great) is affirmed with the words that up until that time the "prophets prophesied through the medium of the Holy Spirit. . . ." (*Seder 'Olam Rabba,* vi, ed. Ratner, p. 140). See Urbach, *Sages,* vol. 1, pp. 565, 943. This claim, of course, means that Hillel did not receive the Holy Spirit.

204. The evidence that John the Baptizer spoke about "the Holy Spirit" seems, therefore, questionable (see Mk 1:8 = Mt 3:11 and Lk 3:16; Jn 1:33). It is another indication of the "christianizing" of the traditions related to John the Baptizer.

205. As H. C. Kee clarifies, the "most telling feature against any simple identification of the Qumran community and early Christianity is the sharp difference in their attitudes toward the world." Kee, *Jesus in History* (New York, 1977 [2d ed.]) p. 57.

206. See V. Turner, "'Liminal' to 'Liminoid' in Play, Flow and Ritual: An Essay in Comparative Symbology," *Process, Performance, and Pilgrimage: A Study in Comparative Symbology* (New Delhi, 1979) pp. 11–59.

207. J. M. Casciaro Ramírez discusses the concept of community salvation at Qumran. See his *Qumrān y el Nuevo Testamento (Aspectos Eclesiológicos y Soteriológicos* (EUNSA 29; Pamplona, 1982).

208. As J. Riches stated, the Qumran community's insistence on "secrecy about its own teaching" kept "the barriers between itself and other Jewish groups as strong as possible." Riches, *Jesus and the Transformation of Judaism* (London, 1980) p. 130.

209. This passage is omitted by Matthew and altered by Luke; it has all the

traits of the historical Jesus and reflects his time; moreover, it mirrors a situation unlike the post-Easter Palestinian Jesus Movement. In that movement, perhaps under the influence of some Essenes after 70 c.e., the boundaries of community were marked with a strong liminality; love of another was altered to mean love of a member of the "in group" who confessed acceptable christology (see esp. the Johannine epistles).

210. D. N. Freedman, "Early Christianity and the Scrolls: An Inquiry," in *Jesus in History and Myth*, ed. R. J. Hoffmann and G. A. Larue (Buffalo, N.Y., 1986) pp. 97–102; quotation from p. 97.

211. See G. Klinzing, *Die Umdeutung des Kultus in der Qumrangemeinde und im Neuen Testament* (SUNT 7; Göttingen, 1972); and J. Coppens, "Où en est le problème des analogies qumrâniennes avec le Nouveau Testament?" in *Qumrân*, ed. Delcor, pp. 373–83, esp. p. 378.

212. See S. Légasse, "Amour des ennemis," in *Études sur le judaïsme hellé-nistique* (LD 119; Paris, 1984) pp. 328–38.

213. Josephus also mentions the hate of the Essenes: before the initiate may be a full member of the Essene community he must, among other tasks, swear "that he will ever hate the unjust . . ." (*War* 2.139). K. Stendahl has argued persuasively that this hatred is not entirely novel but is a blending of two different elements found in scripture (nonretaliation [Deut 32] and hatred of God's enemies [see Pss 139, 79]). The Qumranic eschatological intensity clarifies how these two apparently opposite ethical norms can be combined. As Stendahl states, "Why walk around with a little shotgun when the atomic blast is imminent?" See Stendahl's "Hate, Nonretaliation, and Love: Coals of Fire," in *Meanings: The Bible as Document and as Guide* (Philadelphia, 1984) pp. 137–49; quotation from p. 139. Stendahl's insight is endorsed by J. L. Kugel, who shows that the exhortation *not* to hate one's brother (Lev 19) means not to let hatred "simmer inside of you" and that this understanding was developed at Qumran (1QS 5–6; CD 9) so that one is exhorted to reproach a brother so that hatred cannot build up in one's heart. See Kugel's *In Potiphar's House: The Interpretive Life of Biblical Texts* (San Francisco, 1990) pp. 214–25. See also the Ph.D. dissertation by G. Zerbe, " 'Leave Room for Wrath': Paul's Ethic of Non-retaliation in the Context of Early Judaism and Early Christianity" (Princeton Theological Seminary, 1989).

214. As C. Rowland states, the Qumran Essenes "had an extremely hostile attitude towards other Jews. . . ." Rowland, *Christian Origins*, p. 73.

215. Or, "be accursed" (z'wm).

216. In *Every Good Man Is Free* 78 Philo reported that the Essenes do not possess any weapons (no "darts, javelins, daggers, or the helmet, breastplate or shield"). It is not easy to reconcile this report with the militancy of 1QM, which I do not think we can dismiss as only idealistic or only for a far-off future. Perhaps Philo had written more fully on the subject in a presently lost treatise. See

P. Borgen, *Philo, John and Paul: New Perspectives on Judaism and Early Christianity* (BJS 131; Atlanta, 1987) p. 43.

217. K. Schubert, "The Sermon on the Mount and the Qumran Texts," in *The Scrolls and the New Testament,* ed. K. Stendahl (New York, 1957) p. 120.

218. Yadin, *The Temple Scroll* (London, 1985) pp. 241–42.

219. W. H. Brownlee thought it "too daring" to see the Essenes and their teaching behind Jesus' words in Mt 5:43. See Brownlee, "Jesus and Qumran," in *Jesus and the Historian,* ed. F. T. Trotter (Philadelphia, 1968) pp. 52–81, esp. p. 73.

220. Mk 2:18–22; Mt 6:16–18.

221. Mk 7:2–4.

222. See 1QS (and other copies of the Rule), CD, 4QMMT, 5Q13, 4Q181, 4Q159, 4Q513–514, 1QH, 4Q512. As M. Newton states, "the concept of purity is central and governs much of the Qumran community's life." See Newton, *The Concept of Purity at Qumran and in the Letters of Paul* (SNTS Monograph Series 53; Cambridge, 1985) p. 116.

223. For the text see E. M. Schuller, *Non-Canonical Psalms from Qumran: A Pseudepigraphic Collection* (HSS 28; Atlanta, 1986).

224. This provisional title is taken from the beginning of line 29 of the fragment that supposedly concludes the "letter." I am grateful to Professors Strugnell and Qimron for discussing the text of this document with me.

225. For a photograph, see Charlesworth, *Jesus Within Judaism,* opposite p. 46, or illustration no. 1.

226. See 1QS 6.27; Josephus, *War* 2.145; cf. Lev 24:6.

227. See L. H. Schiffman, *Sectarian Law in the Dead Sea Scrolls: Courts, Testimony and the Penal Code* (BJS 33; Chico, Calif., 1983).

228. An Essene would have been appalled by Jesus' exhortation to rip out an eye or cut off a part of the body lest they cause one to sin (Mk 9:42–47).

229. G. Jeremias, *Der Lehrer der Gerechtigkeit,* p. 353.

230. See the important discussion on purity and danger by M. Douglas. Apposite in comprehending the rules for removing impurity in the community is Douglas's insight that a "polluting person is always in the wrong. He has developed some wrong condition or simply crossed some line which should not have been crossed and this displacement unleashes danger for someone." Douglas, *Purity and Danger: An Analysis of the Concepts of Pollution and Taboo* (London, Boston, 1966, 1985) p. 113. These anthropological and sociological insights are important in the attempt to comprehend many of the Dead Sea Scrolls, especially 1QS and 11QTemple.

231. In perhaps the best summary of Jesus' life and teachings, G. Bornkamm stressed the importance of the Dead Sea Scrolls for understanding Jesus' environment and pointed out that there are "a few scattered parallels"; but he rightly saw the vast chasm that separated Jesus from most pious Jews, and this proves "that he

stands in complete contrast to these separate circles of" the Essenes "as well as to the representatives of official Judaism." Bornkamm, *Jesus of Nazareth,* trans. I. and F. McLuskey with J. M. Robinson (New York, London, 1960) p. 43.

232.   J. D. M. Derrett points out the extreme difference between Jesus and the Essenes on the question of repentance and social behavior. See his "New Creation: Qumran, Paul, the Church, and Jesus," *RQ* 13 (1988) 597–608, esp. pp. 605–7. Sanders opines that "Jesus did not call sinners to repent as normally understood, which involved restitution and/or sacrifice, but rather to accept his message, which promised them the kingdom. This would have been offensive to normal piety." Sanders, *Jesus and Judaism,* p. 210.

233.   See N. Avigad, *Discovering Jerusalem* (Jerusalem, Nashville, 1983).

234.   G. Vermes, *The Dead Sea Scrolls: Qumran in Perspective* (Cleveland, 1978) p. 220.

235.   R. Hamerton-Kelly, *God the Father: Theology and Patriarchy in the Teaching of Jesus* (Philadelphia, 1979) p. 60.

236.   B. Witherington, *Women in the Ministry of Jesus* (SNTS Monograph Series 51; Cambridge, 1984). See esp. p. 126: "Jesus' views of women and their roles do not fit neatly into any of the categories of His day. He was not a Qumranite, nor was he a traditional rabbi in these matters, though he had certain things in common with both groups." E. Schüssler Fiorenza, *In Memory of Her: A Feminist Theological Reconstruction of Christian Origins* (New York, 1987). See esp. p. 151: "Thus liberation from patriarchal structures is not only explicitly articulated by Jesus but is in fact at the heart of the proclamation of the *basileia* of God."

237.   This prohibition raises major problems for Essenes living in Jerusalem. See also the numerous similar rules in the Temple Scroll.

238.   See J. M. Allegro and A. A. Anderson in DJD 5 (1968) pp. 82–85 and J. Strugnell's critical review in "Notes en marge du volume V des 'Discoveries in the Judaean Desert of Jordan,'" *RQ* 7 (1970) 263–68.

239.   Except "one born of a woman" in the concluding hymn of 1QS at 11.21, as Vermes notes in *The Dead Sea Scrolls in English* (London, New York, 1987 [3d ed.]) p. 9.

240.   Josephus mentions that the Essenes did not marry (*War* 2.120) and refers to the simplicity of their life (*War* 2.151). This description fits 1QS and the Qumran Essenes. He also mentions another order of Essenes who did marry (*War* 2.160–61), which resembles what we know from CD. See the comments by G. Bickford in "Some Thoughts on the Dead Sea Scrolls," *Vocatus* (1958) 32–33.

241.   J. Murphy-O'Connor thinks that CD 2.14–6.1 is a missionary document; but he argues that the setting for this section of CD is pre-Qumranic, and even before the leadership of the Righteous Teacher. See Murphy-O'Connor, "An Essene Missionary Document? CD II,14–VI,1," *RB* 77 (1970) 201–29, esp. p. 227. See also Murphy-O'Connor, "The *Damascus Document* Revisited," *RB* 92 (1985) 223–46.

242. Meyer suggested that the Qumran Essenes "frankly appealed to pious Jews to join 'Israel'!" Meyer, *Aims of Jesus*, p. 233. He does not explain this claim. H. Braun mentioned the unmistakable affinity between Jesus and the Qumranites and claimed that "both preach the intensified law against the horizon of a final salvation and judgment imminently awaited." Surely "preach" is a mistranslation of the German word. Braun, "The Significance of Qumran for the Problem of the Historical Jesus," in *The Historical Jesus and the Kerygmatic Christ: Essays on the New Quest of the Historical Jesus*, eds. C. E. Braaten and R. A. Harrisville (New York, 1964) pp. 69–78; quotation from p. 74.

243. See M. Hengel, "Die Einladung Jesu," *Theologische Beiträge* 18 (1987) 113–19.

244. S. McKnight concludes that "Judaism was not a missionary religion." McKnight, *A Light Among the Gentiles: Jewish Missionary Activity in the Second Temple Period* (Minneapolis, 1991) p. 88. He also argues that the Essenes had converts but no adherents (p. 91).

245. J. Allegro was confused. He tried to show that the Gospels were difficult to decipher "and were intended to be so, just as the Essene secrets were not for the eyes of the uninitiated. . . ." Allegro, "Jesus and Qumran: The Dead Sea Scrolls," in *Jesus in History and Myth*, ed. R. J. Hoffmann and G. A. Larue (Buffalo, N.Y., 1986) pp. 89–96; quotation from p. 93.

246. Some passages in the Qumran Scrolls are pictorial; for example, the poem in 1QapGen 20.2–8a offers significant data for understanding Jesus' fondness for poetry, which he uttered in Aramaic. See J. C. VanderKam, "The Poetry of I Q Ap Gen, XX, 2-8a," *RQ* 10 (1979) 57–66.

247. There are, of course, well-known exceptions to this generalization. It is also conceivable that Jesus explained some of his parables to his disciples (as we know from numerous pericopes in the New Testament). There was ample time for such in-depth discussion, especially at night around the common fire.

248. Vermes, *The Dead Sea Scrolls in English*, p. 294. According to this text there were Zadokites who did not join the Qumran community in desert exile.

249. This saying, especially in its negative form, is found in many cultures and is customarily attributed to the wisest person. It is conceivable that it was added to the Jesus traditions and later to the Hillel traditions. It is also possible that, as intelligent individuals with unusual gifts, they would have quoted the saying and made it their own.

250. See A. Dihle, *Die goldene Regel: Eine Einführung in die Geschichte der antiken und frühchristlichen Vulgärethik* (SA 7; Göttingen, 1962).

251. E. Qimron rightly stresses that the Essenes increased the concept of holiness, so that the holiness once reserved for the Temple was expanded to include "the whole of Jerusalem and to a much lesser extent . . . the other cities of the Land of Israel." Qimron, "The Holiness of the Holy Land in the Light of a New Document from Qumran," in *The Holy Land in History and Thought*, ed. M. Sharon (Leiden, New York, 1988) pp. 9–13.

252. The followers of Jesus, especially after 70 C.E., obviously forgot (or felt compelled to modify in light of their own understanding of the eschaton) Jesus' penchant for including even those who would be disruptive. Certainly Jesus did not have the luxury of choosing for his closest followers only those who grasped his message. Mark, and even Matthew and Luke, indicate that Jesus' disciples did not understand his concept of suffering. It was remembered that Peter rebuked Jesus (*epitiman autō*) for some of his teachings (see esp. Mk 8:31-33; cf. 10:37; 14:41). Thus, the major battles in the Palestinian Jesus Movement over who belongs "in" the Jesus group do not imply that Jesus himself was vague on who should be called. Jesus may not have included Gentiles, but he called all Jews to prepare for the dawning of God's rule; and he did not require them to pass an entrance test.

253. H. Mol, *Identity and the Sacred* (Oxford, 1976) see esp. p. 233. I am indebted to J. D. G. Dunn for drawing my attention to this study. Dunn rightly states that "'boundary' is closely linked with . . . 'identity.'" Dunn, *Jesus, Paul and the Law* (Louisville, 1990) p. 216.

254. 1QS is composite; it evolved in light of the needs of the Qumran community.

255. Douglas, *Purity and Danger*, p. 124.

256. There is no clear evidence that Eleazar, whom Josephus knew and allegedly saw cure a demon-possessed person, was an Essene. See the account in *Ant* 8.45-49. The passage is important because Jesus may have been seen as a miracle worker, endowed with Solomonic knowledge to cure demon possession. Is that what is sometimes meant when he was hailed as "son of David"? That means intermittently this affirmation may have medicinal and not messianic overtones. M. Smith is famous for his insistence that Jesus be seen in terms of magic. See his chapter in this book and his *Jesus the Magician* (Cambridge, New York, 1978).

257. See now 4Q266, 4Q268, and 4Q272. Consult J. M. Baumgarten, "The 4Q Zadokite Fragments on Skin Disease," *JJS* 41 (1990) 153-65.

258. See the texts reproduced in D. R. Cartlidge and D. L. Dungan, *Documents for the Study of the Gospels* (Philadelphia, 1980) pp. 205-42.

259. G. Vermes, *Jesus the Jew: A Historian's Reading of the Gospels* (London, 1973).

260. See Charlesworth, "Hanina ben Dosa," in the *Anchor Bible Dictionary*. See also D. L. Tiede, *The Charismatic Figure as Miracle Worker* (SBLDS 1; Missoula, Mont., 1972); G. Theissen, *The Miracle Stories of the Early Christian Tradition*, trans. F. McDonaugh (Edinburgh, 1983); J.-M. Cangh, "Miracles de rabbins et miracles de Jésus: La tradition sur Honi et Hanini," *RTL* 15 (1984) 28-53; P. Sacchi, "Gesù l'Ebreo," *Henoch* 6 (1984) 347-68.

261. Jesus' manner of healing, the laying on of hands, is also the means by which Abraham heals Pharaoh of an evil spirit, according to the 1QapGen 10.21-29. This link is generic; it was probably the customary means for healing.

It is possible that "Essenes" derives from the Aramaic participle *'āsê, 'āsyā,* "healer." Philo, however, understood "Essene" to mean "holiness"; see *Hypothetica* 11.1.

262. See chapter 2 below; see also O. Betz, "The Miracles of Jesus," *What Do We Know About Jesus: The Bedrock of Fact Illuminated by the Dead Sea Scrolls* (London, Philadelphia, 1968) pp. 58–71.

263. See the corroborating report on the Essenes by Josephus in *War* 2.138–39; especially ". . . after this demonstration of endurance, his character is tested for two years more, and only then, if found worthy, is he enrolled in the society." Earlier in this same book Josephus mentioned how admirable were the Essenes' "community of goods" (*War* 2.122).

264. I realize that this generalization is valid only when a vast amount of data is systematized. See the similar summary by M. Wilcox, in *ANRW* II.25.1 (1982) 164–65.

265. The same point is made by W. R. Farmer, *Jesus and the Gospel* (Philadelphia, 1982) p. 38; see also Hengel, *The Charismatic Leader and His Followers.*

266. This conclusion is obtained independently by numerous scholars. See R. P. Meye, *Jesus and the Twelve: Discipleship and Revelation in Mark's Gospel* (Grand Rapids, 1968) pp. 200–202; L. Gaston, *No Stone on Another: Studies in the Significance of the Fall of Jerusalem in the Synoptic Gospels* (NTS 23; Leiden, 1970) p. 147; Sanders, *Jesus and Judaism,* pp. 100–101; and Charlesworth, *Jesus Within Judaism,* pp. 136–38.

267. The attempt to link Jesus' twelve within which there were three special disciples with the composition of the Qumran Council of the Community, specifically "twelve men and three priests" (1QS 8.1) has proved to be unfruitful. The Qumran Rule of the Community probably denoted fifteen men. Moreover, Jesus' group constituted a lay movement; the Qumranites originated and continued to emphasize the priestly quality and perception of their community.

268. This saying rings of authenticity; the post-Easter community needed leaders and more organization as the movement became an institution. Note how Matthew, and his community, slightly altered the saying: "He who (is) greatest among you shall be your servant" (Mt 23:11).

269. See the reflections of the sociologically trained New Testament historian R. A. Horsley in *Jesus and the Spiral of Violence: Popular Jewish Resistance in Roman Palestine* (San Francisco, 1987) p. 240. Also see number 4 under "Major Differences" above.

270. See Dimant, "Qumran Sectarian Literature," in *Jewish Writings of the Second Temple Period,* ed. Stone, pp. 489–503.

271. H. G. Kippenberg, *Religion und Klassenbildung im antiken Judäa: Eine religionssoziologische Studie zum Verhältnis von Tradition und gesellschaftlicher Entwicklung* (SUNT 14; Göttingen, 1982 [2d ed.]) pp. 157–63.

272. R. B. Y. Scott, "The Meaning for Biblical Studies of the Qumran Scroll Discoveries," *Transactions of the Royal Society of Canada* 50 (1956) 39–48, esp. p. 47.

273. See Kee, "The Bearing of the Dead Sea Scrolls on Understanding Jesus," *Jesus in History,* pp. 54–75.

274. In his inaugural lecture, J. C. O'Neill stated that he agreed with Dupont-Sommer and thought that "the Essenes believed the Teacher of Righteousness was the Messiah." O'Neill, "A Sketch Map of the New Testament," *ET* 99 (1988) 199–205, esp. p. 202. See Dupont-Sommer, "Le maitre de justice," *Les Écrits Esséniens découverts près de la Mer Morte* (Paris, 1980 [4th ed.]) pp. 369–79.

275. See A. Jaubert's article in *John and the Dead Sea Scrolls,* ed. Charlesworth, pp. 62–75.

276. C. Newsom, *Songs of the Sabbath Sacrifice; A Critical Edition* (HSS 27; Atlanta, 1985).

277. As S. Talmon stated in a paper at Mogilany, Poland, "the solar calendar must be considered a most important heuristic instrument for defining the very nature of the *Yahad.*" At this Qumran conference Talmon distributed the text and English translation of the first two columns of Mish Ba (4Q83), which is a calendrical scroll. He is publishing it with the assistance of I. Knohl.

278. H. Stegemann, "Die Qumrantexte und ihre Bedeutung für das Neue Testament," in *Georgia Augusta: Nachrichten aus der Universität Göttingen* (May 1983) 17–29, esp. p. 25.

279. Consult the incisive comments by S. Talmon in *The World of Qumran from Within,* esp. pp. 147–85. See also Talmon's *King, Cult and Calendar in Ancient Israel: Collected Essays* (Jerusalem, 1986). Talmon speculates that the Qumran covenanters "did not reckon the beginning of the day from sunset, as is Jewish custom, but rather from sunrise, like the Christians." *The World of Qumran from Within,* p. 173.

280. I consider this statement incontestable. Obviously, his followers felt compelled to write epistles, gospels, ethical tracts, and apocalyptic works. Perhaps it is important to stress, again, that my comparison is with Jesus and the Qumran Essenes (not Jesus' followers and the Essenes).

281. I consider it strange that this fact is either not perceived or considered too obvious to mention. R. Leivestad rightly observes that the Qumranites were "intensely occupied by theological work. . . ." Leivestad, *Jesus in His Own Perspective,* trans. D. E. Aune (Minneapolis, 1987) quotation from p. 21. A. Paul correctly stresses that the Qumranites were "gens du Livre" and that "one is astonished also by the place occupied in the Qumran library by biblical commentaries." Paul, *Le judaïsme ancien et la Bible* (RE 3; Paris, 1987) p. 41.

282. Philo, *Every Good Man Is Free* 80. Josephus, *War* 2.136.

283. This pericope, while shaped by Marcan vocabulary, has impressive evidence of being authentic. The post-Easter community was embarrassed by Jesus' rejection at Nazareth. The interrogatives concerning him are usually pre-Easter.

284. Of course, we must guard against claiming too much about Jesus' authority. H. Anderson rightly warns us to be aware of "the uncritical conceit that what

overwhelmed those around Jesus was the sheer unprecedented *sovereignty* of his presence and being." See Anderson, "Jesus: Aspects of the Question of His Authority," in *The Social World of Formative Christianity and Judaism*, ed. J. Neusner et al. (Philadelphia, 1988) pp. 290–310; quotation from p. 291.

285. Palestinian Talmud Pes 6.1.

286. Philo, *Every Good Man Is Free* 85.

287. Obviously Boers was using this insight to make a theological, not a historical, point; but it is appropriate also as a historically valid conclusion. See Boers, *Who Was Jesus?*, p. 92.

288. The Greek verb *omnyō* means "swear, take an oath."

289. There is no reason to conclude that the thrust of this saying originates only in Matthew's community. The prohibition of oaths fits much better into the sociological crises and eschatological fervor of Jesus' life and teachings than into the Matthean community that was developing binding rules—and allegiances (or oaths)—to the community of Jesus that was buffeted by persecutions I do not think the prohibition is related to the anti-Judaisms in Matthew.

290. W. D. Davies rightly perceived that the Sermon on the Mount "reveals an awareness" of the Essenes "and perhaps a polemic against it." Davies, *The Setting of the Sermon on the Mount* (Cambridge, 1966) p. 235. K. Stendahl concluded that the means of interpreting scripture in Matthew were influenced by Essene methodology. Stendahl, *The School of St. Matthew and Its Use of the Old Testament* (Philadelphia, 1954; repr. 1968). Stendahl clearly points to a school of Matthew, not to a school of Jesus. While both Davies and Stendahl correctly saw a heightened influence of the Essenes in the composition of Matthew, neither would disagree with the suggestion that the Dead Sea Scrolls also help us comprehend the life and teachings of the historical Jesus.

291. Yadin incorrectly reported that "the Dead Sea Scrolls contain strict bans on oath-taking. . . ." Yadin, *The Temple Scroll* (London, 1985) p. 241. This ban is not found in the Dead Sea Scrolls, as far as I know. Josephus (*War* 2.135) and Philo did report that the Essenes shunned oaths (*Every Good Man Is Free* 84); but in tension with this description is Josephus's statement, in line with the Dead Sea Scrolls (especially 1QS), that the initiate "is made to swear tremendous oaths" (*War* 2.139). Apparently, the Essenes swore oaths only to fellow Essenes and only to solidify solidarity with the community. Josephus later mentioned the oaths that the Essenes swear to the community (*War* 2.142). H. Ringgren rightly claimed, "The Dead Sea Scrolls do not know of a prohibition against oaths. . . ." Ringgren, *The Faith of Qumran: Theology of the Dead Sea Scrolls*, trans. E. T. Sander (Philadelphia, 1963) p. 236.

292. Contrast Lev 19:37, according to which the LORD instructs Israel to keep "all my statutes and all my ordinances." See also Deut 6:2, 24–25.

293. Josephus reported that the Essenes were careful to transmit the additional rules and the groups' special books (*War* 2.142).

294. J. Milgrom, "The Qumran Cult: Its Exegetical Principles," in *Temple Scroll Studies* (Sheffield, 1989) p. 178.

295. E. Käsemann, *Jesus Means Freedom*, trans. F. Clarke (Philadelphia, 1969) p. 19.

296. This statement does not imply that Sirach was anathema to the Qumran Essenes. They were indeed fond of it. And, moreover, as J. Priest attempted to show, Sirach in its review of "famous men" alters the order so as to highlight or "bring the priestly element" into prominence. See Priest, "*Ben Sira* 45, 25 in the Light of the Qumran Literature," *RQ* 17 (1964) 111–18.

297. See D. Flusser, *Die rabbinischen Gleichnisse;* B. H. Young, *Jesus and His Jewish Parables* (New York, 1989).

298. As many commentators and exegetes have demonstrated quite conclusively, Mk 4:10–12 reflects the needs of the post-Easter community.

299. Lichtenberger shows that alongside Qumranic deterministic teachings is a Qumran idea that assumes human free will. See Lichtenberger, *Studien zum Menschenbild.*

300. According to Josephus, the Pharisees attribute some events to "fate" but allow for free will. The Essenes, however, contend that all events are determined by fate (*Ant* 13.172). Some of the passages in the Dead Sea Scrolls are studied by E. H. Merrill in his *Qumran and Predestination: A Theological Study of the Thanksgiving Hymns* (SSTDJ 8; Leiden, 1975).

301. M. Broshi in *The Dead Sea Scrolls* (Tokyo, 1979) p. 15.

302. Josephus claims that they believed in the immortality of the soul (*War* 2.154–58) in a way that, like the early Jewish sections of the History of the Rechabites, is in harmony with the Greek concept of the Isle of the Blessed Ones.

303. See 1QH 6.34–35; 11.10–14; also consult Schürer, *The History of the Jewish People,* ed. Vermes et al., vol. 2, pp. 582–83.

304. Michael is not mentioned in the canonical Gospels. Luke mentions "Gabriel" in his infancy gospel in 1:19 and 1:26. Neither Raphael nor Sariel is mentioned in the Bible.

305. See my development of this conclusion in *Jesus Within Judaism.* Wilcox suggests that Jesus saw "the likelihood of a rebel's death before him. . . ." Wilcox, *ANRW* II.25.1 (1982) p. 186. Meyer claims that "it is probable that he conceived his death in sacrificial terms." Meyer, *Aims of Jesus,* p. 252. Acknowledging that the concept of a vicarious and atoning death or suffering of a righteous person was known in early Jewish thought, Hengel is of the opinion that there "is nothing from a historical or traditio-historical point of view which stands in the way of our deriving it [the soteriological interpretation of Jesus' death] from the earliest community and perhaps even from Jesus himself." Hengel, *The Atonement,* trans. J. Bowden (Philadelphia, 1981) p. 64. These new developments are striking in light of the coolness scholars gave to T. W. Manson's and J. Jeremias's conclusion that Jesus saw himself as the suffering servant prophesied by Isaiah. In the foreword to

the paperback issue of Manson's famous work, F. F. Bruce wrote (correctly in my opinion): "It is unfashionable today to hold, as Professor Manson did, that Jesus understood the Son of Man in terms of the Isaianic Servant of the Lord. But unfashionable as it is, Professor Manson's arguments for it are completely convincing." See Manson, *The Servant-Messiah: A Study of the Public Ministry of Jesus,* intro. by F. F. Bruce (Grand Rapids, 1977). Jeremias concluded as follows: "Only to his disciples did he unveil the mystery that he viewed the fulfillment of Isa. 53 as his God-appointed task, and to them alone did he interpret his death as a vicarious dying for the countless multitude. . . ." J. Jeremias and W. Zimmerli, *The Servant of God,* trans. H. Knight et al. (SBT 20; London, 1957 [German original 1952]) p. 104.

306. m. Ta'an. 3:8.

307. See Charlesworth, "Ḥoni," *Anchor Bible Dictionary.*

308. See the Martyrdom of Isaiah, and the Lives of the Prophets.

309. See J. W. van Henten, ed., *Die Entstehung der jüdischen Martyrologie* (SPB 38; Leiden, 1989).

310. R. E. Brown contends that Jesus did anticipate his rejection and death. Brown, "How Much Did Jesus Know?—A Survey of the Biblical Evidence," *CBQ* 29 (1967) 315–45. R. N. Longenecker concludes that Jesus saw himself as the Son of Man, which denoted both suffering and glory. Longenecker, " 'Son of Man' as a Self-Designation of Jesus," *JETS* 12 (1969) 161–72.

311. Allegro, "Jesus and Qumran," in *Jesus in History and Myth,* ed. Hoffmann and Larue, pp. 95–96.

312. This conclusion was tendered by M. Black in his magisterial *The Scrolls and Christian Origins,* p. 163.

313. F. F. Bruce rightly stressed this point in his "Jesus and the Gospels in the Light of the Scrolls," in *The Scrolls and Christianity,* ed. M. Black (London, 1969) p. 80.

314. See R. E. Brown et al., *The New Jerome Biblical Commentary* (Englewood Cliffs, N.J., 1990) p. 1074.

315. See also Philo, *Every Good Man Is Free* 81; cf. *The Contemplative Life* 30–33.

316. S. T. Kimbrough contends that the concept of Sabbath at Qumran was "not so apparently more strict than the Pharisees and the resulting Rabbinical tradition." Kimbrough, "The Concept of Sabbath at Qumran," *RQ* 5 (1966) 483–502; quotation from p. 502. Dimant indicates how CD is no longer easy to align with Pharisaic traditions. Dimant, "Qumran Sectarian Literature," in *Jewish Writings of the Second Temple Period,* ed. Stone, p. 525. Schubert seems more accurately to capture the strictness of Qumran: "The Qumran Essenes were more strict observers of the Sabbath than the Pharisees." Maier and Schubert, *Die Qumran-Essener,* p. 125.

317. The Greek is *anthrōpos* (which can mean "man" or "human being"), but Jesus may well have been directing his remarks at this point to men.

318. Surely it is unwise to attribute this saying to the creation of Jesus' followers or the Matthean church. The context is an intra-Jewish debate regarding Sabbath laws, such as between Hillel and Shammai. The context is thence similar to that of Jesus' day and dissimilar to the time in which Matthew was composed, when "the people" Israel can be portrayed (inaccurately) as shouting "let his blood be on us and on our children" (Mt 27:25). Mt 12:11 does not reflect the Jewish persecution of Christians and etiological interests of Matthew. See D. R. A. Hare, *The Theme of Jewish Persecution of Christians in the Gospel According to St Matthew* (Cambridge, 1967); and N. A. Dahl, "The Passion Narrative in Matthew," in *The Interpretation of Matthew,* ed. G. Stanton (IRT 3; Philadelphia, London, 1983) pp. 42–55, esp. p. 50.

319. The Piel of *yld* means "help to bring forth."

320. E. Zerubavel, *The Seven Day Circle: The History and Meaning of the Week* (Chicago, London, 1985).

321. M. Hengel attempts to show how the title "Son of God" developed between 30 and 50. See Hengel, *The Son of God: The Origin of Christology and the History of Jewish-Hellenistic Religion,* trans. J. Bowden (Philadelphia, 1976). J. C. O'Neill contends that Jesus "went to Jerusalem as God's Son, sent by his Father to sacrifice himself for mankind." This conclusion derives not from confessionalism but from historical research. See O'Neill, *Messiah: Six Lectures on the Ministry of Jesus* (Cambridge, 1980) p. 58.

322. See my attempts to clarify the contours of possibility in *Jesus Within Judaism.*

323. See the earlier discussion on pp. 15–17.

324. Mt 11:25–27; Lk 10:21–22.

325. Flusser, in *Jewish Writings of the Second Temple Period,* ed. Stone, p. 567.

326. O'Neill suggests, on the basis of the Gospel of Thomas, that Jesus may have usually said "the kingdom." See O'Neill, *Messiah,* pp. 116–17.

327. See Charlesworth, "The Historical Jesus in Light of Writings Contemporaneous with Him," in *ANRW* II.25.1 (1982) 451–76.

328. Sif of Lev 20:26, ed. Weiss 93d; *Tanchuma,* ed. Buber *lk lkh* 6; y.Kid 59d; m.Ber 2:2; 2:5; y.Ber 4a, 7b; and the Targumim (Ex 15:18 in Onkelos; Isa 40:9; Mic 4:7). Still valuable is G. Dalman's survey in *Die Worte Jesu* (Leipzig, 1930) vol. 1, pp. 79–83.

329. See esp. 4Q400 1.i; 4Q400 i; MasShirShabb 17–19; 4Q402 1; 4Q403 1.ii; and 4Q405 23.ii, lines 10–11.

330. It is extremely unlikely that Jesus, when he talked about the "plant which my heavenly Father has not planted" (Mt 15:13), was referring to the Essenes, who certainly and frequently referred to themselves as God's eternal planting (1QH 6, 8; cf. CD 1.7–8). This image is also found in many early Jewish texts and derives from the Old Testament. Jesus, moreover, seems to be speaking against the Pharisees, according to Matthew (15:12).

331. F. J. Murphy attempts to show that "any reconstruction that does not see Jesus within first-century Jewish society is unacceptable." Murphy, *The Religious World of Jesus: An Introduction to Second Temple Palestinian Judaism* (Nashville, 1991) p. 341.

332. This is surely a consensus among scholars. See the carefully crafted and informed summary by Wilcox in *ANRW* II.25.1 (1982) 169.

333. Since the early 1950s numerous authors have claimed that Jesus was an Essene and even identified him with the Righteous Teacher. I shall not list these publications, because they are by journalists seeking attention or by scholars who have become confused and even insane. Quite different are the works of Jewish scholars. In the nineteenth century H. Graetz concluded that Jesus adopted the fundamental principles of the Essenes. K. Kohler contended that Jesus exhibited the highest form of Essenism. See Graetz's *History of the Jews* (London, 1891–92) vol. 11, p. 150; and Kohler's "Jesus of Nazareth—In Theology," *JE*, vol. 7, p. 169; and also Kohler's *The Origins of the Synagogue and the Church* (New York, 1929) p. 238. Much more informed and insightful are the comments by J. Klausner in *Jesus of Nazareth*, trans. H. Danby (New York, 1929) esp. p. 211; and S. Sandmel in *Judaism and Christian Beginnings* (New York, 1978).

334. M. Simon wrote, "It appears certain that Jesus knew Essenism, or an environment in which Essenian beliefs were particularly widespread." He continued, "Certain aspects of Jesus' preaching seem to betray a deliberate preoccupation with defining himself over against Essenism." Our research undergirds both insights. See Simon's popular book titled *Jewish Sects at the Time of Jesus*, trans. J. H. Farley (Philadelphia, 1967) p. 148.

335. Yadin, *The Temple Scroll* (London, 1985) p. 241.

336. Sandmel, *Judaism and Christian Beginnings*, p. 305.

337. H. Falk does not claim that Jesus was a Pharisee; but he argues persuasively that Jesus' teachings should be understood in terms of the debates between two groups of Pharisees, the strict Shammaites and the more tolerant Hillelites. In many ways Jesus followed the Hillelite interpretation of the oral law and resisted the Shammaites who "were responsible for handing Jesus over to the Romans for the crucifixion," in violation of Jewish law. See Falk, *Jesus the Pharisee: A New Look at the Jewishness of Jesus* (New York, 1985) p. 8.

338. Schiffman, "At the Crossroads: The Dead Sea Scrolls and the History of Judaism and Christianity," *Network: News of the Faculty Resources Program* (Fall 1988) p. 10.

339. This focus explains why I have not included the claims that Jesus' special meals, especially the Last Supper, were influenced by the Essenes. The meals of the *ḥaberim* need to be more fully understood and assessed. The sacredness of all meals and especially the seasonal feasts was celebrated in every devout Jewish home, including that of Mary and Joseph and of Peter and his family. Possible Essene

influence on the development of the Eucharist would be a phenomenon that postdates Jesus of Nazareth.

340. O'Neill speculates that "most of the Essenes became Christian and brought their distinctive literature with them, with its distinctive christology." O'Neill, *ET* 99 (1988) 203. This hyperbole may be necessary to shake scholars out of their lethargy by pointing to the obvious conversion of some Essenes to Christianity, a high probability that seems obvious—indeed certain—in light of research on 1Cor 6:13–7:1, Ephesians, Acts, Matthew, John, Hebrews, the Didache, and the Odes of Solomon.

341. See J. H. Charlesworth and J. Murphy-O'Connor, *Paul and the Dead Sea Scrolls* (New York, 1990).

342. See Stendahl, *School of St. Matthew;* W. D. Davies, *Setting of the Sermon on the Mount; John and the Dead Sea Scrolls,* ed. Charlesworth.

343. One of the great masters of Qumran research, Father J. T. Milik, concluded at the end of his still-invaluable book, that the new dimensions in Christianity "can only be adequately explained by the person of Jesus himself." This conclusion derives from historical research, not apologetics. See Milik, *Ten Years of Discovery in the Wilderness of Judaea,* trans. J. Strugnell (SBT 26; London, 1959) p. 143.

CHAPTER 2

Jesus and the Temple Scroll

OTTO BETZ

Y. Yadin, who successfully completed the difficult task of editing and interpreting the large and badly mutilated Temple Scroll of Qumran Cave 11 during the last years of his life, illuminated some difficult passages in the Synoptic Gospels with this scroll: (1) the identity of the "Herodians," who appear in the Gospel of Mark among the adversaries of Jesus (3:6; 8:14–21; 12:13); (2) the problem that Jesus was the guest of "Simon the leper" in Bethany when he was anointed by a woman at the beginning of the passion week (Mk 14:3); (3) the much-debated issue of crucifixion as a death penalty in Israel under Hasmonean and Roman rule, which contributes to a better understanding of the trial and death of Jesus; (4) the implicit criticism against the Temple in Jerusalem raised by the author of the scroll, his ideas about the true sanctuary of God, and his program for the worship and purity of Israel. These may be compared with the attitude of Jesus toward the Jerusalem Temple and his ministry of atonement, which pointed to the new covenant for the people of God. The promise of a sanctuary not made with hands (Mk 14:58) will also be taken into consideration.

THE HERODIANS: WERE THEY ESSENES?

The Herodians, who are mentioned only in Mark and Matthew,[1] have always confronted New Testament exegetes with a real problem. Usually one thinks of adherents of Herod (the Great? Antipas? Herod's dynasty?) who made common cause with the Pharisees against Jesus. But this supposition is merely an analytical judgment which yields no factual information. Did they believe that Herod was a kind of Messiah? Were they close to the Sadducees, willing to pay tribute to Caesar (Mk 12:13)?[2] These Herodians could not have been a group with political interests alone, as their name might initially suggest. Since they appear with the Pharisees in the Gospels, they seem to be religiously motivated and concerned with the true interpretation of the Torah.

C. Daniel has recently suggested that the Herodians of Mark were Essenes.[3] He refers to the story of the Essene Manaemos in Josephus (*Ant* 15.371–79). When Herod the Great was still a young boy going to school, Manaemos told him that he would become king. As a result, he won for the Essenes the favor of Herod, who now honored the "prophetic" Essenes (*Ant* 15.373, 378). Hence, it is not unreasonable to suppose that they might have been nicknamed "Herodians" by the common people. The fact that they were the favorite religious party of Herod may also explain why the site of Qumran was not occupied during Herod's reign (31–4 B.C.E.). During this period the Essenes were no longer being forced to withdraw to the wilderness, as was the case under the Hasmoneans, who were sharply opposed to them. They could live in Jerusalem, where they inhabited an "Essene quarter" on Mount Zion, in the southwest corner of the city.[4]

Yadin could confirm the identification of the Herodians with the Essenes by drawing a far-reaching conclusion from a passage in the Temple Scroll (15.9–14). According to this document, the first feast during the year to be celebrated at the sanctuary was the feast of Millû'îm, a dedication of the Temple and the priesthood during the first seven days of the month of Nisan (see Ex 29; Ezek 43:18–27). On each day of the celebration a basket of bread had to be offered together with a ram as a wave offering in the Temple. This offering of seven baskets of bread, not mentioned in the Bible, must have been characteristic of the Essenes and referred to by Jesus in the conversation with his disciples reported in Mk 8:14–21. After the feeding of four thousand people in the wilderness, Jesus warned the disciples to beware of the leaven of the Pharisees and of the leaven of Herod

("Herodians," v. 15). When the disciples did not understand, Jesus reminded them of the feeding of the multitudes and of the baskets full of broken pieces taken up there: twelve baskets at the meal with the five thousand and seven baskets from the seven loaves for the four thousand (vv. 19–20). The reminiscence of these events would help the disciples to understand the warning against the leaven of the Pharisees and that of the Herodians.

According to Yadin, the baskets of bread, gathered together at these two meals of Jesus, pointed to the bread of the Pharisees and the Herodians.[5] The Pharisees emphasized the offering of twelve loaves of bread of the Presence each week in the Temple, loaves that were eaten by the priests, while for the Essenes the seven baskets of bread to be offered during the seven days of the feast of Dedication were characteristic. In the eyes of Jesus, the bread of the Pharisees and the Herodians was "leaven," that is, bread not suited for a sacrifice (cf. 1Cor 5:6–7). On the other hand, the bread distributed by him at the feeding of the multitudes originated from God, pointing to the "bread of life": it is the Son of God, sent by the Father in order to save humanity by offering eternal life (Jn 6:33–35).

The one loaf of bread in the boat of the disciples (Mk 8:14) symbolizes Jesus; therefore it was not necessary to discuss the fact that there was not enough bread in the boat (Mk 8:16). On the basis of Jesus' conversation with his disciples and the Temple Scroll (15.9–14), Yadin concluded that the Herodians in the Gospels must be Essenes and that the miracle of the feeding of the multitudes probably took place on the feast of Ordination, shortly before Passover (see Jn 6:4).

Yadin did not discuss the other passages in which "the Herodians" are mentioned. The identification of the Herodians with the Essenes of the Dead Sea Scrolls seems to correspond to Mark 3:6: together with the Pharisees the Herodians were fiercely opposed to the attitude of Jesus toward the Sabbath and "held counsel . . . against him, how to destroy him." He had healed a man with a withered hand in the synagogue (Mk 3:5), defending this deed with a question on whether it is "lawful on the Sabbath to do good or to do harm, to save life or to kill" (Mk 3:4). The Essenes were concerned with keeping the Sabbath correctly; their interpretation of the commandment not to work on this day of rest was even more strict than that of the Pharisees.[6] This we learn from the Sabbath regulations in the Damascus Document (CD 10–11). Walking about in the field on the Sabbath in order to contemplate the work to be done after the Sabbath was forbidden (CD 10.20–21); according to Mk 2:23–28 Jesus went through the fields with his disciples on a Sabbath. They also did not permit an animal fallen into a pit to be rescued on the Sabbath (CD 11.13, 14); according to Matthew 12:11 this was normally done by the Jews in the time of Jesus.[7] Therefore, we may conclude that "the Herodians" thought that Jesus had profaned the Sabbath; the Torah commands that such an offender be put to death (Ex 31:14; Mk 3:6).

The House of Simon the Leper in Bethany (Mk 14:3)

According to the Gospel of Mark, while Jesus sat at table in the house of "Simon the Leper" in Bethany, a woman came and anointed him with a precious ointment (14:3–9). In Matthew's report, the house of Simon the leper is also mentioned, while according to John, Jesus was in Bethany in the company of Lazarus and Martha, and Mary anointed him (12:1–8).

The fact that Jesus was the guest of a leper in Bethany is quite remarkable. He was not afraid of having contact with lepers who needed his help (Mk 1:40–45 and parallels; Lk 17:11–19). But how could a leper own a house in a village close to Jerusalem and have people such as Jesus and his disciples as his guests? According to the law, lepers had to live in a kind of quarantine "outside the camp" (Num 5:2–3), at the entrance of the gate of a city (2Kgs 7:3ff). The author of the Temple Scroll emphasizes the holiness of Jerusalem. Since this is where God is present in the Temple among humanity, the Temple was to be kept sacred and ritually clean (11QTemple 27.4).[8] The purity required for the priests serving before God (Lev 22:4), for the holy warriors of Israel in their camp (Deut 23:10–11), and the congregation of Israel standing at Mount Sinai and waiting for the coming of God (Ex 19:1–15) served as a kind of obligatory ideal to be observed by the inhabitants of Jerusalem. The holiness of God should not be offended by impurity. Thus "no leper and no man stricken" (by a skin disease) shall enter the Temple unless they have been cleansed. After the cleansing he shall "bring near" (his offering, 11QTemple 45.18; cf. Mk 1:44, where the leper, cleansed by Jesus, is told to show himself to the priest and to offer for his cleansing what Moses has commanded). In the Temple Scroll we read: "And you shall make three places at the east of the city, separated one from another, into which shall come the lepers and the people who have a discharge and the men who had a (nocturnal) emission" (46.16–18). A similar regulation is to be followed everywhere in Israel: "And in every city you shall allot places for those afflicted with leprosy or with plague or the scab, who may not enter your cities and defile them" (48.14–15). According to Josephus (*War* 5.227) the city of Jerusalem was off limits to people with a discharge and to lepers, while the sanctuary could not be entered by women during the time of menstrual uncleanness.[9]

These regulations explain why Simon the leper lived in Bethany, east of Jerusalem. For this is exactly the region where lepers should stay, according to the Temple Scroll (46.16–18). We should not assume that all the concepts and rules of the Temple Scroll were mere theory and pious ideals, never put into practice—which, of course, was true for the program of the true Temple and its cult. But it was the regulations for a life of purity in the Holy City that were followed by the Essenes, of whom a group must have occupied a certain quarter within the walls, most probably in the southwest corner, close to the Essene Gate. Through that gate the Essenes left Jerusalem in order to reach their "place of the hand" (*měqôm yad*=latrine), which was established outside of the city walls in order to keep the holy place clean (46.13–16). In a similar way, quarantine places were established by those Essenes. Therefore, Simon who had a house in Bethany may have been a member of the Essene community who had been obliged to dwell east of Jerusalem because of the disease that rendered him unclean.

THE TEMPLE SCROLL AND THE CRUCIFIXION OF JESUS

In the Mishna, crucifixion is not listed among the modes of capital punishment of the Jewish law, in which burning, stoning, strangling, and beheading are prescribed (m.Sanh 7:1).[10] Like Greeks such as Alexander the Great and the Diadochi,[11] the Romans made ample use of the death penalty of crucifixion, especially when slaves or foreigners had committed violent acts that rendered them *latrones* ("robbers, bandits"). This term could designate not only highwaymen or pirates but also rebellious people such as slaves rising against their masters or guerrilla fighters in the provinces who protested violently against the Roman rule and the foreign soldiers occupying their country. Roman citizens and, in particular, members of the higher ranks of society were normally not sentenced and executed by crucifixion, which in the eyes of the Roman people was the most cruel and disgusting penalty.[12] There was, however, one exception: high treason (*perduellio*),[13] the most serious crime directed against the whole Roman state.

The terrible punishment of crucifixion was used in order to pacify unruly Roman provinces. Judea during the first century c.e. may serve as an example. Josephus reports mass crucifixions in Judea under the Roman prefects Varus (*War* 2.75), Cumanus (*War* 2.241), and Felix (*War* 2.306, 308), and under Titus during the siege of Jerusalem (*War* 5.289, 449–51). In Alexandria too Jews were crucified under the Roman government (Philo, *In Flaccum* 2.84–85).

The Temple Scroll discloses that crucifixion was practiced by Jewish authorities against their own people. We have to analyze in detail an important passage in column 64. It is a kind of midrash, an exegetical explanation of Deuteronomy 21:22–23, presented as an original commandment of God to Moses. It agrees with its context insofar as the last part of the Temple Scroll (cols. 46–67) follows the commandments and ordinances of Deuteronomy 14–22. These regulations are used to safeguard the purity of the Holy City and the People of Israel, which the author of the Temple Scroll has added to his ideas about the true sanctuary and the sacrifices to be offered there. The midrash of column 64 reveals the biblical foundation for the death penalty of crucifixion; in the view of the Qumran covenanters it was already prescribed by God to Moses. Moreover, this midrash determines the crime to be punished by crucifixion and the way in which the execution must be carried out. We also learn that other passages in Jewish writings of that time must be related to the death penalty of crucifixion. Finally, the trial of Jesus can be better understood in light of this text of the Temple Scroll.

While most of the commandments in the Temple Scroll from Deuteronomy 14–22 are taken over with only slight deviations and changes, column 64 offers an interpretation and elaboration of Deuteronomy 21:22. The Qumran author reveals a peculiar interest in this passage and desires to relate it to his community.

Deuteronomy 21:22–23 reads as follows: "And if a man has committed a crime punishable by death and he is put to death, and you hang him on a tree, (v. 23) his body shall not remain all night upon the tree, but you shall bury him the same day, for a hanged man is accursed by God; you shall not defile your land which the Lord your God gives you for an inheritance." The author of the Temple Scroll does not quote this passage but gives the following explanation:

(7) If a man slanders his [=God's] people and delivers his people up to a foreign nation and does evil to his people (8) you shall hang him on the tree, and he shall die. According to the testimony ("mouth") of two witnesses and the testimony ("mouth") of three witnesses (9) he shall be put to death, and they shall hang him on the tree. If a man has committed a crime punishable by death, and has fled unto (10) the midst of the Gentiles and has cursed his people and the children of Israel, you shall hang him also on the tree (11) and he shall die. And you shall not leave overnight their bodies on the tree, but shall certainly bury them the same day for (12) cursed (cursing) by God and men are the ones hanged upon the tree, and you shall not defile the land which I (13) give you for an inheritance. . . .

When we compare this text of the Temple Scroll with Deuteronomy 21:22–23, we can recognize four concerns: to determine the crime to be punished by hanging the delinquent upon a tree, to define this punishment as crucifixion, to clarify some details of the execution itself, and to make sure that the bodies of the delinquents will be buried on the day of the execution. The focal point (see lines 11–13) is in basic agreement with Deuteronomy 21:23; the interpretation of Deuteronomy 21:22 in lines 6–10 is particularly interesting.

The Crime Deserving Crucifixion According to 11QTemple 64:6–10

In my view, Deuteronomy 21:23 has enabled the author of the Temple Scroll to answer the question of what kind of crime should be punished by crucifixion. No explicit statement is made in Deuteronomy 21:22–23 about the crime, which is simply called *ḥēṭěʾ mišpat māwet* ("a sin deserving the death sentence"); this general term is used in 11QTemple 64.9. But it is specified in the Qumran text in a twofold way (lines 6–7; 9–10), whereby the casuistic form of Deuteronomy 21:22–23 is retained. In the first case, three verbs are used to describe the crime: a man slanders "his people"; he delivers it to a foreign nation; he does evil to it (lines 6–7). According to the second case, a man who has committed a crime deserving death may "flee unto the midst of the Gentiles and curse 'his people' and the sons of Israel" (lines 9–10). In both cases the victim of the crimes committed is "his people" ('*ammô*). The suffix may refer to the evildoer who does damage to his own people for the sake of a foreign nation, for the Gentiles. I think, however, that "God's people" is meant as well, that is, the holy ones chosen by him from the Gentile mass of perdition.

High treason is considered to be the most horrible crime, deserving the cruel and shameful punishment of crucifixion. According to the author of the Temple Scroll, high treason committed against the people of God is not merely a political crime but a grave sin as well. It is God who is offended; his holy name is rendered profane before the Gentiles when an Israelite delivers "his people" to a foreign nation or curses it among the Gentiles. The strange terms *hāyâ rākîl*, used in connection with high treason and "delivering his people" (line 7) may have a similar connection, since the noun *rĕkîlût* means "evil gossip."

I think that the crimes of high treason and of delivering up the people of God and cursing it in the midst of the Gentiles must be linked with and even derived from the strange and ambiguous phrase *qilĕlat 'ĕlōhîm wa'ănāšim* (11QTemple 64.12), in which *qilĕlat 'ĕlōhîm* denotes that those committing high treason are accursed "by God and men"; they have cursed God and his people.

In this way the phrase *qilĕlat 'ĕlōhîm* became the biblical foundation for the crime of high treason: cursing God and committing the sin of blasphemy (Deut 21:23) can be done by cursing "his people" or by delivering Israel to a foreign nation.

High treason is not dealt with in the Torah, nor is it found in the Old Testament. But this crime must have been well known, having become a real problem in Early Judaism and for the author of the Temple Scroll; this state of affairs is also transparent through other texts to which I shall refer below. In Roman law, crucifixion was the punishment for high treason. The author of the Temple Scroll discovered a similar regulation in the law of Moses in Deuteronomy 21:22–23. He derived a religious interpretation from the words *qilĕlat 'ĕlōhîm*. Deuteronomy 21:23 merely explains the necessity to bury a criminal hung upon a tree on the day of execution; the author of the Temple Scroll found in them the blasphemous character of high treason to "curse" (*qillel*) God and humanity. He gave a new interpretation of Deuteronomy 21:22–23 and issued it in the Temple Scroll as a commandment that God had given to Moses.

This interpretation of *qilĕlat 'ĕlōhîm* is found also in the Mishna: the man to be hanged is "a curse against God, as if to say that because he blessed (i.e., cursed) the Name and the Name of Heaven was found profaned." The Hebrew *qilĕlat 'ĕlōhîm*, in effect, meant blasphemy; that is why a blasphemer should be hanged. The death of Ḥoni (or Onias) (mentioned in *Ant* 14.22–24) may illustrate this interpretation of Deuteronomy 21:23. The Jews, who together with the Arab king Aretas besieged Aristobulus II in Jerusalem, forced the great intercessor Onias "to place a curse" on Aristobulus II and his fellow rebels (*Ant* 14.22). But he refused to do so and prayed: "O God, king of the universe, since these men standing beside me are Thy people, and those who are besieged are Thy priests, I beseech Thee not to hearken to them against these men nor to bring to pass what these men ask Thee to do to those others" (*Ant* 14.23–24). After this prayer he was stoned (and possibly hanged on a tree) by "evil" Jews, but Josephus also tells how God exacted satisfaction for the murder of Onias (*Ant* 14.25–28). This report justifies my translation of *'ammô* as "people of God" in 11QTemple 64.7, 10; for Onias speaks in his prayer of "Thy people" and "Thy priests" (*Ant* 14.24).

The Execution: Hanging a Man upon the Tree = Crucifixion

The punishment for the crimes of blasphemy and high treason is prescribed in two main clauses in the Temple Scroll (64.8b–9a and 10b–11a). In both cases it is "hanging" the delinquent "upon the tree" (*tālâ 'al hā'ēṣ*). This phrase is taken from Deuteronomy 21:22: A man "who has committed a sin deserving death shall die and you shall hang him upon the tree" (*wĕhûmāt wĕtālîtā 'al hā'ēṣ*). The Temple Scroll gives a different sequence for the verbs "to hang" and "to die": "you (plur.) shall hang him upon the tree and he shall die" (i.e., "in order that he may die," *wtlytmh 'wtw 'l h'ṣ wymt*). This change of word order is very important; Deuteronomy 21:22–23 could be understood in the way we find it in the Mishna (m.Sanh 16:4). There the capital punishment of stoning is prescribed and the problem is discussed whether "all that have been stoned must be hanged" or whether hanging should only be applied to the grave crimes of idolatry and blasphemy. This means that the corpse of a man executed by stoning must be hanged upon a tree; it has to be exhibited publicly in order to warn the people by showing them the severe consequences of sin. The sequence of the verbs "to die" and "to hang" in Deuteronomy 21:22 is taken seriously by the rabbis. To them, hanging is not a mode of execution. According to the Mishna (m.Sanh 16:4) the shameful exhibition of the corpse should take place for a short while and only in extreme cases.

In the Temple Scroll, however, the sequence "hanging-dying" indicates that the delinquent shall be hanged alive upon the tree, death being the result of this punishment. Hanging is here the way of carrying out the death sentence and not an additional act of exhibiting the corpse of the delinquent, as the rabbis interpreted Deuteronomy 21:22–23. This becomes evident from the role of the witnesses which is introduced into the text of the Temple Scroll (lines 7–9): "On the testimony of two witnesses and on the testimony of three witnesses he shall be put to death." Through their testimony they will cause the death sentence of the trial (lines 7–8) and they will also carry out the execution: "And they (wĕhēmâ) shall hang him upon the tree" (line 9). In Deuteronomy 21:22–23 no witnesses are mentioned. The author of the Temple Scroll has introduced them into the text about high treason in dependence on Deuteronomy 17:6–7 (cf. 19:15): "On the testimony (literally, "mouth") of two witnesses or of three witnesses he that is to die shall be put to death; a person shall not be put to death on the evidence of one witness. The hand of the witnesses shall be first against him to put him to death, and afterward the hand of all the people." The text of the Temple Scroll says that "two and three witnesses" are required for the sentence of "death by hanging"; five witnesses have to agree in their testimony and to carry out the execution. The very fact that witnesses are introduced into this midrash on Deuteronomy 21:22–23 reveals that this text is understood as an ordinance of judgment and the act of hanging upon the tree as execution. The delinquent has to be hanged alive in order that he may die. This amounts to crucifixion, the Roman punishment for the crime of high treason.

As a matter of fact, there is another text of Qumran that confirms this interpretation of the Temple Scroll (64.6–13) and may be taken as evidence that crucifixion was practiced in Early Judaism: the fragment 4QpNah.[14] In this text, a "Lion of Wrath" is mentioned who "used to hang men alive" (yitleh ʾănāšîm ḥayyim, line 7). The next fragmentary line speaks of "a man hung alive on the tree" (tālûy ḥay ʿal hāʿēṣ, line 8). Again, we have a clear reference to Deuteronomy 21:22–23, but here, too, "hanging men alive" means crucifixion. The Lion of Wrath must be identified with the Hasmonean king Alexander Janneus, who crucified eight hundred of his Jewish enemies because they had called the Syrian king Demetrius III Eukairos for help against their own tyrannical ruler (*War* 1.92–97; *Ant*

13.376–81). Whereas Josephus condemns this atrocious act, the Qumran author seems to justify it by pointing to Deuteronomy 21:22–23; Alexander had punished the crime of high treason by crucifixion.

The passage in the Temple Scroll (64.6–13) is most valuable to us because it is a legal (halakic) text of Early Judaism that deals with the penalty "of hanging men alive."[15] This does not mean "hanging by the neck," for this kind of punishment was not known in antiquity; strangulation was carried out at that time without gallows. Instead, we have to think of crucifixion. The few other texts relating to this issue are either brief exegetical notes[16] or anecdotes.[17]

A Story about Sorcerers   In addition, there is the incredible remark about the rabbi and Pharisaic leader Simon ben Shetaḥ who had hanged eighty women (witches) at Ashkelon (*tālâ šĕmōnîm nāšîm bĕʾašqĕlôn*).[18] In an important study, M. Hengel has shown that the historical truth has been obscured polemically in this text.[19] In actuality, influential men and political enemies of the Pharisees, not women practicing sorcery, must have been "hanged" (=crucified) under the rule of the Queen Alexandra Salome, the wife and successor of Alexander Janneus; this is the event behind the rabbinic tradition about Simon's mass execution. According to Josephus, the Pharisees became highly influential and politically powerful after the death of Janneus. They persuaded the queen to eliminate those who had participated in the crucifixion of the eight hundred adversaries of Janneus, mentioned by Josephus (*War* 1.79–80; *Ant* 13.380ff. and in 4QpNah). Most probably Simon ben Shetaḥ, who was famous for his antagonism toward Alexander Janneus and for his insistence on justice,[20] was mainly responsible for this act of retaliation. The powerful personality of Simon and his role in history soon became the source for legendary stories;[21] to these belong the remarks about his hanging eighty women (witches) upon the tree.

Exaggerations   I want to follow up Hengel's analysis and show that the rabbinic way of speaking about this event and the polemic distortion of the historical truth reveal the influence of Deuteronomy 21:22–23 and its interpretation in the Temple Scroll. The rabbis tried to justify the action of Simon with the "necessity of the hour" (*haššāʿâ sĕrîhâ*), demanding such an illegal procedure. This points to a political decision rather than to a condemnation of witchcraft. The elimination of prominent members of the Sadducean party was a political necessity for the Pharisees, who had to establish and to strengthen their newly acquired leadership. The number "eighty" may correspond to the eight hundred victims of Alexander Janneus; other valuable suggestions are made by Hengel.[22] We have, in any case, to reckon with exaggerations.

Witchcraft   The motif of witchcraft (according to y.Hag 77d and y.Sanh 123d) may be secondary; Hengel points to the saying in Abot 2:7: "Where there are many women there is much witchcraft."[23] In my opinion, the motif of witchcraft was introduced in order to justify the penalty of crucifixion. The practice of sorcery and witchcraft could be condemned as blasphemy, because the secret name of God was used in incantations (cf. b.Shab 75a).[24] Thus, the crime of *qilĕlat 'ĕlōhîm* (Deut 21:23) was committed, which had to be punished by crucifixion. On the other hand, Simon ben Shetaḥ was praised for having restored the authority of the law. Great teachers of the law were celebrated as having control over supernatural powers such as demons. The charismatic rabbi Ḥanina ben Dosa gave orders to Agrat bat Machlat, the princess of demons (b.Pes 112b/113a). Hanging witches, then, meant to triumph over the world of demons in the name of the Torah.

Ashkelon   From a historical point of view, it is very doubtful that the city of Ashkelon was the location of a trial by Jewish authorities in the first century B.C.E. Ashkelon had not been conquered by the mighty warrior Alexander Janneus. It remained a Hellenistic, Gentile city, protected by the Ptolemies and strongly anti-Jewish; it had its own jurisdiction even under the Roman rule of Palestine.[25] According to Hengel, Jerusalem, not Ashkelon, must have been the place of that mass execution under Simon ben Shetaḥ.[26] How, then, can we explain the introduction of this Gentile city into the tradition of Simon ben Shetaḥ? I have suggested elsewhere a play on the words *'ašqĕlôn* and *'îš qālôn* ("man of shame").[27] Hengel has had a similar idea, referring to the passage 1QpHab 11.12, in which the Wicked Priest is mentioned "whose shame was greater than his honor."[28] These solutions, however, do not exhaust what can be further learned from Deuteronomy 21:22–23. The strange phrase *qilĕlat 'ĕlōhîm* could have been the source for choosing this Gentile city: *'ašqĕlôn* had seen the crucifixion of the "men" (*'îš*) who had "cursed" (*qillēl*) God and "his people." If we follow the text in the Temple Scroll (col. 64), they had done this "in the midst of the Gentiles," to whom they fled after they had committed a sin deserving death (lines 9–10). There may, however, be some historical truth in the name Ashkelon. Hengel is certainly correct with his hypothesis that the victims of Simon ben Shetaḥ were Sadducees and former members of the Sanhedrin under Alexander Janneus. Together with the presiding king, they had been responsible for the death sentence of crucifixion, by which the revolting Pharisees were punished for high treason and blasphemy. But after the death of their protector, some of the Sadducees may have fled to the non-Jewish, Gentile city of Ashkelon in order to find refuge, since they had committed "a sin deserving death." But there was not sufficient reason for the citizens of Ashkelon to defend those Jews who had been counselors of the king Janneus; consequently, they were handed over to Simon ben Shetaḥ. In any case, the Sadducees certainly were caught by surprise by the sudden change after the death of Alexander and were unable to resist the call for vengeance by the victorious Pharisees. Their helplessness may have been one of the reasons for calling them "women"; Hengel points to passages such as Jeremiah 50:36–37; 51:30; and Nahum 3:12, which speak of "men becoming women" in the hour of sudden crisis.[29]

Thus we have two important sources in Early Judaism that prove that Deuteronomy 21:22–23 was consciously appropriated and interpreted in the first century B.C.E. in relation to the penalty of crucifixion: (1) 11QTemple 64.6–13 and, together with it, the fragment 4QpNah; and (2) the rabbinic tradition on Simon ben Shetaḥ and the eighty women. They come from different groups and times, and both are somewhat enigmatic and distorted by polemic. But they allude to historical facts that belong together as cause and effect, the latter being an act of revenge for the former deed. In both sources the passage in Deuteronomy 21:22–23 is understood as crucifixion. This is important for the New Testament and the trial of Jesus.

11QTemple 64.6–13 and the Trial of Jesus

That crucifixion in Judaism of the first century B.C.E. could be regarded as a divine commandment and as a legal penalty for high treason and blasphemy is important for reevaluating the trial of Jesus. One can no longer argue that the fact of Jesus' crucifixion excludes Jewish participation in his trial and death; the Romans were not the only ones to use execution. We must admit, of course, that the Roman prefect Pontius Pilate condemned Jesus to be crucified and that Roman soldiers carried out the execution. The Jews did not have the *ius gladii* under the Roman administration; it was reserved for the prefect (*War* 2.117; *Ant* 18.2; Jn 18:31;

19:10).[30] In the provinces, however, the local courts were kept intact and often cooperated with the Roman prefect. Therefore, in the trial of Jesus the Sanhedrin of Jerusalem may have formed a kind of *consilium iudicum* which did the investigation of the case (*cognitio*) and prepared the accusation (*accusatio*) for the court of the prefect. That is why the nocturnal hearing of Jesus, carried through by a commission of the Sanhedrin under the high priest (Mk 14:53–65), and the morning session of the Sanhedrin (Mk 15:1) should not be treated as unhistorical creations of the Christian community; these events fit the legal situation in a Roman province of that time.[31]

The Sanhedrin   The Jerusalem Sanhedrin in the time of Jesus was held responsible for the maintenance of law and order in Judea. It was headed by the high priest, who followed the principles of the Sadducean understanding of the law. With regard to crucifixion, the Sadducees may have been in basic agreement with 11QTemple 64.6–13, that is, with the view that crucifixion was to be considered a legal penalty. In the trial of Jesus this is confirmed by John 19:7, where the Jews declare to Pilate: "We have a law, and by that law he ought to die, because he has made himself the Son of God" (cf. 18:31). Deuteronomy 21:22, as understood by the Sadducees, must have been alluded to as we have it in 11QTemple 6.6–13. This means that Jesus ought to die by "being hanged alive upon the tree," since his false claim to be the Son of God was both blasphemy and high treason. When in the trial Jesus confessed to being the "Son of God" and "Son of Man," he had uttered "a blasphemy" (Mk 14:62–64). God had promised to David that he would protect his son (2Sam 7:12–15). Furthermore, a man cannot make himself the Son of God and Messiah, for only God will do that (2Sam 7:12–14; Ps 2:7; 110:1).[32] A false messiah and Son of God is guilty of committing high treason. This becomes evident from the word of Caiaphas about Jesus: "If we let him go on thus, everyone will believe in him, and the Romans will come and destroy both our holy place and our nation" (Jn 11:48). A false messiah may cause a revolt and finally "deliver his people" to the Gentiles (11QTemple 64.7). That is why Caiaphas said, "It is expedient for you that one man should die for the people, and that the whole nation should not perish" (Jn 11:50). In this way the Jewish court reached the conclusion that Jesus "was deserving death" (*hayyab mîtâ; mithayyab běnapšô;* see Mk 14:64b); he had committed a "sin deserving death" (*ḥēṭē' mišpat māwet,* cf. Deut 21:22). For this sin, the death penalty had to be crucifixion.[33] The Jewish court had no authority to carry out the death sentence, but it could expect the sentence "death by crucifixion" (*ibis ad crucem*) from the Roman prefect were Jesus handed over to him (Mk 15:1). This expectation probably explains why some Jews could ask Pilate to crucify their false king (Mk 15:13).

Golgotha   We also find in the Gospels a passive interpretation of the term *qilĕlat 'ĕlōhîm:* the man hung on the tree is "cursed by God and men" (*mĕqōlĕlê 'ĕlōhîm wa'ănāšîm*). This brings us to the hill of Golgotha. Mark reports that the people passing by, the chief priests and the scribes derided the crucified Jesus for having claimed to be the Son of God and to be able to destroy and rebuild the Temple (Mk 15:29–32). For the evangelist, this was an act of blasphemy and cursing, just as in the Temple Scroll cursing God's people is blasphemy (11QTemple 64.10); the Messiah is the king of Israel and the Son of God (Mk 15:39). I think, however, that the Jewish officials at Golgotha, repeating the charges of the trial, tried to urge Jesus to confess his sins and publicly deny his claim to be the Son of God. According to the Mishna (m.Sanh 6:2), the confession, with the petition that God may reckon the death penalty as atonement for the committed sin, gives the criminal the chance to obtain a share in the world to come (m.Sanh 10:1). In Luke 23:40–42 one of the two "robbers" crucified together with Jesus (vv. 32–33) confessed his guilt and asked Jesus to remember him in his realm. Jesus promised him participation in paradise (v. 43), that is, in eternal life. In the eyes of the evangelists Jesus did not have to confess any sins; he was the righteous one who made people righteous (Isa 53:11), even in the hour of his death. Instead of making a confession, Jesus commended his spirit into the hands of his heavenly Father (Lk 23:46).

Crucifixion in the Pauline Writings   The apostle Paul also related the cross of Christ to Deuteronomy 21:22–23. He quoted it in Galatians 3:13: "Cursed be everyone who hangs on a tree." More than any other passage of scripture, Deuteronomy 21:22–23 may have convinced Paul that it was necessary to persecute the Christians. Belief in a crucified Messiah was a dangerous superstition; it was even blasphemy. But, the claim to have experienced the risen and exalted Lord on the road to Damascus gave Paul a new understanding of Jesus and his cross. From now on he no longer regarded Christ "according to the flesh" (2Cor 5:16), that is, from a Jewish point of view.

In light of his Damascus experience, Paul regarded Jesus as the Son of God despite his crucifixion. This meant that Deuteronomy 21:22–23 had to be interpreted in a new, soteriological way. Paul did not simply abolish this passage; he was not about to deny its validity. He came to the conclusion that Christ had suffered for sinners and fulfilled the prophecy of the Servant of the Lord in Isaiah 53: He "bore our sicknesses (= sins)" (Isa 53:4). Thus, according to Paul, Christ redeemed sinners from the curse of the Law by becoming the *taluy*, the man accursed by God for sinners' sake, so that in him the blessing of Abraham might come upon the Gentiles (Gal 3:14): "For our sake he made him to be sin who knew no sin, so that in him we might become the righteousness of God" (2Cor 5:21; cf. Isa 53:10–11; Deut 21:22–23).

I think that Paul understood Isaiah 53:5 in a new way. It says that the Servant was "pierced (*mĕḥōlāl*) for our transgressions." Paul may have read *mĕqōlal*, that is, "cursed" for our transgressions. This understanding would explain "the curse" = *mĕqōlal* in Galatians 3:13 and would agree with *mĕqōlal* in 11QTemple 64.12. In addition, the Targum (*TargJon* to Isa 53:5) does not render *mĕḥōlāl* as "pierced" but speaks of the "profanation" of the Temple.

The Burial of the Body

The main point of Deuteronomy 21:22–23 is the commandment in v. 23b to bury the body of a hanged criminal "on the same day": he shall not remain all night upon the tree; otherwise the land which God will give Israel for an inheritance will become defiled. In 11QTemple 64 this commandment is repeated without any comment (lines 11–13). For the author of the Temple Scroll, then, the burial of the criminal did not constitute a problem; for him the important and controversial matter was the penalty of hanging a man upon a tree and the crime that deserved this punishment.

Unlike the Temple Scroll, however, the impact of Deuteronomy 21:23 emerges in the passion story of the Gospels. The Gospels emphasize the fact that the body of the crucified Jesus was taken down and buried immediately after his death, that is, "on the same day." Joseph of Arimathea had asked Pilate for "the body of Jesus" (Mk 15:43), took it down and laid it "in a tomb hewn out of a rock" (v. 46). According to the Gospel of John the Jews insisted on strict obedience to the commandment in Deuteronomy 21:23b. They wanted "to prevent the bodies from remaining on the cross" (cf. 11QTemple 64.11), because it was the day of Preparation for the great Sabbath (Jn 19:31), that is, the first day of Passover. Joseph of Arimathea, then, "took away the body of Jesus" (v. 38); together with Nicodemus he anointed it, bound it in linen clothes, and buried it in the garden tomb which "was in the place where he was crucified" (v. 41).

The fourth evangelist wants to make sure that everything was done according to Deuteronomy 21:23b. For him, however, Jesus was the "king of the Jews" (19:19–22), who therefore was placed in a new tomb (v. 41) after he had been anointed with a great wealth of spices (vv. 39–40). John indicates that he was buried in royal fashion. Moreover, the corpse of Jesus did not defile the land (Deut 21:23b). Clearly the opposite was the case. When one of the soldiers "pierced" Jesus' body with a spear, "at once there came out blood and water" (19:34), the symbols of sacramental salvation. To John this was the fulfillment of Isaiah 53:5: "He was pierced for our transgressions."

THE TRUE TEMPLE
ACCORDING TO THE QUMRAN TEXTS
AND THE TEACHING OF JESUS

The Temple in 11QTemple and the Sanctuary of God at the End of Time

The Temple Scroll claims to be a kind of *Tritonomium*, a law commanded by God to Moses.[34] The Temple that this document prescribes should have been built by the people of Israel on Mount Zion. When compared with this ideal sanctuary, the Temple of Solomon and the Second Temple do not have the correct measurements, courts, and installations; moreover, the festivals of Israel are not celebrated at the right times and in the way God had actually ordered them. The plan and program of the Temple Scroll were not intended to be realized at the end of times and in a renewed land as, for example, the program of Ezekiel 40–48. This is clearly indicated by the Temple Scroll (29.7–10), in which a sanctuary is promised that God himself will build for Israel in the final age. This text begins with the classical covenant formula: "And they shall be a people to me and I shall be (God) for them forever (cf. Ezek 36:28). And I shall dwell with them forever and ever." The permanent presence and close communion of God with a renewed Israel are foreseen; God shall dwell (*šākantî*) with them forever. This dwelling of God is guaranteed by a new sanctuary: "And I shall consecrate (' *āqaddēšâ*) my sanctuary by my glory [the Temple], on which I let dwell my glory (9)[35] until the Day of the [new] Creation [or: "Blessing"] on which I myself (*'ānî*) shall create my sanctuary and (10) establish it for myself for all days, according to the covenant which I have made with Jacob at Bethel." This is the only passage in the Temple Scroll in which God speaks of the eschatological future.[36] This is done with terms and concepts that cannot be found in the other Qumran texts known to us. In the latter, we do not hear anything concerning a covenant made with Jacob at Bethel or concerning the consecration of a sanctuary by the glory of God and the "creating" of a new one on the "day of creation."[37] Instead, the Qumran texts normally speak of "the end of days" (*'aḥărît hayyāmîm*), which serves as a hermeneutical device to relate passages of scripture to the future. The promise of a new Temple can be found in the Apocalypse of Weeks of 1 Enoch and especially in the book of Jubilees, which emphasizes and elaborates the revelation of God to Jacob at Bethel.[38] But only in the Temple Scroll can one find that the final covenant will be the fulfillment of a covenant with Jacob at Bethel. And only there does God declare that God himself will "create" a sanctuary as one of the most important symbols for his covenant with Israel.

But we have some texts from Caves 1 and 4 in which God appears as a builder of both a holy city existing in the present (1QH 6) and a sanctuary serving his elect in the messianic age (4QFlor). The strong city established by God is the symbol for the Qumran community, which will resist the powers of hell (*Sheol*) and destruction at the end of times (1QH 6.25–29).

What will the new Temple, built by God for the messianic age on the "day of blessing (creation)," be like? Yadin thought of a real sanctuary in Jerusalem with a sacrificial cult, as commanded in the law of Moses. Accordingly, the blood of animals is expected to atone in the new age, as is integral to the cult program specified in the Temple Scroll. Yadin held that the Essenes were so faithful to the Torah that they could not envision a time when the sacrificial laws of the Torah would be invalidated, that is, when a sanctuary would be without animal sacrifices. He saw this view confirmed by the War Scroll (1QM), which prescribes the rules for the final war between the powers of light and darkness. At that time, the priests, assisted by the Levites, will serve in twenty-six classes and offer burnt offerings and sin offerings in order to make atonement for the whole community (1QM 2.2–5).[39]

Thus, the present cult of the Qumran community, characterized by a spiritual worship of prayer and obedience to the commandments of the law, must be understood as an interim cult, forced upon the sect by its criticism of the priesthood in Jerusalem and its withdrawal into the desert. If we follow Yadin, the exiles at Qumran and their adherents in the cities of Palestine must always have sustained the hope that they would be able to participate fully in a sacrificial cult in Jerusalem, where a legitimate high priest and a law-abiding priesthood would render an efficient service of atonement for Israel.

The Spiritual Worship at Qumran

I wonder, however, whether for the Qumran Essenes such a sacrificial Temple cult with streams of blood was really the ideal way of worshiping God both in the present and in the eschatological future. The Rule of the Community and the writings attached to it (1QSa, 1QSb), the Thanksgiving Hymns, and a fragmentary midrash on 2 Samuel 7 (4QFlor) all give the impression that the spiritual interpretation of the Temple and its worship at Qumran was not merely an interlude that would come to an end in the messianic age. Rather, they would prepare the way for true worship in the future, for the full realization of the fellowship of the saints in heaven and on earth in a worshiping community at the end of time. Certainly God would bring about a complete change in the future, especially with regard to the practice of piety. In the messianic age there would even be new rules, which will arise from new insights and the full revelation of righteousness and truth (1QS 9.10–11). But it was also thought that there would be some continuity. The covenant represented by the Qumran community is the eternal covenant, the "new covenant in the land of Damascus" (CD 8.21). Its basic structure, including the groups of priests and laymen, was expected to remain intact and be strengthened by the two messiahs of Aaron and Israel.

The priestly members of the Qumran community played an important role in the life of these people. But their function was spiritual: teaching, blessing, and presiding at the meals and assemblies. Even the priestly rules for the purity of service in the Temple became extended to the lay members of the Qumran community. In my view, this extension was due to the expectation of an imminent coming of God; one has to prepare for God a way in the wilderness (1QS 8.13–14; cf. Isa 40:3). The manifestation of the glory of God at his final coming would be similar to the theophany at Mount Sinai (CD 20.26). Therefore, preparation for the second advent of God must be oriented to Israel at Mount Sinai.

The "standing of Israel" in Exodus 19 served as a kind of model for the life of the Qumran community and justified their attempt to apply the rules of priestly purity to the lay members as well. Everyone had to be as holy as the priests serving before God. The organization of Israel at Mount Sinai—the division of elders (Ex 19:7; cf. 1QS 6.8), priests, and laymen (Ex 19:21–22) in groups of ten, fifty, and one hundred (Ex 18:21); living in camps (Ex 19:2); and the necessary ritual purity and abstinence from sexual intercourse (Ex 19:14–15)—was followed at Qumran and instituted as a permanent order of the life of the community in expectation of the second coming of God. Hence, the ideal of becoming a kingdom of priests and a holy people (Ex 19:6) was pursued at Qumran.

The well-known words in Exodus 19:8 should be considered the origin of the self-designation *yaḥad* ("togetherness, union"). In this passage Israel "together" (*yaḥdāw*) made the following promise: "Everything that the Lord says we will do!" Everyone who joined the Qumran *yaḥad* and entered the covenant had to confirm by an oath the obligation "to return to the law according to everything that is commanded with his whole heart and soul" (1QS 5.8–9); one had to live and to pray "together" (*yaḥad;* 1QS 6.2–3).

The emphasis on doing the whole law and the designation of the would-be members as "willing ones, volunteers" (*mitnaddĕbîm, niddābîm*) may have been suggested by Israel's willingness "to do all that the Lord says" (Ex 19:8). Significant in the Sinai pericope of Exodus 19–20, however, is that neither sacrifices nor atonement by blood is mentioned. The same holds true for the promise of the new covenant and the new Israel in Jeremiah 31:31–34 and Ezekiel 36:27ff. The cleansing of Israel with water and the spirit (Ezek 36:25ff.) is what the Qumran people expected in the future of God's activity (1QS 4.20–22). In the present the spirit was already experienced as the most effective power in making atonement for sins (1QS 3.6–9). The Qumran people offered themselves as a kind of living sacrifice to God; those who are "willing for his truth" shall bring all their knowledge, strength, and property into the *yaḥad* of God (1QS 1:11–12).

The spiritualization of the cult among the Essenes was praised by Philo. Their exemplary piety expressed itself not in sacrificing animals but in rendering their minds holy (*Every Good Man Is Free* 75). This spiritual worship served as a bridge between the present and the future. According to the blessing of the high priest (1QSb 4.20ff.) this highest representative of the community will serve God like an "Angel of the Presence" in the holy dwelling place for the glory of God and "cast his lot together with the angels." The spiritual cult as practiced in the present of the living sanctuary of Qumran could foreshadow the things to come. A worship in the fellowship of the angels cannot use animal sacrifices.

The Spiritual House of the Qumran Community

The community of holy men at Qumran, who offered their whole existence as a kind of sacrifice to God, attempted to fulfill the function of the Jerusalem Temple by making "atonement for the land" (1QS 8.6, 10). They believed that God would accept their obedience to the law and their prayers like incense and the fat of sacrifices (1QS 9.3–6). Therefore the community could understand itself as a holy house for Israel and as the foundation of a Holy of Holies for Aaron (1QS 8.5–6). This holy house and living sanctuary was eschatologically significant. It could neither be destroyed nor shaken in the coming catastrophe of judgment; its walls and foundations will not move from their place (1QS 8.7–8). And God was being praised as the builder of a city on the rock that cannot be swallowed by the gates of hell (1QH 6.24–29). Thus the famous oracle in Isaiah 28:16–17 was thought to be fulfilled in the Qumran community.

The fragmentary text of 4QFlorilegium seems to promise a spiritual sanctuary for the messianic age. There the 2 Samuel 7 oracle, announced by the prophet Nathan to King David, is quoted, combined with other biblical passages, and related to the end of days. God will establish a sanctuary (cf. Ex 15:17–18 in line 3) which no strangers, such as Moabites or Ammonites will enter (see Deut 23:3 in line 4); only holy ones are there.[40] This sanctuary will never be destroyed, unlike the first Temple, which fell because of the sins of Israel (line 5).[41] God had commanded "to build for him a sanctuary of men (*miqdaš 'ādām*) so that they will offer him words of the law as incense before him" (line 6). The designation *miqdaš 'ādām* is difficult to interpret. Does it refer to a sanctuary that God commanded to be built by human hands? Or is it a "sanctuary (consisting) of human beings (men)" that God promised to build himself? Usually the first rendering is chosen, but I think that the latter is preferable. This promise is preceded by an exegesis of 2 Samuel 7:10 ("I will appoint a place for my people Israel . . . and wicked men shall not afflict it any more") and by the quotation of Exodus 15:17–18 ("The sanctuary, O Lord, Thy hands establish"). In my view this sanctuary will be a spiritual house and living Temple in which deeds of the law will be offered as incense (lines 6–7).

The eschatological and spiritual nature of this sanctuary is further evident from the following facts: (1) In the second half of 4QFlorilegium the author quotes and explains parts of 2 Samuel 7:12-14 (lines 10-13), which he relates to the coming of the Messiah, the scion of David and savior of Israel. For this reason, we surely do not err in supposing that the earlier part of the document deals with the messianic future as well. The sanctuary promised here applies not to the present Qumran community, but to the future. (2) The priestly Messiah, that is, the companion of the Davidic Messiah—is called "the Interpreter of the Law" (dôrēš hattôrâ, line 11). His function is suited to the spiritual worship in the "sanctuary of man," where "works of the law" are offered as incense. In corollary fashion, the worship of angels occurs in prayers of praise and intercession with incense. Such interpretation of the law is less appropriate for a high priest in a real temple. (3) The enemies of Israel are also spiritualized. They are no longer identified with foreign nations such as the Philistines, the Babylonians, or the Romans. The author describes them as agents of Belial who try to seduce the true people of God and to let them stumble in order to deliver their souls to Belial (lines 7-9). In the present, Belial is ruling in the world (1QS 1.18). He has taken captive the priests of Jerusalem with three nets (CD 4.12-18); that is why the Temple service can no longer atone for the land. (4) The "holy ones of the name" (line 4) may refer to the angels or to the holy community that has fellowship with the angels. The "community of Israel at the end of days" (1QSa 1.1) will have fellowship with angels; therefore, people with physical defects cannot be in its assemblies (1QSa 2.5-9).

The evidence adduced above leads us to ask the following question: Will the new sanctuary, promised by God in 11QTemple 29.7-10, actually replace the Jerusalem Temple and set forth its sacrificial cult? This passage has no explicit reference to the cult, and the allusion to the covenant with Jacob at Bethel does not provide any clue. But the analogy to and continuity with the Temple program given in the Temple Scroll may justify such an assumption. If this suggestion should prove to be true, then two different views on Temple and sacrifice become apparent in the Qumran writings and the Pseudepigrapha: (1) A real Temple with animal sacrifices and blood atonement. This view emerges in the War Scroll, the Temple Scroll, the book of Jubilees and the Testaments of the Twelve Patriarchs. (2) A living temple with a spiritual worship, reflected in Qumran texts such as 1QS (together with 1QSa and 1QSb), 1QH, CD, and 4QFlorilegium. The long exile at Qumran and its opposition to the Jerusalem priesthood led to a spiritualization of the Temple of God and the cult. This tendency

was strengthened by efforts to link worship on earth with
which fostered a further expectation of the messianic
fellowship with the angels. If the efficiency of the Jerusalem ᴛᴇᴍᴘᴌᴇ
depended so much on the purity and integrity of the officiating priests,
then a living temple built by God had to be preferred as a better means of
atonement. Among the saints at Qumran the "standing of Israel at Mount
Sinai," not Israel's sacrificial worship in the Jerusalem Temple, became the
model for genuine eschatological existence.

Jesus and the Worship in the Temple

Jesus' view of the Temple in Jerusalem was different from that of the
Qumran community. He was not concerned with correct measurements of
the Temple courts and never complained about the ritual impurity of the
priests, because in light of the coming kingdom purity of the heart was
decisive (Mk 7:21). For this reason, atonement for the land of Israel was not
as important to him as the forgiveness of God for the people of Israel,
forgiving one's fellow human being and peace among humanity (Mt 5:9; cf.
Lk 2:14). Reconciliation among people must precede an offering that
should reconcile humanity with God (Mt 5:23). For Jesus, the Jerusalem
Temple was primarily meant to be a house of prayer (Mk 11:17). In a
parable on prayer (Lk 18:9–15) Jesus has a Pharisee and a tax collector go
up to the Temple (Lk 18:10). The tax collector "went down to his house
justified," not because he had offered a sacrifice but because of his prayer of
sincere repentance (Lk 18:13–14). This prayer is reminiscent of Psalm 51:17:
"The sacrifice acceptable to God is a broken spirit; a broken and contrite
heart, O God, Thou wilt not despise." Jesus contended that God does not
desire sacrifice, but mercy (Mt 9:13; 12:7), that is, a merciful heart of repentance: "There will be more joy in heaven over one sinner who repents than
over ninety-nine righteous ones" (Lk 15:7, 10). The Temple should not
merely gather and serve Israel, but unite all nations in prayer (Mk 11:17).
It is for this reason that Jesus cleansed the Temple by driving the merchants
and money changers out of the court of the Gentiles (Mk 11:15f.).

Jesus offered forgiveness apart from the Temple cult (Mk 2:5; Lk 7:47).
His forerunner, John the Baptist, had preached a baptism for the forgiveness of sins (Mk 1:4) which did not require sacrifices but "fruit that befits
repentance" (Mk 3:8). This fruit may be compared to the "works of the law"
offered in the Qumran sanctuary (4QFlor, lines 6–7). The forgiveness

brought by Jesus rested on the authority of the Son of Man (Mk 2:10; cf. Dan 7:14), who was sent by God and acted on his behalf (Mk 2:7-11; cf. Ps 103:3).[42] In an indirect way, Jesus also pointed to the prophecies about the new covenant, using their language of God's giving and forgiving. The forgiveness of sins (Jer 31:34) and the giving of a new heart and spirit (Ezek 36:27), not a sacrificial cult offered in a temple, will be the characteristic features of the new covenant (Mk 14:24; see also chapter 1 above).

As for the Qumran community, the "standing" of Israel at Mount Sinai was important for Jesus as a model for eschatological existence. Matthew, at least, understood Jesus in this way. The Sermon on the Mount, in which the law of the new covenant is proclaimed, is structured after Exodus 19. This dependence is quite evident in the prelude to the sermon (Mt 5:1-20), whose background must be found in Exodus 19:1-8.

Jesus and the Temple of the Messianic Age

The criticisms that Jesus raised against the Jerusalem Temple were independent of and different from those of the Qumran community. But he came quite close to the Qumran vision of a spiritual sanctuary. His promise to build a "temple not made with hands" (Mk 14:58)—that is, to build his "church" (Mt 16:18)—presupposes some of the scriptural references that were used in Qumran. The Messiah, however, will be the Lord of the Temple. This Temple saying of Jesus is very well attested (Mk 14:58 and parallels; 15:29 and parallels; cf. Jn 2:19; Acts 6:14; Mt 16:18).

In the trial of Jesus it served as a testimony for the claim of messiahship. After the witnesses had failed to report the claim correctly, the high priest directed the decisive question to Jesus: "Are you the Christ, the Son of the Blessed One?" (Mk 14:61). The oracle of Nathan stands behind this question; as in 4QFlorilegium it is related to the messianic son of David (cf. Mk 12:35-37; Rom 1:3-4). This connection explains the messianic implications of the Temple saying of Jesus. The son promised to David by Nathan will build a house for God (2Sam 7:13). This is the "temple not made with hands" as promised by Jesus. It will be a "sanctuary of man," as the Temple which the hands of God will build (4QFlor 1). Jesus could call it his "church" (Mt 16:18). That is why he could confirm the confession of Peter ("You are the Christ, the son of the living God!") by the announcement to build his church (Mt 16:17-18).

This church, the new temple not made with hands, consists of people who want to return to the Lord. This is revealed by the time span of three days, which most probably points to Hosea 6:2: the one of Israel who repents will be "raised" by God "on the third day." Matthew 16:18 is dependent on Isaiah 28:16; God will lay a sure foundation and a precious cornerstone on Mount Zion. We have noted above that this oracle was thought to have been fulfilled in the community at Qumran, which is a "strong city," built on a rock, and a holy house for Israel and Aaron (1QH 6.25–29; 1QS 8.5–8). This foundation of God and its members stand in opposition to those who made a covenant with death and who have their refuge in lies—they will be swept away (Isa 28:15–19). But the foundation of God will remain firm during the final catastrophe (1QH 6.29), untouched by the "gates of Hades" (ša'ārê māwet, 1QH 6.24; cf. 3.17–18).

In my view Jesus also had Isaiah 28:16 in mind when he announced a temple and a church on the rock, against which the gates of Hades cannot prevail (Mt 16:18; cf. Isa 28:15). But for Jesus the second part of Isaiah 28:16 was important as well: "He who believes will not be in haste" (yāḥîš=he will not yield to the assault of evil).

Faith participates in the strength and stability of the firm foundation of God to which it is directed. In a further word to Peter, Jesus alluded again to this Isaianic passage: "Simon, Simon, behold Satan demanded to have you, that he might sift you like wheat; but I have prayed for you that your faith may not fail. And when you have turned again, strengthen your brethren" (Lk 22:31–32). Here too Peter is supposed to be the rock of the living sanctuary of God (cf. Isa 28:16a). However, he must face the heavy attacks of Satan and Hades (cf. Isa 28:15). Jesus, acting as an intercessor, will lay his hands upon the rock; he will ask that Peter's "faith may not fail" (Isa 28:16b).

Later on, Isaiah 28:16 became important scriptural testimony for the fundamental role of Jesus in relation to the church. He was believed to be its foundation (1Cor 3:11; Rom 9:33; 10:11; 1Pet 2:6, 8; Mt 21:42), the precious cornerstone laid by God in Zion. As the Epistle to the Hebrews suggests, the Christian vision of the heavenly Jerusalem and city of God, being the goal of Christian pilgrimage and the final refuge and resting-place, is a development of Isaiah 28:16 (cf. Heb 11:10; 12:22; 13:14) and also the attitude of hope and faith directed toward it. I think that the famous "definition" of faith in Hebrews 11:1 has Isaiah 28:16 as its scriptural background.

The Atoning Death of Jesus

According to the Epistle to the Hebrews, Jesus was the blameless high priest at the end of times. He had no need to offer daily sacrifices for his own sins and for those of his people; "he did this once for all when he offered up himself" (7:27). The message of the author of Hebrews is reflected in the sayings of Jesus such as Mark 10:45 and 14:24; the Son of Man gives his life as "a ransom for many."[43]

For this reason the disciples were promised (Jn 1:51) that they would "see heaven opened and the angels of God ascending and descending upon the Son of man." The Son of Man, the Logos incarnate, is the true place of atonement and therefore the "Beth-El" of the messianic age and of the new covenant. He is the divine Word who dwelled among humanity; through him the glory of God became manifest (Jn 1:14; cf. 11QTemple 29.7–10). His body is the temple, destroyed by humans, but raised again within three days (Jn 2:19–21). By giving his life Jesus carried away the sins of the world (1:29) and through his death and resurrection the worship in spirit and in truth was made possible (4:23–24).[44]

Notes

1. Mk 3:6; 12:13; Mt 22:16. In Mk 8:15 the "leaven of Herod" is the reading offered by important codices such as Vaticanus and Sinaiticus. It seems to be a more difficult reading than the one in Papyrus 45 and other manuscripts. But "Herod" does not make much sense; consequently, Yadin's choice of "Herodians" is to be preferred.

2. See S. Sandmel, "Herodians," in *The Interpreters Dictionary of the Bible* (Nashville, New York, 1962) vol. 2, pp. 94–95.

3. C. Daniel, "Les Hérodiens du Nouveau Testament, sont-ils des Esséniens?" *RQ* 6 (1967) 31–53; 7 (1979) 397–402.

4. B. Pixner, *An Essene Quarter on Mount Zion?* (Jerusalem, 1976).

5. Y. Yadin, *The Temple Scroll* (English edition) (Jerusalem, 1983) vol. 1, pp. 138–39.

6. L. H. Schiffman, *The Halakhah of Qumran* (Leiden, 1975) pp. 77–133.

7. According to CD 11.16–17 it was permitted to help a man who had fallen into a place full of water or into a pit from which he could not get up by himself.

It was forbidden to speak of matters of labor and work to be done on the next day (CD 10.19). Jesus declared that it was lawful to do good on the Sabbath (Mk 3:4). According to John 5:17 he said, "My father is still working, and I am working," even on the Sabbath.

8. Cf. 11QTemple 45.13–15: "No blind man shall come into it all his life and they shall not render unclean the city where I am dwelling in her midst, for I shall dwell in the midst of the children of Israel forever" (cf. 46.11–12).

9. See m.Kelim 1:8; m.Baba Qamma 1:14; m.Nidd 7:4; Josephus, *Ant* 3.261; Yadin, *The Temple Scroll*, vol. 1, pp. 304–5.

10. They are given in the order of gravity. Burning, mentioned first, is the most painful. On the other hand, the death penalty of beheading, considered less severe, is said to be very shameful, especially with regard to the way the Romans did the execution.

11. See M. Hengel, *Crucifixion* (London, 1977) pp.74–75.

12. See Cicero in his speech against Varus (2.5.165), who calls it the *crudelissimum taeterrimumque supplicium*, "the most inhumane and disgraceful (form) of capital punishments." In the *Sententiae*, a work compiled by the Roman jurist Lucius Paulus (300 C.E.), the three *summa supplicia*, "the ultimate capital punishments" are crucifixion (*supplicium crucis*), burning (*crematio*), and decapitation (*decollatio*). See Hengel, *Crucifixion*, pp. 8, 33–34; see also chapter 10.

13. Hengel, *Crucifixion*, pp. 39–45; cf. Livy 30.43.13; Cicero, *Pro Rabirio* 9–17, esp. 16; Paulus, *Digesta* 48.19.38.1.

14. This text was first published by J. M. Allegro in *JBL* 75 (1956) 89ff. He pointed to Alexander Janneus and to Josephus, *War* 1.92–97; *Ant* 13.316–81. See chapter 10 in this volume.

15. There is, of course, the halakah of m.Sanh 6:4, which prescribes the execution of hanging a man on a tree. But we have already seen that this text offers a different interpretation of Deuteronomy 21:23, in which the hanging of a corpse is meant, not crucifixion.

16. 4QpNah, confirmed by Josephus (*War* 1.79–80; *Ant* 13:380ff.); Targum Yerushalmi on Num 25:4; Sifre Num 13 (the punishment of Jews worshiping Baal Peor).

17. See GenR 65:22 (2:741–42) on the death of the rabbi Yose ben Yoezer, who was crucified under the rule of Antiochus Epiphanes, or the parabolic story t.Sanh 19.7: the twin brother of a king was crucified, and the people passing by say, "It seems that the king is crucified." This is blasphemy, that is, "cursing God," since the king is God, and the human being, created in the image of God, looks like his twin brother. This story seems to illustrate the term *qilĕlat 'ĕlōhîm* of Deut 21:23: a crucified man, a *tālûy*, is an offense to God. A similar interpretation of *qilĕlat 'ĕlōhîm* is given in m.Sanh 6:7: seeing a crucified man, God says "Qalani (*meroši*)"="I am suffering from my head" (because of that horrible sight of a suffering "image of God").

18. m.Sanh 6:5; cf. Sif Deut 22:22; y.Hag 2.2 (77d 28f).

19. M. Hengel, *Rabbinische Legende und frühpharisäische Geschichte: Schimeon b. Schetach und die achtzig Hexen von Askalon* (Heidelberg, 1984).

20. Ibid. pp. 37–38.

21. Ibid., pp. 38ff.

22. Ibid., pp. 44–45.

23. Ibid., p. 45.

24. Ibid., pp. 22–23.

25. Ibid., pp. 41ff.

26. Ibid., p. 55.

27. See O. Betz, "Probleme des Prozesses Jesu," in *ANRW* II.25.1 (1982) 609.

28. Hengel, *Rabbinische Legende,* 43.

29. Ibid., p. 49. This may have caused the "tendentious metamorphosis" of the historical fact.

30. See my "Probleme des Prozesses Jesu," p. 641. For a different view, see, among others, M. Lietzmann, "Bemerkungen zum Prozess Jesu," *ZNW* 30 (1931) 211–15; 31 (1932) 78–84; P. Winter, *On the Trial of Jesus* (Berlin, 1961).

31. See A. N. Sherwin-White, *Roman Society and Roman Law in the New Testament* (Oxford, 1963); S. A. Fusco, *Il dramma del Golgota nei suoi aspetti processuali* (Bari, 1972), whose argument is based essentially on the Cyrenaika (7–6 B.C.E.) and on the *Consilia*, which consisted of Greek and Roman members in equal numbers (pp. 9–10).

32. The charge of blasphemy in the trial of Jesus is very strange, unless we relate the claim of messiahship to Deut 21:22–23 and to the term *qilĕlat 'ĕlōhîm*. A false Son of God has cursed God and dishonored his holy name. The high priest says to his colleagues, "You have heard the blasphemy" (Mk 14:63). For the members of the court who have to decide on blasphemy, it is very important to have heard the utterance, which suggests that they have witnessed the crime (m.Sanh 7:6). After they heard the blasphemy, they did not "need witnesses any more" (Mk 14:63). The rite of tearing the clothes when hearing a blasphemy (Mk 14:63) is prescribed in m.Sanh 7:5.

33. According to m.Sanh 6:4, too, the crime of blasphemy must be punished by hanging the blasphemer upon the tree, but only after he has been executed by stoning. The same is done in the case of idolatry; blasphemy and idolatry are understood as *qilĕlat 'ĕlōhîm*.

34. In this regard it can be compared with Jubilees, which claims to be a revelation given by the angel of God (Michael) to Moses.

35. The terminology of this promise is strongly reminiscent of John 1:14: *šākan=skēnoō* ("to dwell"), *kābôd=doxa* ("glory").

36. This is indicated by the structure of the promise, which is the same as that of the oracle in Genesis 49:10, widely used during the Second Temple period and in the New Testament. The status of the present must be maintained until the time

of the new (messianic) age, which will usher in a new order, kingship, priesthood, and so on.

37. The damaged text may be read either as *yôm habbĕrākâ* (so in Yadin's Heb. edition of the Temple Scroll) or as *yôm habbĕrî'yâ,* suggested in Yadin, *The Temple Scroll: The Hidden Law of the Dead Sea Sect* (London, 1985) p. 113. Yadin showed that the Temple of 11QTemple has some similarities with that of Ezekiel 40–48, but also striking differences. The same holds true for the description of Solomon's Temple given by Josephus (*Ant* 8.61ff.), according to which it contains three concentric square courts like the Temple of 11QTemple (ibid., pp. 167–69).

38. The sanctuary of God will be built for all eternity, since "the God of justice will be their God and dwell together with them" (Jub 25:21; cf. 27:27). This means that God himself, not merely his glory, will dwell with his people; cf. Genesis 28:16: "The Lord is in this place!" Jacob was forbidden to build a sanctuary at Bethel (Jub 32:22), obviously because the place for such a sanctuary was Jerusalem. But Jacob had established a court at Bethel, surrounded by a wall, and he had sanctified this place for him and his sons forever (Jub 32:16–17; cf. Gen 35:13). Therefore the new name "Israel" was given to him (Jub 32:16–17; cf. 25:21), which to the author of Jubilees already must have indicated the "man who sees God." For according to Jubilees 32:20, Jacob "saw," until God had ascended to heaven (cf. Philo, *On the Confusion of Tongues* 146). According to Wisdom 10:10, Wisdom had "appeared" to Jacob at Bethel, had "showed" him the kingdom of God, and had given him the knowledge of holy things (or, "the angels" = the holy ones). See S. Kim, *The Origin of Paul's Gospel* (Tübingen, 1980) p. 222. As in Genesis 31:13 (LXX: "I am the God who appeared to you." The "appearance" of God to Jacob is another explanation for his name "Israel": he was the man to whom God "appears" (*yērā'ēh*). No covenant with Jacob is mentioned in the book of Jubilees.

39. Yadin, *The Temple Scroll: The Hidden Law,* p. 235.

40. Line 4: *qĕdôšê šem* ("holy ones of [the] name"). The reading *qĕdôšay šam* ("my holy ones are there") seems to be better, but in the context God is spoken of in the third person.

41. See also TargJon to Isa 53:5; SifDeut 61 (ed. Friedmann, p. 87b to Deut 12:2).

42. See my article "Jesu Lieblingspsalm: Die Bedeutung von Psalm 103 für das Werk Jesu," in *Theologische Beiträge* 15 (1984) 253–69.

43. S. Kim, *The Son of Man as the Son of God* (Tübingen, 1983) pp. 38–66.

44. See my article "To Worship God in Spirit and in Truth," in *Standing Before God: Festschrift for John Oesterreicher* (New York, 1981) pp. 53–71.

A bibliography of books and articles written on special problems of the Temple Scroll and a fine survey on different views is given by L. H. Schiffman in *BA* 48 (1985) 122–26.

CHAPTER 3

Membership in the Covenant People at Qumran and in the Teaching of Jesus

HOWARD C. KEE

Analysis of membership in various Jewish and Christian groups around the beginning of the Common Era can benefit from the use of categories and analytical modes that derive from the social sciences. These methods help sensitize the interpreter of the evidence to recognize facets that may otherwise have been overlooked. Attention to these dimensions of the data are of value in a comparative analysis of the respective communities that are implicit in the Dead Sea Scrolls and in the earliest strata of the gospel tradition. Seven such analytical modes[1] are (1) boundaries: defining participation in the community; (2) status and role: the pattern of leadership and the ranks of membership within the community; (3) authority: the criteria by which decisions are made; (4) ritual: the formal corporate and individual acts by which participation in the community is gained or reinforced; (5) group functions: the means of maintaining the identity and integrity of the membership; (6) the symbolic universe: the stated and implicit understandings and assumptions about the world and the place of the community within it; (7) literary modes of communication: how the community conveys and interprets its corporate self-understanding to its members and others. In the analysis that follows, a comparison is offered with respect to the evidence in each of these categories.

BOUNDARIES

The Qumran community is defined by response to the revised understanding of God's covenant with his people as set forth by the so-called Teacher of Righteousness. His title would be more accurately rendered by a paraphrase: the one whose teaching is right. While there is concern in his teaching for "righteousness" in the sense of purity of life, what characterizes his message is correct against incorrect understanding and implementation of the covenantal tradition. Those who agree that he has the right perceptions of the purpose of God for his people are the ones who have joined to form this new community. What is required is not ethnic identity as part of Israel genetically or participation in the Temple cult, but, as the Rule of the Community sets forth, to pledge in the presence of the whole community total obedience to the law of Moses, as interpreted by the Teacher and the priests who now preserve the covenant traditions. Separation is to be maintained from all nonmembers. The latter cannot enter the ritual waters nor share the common meal of the community; their doctrines and their system of justice, their food and drink are to be avoided. The members are to obey "the sons of Aaron," those priests who are considered to have the true interpretation of scripture and tradition, one of whom is assigned to supervise each group of ten members. When the children of members reach "the age of enrollment,"[2] they are to take the oath of the covenant. The same public affirmation is required of adults who at any time desire to join the community.

We shall consider below the functions for maintenance of membership and the penalties for violation of the rules. But it is essential to note the categories of people that were automatically excluded from participation in the common life. In the Damascus Document (16) it is stated that "no madman, or lunatic, or simpleton, or fool, no blind man, or maimed, or lame, or deaf man, and no minor shall enter into the community, for the angels of holiness are with them." The Temple Scroll asserts that only pure Israelite males may enter the Temple courts; the blind are not to have access to the renewed Temple of the endtime, nor women, nor children under the age of twenty, nor proselytes before the fourth generation (11QTemple 38–40). Persons who fall into these categories are not to be given a share in God's covenant people. Indeed, the possibility of participation in the community is predetermined. There are only two kinds of human beings:

those ruled by the Prince of Light and those ruled by the Angel of Darkness (1QS 4). For the latter, there is no hope of redemption. The former manifest their foreordained destiny by submitting themselves to the sons of Zadok, who will guide them into true obedience to the covenant (CD 5).

As at Qumran, the crucial figure for early Christian definition of covenant community is one who reinterprets the traditions of Israel and claims to be a divinely endowed agent of renewal. A more shocking contrast with the separatist purity requirements for admission laid down by the Teacher could scarcely be imagined that Jesus' self-description in response to the questioners who come to him from John the Baptist asking if he is indeed the Coming One who will renew God's people: "A glutton and a drunkard, a friend of tax collectors and sinners" (Lk 7:34). Placed as it is in the context of fulfillment of prophetic hopes about the coming of God's agent for establishing the kingdom (Lk 7:26–27), and linked with Jesus' implicit self-identification as the Son of Man, what we see in him is a radical openness with regard to potential participation in God's people. The contrast is heightened when we recall the answer that Jesus sent back to John about his role. It calls attention to what Jesus has been doing: "the blind receive their sight, the lame walk, the lepers are cleansed, and the deaf hear, the dead are raised up, and the poor have good news preached to them" (Lk 7:22). Jesus is here seen as fulfilling the eschatological promise of renewal uttered by the prophets,[3] rather than as excluding from a share in the new age those with these physical disabilities. Similarly, Jesus is depicted in Mark as having physical contact with the dead (Mk 5:1–20, 21–43), lepers (Mk 1:40–45), Gentiles (Mk 7:24–30) and as enjoying table fellowship with such betrayers of Jewish integrity as the tax collectors—to the extent of admitting one of them to the inner circle of his followers (Mk 2:13–17). His summons to share in the life of God's people is to those in physical, moral, and social need, not to those who have gained and seek to maintain their ritual and legal purity: "I came not to call the righteous but sinners." The potential participants in these two communities—Qumran and the Jesus Movement—are very different, even though both are building on the scriptural and covenantal traditions of Israel.

AUTHORITY

The basic criterion for authority in the Dead Sea Scrolls is scripture (see chapter 1 above), although there are important supplemental factors as well that are drawn upon in setting forth the aims and structure of this community. This combination of elements is vividly and succinctly set out in 1QS 5. Anyone who enters the covenant "shall undertake by a binding oath to return with all his heart and soul to every commandment of the law of Moses in accordance with all that has been revealed of it to the sons of Zadok, the keepers of the covenant and the seekers of his will, and to the multitude of the men of their covenant who together have freely pledged themselves to his truth and to walking in the way of his delight." The same point is made earlier in that document (1QS 3), where anyone converted to the community is instructed "to walk perfectly in all the ways commanded by God concerning the times appointed for him, straying neither to right nor to left and transgressing none of his words. . . ." What is at stake is not only the law, but the understanding of it in the present time of transition, when God has disclosed his purpose to the Teacher and when that divine plan is about to be consummated.

In the detailed explanation of the responsibilities and destiny of the community, there is extensive appeal to the prophets as well, both by explicit quotation and by unmistakable allusion. The withdrawal of the community to the Wilderness of Judea is seen to be in fulfillment of Isaiah 40 (1QS 8). The defection of the mainstream of Israel from the purpose of God is seen to be in accordance with the prophets (CD 1; cf. Isa 30:10, 13). The vision of the throne of God in 4Q405 obviously builds on the model of Ezekiel's vision of the chariot throne of God in Ezekiel 1. It is significant that prominent among the Qumran documents are commentaries which show the direct relevance of these ancient texts for the circumstances and prospects of the new covenant people. They include commentaries or expansions on Genesis, Isaiah, Hosea, Micah, Habakkuk, and the Psalms.

In addition to the divinely granted insights into the meaning of scripture that the community is convinced have been given to the Teacher, there are documents in its library which closely resemble scripture in form and content but which were produced by the Teacher or his successors in the leadership of the group (see chapter 5 below). These include psalms and reports of visions, which heighten or expand on scriptural themes. Above all, there is the lengthy collection of Thanksgiving Hymns, which echo the style of the biblical Psalms but convey the hopes, fears, and prospects of the community as God brings to fulfillment his purpose through and for them. It is this combination of scriptures, interpretations of scripture, and supplemental writings providing insight into the direct meaning of scripture for this group that is the ground of decision making and the justification for the community's claims about who its members are and what God disclosed through the Teacher and is now at work accomplishing in spite of misunderstanding and hostility on the part of the official leaders of Israel.

Formally, there are many points of similarity between the authority of scripture in the Dead Sea community and in the early gospel tradition. Throughout Mark the details of what Jesus does, of who he is, and of what God is accomplishing through him are correlated with scripture, either by direct quotation or by clear allusion. This is evident from the confirmation of John the Baptist (Mk 1:2) and of Jesus (Mk 1:11) in their respective roles, through Jesus' explanation about the Son of Man rising from the dead in Mark 9:9–11, to his crying out to God on the cross (Mk 15:34) in the words of Psalm 22. There are important analogies with scriptural events, such as the Q sayings about the sign of Jonah and about the queen of the South seeking wisdom from Solomon (Lk 11:29–32) and the two stories of miraculous feeding of the throngs in Mark 6:30–44 and 8:1–10, both building on the account in Exodus 16 about the manna provided by God for the covenant people in the desert. As at Qumran, the meaning of scripture is not seen as self-evident, but requires special interpretation for the members of the group. This is the case with Mark's account of Jesus explaining the meaning of his parables to the disciples (4:10–12, 33–34) and in the Q saying that God has revealed truth to the "babes" who comprise the community but has hidden truth from those who claim to be wise and to possess understanding (Lk 10:21–22). Thus, the authority of scripture is basic, but the interpretation of it is also seen as a divine gift through Jesus to the members of the Christian community.

The authority of Jesus as agent of God and interpreter of his will is asserted in three different ways in the early gospel tradition. At baptism and on the mount of transfiguration Jesus is acclaimed by a heavenly voice as Son of God (Mk 1:9–11; 9:28). As in the Scrolls, the vision of the heavenly figures and the transformation of the appearance of Jesus build on the prophetic tradition which in Judaism became what is known as Merkabah mystical experience.[4] Then there is the testimony from the demons that Jesus—whom they address as Son of the Most High God—is their conqueror (Mk 5:7; Lk 8:28). Elsewhere in Mark it is noted that the demons recognize Jesus as the instrument of God (1:34; 3:11). The third strand of tradition concerning the source of Jesus' power reports that he made explicit claims to have been granted authority from God: to be the prophet for God (Mk 6:4), to be able to expel demons "by the finger of God" (Lk 11:20), and finally to be the Messiah, the Son of the Blessed (Mk 14:62). These claims, of course, go beyond those made by or in behalf of the Teacher, whose roles are primarily leader of the community and interpreter of the purpose of God for them. It is the more ironic that requests to Jesus to perform signs in order to demonstrate publicly his divine connections are dismissed by him (Mk 8:11–13; Lk 11:29–32). Nevertheless, Jesus is depicted as claiming that there will be confirmation of his special relationship to God on the day of consummation: "You will see the Son of Man sitting at the right hand of Power, and coming with the clouds of heaven."[5]

STATUS AND ROLE IN THE COMMUNITY

In the Dead Sea material, the authority of the Teacher is transmitted to the council, which guides the common life of the community. According to the Damascus Document (1), God raised up the Righteous Teacher 390 years after the exile in order to restore Israel from its period of disobedience. This would be achieved through a faithful remnant to whom God had revealed his purposes. The majority of Israel will continue to disobey the law, but the Teacher will—through the priests and Levites who left their roles in the Jerusalem Temple and its establishment—restore the true sons of Zadok, the elect of Israel. The Damascus Document builds on the imagery of Yahweh's instruction to Moses at Beer (Num 21:18): the well from which they are to draw is the law; the stave is the interpreter of the law, and the nobles of the people are the faithful remnant (CD 7). There is a well-defined hierarchy: the Teacher is the venerated founder and prime interpreter of the law and of God's purpose for his people. Replacing him is the Master, or Guardian, who is to be thirty to fifty years of age and whose responsibilities and powers are detailed in 1QS 9. He must see to it that the will of God is obeyed, that revealed knowledge is meted out and that all are instructed in the mysteries, that the members of the community are evaluated, and that the truth is kept from outsiders. In the assembly, the priests, who are to be thirty to sixty years of age, are first in authority, with ten members assigned to each priest. These "sons of Aaron" are in command with respect to justice and property. They set the examples for the other members. Within the Council of the Community there is to be a group comprised of twelve men and three priests; its responsibility is to be knowledgeable about the law, to preserve the faith, to atone for sin, and to walk according to the standard of truth (1QS 8).

According to the Rule of the Congregation, to gain membership in the group, one must have received instruction in the statutes of the law and the precepts of the covenant for at least ten years. At age twenty, admission was granted, although family duties and sexual relations with women were to be carried out. At age twenty-five, the novice could take his place in the lower ranks of the congregation and work for its benefit. At thirty, he could take part in the decision making of the community, finding his place in the ranks of members. All members of the community were to be ranked on admission, and each was to be obedient to his superior. Yearly there was to be a reexamination of each and a reclassification. Special provisions were made for simpletons (no responsibilities assigned) and the elderly (work commensurate with their abilities). The "sons of Levi" who preside over the community were themselves subject to the "sons of Aaron," that is, the priests. Anyone in the council who deliberately violated "one word of the law of Moses" (1QS 8) was to be permanently expelled; an inadvertent infraction led to a two-year period of penitence before restoration.

This structure and function of the community were to continue until the time of renewal (1QS 4), when the eschatological prophet would come, together with the messiahs of Aaron and Israel, who are the priestly and royal rulers, respectively. The chiefs of Israel will be assembled before him, and the heads of all the families of the congregation according to rank. The climax of this consummation (which was probably performed as an anticipatory ritual) will be the table where bread and wine will be set out. The priest (Messiah of Aaron) will bless the wine first; then the Messiah of Israel, to which the congregation responds by uttering a blessing.

The transmission of authority is significantly different in the older gospel tradition. There Jesus calls his followers without any apparent advance notice or prior association.[6] They are called directly from secular occupations—fishing and tax collecting, for example (Mk 1:16–20; 2:13–17)—to associate with him in his itinerant ministry. Initially they merely accompany him (Mk 1:39), but then he appoints the twelve "whom he desired" to be with him and sends them out to preach and to have authority over demons (3:13–14). Later in the Marcan account (6:6–13) he sends them out in pairs, with authority over the unclean spirits. They are to take no provisions for daily needs but are to rely on the generosity and hospitality of those whom they meet on the road. Their work is said to have consisted in preaching repentance, expelling demons, and healing the sick.

Jesus' own authority is reported in a number of different modes. He pronounces the forgiveness of sins (2:1–12) and then defends what he has been challenged for doing on the ground that as Son of Man he has authority on earth to forgive sins. In what we would call the realm of nature he has authority as well, according to Mark 4:35–41. At his commanding word the storm at sea is stilled, and in Mark 6:45–52 he walks across the Sea of Galilee. The disciples are portrayed as astounded by this power and puzzled about who he is that can perform these acts. The populace is likewise amazed at his powers of healing and exorcism and try to touch him that they might benefit from his extraordinary capabilities (Mk 6:53–56).

The call to discipleship is not an offer of privilege but a commitment to what would be generally regarded as deprivation. These demanding accompaniments of discipleship include a break with one's family (Mk 3:32–35) and the possibility of loss of one's life (Mk 8:34–37). It requires the abandonment of personal ambition and of striving for positions of power (Mk 9:33–37; 10:35–45). The seriousness of the threat to stability and tranquillity that discipleship constitutes is apparent in the hostile reaction to Jesus on the part of the religious and political authorities, including groups as diverse as the separatist Pharisees and the Herodian collaborators with the Roman overlords (Mk 3:6), as well as the scribes who accuse him of being in league with the prince of demons (3:22). The thrice-repeated prediction of his death expects a coalition of these hostile authorities: the elders, the chief priests and the scribes (Mk 8:31; 9:31; 10:33), together with Gentile powers. Yet Jesus is quoted as affirming that God will in the future confirm his authority. This is implicit in his declaration about the Messiah, the Son of David (Mk 12:35–37), as well as in his prediction that, beyond the cosmic disturbances that are to mark the end of the present age, the Son of Man will come "with great power and glory" and "send out the angels to gather his elect from the ends of earth to the ends of heaven" (Mk 13:26–27). Thus the Jesus community is perceived as being constituted of members whose origins are worldwide. Yet those who have failed to fulfill their obligations toward the Son of Man will be put to shame on the last day (Mk 8:38). All who follow him are required to be willing to take up the cross in their allegiance to him (8:34).

RITUAL AND SABBATH REQUIREMENTS

A major factor in the Dead Sea community's break with the Jewish religious establishment is what is seen as the latter's failure to fulfill the divinely intended provision for gaining and maintaining purity. As is evident from both the Rule of the Community and the Damascus Document, total obedience to the law of Moses—"walking perfectly in all his ways" (1QS 2)—includes conformity to the cultic as well as the ethical obligations. The cleansing by the Spirit of Holiness that members experience and exemplify begins with purification by immersion in the purification water, but it includes observing the divinely determined times (1QS 3), avoiding the sharing of food and drink with nonmembers (1QS 5), and eating meals only within the community (1QS 6).

Chief among the appointed times is the Sabbath (CD 10–11). The prohibited activities on the Sabbath include conversations on anything more than essential matters, any form of financial transactions, and extensive "walking." Nothing found lying in the fields is to be eaten, and food is to have been prepared prior to the Sabbath. Water may be drunk from streams but not drawn from wells. Even taking beasts out to pasture is strictly limited, and no help is to be offered to a female animal who is giving birth or to any beast in a ditch. Servants are not to be chided. Nothing is to be brought into a house, and sealed vessels are not to be opened. The day is to be spent well out of contact with Gentiles. A notable exception to rules against physical activity on the Sabbath is the permission to help someone whose life is at risk in fire or water.

Strict ritual cleanliness must be observed in sending gifts to the altar and in entering the house of worship. Avoidance of Gentile associations includes the prohibition against selling animals, grain, wine, or servants to them, or even stealing from them! The purity rules extend to the eating of fish and locusts, and the possible defilement from wood stoves, dust, or the pegs and nails in the house of a dead man. Clearly the aim of these expansions and specifications of the Sabbath laws against work and of ritual cleanliness is the establishment and maintenance of the distinctive purity of God's people.

Jesus, by contrast, is reported in the gospel tradition as often under attack for violation of both purity and Sabbath laws. He defends his followers by appeal to scriptural precedent when they pluck grain and eat it as they pass through a field (Mk 2:23), on the principle that human hunger has priority over religious rules.[7] Similarly, Jesus' Sabbath-day healing of the man with the withered hand (Mk 3:2) puts human need above even such a basic law as Sabbath observance.

On purity issues the perspective in the gospel tradition is similar. The concern that physical contact with the ill would result in defilement and therefore with disqualification for participation in the covenant people is simply brushed aside by Jesus in face of the need for human health and wholeness. According to Mark's narrative, Jesus touches Peter's ailing mother-in-law (1:31), the leper (1:41), the dead girl (5:41), the deaf man (7:33), and the epileptic boy (9:27). He allows the menstruating woman to touch him (5:21), and he heals the multitude of sick and possessed who come to him from Gentile territories (3:7–10). When the issue of ritual purity is raised by the Pharisees and scribes (Mk 7:1–25), it is fully acknowledged that neither he nor his disciples follow these traditions. Jesus is reported to have made a public utterance denying that defilement comes from what human beings touch, insisting rather that the source of corruption is the human heart, from which all sorts of personal and social wickedness originate. Mark has inserted a parenthetic phrase: "Thus he declared all foods clean" (7:19). This statement is obviously from the evangelist or his community, but it is not incompatible with the tradition itself.

The Q tradition makes the same point in different words (Lk 11:37–40), stressing the incongruity with concern for the exterior of dishes and cups while neglecting the unclear interior of the pious individual preoccupied with ritual matters. Indeed, these self-styled interpreters of the law lay burdens on others that they do not assume for themselves and stand in the tradition of those who in the past have put to death the prophetic critics of the religious leaders (Lk 11:46–48). In sharp contrast to these regulation formulators who see themselves as the guardians of covenantal purity, Jesus describes God in parables as the one who seeks out the lost (Lk 15:4–7) and as the one who sends messengers to urge the outsiders and the rejected to share in the common life of God's people (Lk 14:15–24).

The most striking contrast between Jesus and Qumran with regard to ritual is in the respective attitudes toward the future of the Temple. The Temple Scroll (11QTemple) is devoted to a description in great detail of the reconstructed Temple in Jerusalem in the new age, when all the qualified priestly leaders will be in charge and when the divinely intended requirements for the function of the Temple and the behavior of the inhabitants of the Holy City will be in force. The Temple, its priesthood, and the bread of the covenant will be established forever (11QTemple 8; 21; 29). The qualifications for entering the Temple are explicit: only Israelite males (39); no blind men (45), none who come into contact with lepers or graves (45; 50). If God is to show mercy to Israel, all the commandments must be kept, and those who violate his statutes are to be stoned (55). God will establish a king over Israel, but priests and Levites are to write the laws for him (56) and to sit with him in judgment (57). They must share in the decision about going to war (58). King and people will be preserved if they obey the law (59). Every non-Israelite in the cities that God has given to his people is to be destroyed (62). Anyone who threatens the political or ritual integrity of Israel "you shall hang on a tree." If he has defected to the nations or has cursed his people, "you shall hang him on a tree, and he shall die. And the body shall not remain upon the tree all night, but you shall bury him the same day," lest the exposed body defile the land (64). A false prophet whose guilt is established by two or three witnesses who testify that his predictions have not come true is to be shown no mercy: "a life for a life, an eye for an eye, a tooth for a tooth, a hand for a hand, a foot for a foot" (61; cf. Deut 19:21).[8] Nothing must defile the Temple or the city where God dwells among his people (45).

In the older gospel tradition Jesus simply announces that the Temple is to be destroyed totally: "not one stone on another" (Mk 13:2). Earlier he is said to have cleansed the Temple, denouncing it as an institution of commerce, which stands in the way of one of its divinely intended functions— to provide access for Gentiles through it to the God who is said to dwell there (Mk 11:15–17). In the apocalyptic discourse that follows in Mark (13:5–37) there is an unmistakable reference to the desolating sacrilege in the Maccabean period as reported by Daniel (9:27; 12:11). This violation of the Temple took place when the image of Zeus was ordered to be erected ir the Temple precincts by Antiochus Epiphanes in 168 B.C.E. The issue arose again when Gaius Caligula in 40 C.E. issued a similar decree. Although it is difficult to determine the extent to which an original core of predictions by Jesus about the destruction of the Temple may have been expanded in light of the Roman invasion of Judea in 67–70 C.E., there seems for certain to be a basic prophetic oracle by him that the Temple would be destroyed. It is noteworthy that there is no correlative prophecy of its reconstruction, just as there is only the proclamation of a curse on the fig tree (apparently an image of Israel as God's potentially fruitful people) and no hint of its renewal (Mk 11:12–14). Thus there is in this tradition no prediction of the restoration of the cultic system or of the supposed dwelling place of God in the Temple.

GROUP FUNCTIONS

The main activity which constitutes the covenant people according to the Dead Sea Scrolls and which justifies the existence of this new community is that they do what is commanded by the law and the prophets (1QS 1). They are to love all whom God has chosen and hate all he has rejected; to love the "sons of light" and hate the "sons of darkness." This includes the observing of the appointed times and the pooling of their material resources (1QS 6). Those who walk in the stubbornness of their hearts are to be excluded. There are two kinds of human beings: the "sons of light," who are guided by the angel of truth, and the "sons of darkness," who are led by the angel of darkness. God loves the former and loathes the latter (1QS 3). The qualities that are to characterize God's sons are humility, patience, love, goodness, understanding, intelligence, discernment, zeal for the laws, a holy intent, and the spirit of wisdom. Conversely, the "sons of darkness" are dominated by a spirit of falsehood, greed, lethargy, wickedness, haughtiness, cruelty, brazen insolence, abominable deeds, lewdness, and blasphemy. They are blind of eye and dull of ear, stiff-necked and in the dark (1QS 4). The enlightened will be instructed in divine knowledge and have been chosen for an everlasting covenant through which they will attain to the glorious image that God first granted to Adam. One of their major responsibilities is to establish and maintain separation from all nonmembers, avoiding social or physical contact with them and eschewing their doctrines and their concepts of justice (1QS 5). The sons of Aaron will be their guides to understand and live by the law of God.

The erring are to be rebuked in charity, initially before eyewitnesses and then before the congregation.[9] Specific penalties are laid down for various violations of the community and its understanding of the law of God. One who lies is excluded from the common meal for one year, as is one who displays obstinacy or impatience or utters a word against the priest. Lesser faults with milder sentences of exclusion from the common life include interrupting a companion who is speaking (ten days), sleeping through an assembly (thirty days), leaving the assembly three times (ten days), being poorly dressed or guffawing (thirty days), slandering a fellow member (expulsion). Anyone who betrays the truth of the congregation will be put on probation for two years and reexamined and reclassified before readmission. Anyone who shares food or property with a member on probation will be expelled. Vowing the destruction of another member by appeal to the laws of the Gentiles is to be punished by death, as is the recanting of an oath (CD 9; 16).

The community perceived itself as the "house of holiness" (1QS 8), a precious cornerstone (Isa 26:16), a perfect dwelling place for Aaron, as the embodiment of the everlasting knowledge of the covenant of rightness, as the house of perfection and truth in Israel. The community believed that it was atoning for the land even as it was identifying and judging wickedness. In the last days, the community is to assemble—including women and children—to hear the covenant and its exposition, which are binding on everyone born in Israel (1QSa 1).

In preparation for the new age, the community is instructed in detail about the war that will take place between the force of evil and the people of God (1QM). Angels will battle the heavenly hosts of evil, as the priests and the community's soldiers fight the earthly foes. Indeed, the war of the faithful remnant of Israel is to be fought against all nations: "There shall be eternal deliverance for the company of God, but destruction for all the nations of wickedness" (1QM 15). The priests, and especially the high priest, will strengthen the troops for the final battle against the nations of the world. Rome—referred to regularly as "the Kittim"—will fall, while the chief priest, the priests, and the Levites will sound the trumpets to aid the troops. In preparation for this final war details are given even to the sizes of the standards, shields, spears, and swords of the army. These divinely endowed forces are identified as "the divisions of God for the vengeance of his wrath on the sons of darkness."

Here too a sharp contrast is seen with the gospel tradition. In addition to encouraging his followers to pay their taxes to Caesar (Mk 12:13–17), the Q tradition reports Jesus as calling his hearers to love their enemies and to pray for those who persecute them. In so doing they manifest the qualities of God, their Father, who showers benefits on the just and the unjust. This love is to expect nothing in return from the objects of that love, but the promise is that God will reward his people for manifesting this quality, which is essential to his very nature (Lk 6:27–36; Mt 5:43–48). This attitude of love that Jesus enjoins toward one's neighbor contrasts with the sharp ritual differentiation enjoined at Qumran (Mk 12:31).[10] That this love is not to be limited to Jewish neighbors is evident from the gospel image of Jesus as one who takes initiative in reaching out to Gentiles and to marginal people within the dominant Jewish society. These attitudes and modes of relationship are offered by Jesus not merely as noble concepts but as akin to the love of God and as manifestations of the fulfillment of the prophetic promises (as we noted in our consideration of Jesus' response to the questioners from John the Baptist about his role in the redemptive purpose of God). This matches precisely with the injunction noted above that one is to love one's enemies, thereby reflecting the gracious action of God toward all humanity.

Not only on this specific issue of attitude toward one's enemies but also with regard to the structure, functions, and ethos of the community as reflected in the early gospel tradition, the contrast with Qumran is very great. The fact that Jesus chose twelve men to form the basic leadership for the movement he launched recalls, of course, the tribes of Israel, but the only explicit link between these two groups appears in the Q tradition, where the disciples are promised that on the day of the Son of Man (or the kingdom of God) they will "sit on twelve thrones judging the twelve tribes of Israel" (Mt 19:28; Lk 22:28–30). Their role is thus linked with the destiny of the covenant people as Jesus defines and constitutes it.

In the older layers of the gospel material, however, there is no hint of authoritarian or even distinctive leadership roles for the twelve. Rather, they are to extend the ministry of Jesus in preaching the good news of the kingdom, in calling for repentance in view of the coming new age, and in healing and exorcisms through which the powers of evil are overcome and the wholeness of human existence is experienced. The summoning of people to participate in the new community who are ethnically, socially, ritually, occupationally, and even morally marginal by the standards of the Pharisees or the Dead Sea sect heightens the differences between Jesus and his Jewish contemporaries. Although the symbolic act by which the unity of the covenant people is celebrated in the Dead Sea community and in the Jesus tradition are virtually identical—a meal of shared bread and wine in expectation of the coming of the Messiah—the ground of participation is fundamentally different. For the Dead Sea group, partaking in this meal was a sign of their having found acceptance through conformity to the purity requirements. For the Christians, it was an expression of their reliance on the sacrifice of Jesus which ratified the new covenant.

THE SYMBOLIC UNIVERSE

The Dead Sea Scrolls display a clearly defined view of the world. Although God is the ultimate power in the world, there are operative in the universe the *two spirits:* one of light, the other of darkness. God has been at work in human history, disclosing his purpose for humanity to such chosen instruments as Abraham, Moses, and David, as well as to the prophets. The people of Israel have almost wholly strayed from the divine plan, led by evil and perverse leaders, especially the official priests. This disobedience culminated in the exile of Israel, from which the people returned but were leaderless for nearly four centuries (CD 1). Now, through the Righteous Teacher whom God raised up, the proper understanding of God's purpose and the appropriate response of his people to that plan have been revealed.

The divinely intended structure for community leadership has been provided through the faithful priests and Levites. If the people will conform to the law as interpreted by the Teacher and the leaders who have succeeded him, they will share in the blessings of the new age which God is about to establish. The initiation into the community through baptism is to be followed by instruction and guidance by the sons of Aaron and the Levites and confirmed through the obedience of initiates to these regulations as well as the symbolic participation through the pooling of possessions and sharing in the repeated meals of bread and wine. By maintaining obedience to the ritual requirements and a proper distance from non-members—Jewish or Gentile—members can be assured of a part in the age to come as the true Israel of God. In a final cosmic conflagration, the human and angelic (or demonic) enemies of the community will be destroyed, and God's will shall triumph over his faithful people and the whole of the creation. The fidelity of the community will be rewarded when the promised prophet comes, together with the messiahs of Aaron and Israel, who will lead the faithful in the fulfillment of this symbolic meal of covenantal identity.

Formally, important features of this symbolic picture have counterparts in the gospel tradition's depiction of the role of Jesus, the summoning of a new people of God, the conflicts with the evil powers, and the consummation of the divine purpose. As in other Jewish groups in the first century C.E., there was a common aim to redefine the covenant people—although from group to group there were important differences in specifics. Later in the first century, the Zealots focused on political autonomy achieved by military effort as the means of accomplishing Israel's promised destiny. For the Sadducees, the aim was to maintain the vitality of the cultic system centered in the Temple, in the assurance that here God was in their midst and that by the sacrificial system the right relationship of God with Israel could be carried forward. For the Pharisees, the public cultus needed a supplement which embodied personal commitment on the part of participants, through informal gatherings for study and appropriation of the scriptural tradition and through maintenance of a separate identity in a culture increasingly dominated by Greco-Roman values and mores. The unity of the Pharisaic groups was celebrated through table fellowship. The Qumran covenanters, as sketched above, offered yet another alternative mode of appropriating the covenantal identity.

Over against these, the Jesus Movement as we see it in Mark and Q shared with the Pharisees the belief that the people of God should not actively oppose the political power (Rome), nor should they passively adopt its cultural and social standards and values. An attempt is made to preserve a balance between acquiescence in certain demands of the pagan rule and the conviction that the God of Israel is the supreme power who will ultimately establish his rule on earth. This nonaggressive attitude on the part of the Pharisees doubtless accounts for what seems to have been Roman encouragement of the rabbinic movement in the time after the fall of the Temple. In the gospel tradition, Jesus is the one through whom the coming of God's kingdom will be achieved. His followers meanwhile have the task of preparing for that event through their ministry of preaching and healing. Because the time is so short, what is required of them is effectiveness and seizing opportunities for witness, rather than erecting barriers at Qumran by laying down rules for admission and maintaining status within the community.

LITERARY MODES OF COMMUNICATION

The literary genres employed by religious groups to convey their convictions to members and other inquirers reveal important features of their aims and rationale. The Qumran group had in its two basic documents—the Rule of the Community and the Damascus Document—some elements of the historical origins of their movement, but the preponderance of the material in both writings concerns the requirements for admission, the structures of authority and decision making, the basic pattern of proper performance by the adherents, the criticisms of what we may in retrospect regard as the mainstream Judaism of the period, and indications of the hopes that the group held concerning its future in the purpose of God. These two writings serve as examples of what anthropologists have called "foundation documents," in that they trace the origins of the group, the guidelines for the ongoing life of its members, and the shared expectations for the fulfillment of what they see as their divinely given destiny. The commentaries on the biblical prophets that have been found at Qumran provide the clues to how scripture is to be interpreted within the community and to what the group's norms and values are in its claim to be the true heir of the biblical tradition. There are also supplements to what Judaism and Christianity came to regard as scripture, ranging from additional psalms to prophetic utterances and accounts of visions. These extra-biblical writings likewise serve to articulate the specific norms and perspectives in terms of which the group lays hold of, and exploits for its purposes, the older traditions of Israel.

By the time the Gospel of Mark was written and the Q tradition had taken the shape it had when it served as a source for Matthew and Luke, the letters of Paul had been written but not brought together as was later to occur. There are no existing Christian scriptures on which the gospel tradition can draw or comment. Instead, Mark and Q serve many of the same ends for the early Christians as did the basic Qumran documents. They indicate links between Jesus and his followers on the one hand and the earlier history of God's people on the other. These sources then move to provide detail as to how the movement began and how it was carried forward by those who chose to work with the founder. The gospel differs basically from the Qumran convenanters' foundation documents in that Mark is far more explicitly biographical. Later gospels were to expand precisely those dimensions, including accounts of the parentage, birth, childhood, and postresurrection appearances of Jesus, as is evident in Matthew and Luke.

As for other possible analogies with the Dead Sea Scrolls, there are in the first century c.e. no Christian commentaries on the Jewish scriptures. Mark and Q have many quotations from them, however, and even more allusions, in some cases by reference to biblical figures or imagery or events that are seen as precedents of what God is doing or about to do through Jesus.

There are traces of poetic or hymnic style in some of the gospel material, which probably reflects the corporate religious gatherings of the community. Again, these features are greatly expanded in the Gospels of Matthew and Luke. Central to the gospel tradition is the factor of divinely granted vision, through which the future purpose of God is disclosed to Jesus and his followers, both as a guide to their behavior and as a clue to their appropriate activity in the interim before the new age arrives. It is consonant with this view that the two most extended units of proclamation in Mark are the parables (Mk 4) and the apocalyptic discourse (Mk 13). Both require private explanation to members of the community. The apocalyptic pronouncements foretell the end of the then-operative religious system—the Temple and the priestly establishment—and its replacement by the new covenant community.

One should not be misled by the formal similarities between the literary modes at Qumran and in the early gospel tradition, however. To assume simple identity of these features would be to miss the basic differences in community concept between these two bodies of literature, in each of which the apocalyptic tradition has been adapted and transformed to serve the peculiar interests of the respective communities. Through the use of these questions, which arise from social methods in exploring these two sets of texts, the historian is able to see specifically the distinctive structures, norms, aspirations, goals, and leadership patterns that characterize each of these communities. In this way one can discern how each of them— the Qumran community and the Jesus Movement—saw and articulated its claim to be the true heir of "the new covenant."[11]

Notes

1.   These categories were developed at a seminar that I led at Boston University in 1986, which was sponsored by the National Endowment for the Humanities. They are set out in fuller form in my book *Knowing the Truth: A Sociological Approach to New Testament Interpretation* (Minneapolis, 1989) pp. 65–69.

2.   CD 15. The Rule of the Congregation (1QSa) indicates that the age of enrollment was twenty years.

3.   The saying of Jesus is a composite of elements from Isaiah 29:18–19; 35:5–6; and 61:1.

4. Discussed in my essay "The Transfiguration in Mark: Epiphany or Apocalyptic Vision?" in *Understanding the Sacred Text* (Valley Forge, Penn., 1972) pp. 135–52.

5. The attempt of R. Bultmann to classify these future Son-of-Man sayings as references by Jesus to some future figure other than himself is more ingenious than persuasive. Whatever the origin of these sayings, the old gospel tradition attributed to Jesus the expectation of divine confirmation.

6. Scholars have sometimes suggested that Jesus was earlier associated with at least the core of his disciples at the time when they were all part of the movement led by John the Baptist. There is no direct evidence for this theory, however, though it might be inferred from the Gospel of John, in which Jesus and the disciples were carrying on baptismal activity prior to the launching of his public ministry (3:22–23; 4:1).

7. In 1Sam 21:1–7, David and his companions violate the law regarding sacred bread, but the Marcan tradition sees the principle of the priority of human need as identical.

8. The theme of nonretaliation in the Q tradition (Lk 6:29–30) is expanded in Matthew 5:38 to explicit rejection of this principle of "an eye for an eye and a tooth for a tooth."

9. A similar arrangement for calling to account a member of the community— first on a one-to-one basis, then before witnesses, and finally before the congregation—appears in a unique gospel pericope: Matthew 18:15–20. There is nothing comparable in Mark or Q.

10. See the similar discussion on this point in chapter 1 above.

11. See the discussion of "the new covenant" in chapter 1 above.

CHAPTER 4

Recovering Jesus' Formative Background

PAOLO SACCHI

Today it is widely acknowledged, and certainly not for the first time, that Jesus was a first-century Palestinian Jew.[1] This fact means that his work and his teaching must be studied and interpreted within the context of the history of that first-century society of the Near East. As a result, our questions concerning Jesus and his teachings must be framed in terms of his own time. This approach inevitably minimizes Jesus' uniqueness, though it would be a mistake to think that Jesus' character and significance are thereby simply identified with his context and, hence, generalized. Indeed, human beings, no matter how tied to a particular historical context, cannot be grasped by mere abstraction or reduction to a product of their ideological background. In Jewish society, there exists an overarching level of ideas that distinguishes Jews from all others. These are self-defining ideas, which include notions of faith in a God who is revealed in history, God's ultimate judgment of the world, the importance of law, the threat of impurity, a deep sense of sin, the problematic nature of evil, and a messianic expectation. A further level has to do with ideas that distinguish different groups within Judaism itself. Finally, we may speak of even smaller subgroupings all the way down to individuals, with their distinctive beliefs and ideas.

Christianity, through the medium of the Palestinian Jesus Movement, received formative teachings from Jesus. Jesus' ideas were original enough to give rise, even through the reappropriation and interpretation of his followers, to a distinct movement that may be identified as "Christian."

The perennial problem of Jesus' uniqueness has certainly not disappeared, despite the reaffirmation of his first-century Jewishness. Reimarus,[2] who lived in the eighteenth century, was the first to approach the problem from a historical-critical perspective. He argued that the rise of "Christianity" and its break with Judaism had its origin in the discontinuity between Jesus and his disciples. Today, however, the problem can be addressed in a better way; we have at our disposal many more documents from Jesus' time than were in the hands of scholars two centuries ago.

In this essay, my goal is not to deal with problems presented by such an alleged discontinuity.[3] Rather, I would like to discuss the place of Jesus within the ideological movements of his time. This might be a first step in overcoming the rigidity with which Jesus' uniqueness has been assessed.

We have several sources at our disposal that shed light on this problem. Although it is difficult to distinguish between Jesus' authentic teaching and the theology of the early Christian community, the New Testament documents remain the most important sources for Christian origins. When used with caution, they provide some information on the Pharisaic movement as well. The New Testament, however, may be considered a reliable source on the Pharisees only when it comes to certain distinctive points of their doctrine. This evidence must, of course, be treated critically and be carefully compared with other evidence, especially that of the Mishna.

The Mishna provides us with perhaps the best literary witness to Pharisaic thought contemporary to Jesus. The central problem in using this material is how to date the passages in which the evidence appears. Research on the stratification of material in the Mishna is just beginning and is fraught with many difficulties.

In the case of Jewish pseudepigraphical writings, I do not think that the problem of Christian interpolations is as serious as some scholars believe. Such interpolations are often easy to detect. Applying an attitude of "systematic doubt" as a starting point in determining the "authentic" or "non-Christian" materials in this body of literature may not be the most appropriate approach. While such a critical method may be essential in an initial philosophical investigation, it should be employed with caution in historical and philological studies.

Finally, we have in our possession the Qumran literature as well as the body of historiography, philosophy, and other works by Jewish authors such as Josephus and Philo, which were written in Greek. However, this considerable body of literature, which consists of both well-known texts and recently discovered or little-studied materials, awaits thorough scholarly assessment of its value for reconstructing Jesus' context. From the still frequently cited Strack-Billerbeck parallels,[4] one might easily gain an impression that the Gospels contain nothing that does not appear in rabbinic literature. Narrative descriptions as well as individual sayings of Jesus can be found in similar or sometimes identical forms in both *corpora*. But, as observed by S. Ben-Chorin, it is the "concentration" of a certain type of saying or thought in the New Testament that distinguishes its meaning or use within this context as opposed to that of rabbinic tradition.[5]

As is well known, Jewish literature employs a wide repertoire of common literary *topoi*, many of which survive into the relatively late, talmudic material (Gemara). Within an immense and diverse number of Jewish literary works and traditions, the same saying could be used to express a wide range of ideas.[6] Consequently, comparisons should extend beyond individual *topoi* that appear in various works or traditions; they should also involve the different contexts within which the given *topoi* are found. In this way, one exposes the sometimes disparate ideas underlying the use of similar *topoi*. An analysis based on verbal, linguistic, or phraseological similarities all too often fails to stress or even make as its goal a determination of the nature and identity of ideas expressed within traditions of Jewish thought taken as a "whole."

The analysis I propose would focus, by contrast, on how similar or even identical *topoi* were used and interpreted by various groups within Judaism. Thus the remainder of this article will be addressed to a few elements or *topoi* that enable us to identify clearly different groups or currents of thought within Judaism. In fact, these often-identical *topoi* can be said to constitute boundaries between the communities that appropriated them. The delineation of separate groups can be determined by the way the *topoi* function within different contexts and their significance for both religious life and secular behavior.

Jewish thought contemporary to Jesus' teaching was confronted by many difficult issues. Yet it dealt with them under the aegis of a limited number of themes including those mentioned above. Not all of these themes are reflected in Jesus' teaching in a direct manner. Consequently, we will limit our discussion to a few cases in which Jesus' thought, in light of these themes, may be grasped in a clear way.

In order to simplify our discussion further, we will focus on the Gospel of Mark. While the four New Testament Gospels all contain a considerable amount of material based on authentic Jesus tradition—each does so within a very different theological framework—the Gospel of Mark, widely considered to be the oldest of the Gospels,[7] seems to provide a suitable *initial* approach to our study.

It is not easy to make distinctions between authentic Jesus tradition and that which properly belongs to the early community. The problem probably does not have a definitive solution, at least with respect to recovering the *ipsissima verba* of Jesus. But this is not as serious a problem as it may at first seem. The antiquity of the Gospels and the osmosis between master and disciples are sufficient to ensure a fairly close representation of the teaching of Jesus. Since Jesus lived together with his disciples and hence created a type of community even before his death, there existed an adequate medium for the transmission of his teachings.[8]

MARK 2:1–12:
THE HEALING OF THE PARALYTIC

In this passage Jesus identifies himself with the "Son of Man": "But so that you may know that the Son of Man has authority on earth to forgive sins"—he said to the paralytic—"I say to you, stand up, take your mat and go to your home" (2:10–11; NRSV; cf. vv. 5, 7). Jesus ascribes to himself functions that in contemporary Jewish literature are attributed to the "Son of Man." This figure is known to us from the Similitudes of Enoch (chs. 37–71), in which he acts as the universal judge at the end of time.[9] The Son of Man knows all the secrets of justice, for he was created for all time. We are not in a position to know whether acquaintance with the details of the theology of the Similitudes was widespread, but it seems certain that, at the very least, many Palestinian Jews thought the "Son of Man" would function as supreme judge; otherwise, there is no basis for the interchange between Jesus and his audience in Mark.

In this case the connection between the Similitudes and Jesus is clear; however, this should not be construed as a literary relationship. We cannot infer from this text that Jesus knew the Similitudes; we can only assume that, at least in Galilee, the notion of a superhuman figure called the "Son of Man" who functioned as supreme judge of all humanity circulated widely.

This point is where the problem arises. Modern scholars have maintained that the Similitudes constitute an "apocalyptic" book; at the same time, this category of thought is quite anachronistic. It is both an appropriate and useful category through which to approach the interpretation of ancient literature in terms of modern categories of thought. Yet we must not confuse our own terminology, which is a modern creation, with ancient habits of thought and categorization. Otherwise it becomes impossible to make proper use of ancient sources. Our interpretative language is not the same as that of the ancients. Consequently, we might be tempted to think that the ancients did not know certain works we call "apocalyptic." However, apocalyptic thought represented too important a phenomenon to have been ignored by the majority of those living in the contemporary Jewish environment. We shall see the significance of this fact at a later point in our discussion.

A further question arises from the text in Mark. In v. 1 Jesus says that he is able to forgive sins; he freely and graciously "justifies" sinners in his life. The problem of liberation from evil, especially from sin, was strongly felt by Jesus' contemporaries. Indeed, this issue already had a long history before the time of Jesus. Sin was perceived as the only real obstacle to salvation. One thinks of the emphasis placed on Yom Kippur and the central role this festival is given in Jubilees 5:17–18.

A notion of free or gracious justification existed among the Essenes. All those who became members of the Qumran group and who had faith ('*ĕmûnâ*) in the Righteous Teacher obtained justification (1QpHab 8.2–3). Similarly, we read in the Rule of the Community (1QS 3.6): "For the spirit of the *true* counsel concerning the ways of man, all his sins are cleansed." We find similar notions elsewhere in the Rule of the Community:

> Through his righteousness he wipes out my sins, for from the source of his knowledge he let spring my light . . . and from the source of his righteousness is my justification. . . . As for me, if I stumble, *the mercy of God* always saves me. If I stagger because of the evil of the flesh, my justification is the righteousness of God, which always endures. . . . Through the greatness of his goodness he always cleanses all my sins. Through his righteousness he cleanses me of the uncleanliness of man and of the sins of the children of men. (1QS 11.3, 5, 12, 14–15)

Finally, in the Thanksgiving Hymns we read: "You *purify* the iniquity and *clean[se]* the children of me[n] of sin through your righteousness . . . for you have created the just and the wicked" (1QH 4.37–38).

The translation of these passages is not always certain, especially in the instances indicated by italics, but the general sense is quite clear. The story, as recounted in Mark, portrays Jesus as one who, at the very beginning of his teaching and preaching activity, holds the position that a free and gracious justification from sin is the only way to salvation from evil. In the case of the Righteous Teacher, the concept of justification is related to his notion of predestination and to his own understanding of knowledge as enlightenment. These elements cannot be found in Jesus' thought. Yet Jesus, as well as the Teacher, maintained that the way to salvation consists in obtaining free and gracious forgiveness from God. It may well be that at the beginning of Jesus' preaching ministry, the way to such salvation was not clear. Nevertheless, the centrality of a salvation through forgiveness is already established at the very beginning of his teaching activity. The presence of this theme of justification locates Jesus as closer to Essenism than to apocalypticism[10] or Pharisaism.

The Calendar

According to the Synoptic tradition, Jesus celebrated the Passover on the eve of his crucifixion. In the Gospel of John, however, this feast does not occur until the Sabbath (Friday evening/Saturday). The Johannine chronology synchronizes the hour of Jesus' death with the time when the paschal lamb was being slaughtered. Consequently, the Fourth Gospel does not report that Jesus already celebrated the Passover; the supper recounted in chapter 13 is more of a farewell meal. This contradiction among the Gospels has always troubled scholars. I think that the most reasonable resolution to this problem has been suggested by A. Jaubert.[11] According to her hypothesis, Jesus followed not the calendar of the Pharisees but another calendar tradition. This position has been repeatedly criticized; however, in my opinion, it has withstood this criticism and is unquestionably the best approach to the problem of the dating of the Passover relative to the death of Jesus.

The existence of two different liturgical calendars in Jesus' time is certain. On the one hand, there was a more ancient solar calendar, which had been used by the Judean administration because it was the calendar used by all the surrounding peoples. On the other hand, the lunar solar calendar, which existed in Jerusalem at least since the reign of Menelaus (171–164 B.C.E.)[12] was introduced toward the end of the first century B.C.E. as a means of determining the liturgical year. This information can be inferred from a judgment attributed to Hillel the Elder reported in rabbinic works. It is said that Hillel was consulted on the issue of whether the law of the Sabbath was stronger than the law of Passover, because the norm had been forgotten. Since Passover not infrequently falls on a Saturday, it is unlikely that many were really at a loss as to how such an occurrence was to be handled. Consequently, a halakic judgment would have been necessary only if Passover had never before occurred on a Saturday.[13]

The phenomenon of a double calendar is a reflex of a divided society. On the religious level, this division was constituted by those who followed Pharisaic innovation and those who did not.

IMPURITY (MARK 7)[14]

By the time of Jesus, impurity had been a long-standing issue. In the Letter of Aristeas the problem of impurity arises out of contact with non-Jews. In this document the laws of impurity are assumed and, hence, go unquestioned.[15] Subsequently, however, this issue arose from within Jewish society itself. The question was no longer how to answer the non-Jew concerning the law, but how to find out what the value of purity meant from a more "existential" point of view. R. Ḥanina ben Dosa, who dates to the first half of the first century C.E., was once seen carrying the unclean carcass of a snake upon his shoulder, his behavior implying that impurity[16] does not exist. It is interesting to note that R. Ḥanina's thought is inferred only from his action. Some of Jesus' actions may also be analyzed in the same way.

Essenism, however, developed the notion of impurity in an opposite sense. Impurity not only exists but is synonymous with sin and is an evil force. Thus the author of one of the Thanksgiving Hymns was able to write that "man is in iniquity from the womb" (1QH 4.29–30). In this passage, "iniquity" does not mean "transgression"; it has a wider meaning. Impurity is a force somehow invading humankind since its conception. In the Rule of the Community we read that the one who does not join the sect "is not justified because of the great (?) stubbornness of his heart. . . . He is not sanctified by the water of the sea and of the rivers. He shall remain completely unclean as long as he rejects the will of God" (1QS 3.3–6). The way to salvation from sin coincides with purification. The norms of purity were extremely important for the Essenes. Impurity was sin itself.

According to the Jesus tradition in Mark 7:1–23, impurity is a reality.[17] Jesus seems only to have denied the existence of unclean foods; in any case, he denied that any impurity they might have could defile humans. We do not know precisely what Jesus thought about contact with impurity,[18] but on the whole it is clear that for him humans are defiled only by sin. A new problem emerges at this point: What is sin? That is, is transgression of the norms governing purity to be equated with sin?

From Jesus' teaching to his disciples we can infer that he considered the purity rules to be suspended. The basic concept underlying the purity rules in Jesus' time is difficult for us who live twenty centuries later to comprehend. The society in which Jesus lived was not used to precise conceptual definition. The norms governing purity were a matter of law. A term referring to "purity rules" in the sense in which we use it today did not exist. Our modern terminology is derived from a process of conceptualization that is anachronistic to the time of Jesus. It is a different matter to say simply that "purity exists" or that "it does not exist," or even to say that "impurity exists." Therefore, it would have been necessary to indicate those things which were thought to defile but which in fact did not defile.

Jesus' dismissal of purity rules made his teaching ambiguous, as can easily be seen from the problems that the early church encountered in this respect. For instance, in Caesarea Maritima Peter did not know whether to go into a nonbeliever's house (Acts 10), and in Antioch his actions demanded that Gentiles adopt the Jewish Christians' practices for the sake of purity (Gal 2:11–14).[19] In any case, impurity did exist for Jesus, who, in accordance with his own understanding, regarded it as a negative force linked with sin.

In the second half of the first century, Johanan ben Zakkai dealt with the problem of impurity again. Following R. Ḥanina, he stated that impurity does not exist: "It is neither the corpse which renders a man unclean nor the waters which purify."[20] At the same time, however, he insisted that everything concerning purity is contained in the Torah and that therefore humankind must observe the will of God.

As in other instances, we can distinguish between two divergent attitudes among the Jews. There were those who thought that impurity is a reality or even an entity, while others considered it to be only a matter of law. Here again, this differentiation contrasts the Pharisees with the Essenes. It is not clear which position the so-called apocalyptic texts take on this matter. To my knowledge, they do not explicitly deal with this issue.

MESSIANISM

For the many Jews of Jesus' time, the Messiah who was to come had to be the descendant of David, who would ascend to his throne in order to restore the destiny of Israel (see PssSol 17). If this understanding of the Messiah was common to all first-century Jews, then the early church's claim that Jesus was the Messiah would have been completely new within Judaism. It would have been so novel as to be even beyond the usual categories of Jewish thought.

In the Gospel of Mark the theme of the messianic secret may indicate that Jesus' thought concerning his mission was not well understood by some of his contemporaries. This lack of understanding may well have derived from a certain ambiguity in Jesus' own thought on the matter. Mark's presentation of Jesus' self-understanding seems closer to the facts than that of the Fourth Gospel. John's interpretation of Jesus is clear-cut: Jesus, whose kingship was not of this world (Jn 6:15; 18:36), did not want to be a king. In fact, not all Jews anticipated a warrior messiah as did R. Akiba. In Jesus' time there were also other types of messianism in Palestine, in which, for instance, the figure was connected with priesthood or with a superhuman being.

Jesus' thought concerning the Messiah is clearly expressed in Mark 12:35–37. Whether Jesus felt he was the Son of David or not, he made it clear that the Messiah was superior to David, who called him "my Lord." Here we are not interested in establishing whether the interpretation of the psalm given by Jesus is the correct one. It is enough to say that, historically speaking, it was his own interpretation. He felt he was the Son of God[21] and therefore superior to David. This conclusion is to be combined with the observation that, according to the Jews, the title "Son of God" was not to be understood literally and that it was not attributed to Jesus alone.[22]

Jesus also identified himself with the Son of Man, the eschatological judge. Yet that judge in the person of Jesus is also the one who graciously forgives. If Jesus considered himself to be the Messiah, he then identified himself with a supernatural being. Among the titles attributed to Jesus, the one that prevailed in the early Christian community was "the Messiah." The title endured because many Jews believed that the Messiah would have a superhuman character rather than a mere natural royal function.

Today it may seem a bit strange that anyone could believe in the existence of superhuman beings. Yet it was a common notion in the first century of our era. Every Jew believed that Elijah was to come back to earth. It was written in scripture (Mal 3:23–24); and, if he was to return, this meant that he, though a mortal, was not dead. All Jews also believed that Enoch was not dead (Gen 5:24). The so-called Enochic traditions give evidence that many thought Enoch existed somewhere in the cosmos and performed special cosmic functions. Recent discoveries near Qumran have brought another heavenly figure to light: Melchizedek,[23] who was considered an 'ĕlōhîm (literally, "a god").[24] The Son of Man was even said in the Similitudes to have been created before time (1En 48:3). While the belief in superhuman figures was common to the whole of Judaism, the definition of their functions and their increasing importance were specific to various ascetic and apocalyptic groups.

Many of Jesus' contemporaries believed that some of these figures might come to earth and serve some salvific function. We read in Matthew 11:14 that "this is Elijah who has come," and in Matthew 16:4 that "some say that you are John the Baptist; some Elijah; and others, Jeremiah or one of the prophets" (see also Lk 4:18–19; 9:7; Jn 1:19–21). Whatever the exact interpretation of these passages, it is clear that Jesus interpreted his function in God's design as messianic. The figure of the Messiah for Jesus was decidedly closer to the superhuman character of asceticism and of apocalyptic thought than to the rather human royal messiah (Davidic or not) of the Pharisees. In any case, Jesus identified himself with the greatest of all superhuman figures, a claim implicit in Mark and later explicit in John,[25] as noted above. On the one hand this shows the novelty of Jesus' thought, but on the other hand it is clear within which sphere of thought Jesus moved.

AN IMPORTANT CASE OF HALAKAH: DIVORCE

There is no doubt that for the Pharisees divorce—or rather the repudiation of a marriage—was permitted in accordance with the Mosaic law. The justification for this could be discussed, but not the principle.[26] It is also clear that repudiation of a marriage was not allowed among the Essenes, who probably even refused a widow or widower's right to a second marriage.[27] In Mark's Gospel, Jesus' attitude seems the same as that of the Essenes with the possible exception of the problem of a widow or widower's second marriage, which is not mentioned. Paul allows for it, but insofar as he presents arguments in its favor, it seems that for him it remained an unresolved problem. Paul makes a concession in light of the principle that "it is better to marry than to be aflame with passion" (1Cor 7:9; NRSV).[28] The restrictiveness of Jesus' attitude toward marriage, then, is closer to the ascetic spirituality than to the Pharisaic.

From this analysis concerning fundamental aspects of Jewish thought in the time of Jesus, Judaism appears to be divided into two main types. The distinction between them lies not in the solutions they give to each of the problems confronted but in their general approach and the leading ideas they used to reach their solutions. The importance of messianism ultimately derives from an attitude of mistrust in human ability to cope with sin. Thus, the human being looks for a way of salvation only through divine goodness and mercy. This attitude tends to conceive of impurity as a reality, because impurity in this sense truly limits humanity, which according to some extreme Essene ideas seems in some essential way to have been annihilated.

These two opposing attitudes existed in the Jewish world long before Jesus' day, though they were often not clearly conceptualized. The author of Isaiah 11, who expected salvation from a royal messiah, had a different form of piety from that of the author of Deuteronomy 3:5: "See, I have set before you life and good, death and evil."[29]

The notion that in ancient Palestine there were two main types of Judaism is confirmed by the historian Flavius Josephus, who may be regarded as a direct witness to the period under consideration, even if he lived toward its close. Josephus distinguishes only three groups within Judaism: the Pharisees, the Sadducees, and the Essenes. The Jewish currents of thought (*haireseis* or *philosophiai*) are always three for Josephus. In *Antiquities* he introduces a fourth: "The Jews . . . had three philosophies . . ." (18.11); "as for the fourth of the philosophies . . ." (18.23).

Even if Josephus gives considerable information concerning these "sects," and especially the Essenes, he always summarizes his thought according to what he considered to be the root of all their differences of opinion. He organizes their variety of beliefs according to attitudes held with respect to divine and human action. At the two extremes lie the Sadducees and the Essenes. The Pharisees lie in the middle—and for Josephus this was perhaps an indication of their superiority. Josephus explains that from a historical point of view the Sadducees are (or were) irrelevant (*Ant* 18.17); they were in fact absorbed by the Pharisees. Consequently, he thought that the Jewish ideologies of Palestine, at least until 7 C.E., could be classified in two main groups: the Pharisees and Sadducees versus the Essenes. According to Josephus, the two groups differed because the former attributed most (or all) destiny to human will, whereas the latter denied that destiny was dependent on human will. Clearly, this classification is speculative and not historical.

The Jewish groups prior to 70 C.E. were more than two or three in number. Josephus knew this very well, but when he wanted to present the main character of thought of his people to western Greco-Roman civilization, he found it natural to divide Judaism into two main groups, that is, into two Judean "philosophies" corresponding only partially to historically active groups. It is interesting to note that the term "philosophies" appears only in the last text he wrote. At first they were called *haireseis,* a term which assumed a more historical and more concrete character and which at last appeared to Josephus as inadequate.

Antiquities 13.172–73, which is the shortest discussion of these matters and therefore the most schematic one, is clear. The core of the problem for Josephus is the attitude of the Jew toward what he calls Destiny. The Pharisees, Josephus says, think that only some things are due to destiny (that is, to the will of God);[30] the Sadducees deny this destiny and maintain that the human factor is responsible for all occurrences within an individual's life; by contrast, the Essenes declare that Destiny is the master of everything.[31]

Josephus' division of Judaism into two main factions may derive from his personal experience of a problem that was particularly felt at the time, one acute enough to create significant differences of opinion. Thus Josephus' distinction is not one made solely by moderns, of which the ancients were unaware. If we were the only ones aware of it, it would be important only for the sake of writing the history of thought; but if Josephus' contemporaries were also aware of it, it means that it belongs also to the evidence of history.

Josephus' classification was based on theoretical principles, even though they derived from observation of historical parties. This conclusion is confirmed not only by the fact already referred to—that the ancients knew many more names of Jewish groups than the three used by Josephus[32] — but also by the complementary fact that we modern scholars use at least one term that was unknown to the ancients: apocalypticism.

Yet the texts we characterize as "apocalyptic" show the existence of a current of thought that could hardly have been unknown to Josephus, given the volume of the works belonging to the tradition and their originality within Judaism. Today we relate some, but not all, of the apocalyptic works to Essenism, and this identification may explain why Josephus ignored this current of thought. Apocalyptic works were for him either on one side or the other.[33]

On the basis of this short analysis, therefore, it appears that Jesus' formative background was of an Essene type. His uniqueness must be sought within this kind of thought, which necessarily led to confrontations with his "Pharisaic" contemporaries. I speak of a confrontation and not a clash, because there was always an ongoing dialogue among Jewish groups, a dialogue which according to the Jewish mentality of that time did not deal with abstract principles but with many specific issues and problems. This gave room for flexibility. Although Jesus' thought had an Essene background, it was always far from the rigidity and extremism of the Essenes themselves.

Notes

1. All translations in this article are my own, unless otherwise indicated.

2. H. S. Reimarus, *Reimarus: Fragments,* ed. C. Talbert (Philadelphia, 1970) p. 71; cf. p. 64.

3. An excellent synthesis of this question can be found in F. Parente, "Il problema storico dei rapporti tra essenismo e cristianesimo prima della scoperta dei Rotoli del Mar Morto," *La Parola del Passato* 86 (1962) 333–70; 95 (1964) 81–124.

4. H. L. Strack and P. Billerbeck, *Kommentar zum Neuen Testament aus Talmud und Midrasch* (Munich, 1922–28).

5. S. Ben-Chorin, *Bruder Jesus: Der Nazarener in jüdischer Sicht* (Munich, 1969).

6. G. Vermes, "Jewish Literature and New Testament Exegesis," *JJS* 33 (1982) 361–78, esp. 372ff.

7. W. Schmithals, *Einleitung in die drei ersten Evangelien* (Berlin, New York, 1985). Concerning the possibility of an early date for Mark's Gospel, see

J. Carmignac, *La naissance des évangiles synoptiques* (Paris, 1984); and J. A. T. Robinson, *Redating the New Testament* (London, 1976).

8. G. Theissen, *Sociology of Early Palestinian Christianity*, trans. J. Bowden (Philadelphia, 1978) p. 18. I am persuaded that the criterion of dissimilarity must be applied with caution.

9. I accept the interpretation of the Son of Man in Daniel 7 as a symbol for the whole people of Israel. Later the Son of Man came to represent an autonomous and real figure. The recent attempt to explain the Son of Man in the Similitudes as a collective symbol for Israel has no basis in the text. See G. Segalla, "Le figure mediatrici di Israele tra il III sec. a.C. e il I sec. d.C.: progettazione e illustrazione del tema," *Richerche storico bibliche* 1 (1989) 13–66.

10. See 2 Baruch and 4 Ezra. On this subject both of these works clearly show ideas that contrast with those of Jesus; for them salvation belongs only to the just.

11. A. Jaubert, *La date de la Cène* (Paris, 1957); "Jésus et le calendrier de Qumrân," *NTS* 7 (1960–61) 1–30; "Le mercredi où Jésus fut livré," *NTS* 14 (1967–68) 145–64; "The Calendar of Qumran and the Passion Narrative in John," in *John and the Dead Sea Scrolls*, ed. J. H. Charlesworth (New York, 1990) pp. 62–75; A. Moda, "La date de la cène; sur la thèse de M.lle Annie Jaubert," in *Nicolaus* 3 (1975) 53–116; J. C. VanderKam, "The Origin, Character and Early History of the 364-Day Calendar: A Reassessment of Jaubert's Hypotheses," *CBQ* 41 (1979) 390–411.

12. See R. T. Beckwith, "The Earliest Enoch Literature and its Calendar: Marks of their Origin, Date and Motivation," in *RQ* 10 (1981) 365–403; F. H. Cryer, "The 360-Day Calendar Year and Early Judaic Sectarianism," *Old Testament* 1 (1987) 116–22; P. R. Davies, "Calendrical Change and Qumran Origins: An Assessment of VanderKam's Theory," *CBQ* 45 (1983) 80–89; P. Sacchi, "Testipalestinesi anteriori al 200 a.C.," *RivB* 34 (1986) 183–204; J. C. VanderKam, "2 Maccabees 6, 7a and Calendrical Change in Jerusalem," *JSJ* 12 (1981) 52–74; idem, "The 364-Day Calendar in the Enochic Literature," *SBL 1983 Seminar Papers*, ed. K. H. Richards (Chico, Calif., 1983) pp. 157–65.

13. b.Pes 33a. See also F. Manns, *Pour lire la mishna* (Jerusalem, 1984) pp. 50–51.

14. See R. P. Booth, *Jesus and the Laws of Purity, Tradition History and Legal History in Mark 7* (*JSNT* SS 13; Sheffield, 1986).

15. See LetAris 142ff.

16. See b.Ta'an 25a and b.Ber 33a. See also G. Vermes, *Jesus the Jew: A Historian's Reading of the Gospels* (London, 1982 [2d ed.]) p. 81.

17. See also the parallel in Matthew 15:1–20. The ideology concerning purity and impurity is the same as in Mark, even though the two texts contain differences. The absence of the theme of food impurity in Luke can be explained by the fact that it was written for Gentiles.

18. I find it difficult to interpret some of Jesus' actions that might be concerned with this problem, such as the episode of the woman with an issue of blood

(Mk 5:25–34) or those episodes in which Jesus had no difficulty in meeting sinners. Jesus' actions are not as radical as those of R. Hanina's; nevertheless, as we have already seen, impurity was for Jesus a reality.

19. For a different interpretation of these passages, see Vermes, *Jesus the Jew*, pp. 28–29; idem, *The Gospel of Jesus the Jew* (Newcastle upon Tyne, 1981) p. 39. Among Jesus' actions that may shed light on his conception of impurity, see especially those mentioned in n. 17 (above).

20. This text (Tanhuma Hugat 26 and parallel) is quoted in J. Neusner, *The Idea of Purity in Ancient Judaism* (SJLA 1; Leiden, 1973) pp. 105–6. Neusner has challenged the antiquity of this text. In fact "if Yohanan ben Zakkai had really said such a thing, then his opinion was everywhere ignored for the next four or five centuries. . . . This to be sure is not a decisive argument, for his pro-gentile sayings were similarly ignored." In my opinion, the antiquity of this text, or at least of the ideas expressed by it, is certain, because it answered a precise need of first-century Judaism, within which, as we have seen, the problem had arisen and required an answer. Once the distance between the Jews on one side and the heathens and the *minim* on the other had increased, the problem was no longer relevant as before. The solution of ben Zakkai sufficed for a long time.

21. See chapter 5 below.

22. See Vermes, *Jesus the Jew*, pp. 192ff.

23. See editions of and commentary on 11QMelch (11Q13). See also A. S. van der Woude, "Melchisedek als Erlösergestalt in den neugefundenen eschatologischen Midraschim aus Qumran Höhle XI," *Oudtestamentische Studiën* 14 (1965) 354–73; and recently E. Puech, "Notes sur le manuscrit de 11QMelchisédeq," *RQ* 12 (1987) 483–515. See also Hebrews 7:3: "without father, without mother, without descent, having neither beginning of days, nor end of life" and 2 Enoch 68–73, where Melchizedek was virginally born from Sofonim and was taken by the archangel Mikael into the garden of Eden, where he lives eternally.

24. On Melchizedek as *'ĕlōhîm*, see C. Gianotto, "Melchisedek e la sua tipologia," *Supplementi alla Rivista Biblica* 12 (Brescia, 1984) 64–75.

25. Jesus' identification with the Son of Man is implicit in the Synoptic Gospels (see Mk 2, treated above). It becomes explicit in John, even if here this title is used less often for Jesus than in the other Gospels. See John 9:35–39.

26. See the discussion between the schools of Hillel and Shammai on legitimate grounds for repudiation (cited in m.Gitt 9:10). See Strack-Billerbeck, *Kommentar*, vol. 1, pp. 313ff.

27. See CD 4.20–21: "They take two women during their [related to "men," not to "women"] life, whereas the principle of creation is 'Male and female created he them.'" Though my interpretation is not the one most widely followed, this text can mean nothing else; "their" refers to a masculine noun. The meaning therefore is this: "the guilt consists in the fact that they take more than one wife during their life." The fact that the stress is placed on "during their life" shows that the problem

is not polygamy (simultaneously having two wives) but allowing the second marriage. L. Moraldi affirms that the text is not clear; he makes a list of all the possible interpretations and chooses the one that relates "their" to women. Moraldi, *I manoscritti di Qumrān* (Classici delle religioni; Turin, 1986 [2d ed.]) p. 236. See also H. Braun, *Qumran und das Neue Testament* (Tübingen, 1966) vol. 1, pp. 40–42, 192–93.

28. Paul (1Cor 7) advises unmarried people and widow(er)s to live in continence (v. 9); but at the end of the passage (v. 39) he allows for second marriage, because the wife is bound by the law as long as he lives (which is along the lines of "during their life" of CD). However, if her husband dies, the woman is free. Paul does not have polygamy in mind, but clearly a widow(er)'s marriage: if he has to argue in order to allow it (Paul has already made the concession at v. 8), this means that the matter was not completely settled and that someone probably had denied this widow(er)'s right to marry again.

29. Cf. Sirach 15:11–17. All the variants of v. 15 have to do with the problem of freedom of choice. According to the author, God placed man in the hand of his ability to decide (*diaboulion*); but for some copyists "in the hand of his ability to decide" became "in the hand of his enemy," or also "in the hand of his nature" (later the two lessons were conflated). In addition to the statement that "to do the will of God is intelligence," some manuscripts read "to do the will of God is faith." A human's freedom of choice must have been an important and vexing issue during this period.

30. For "Destiny" Josephus always has *heimarmenē*, a word cherished by the Stoics and perhaps chosen by him not only because it was widely used in his time but also because it most closely expressed the concept of "divine will."

31. See also *Ant* 18.13 (for the Pharisees); 18.17 (for the Sadducees); and 18.18 (for the Essenes). In *War*, 2.119–66 is devoted almost entirely to the Essenes. Josephus devotes only §§162–66 to the Sadducees and the Pharisees and only in these paragraphs does the schematic presentation appear, based on the criterion of freedom of choice. The issue of human freedom is applied to the Essenes only in the shortest texts. This is therefore a recapitulatory and general criterion, but for this reason alone, it is extremely important for any classification of the currents of that time.

32. From Christian sources, as many as thirteen to fourteen names can be derived. Authors generally supply a series of seven names, but the names in the series do not coincide. The various designations for Jewish groups include Ebionites, Hellenists, Hemerobaptists, Herodians, Essenes, Pharisees, Galileans, Genists, Masbateians, Merists, Nazarenes, Sadducees, Samaritans, and Scribes. For the "scribes" as a social group, see J. Neusner, "The Formation of Rabbinic Judaism: Yavneh (Jamnia) from A.D. 70 to 100," in *ANRW* II.19.1 (1972) pp. 3–42, esp. 3, 37–41. Cf. Eusebius, *Historia Ecclesiastica* 4.22.7; Justin, *Dialogue* 80; Epiphanius,

Haereses 1.14ff.; Apostolic Constitutions 6.6; Pseudo-Jerolamus, *Indiculus haereseorum;* and Isidore of Seville, *Origenes* 8.4. Josephus may speak of the Baptist, of Jesus himself, of Jude the Galilean, and of many others, but he does not modify his general classification.

33. To place 1 Enoch 8 and 98:4 in the same current of thought is impossible without appealing to the modern concept of "historical development."

CHAPTER 5

Jesus as "Son" and the Righteous Teacher as "Gardener"

JAMES H. CHARLESWORTH

The foreword to this volume clarifies the basic consensus that now exists among the world specialists on the Qumran Scrolls. With the light provided by such shared insights it is possible to stress how important the Dead Sea Scrolls are for an understanding of Early Judaism and Christian origins.

INTRODUCTION

The Dead Sea Scrolls

The first purpose of this chapter is to seek to discern how and in what ways we might come closer to understanding the devout Jew, the Righteous Teacher, whose name may well have been Zadok.[1] Who did he think he was? Did he refer to himself metaphorically? Did he think he had a special place in God's history of salvation?

Many gifted specialists have come to the conclusion that *some portions* of the Dead Sea Scrolls were written by the Righteous Teacher, the founder of the Qumran Community. Among such specialists are Carmignac, Dupont-Sommer, Jeremias, Qimron, Schultz, Strugnell, Sukenik, Yadin, and others.[2]

Singularly important in this focused research is the scroll known as the Thanksgiving Hymns (1QH). From the beginnings of Qumran research these hymns have caught the eye of specialists as possibly,[3] probably,[4] or certainly[5] composed by the Righteous Teacher. G. Jeremias and others refined the methodology and set conclusions on a firm foundation. Only some of the hymns in this scroll (1QH) were composed by the Righteous Teacher.[6] At the present time, most leading experts on the Scrolls rightly conclude that some of the Thanksgiving Hymns were composed by the Righteous Teacher.[7]

One hymn that is almost certainly to have been composed by him is found in column 8 of the Thanksgiving Hymns. It has a peculiar and distinct use of the first person pronoun and reflects a unique consciousness of being empowered by God and having received revelation from him. It is virtually unimaginable that an ordinary pious member of the community could have composed it. We shall center our research on this hymn, seeking to discern what might be known about the self-understanding of the Righteous Teacher.

The Gospels

The second purpose of this chapter is to examine the parable of the wicked tenant farmers to see if there is embedded in it some precious deposits of Jesus' own self-understanding. To what extent does this parable help us comprehend Jesus' self-understanding?

Numerous New Testament specialists have slowly come to the point where they can no longer agree with the pessimism of Bultmann and others.[8] Chrys C. Caragounis rightly points out that the "basic fault" methodologically is "the unwarrantably negative view that has by and large been taken with regard to the sources."[9] That means, in popular terms, something like the ultra-liberal scholar saying to all others, "I dare you to prove that Jesus actually said these words in precisely that way." With this attitude, precision is dethroned for positivism.

Fortunately, there is no longer a consensus that we cannot discern and discuss Jesus' self-understanding or his purpose. My own research leads me to admit that Jesus never claimed to be the Messiah. That conclusion, however, does not warrant or entail the claim that he could not have had some messianic self-perception. His silence may well be an implicit indication that he may have thought of himself as Messiah.[10] Numerous Jewish texts, like the Psalms of Solomon and 4 Ezra, indicate that only God can declare who is the Messiah. Any self-designation only proves that the proclaimer cannot be the Messiah. This insight certainly helps clarify the reticence (or refusal) of Jesus to accept Peter's confession according to Mark 8.[11]

Like any human being, Jesus had some understanding and perception of himself. But did he have something like a messianic self-understanding?

Numerous research specialists have now come to the conclusion that Jesus may have had some messianic self-understanding. Included in this list would be a wide range of diverse New Testament specialists such as D. E. Aune, D. Flusser, D. R. A. Hare, M. Hengel, R. Leivestad, and B. F. Meyer.[12] E. P. Sanders contends that Jesus accepted the role of king "either implicitly or explicitly."[13] Despite the obvious conflicting textual evidence, H. Boers is forced to admit that Jesus' triumphal entry into Jerusalem at least raises the possibility that Jesus may have intermittently held some messianic self-understandings.[14] M. Hengel points out that Jesus' charismatic role, especially his charge to follow him, discloses his perception of possessing "underivable 'messianic' authority."[15] The excellent Swedish specialist R. Leivestad concludes that Jesus "understood himself as Messiah."[16]

The parable of the wicked tenant farmers, despite signs of some editorial reworking by his followers, seems to derive ultimately from Jesus.[17] He then may have referred to himself with the word "son": "He (the 'man who planted a vineyard' = God)" sent "his son" to the tenant farmers "saying, 'They will respect my son.'" These words are from the canonical version (Mk 12:1–9; Mt 21:33–46; Lk 20:9–19). An early apocryphal work, the Gospel of Thomas, preserves the following version of these words: "Then the master sent his son. He said, 'Perhaps they will respect my son.'"[18]

Is it conceivable that Jesus could have thought of himself as "God's son"? Working on other texts, numerous scholars have come to the conclusion that the answer is a simple yes: Jesus considered himself God's son. Some of the experts who have come to this conclusion are M. J. Borg, D. Flusser, and J. D. G. Dunn.[19]

Final Purpose

The final purpose of the present chapter is to compare what we have learned about the Righteous Teacher with our new comprehension of Jesus. Any influence between them would have to be from the Righteous Teacher, who lived in the second century B.C.E., to Jesus, who lived in the first century C.E.; but while it is possible that Jesus, as a boy, may have known Hillel,[20] there is no evidence to suggest that he knew anything about the Righteous Teacher.[21] It is conceivable[22] that he had heard about him through an Essene. We are finally led to ponder this issue: Did these two different individuals evidence what may be called a prophetic and eschatological charisma?

THE RIGHTEOUS TEACHER

Over forty years of labor on over three hundred scrolls and fragments and archaeological work on Khirbet Qumran and the Qumran caves have produced the following widely recognized portrait of the Righteous Teacher, which may be an honorific title (it appears in CD, 1QpHab, 4QpPs 37).[23] Sometime before 150 B.C.E. he had been an influential priest in the Jerusalem Temple. He may perhaps have even been once an officiating high priest.[24] He and his group claimed to be (and probably were) the legitimate heirs to the high priesthood. They were conscious of being the descendants of Zadok and Aaron. Perhaps the precursors of the Qumran covenanters survived in Jerusalem for "twenty years" (CD 1) before they became coherent theologically and sociologically through the charismatic leadership of the Righteous Teacher. Some of the group who followed the Righteous Teacher were Levites who officiated in the Temple.

Because of a major rift among rival priestly groups, the Righteous Teacher eventually was forced out of the Temple,[25] perhaps sometime before 150 B.C.E. He led a small band of followers into the wilderness around the middle of the second century B.C.E. In the wilderness they eventually found the ruins of an old fortress that clearly, as archaeologists have shown, predates the Babylonian captivity of the sixth century B.C.E.[26] The small band of priests restored these ruins and prepared an area in which to work and worship. They lived in the adjoining caves and on the terraces. In the deep depression of the desert, the lowest spot on earth, they could look either to the west and the sharp and rugged cliffs nearby, or to the east with the lifeless Dead Sea before them and in the distance the horizon over which the light comes each morning.

Subsequently they were harassed by a rival and illegitimate priest in the Temple cult. They called him "the Wicked Priest." He is most likely one of the Maccabees, either Jonathan (c. 160–143 B.C.E.) or Simon (143–c. 135 B.C.E.). While the Qumran covenanters were celebrating Yom Kippur (the Day of Atonement) they, and especially the Righteous Teacher, were persecuted by the Wicked Priest and others from Jerusalem:

> . . . the wicked priest who persecuted[27] the Righteous Teacher at the house of his exile in order to engulf him[28] in the anger of his wrath; and at the time of the festival of rest, the Day of Atonement, he appeared to engulf them and to make them stumble on the day of fasting, their Sabbath of rest. (1QpHab 11.4–8)

Obviously the Wicked Priest could not leave Jerusalem during the time he and his group celebrated the Day of Atonement. The group at Qumran (the place of "exile") clearly followed a calendar different from the one accepted in the Jerusalem cult.

Two calendars clearly were advocated in Early Judaism,[29] a lunar one by the Jerusalem priests, and a solar one by the Qumran group and others. It is possible that on the Day of Atonement, when the Righteous Teacher and his group were dedicated to religious observances, "the Wicked Priest" severely injured the Righteous Teacher. There is no evidence, however, that he was martyred, let alone crucified.[30]

Most importantly, the Righteous Teacher was powerful and created a new means of interpreting scripture (= the Old Testament or Hebrew Scriptures) because he claimed to have received a special revelation (1QpHab 7). This unique revelation empowered him and his followers to contend that God had disclosed all the mysteries in the words of the prophet to him and to him alone.

The death of the founder of this community must have shaken his followers, because they held firmly to the belief that God would soon vindicate them by sending one or, most likely, two Messiahs. As far as we know, they left no record of their reflections on his death. They certainly did not believe that he would return to them, and it remains unclear whether they held to the belief in the resurrection, which was already well known in Early Judaism, as we know from studying the books of Enoch,

Daniel, 2 Maccabees, and many other Jewish works including the Amidah (especially the Eighteen Benedictions said on weekdays).[31]

Sometime around 100 B.C.E. the size of the community was greatly expanded, as we know from the archaeological excavations of Qumran and of Cave 4. Other Jews obviously joined the community and increased the size of the buildings. The physical expansion to Qumran was not due to births within the community, since the original Qumran covenanters were probably celibate priests.[32] These reflections most likely take us beyond the time of the Righteous Teacher, the date and manner of whose death are still unclear.[33]

The Self-understanding of the Righteous Teacher

What did the Righteous Teacher think about his own suffering and humiliation, his exile, and his place in God's holy history? How could he find meaning in a wasteland, far removed from the center of the Holy Land, and the house of God, the Jerusalem Temple? What was the purpose of his priestly lineage? Was there any hope for him and his faithful few? Where was God?

These questions are ours; but surely he must have raised and pondered similar issues. He was certainly a brilliant, highly educated and dedicated Jewish priest of the most prestigious lineage. Is there any evidence of what he might have thought about the problems within Judaism and especially the usurpation of the Holy of Holies? Is there any writing that might disclose his own self-understanding?

For decades some distinguished scholars, especially J. Carmignac, claimed that the Righteous Teacher wrote all of the Rule of the Community, the Thanksgiving Hymns, and even the War Scroll.[34] Other specialists claimed that the Righteous Teacher wrote the Temple Scroll.[35] These scrolls cannot be attributed to the same person; each of them is a composite of traditions that come from different periods. It is equally unlikely that the founder of the community wrote no portion of the extant scrolls. He was well trained and founded a community which above all is distinguished from other Jewish groups by the quantity of documents it copied and composed.

The special hymnbook of the community is the Thanksgiving Hymns or Hodayoth. It is now evident that some of these hymns were composed by the Righteous Teacher. As G. Jeremias has shown,[36] in these hymns we can find the use of the first person singular, which is distinct and represents a unique individual. The most impressive example of a hymn that reflects the self-understanding of the Righteous Teacher seems to be preserved in column 8.[37] Here is my translation:

4 I [praise you, O Lord, because you][38] placed me
        as[39] an overflowing fountain in a desert,[40]
        and (as) a spring of water in a land of dryness,[41]
5   and (as) the i[rri]gator[42] of * the garden.[43]
   You [have plant]ed a planting of cyprus, and elm,
        with cedar together (yḥd)[44] for your glory;
6   (these are) the trees of * life hidden[45]
   among all the trees of the water[46]
   beside the mysterious water source.[47]
   And they caused to sprout the shoot (nṣr)[48]
        for the eternal planting.
7 Before they shall cause (it) to sprout they strike root,
        then send forth their roots to the river (ywbl).
        And its trunk[49] shall be open to the living water;
8   and it shall become the eternal fountain.
   But upon the shoot (nṣr)
        every [beast][50] of the forest shall feed.
   And its trunk (shall become) a place of trampling
9   for all those who pass * over the way (drk).[51]
   And its branches (shall be food)[52] for every bird.
   And all the tre[es][53] of the water
        shall exalt themselves[54] over it,
   because they shall become magnified in their planting.
10 But they shall not send forth a root to the river
        (ywbl).[55]
   And he who causes to sprout[56] the hol[y] shoot (nṣr)
        for the planting of truth is concealed
11 with the result that he is not * esteemed,
        and the sealing of his mystery is not perceived.[57]

This is a remarkable hymn. It is in harmony with what we learn about the Righteous Teacher in other scrolls (1QpHab, CD, 4QpPs 37) and the other hymns that probably derive from him. The hymn is semiallegorical[58] and reflects his self-understanding. He praises God for planting him "as an overflowing fountain in a desert." For him God initiates the eschatological act in the drama of salvation. Although the action in this hymn intermittently shifts to the salvific acts of the Righteous Teacher, the ultimate actor behind all is God, who through this priest of ancient and legitimate lineage is creating the new age.

The Righteous Teacher does not bewail the loss of his high position in the Temple cult. He acknowledges that he is in the desert—perhaps on the marl terrace near Qumran overlooking the Dead Sea. Through eschatological optimism he rejoices in his followers. Using imagery that for centuries had already carried deep symbolic meaning, he affirms that his followers are "the trees of life" that are unrecognized and uncelebrated. They are trees for God's glory but now "hidden among all the trees of the water." These latter trees are perhaps the rival priests in the Temple.[59]

The Righteous Teacher is the "i[rri]gator of the garden." This identification is strengthened by lines 10–11: the Righteous Teacher, under God's power, causes "the hol[y] shoot" to sprout; but he is "not esteemed" because the revelation of his identity is "not perceived" by those outside his group. The identity is confirmed by 8.16:

And you, O my God, have put in my mouth
　　as it were an autumn rain (*kywrh gšm*)
　　　for all [the sons of men],
and as a spring of living waters
　　which shall not run dry.

The author of this line, the Righteous Teacher, returns to the thought with which he opened the hymn. He is clearly the "irrigator of the garden," the one in whom God has placed the "autumn rain," a significant symbolic term,[60] and the "spring of living waters," another highly symbolic phrase. It is easy to imagine such thoughts being prompted by the lifelessness of the Qumran area and by being in exile. The physical setting (dry land) evokes metaphor and symbolism (the irrigated garden, the living hope of his followers, because he has "living water" or charisma).

The theological significance of this hymn is clarified by the content of the Gozan inscription (from Tell Fakhariyeh).[61] The statue on which the inscription is written (in Assyrian and Aramaic) is that of a "king" (in Aramaic) who celebrates his god as one who "irrigates" all the lands. Here is Kaufman's translation of the pertinent lines from the Aramaic:

> The likeness of Had-Yit'i which he placed before Hadad of Sikanu, irrigation master of Heaven and Earth, he who brings down prosperity and provider of pasture and watering place for all the lands, and provider of ritual-sprinkling and libation vessel to all the gods his brothers, irrigation master of all the rivers, he who makes all the lands luxuriant, Merciful God whose prayer is good, resident of Sikanu, Great Lord, lord of Had-Yit'i, King of Gozan, son of Sas-Nuri, King of Gozan.[62]

The god is thus portrayed as a gardener. Other texts also show that in the ancient Near East the deity was the gardener. He is the one who brings rain and provides for the fruitfulness of the land. The Righteous Teacher inherits these thoughts from ancient traditions[63] and projects himself as the one whom God has allowed (or caused) to irrigate the dry land (the parched followers) and plant the eternal planting (the remnant who shall be living trees in God's restored paradise).[64] The Righteous Teacher conceives of himself as the gardener, "the irrigator of the garden" (1QH 8.4–5).

The Righteous Teacher may show the well-known Semitic penchant for paronomasia (a judicious use of a well-crafted pun). He may have obliquely referred to himself when he chose the term for "early rain (or shower)" (*ywrh*),[65] which plays on the term by which his followers called him, "Teacher" (*mwrh* or *ywrh*).[66] The Righteous Teacher may also be "the mysterious source" (8.6).

The present is not the time for lamenting or rejoicing; all meaning comes from the Teacher's vision of the culminating divine drama. The Righteous Teacher is "the eternal fountain"; he and his followers are the "garden," and "the eternal planting." The future of God's promises is grounded in the present actions of the founder of this community. The faith of the Righteous Teacher is firm. His self-understanding as the irrigator of the eternal planting is found in the words of this allegory.

There is more. The suffering of the Righteous Teacher and his followers may also be mirrored in these lines. He portrays himself as the irrigator of the garden which will produce the shoot for the eternal planting. But the "shoot" has endured much suffering: the beasts feed on him; he has become "a place of trampling."[67] The other priests, "the tre[es] of the water" have exalted "themselves over" him, "because they shall become magnified in their planting," that is, in their exalted position in the Temple cult. Again, the Righteous Teacher refers to himself as one who is "concealed," "not esteemed," and "not perceived." Yet he is convinced that he is the one who has been chosen by God to cause "to sprout the hol[y] shoot for the planting of truth," that is, the eternal garden that will surpass in the endtime the paradisiacal state of the garden of Eden.

When one studies the Dead Sea Scrolls and Early Judaism, one can see behind this allegory some of the history of the Dead Sea Scroll community, and even of the self-understanding of its founder. Five distinct and interrelated aspects of the Righteous Teacher's self-understanding appear in these few lines.

First, he begins by using the first person pronoun as a subject and an object: "I [praise you, O Lord, because you] placed me. . . ." He continues to reveal his perception of election; he thinks he has an elevated role in the history of God's majestic and eschatological deeds. He is not the exiled one. He is the chosen irrigator of God's own garden, the faithful remnant of the covenant between the Creator and his chosen nation. The Righteous Teacher portrays himself as "the mysterious water source," the one who "is concealed," and whose "mystery is not perceived." In the sense of these words he is a religious mystic with deep powers of introspection.

Second, he sees his life and work in line with God's past activities, although this dimension is subtle and remains undeveloped. The reference to the "garden" probably was accompanied by thoughts about God's acts at creation, especially the Yahwistic account in Genesis of how God planted a garden for the human in Eden.[68] The quasi allegory of 1QH 8 is paralleled by the allegory summarized by, or hinted at in, Genesis and Ezekiel.[69] The present activity by God for his eternal planting, however, is not seen so much in terms of past activities as in the future dimension of certain fulfillment. The image of planting brings to mind the prophetic message and history of salvation well known to the Righteous Teacher, who must have been especially fond of Isaiah and Ezekiel.

Third, this hymn discloses the eschatological perspective of the Righteous Teacher. The planting is for "the garden," which is none other than "the eternal planting." This is certain because "the shoot," an obviously very complex and symbolic term, is already taking form, since "the trees of life," using the water from the Righteous Teacher, have "caused" it to sprout.[70] The past tense is used to describe either the certainty of a future act or—here more probably—to reveal the hidden, mysterious activity that has already commenced. The end of time will see the return of "the garden," "the eternal planting."

This planting will not be like the garden of Eden. It will be "the planting of truth," and hence devoid of any possibility of division between Creator and creature. There is no possibility of a fall or disobedience in "the eternal planting." The adjective "eternal" clarifies this dimension of the history of salvation.

Fourth, it is abundantly clear that the Righteous Teacher has a major source for his confidence. It is the feeling of God's continuing revelatory activity evident in his own group and his relationship to his community that give him assurance and confidence. He obtains meaning in and through his insoluble link with one specific community. His life obtains meaning because he is God's irrigator, because there are around him "trees of life" which need and flourish from his work. He is closely linked with God, but the one "who causes to sprout the hol[y] shoot" is not God but the Righteous Teacher, who is God's instrument.

His humility before God turns to pride before the community. It is from his followers and their recognition of his charisma that he is sustained and becomes boastful. It is conceivable that he gave to this group of priests the unique dimension of being the *yaḥad*, which means "oneness" but is rightly translated "community."

Fifth, he had a clear expectation. His words do not convey an ephemeral dream. They embody the assurance that his life and teaching have produced the eternal planting of truth.

THE HISTORICAL JESUS

Research on the historical Jesus for more than two hundred years has shown one perennial penchant: to portray Jesus in terms of one's own ideals and customs. It is certain that Jesus' authentic words were altered significantly in the forty years that separated his crucifixion from the composition of the first Gospel. It is equally certain that Jesus' followers were not only interested in the Lord they affirmed was raised from the dead by God. They were also interested in the Jesus they had known earlier, and they always identified the risen Christ with the one they had known in Galilee and Jerusalem. For them the identity was not ideological but ontological.[71]

In the last ten years scholars have shown far more confidence than their former teachers in knowing something with confidence about the pre-Easter Jew called Jesus. This confidence is due not only to refined methodology but also to an enlightened perception of pre-70 Palestinian Judaism, thanks to the fruitful work on the Dead Sea Scrolls and other pre-70 Jewish writings.[72]

The following portrait of Jesus seems now to be widely accepted by many New Testament specialists. Jesus had some relationship with John the Baptizer, who certainly baptized him. He began his public ministry in or near Capernaum and took the initiative in calling men and women to follow him.

He did select a special group, the twelve, and this action seems to indicate some revolutionary purpose to "restore Israel." He performed healings and probably also exorcisms. He was an itinerant preacher who proclaimed the nearness (even presence at times) of God's kingdom. He insisted that God is a loving Father; his favorite word for God was not the ineffable and common Jewish name for God, Yahweh, which according to our sources he never used. He customarily called God "*Abba*," the Aramaic noun which for him denoted a beloved and intimate Father. He also taught his disciples, in the Lord's Prayer, to call God by this unsophisticated term of endearment.

He possibly faced without fear the premonition that he would be murdered, perhaps stoned. After an unknown period of public teaching in Galilee he moved southward to Jerusalem, where he boldly and successfully demonstrated his disdain for the corruption in the Temple during a public confrontation with the priestly establishment. He suffered through rejection by two especially close disciples (James and John the sons of Zebedee), the betrayal of Judas, and the denial of Peter. He eventually died ignominiously on a cross, outside the western wall of Jerusalem in the spring of 30 C.E.

Within a very short interval of time his followers began to claim boldly and openly that God had raised him from the dead. The memory of him lingered on among those who had lived with him. Slowly this memory faded in the claim to have met him alive in a resurrected form, in the daily endeavors to proclaim his messiahship, sonship, and lordship, and especially in the fervent belief that he was about to return as judge and fulfiller of God's promises.

The Self-understanding of the Historical Jesus

Obviously Jesus did not proclaim himself.[73] That fact does not mean that Jesus had no understanding of who—or whose—he was. He certainly possessed some self-understanding.

What did Jesus think about his inability to reach others and to convince his closest disciples that he must face a life of suffering? What did he think about himself as he proclaimed that the rule of God was beginning to break into the present? What did he think about his rejections, first by scribes, some Pharisees, and then finally by his closest disciples and friends, including Judas and Peter? What was his purpose in the Temple when he attacked the money changers?[74] How was his self-perception shaped by reflections on his role in the rule of God (the kingdom of God) and on the miracles performed through him?

Clearly he was not preoccupied with his self-understanding, but did he never ponder who he was and what his role was in God's drama of salvation? Surely his dynamic, underivative, and authoritative speech reflects a very strong ego. His ability to perform exorcisms and other "mighty works" would have forced upon him some self-reflections. To think otherwise, far from attributing messianic overtones to him, portrays him as an otherworldly figure. His expectation of being martyred must have evoked some reflections on who he was. The salutes and titles attributed to him by other Jews, whether Peter or the crowds,[75] must have caused some self-reflections.

An answer to our search for Jesus' self-understanding is hidden in one of his parables, which are well-known art forms typical of Jesus' teaching.[76] The parable of the wicked tenant farmers, though obviously edited by the evangelists (including Mark), probably derives ultimately from Jesus for the following reasons.

First, it is widely attested and cannot be attributed to the creativity of one evangelist. It is found within (Mk, Mt, Lk) and without the Christian canon (GThom).[77]

Second, the essential core of this parable is different from the proclamations (kerygmata) of Jesus' earliest followers. The review of history seems more typical of tendencies in the Jewish apocalypses[78] than the essential thrust of the *kerygma,* which was focused more on Jesus than on the past history of salvation.[79]

The concept of "son" is thoroughly Jewish and contains none of the early christological reflections. The death of the "son" in the parable is not by crucifixion; the corpse is dishonored; and the death is in no way efficacious. The expectation that the Jewish tenants "will respect" Jesus clashes with the anti-Jewish polemic of the evangelists, especially Matthew and John.[80]

Third, the parable bears the stamp of Jesus' own genius; it was not transferred to him from an unknown Jewish source.[81] It is an eschatological parable and thus coheres with other well-known parables that are authentic to Jesus. The reference to killing the envoy, especially the son, coheres with other passages that clearly go back to Jesus and reflect his premonition of impending martyrdom. The mention of "last (of all)" may be in harmony with Jesus' futuristic eschatology; if so, it clashes with Matthew's, Luke's, and especially John's tendency to shift the spotlight from the future to the present. The ambiguity of some parts of the parable, especially the exact meanings of "heir" and "inheritance," is in line with many of Jesus' sayings, which are sometimes opaque. The vagueness also clashes with the attempt by the evangelists to clarify ambiguities. The focus on God as the owner (*kyrios,* "Lord") of the vineyard fits better within Jesus' theocentric theology and his dependence on early Jewish theology and its development of Old Testament motifs than it does within the focus on Jesus by the post-Easter church.

Fourth, the setting of the parable, especially the social and economic conditions portrayed, represents Jesus' own time and not that of the evangelists. The fruitful fields are owned by absentee landlords, which describes rural Palestine beginning with the heavy taxations by Herod the Great.[82] It does not so representatively describe Palestine after its devastation by the Romans in 66–70 C.E.[83] The ambience is that of Palestinian Jews from the time of Herod the Great until 70,[84] when they, like Job, felt unjustly persecuted,[85] and not that of the post-Easter community, which claimed to be justified by Christ's death and resurrection.

The refusal of the tenant farmers to pay what is owed to the landlord makes adequate sense only in Jesus' time; the land rightfully belonged to the so-called tenant farmers, who believed that their religious and legal right had been unjustly robbed from them. Such history fits precisely both the parable and the Palestinian countryside after 38 B.C.E. Seen with this perspective the parable rings with meaning.

The imagery—notably the reference to the meaning of "trough," the time for harvesting, and the portion of the harvest due the landlord—would have been familiar to Jesus' hearers, but it would have needed explanation to many readers of the Gospel of Mark in Rome, Alexandria, or Antioch. The economic setting is rural, not urban,[86] and goods are unequally distributed. Such is the setting of Jesus' authentic parables,[87] which evoke empathy in the hearers.

Fifth, the reference to the "son" is impressively undeveloped and ambiguous. This factor accords well with the use of "son" in early Jewish theology, and especially with the words of some Galilean charismatics contemporaneous with Jesus, notably Ḥoni (m.Taʿan 3:8), or the tradition that one of the Galilean charismatics, namely Ḥanina, was called "my son" by God (b.Ber 17b).[88]

Sixth, the parable is one piece of cloth. In Mark it does reflect some editing (only interpolations and an expansion at the end), but it does not evidence reweaving. It is as if new threads were sewn into the whole cloth; it is not as if a new garment is woven out of reused pieces.

It is wise now to present the parable of the wicked tenant farmers, which is recorded in Mark 12:1-12; Matthew 21:33-46; Luke 20:9-19; and also in the Gospel of Thomas 65. Previous studies, confirmed by my own research, have disclosed that the two primary records of this parable are in Mark, which was the source for Matthew and Luke, and in the Gospel of Thomas, which does not contain the edited portions of Mark's account.[89] Both Mark and Thomas preserve early and independent versions, and they are strikingly similar.[90] Here is my translation of Mark's tradition:

He began to speak to them in parables. "A man planted a vineyard, and set a fence[91] around it, and dug a trough (for the wine press). Then[92] he built a tower (to protect it); finally,[93] he leased it to tenants, and went away. When the time came (for the harvest), he sent a servant to the tenants, to collect from them (his portion) of the fruits of the vineyard. But they took him, beat (him), and sent (him) away empty-handed. Again he sent to them another servant; him they wounded in the head, and treated shamefully. Then[94] he sent another; him they killed; (he even sent) many others; some they beat and some they (even) killed. He[95] had still one other (he could send): a beloved son (*huion agapēton*). He sent him to them last (of all, *eschaton*) saying, 'They will respect my son.' But those tenants said to one another, 'This is the heir; come, let us kill him, and the inheritance will be ours.' And seizing (him), they killed him, and cast him out of the vineyard. What will the owner (*ho kyrios*)[96] of the vineyard do?[97] He will come and destroy the tenants, and give the vineyard to others." (Mk 12:1-9)

A form-critical analysis clarifies that this story has a well-defined beginning and ending and is a short, self-contained unit of thought. The form is a fully developed parable.

There is impressive evidence that it once circulated in an Aramaic oral form.[98] Note the undeveloped sentences and the need to supply within parentheses the full meaning. The audience knew the historical setting; it was familiar to them from their daily lives. Note especially the need to supply objective pronouns within parentheses: "him" must be added for meaningful English not fewer than three times. Recall the following sentence: "But they took him, beat (him), and sent (him) away empty-handed." Like English, Greek usually presents these objective pronouns, but Aramaic, Jesus' own language, frequently assumes them in oral and written language.

What is most impressive is the lack of expansion of the story from the editing of the evangelist Mark. He has clearly supplied only "beloved" before son. This adjective was one of Mark's favorites, as we know from the theophanic voice in his account of Jesus' baptism and transfiguration: "You are (or this is) my beloved (*agapētos*) son" (Mk 1:11 [the baptism] and 9:7 [the transfiguration]). No other clear Marcan expansion is evident, except perhaps the ending.[99]

The theologian Mark did not clarify how the son was killed, and that is impressive.[100] For Mark the death of Jesus was extremely important. It was one of the key reasons he composed his Gospel. For him Jesus' death on a cross was salvific and essential for the forgiveness of sins; but according to this parable the death of the son benefits no one. Moreover, the death occurs within the vineyard, and the corpse is hurled over the fence that surrounds it. Jesus' crucifixion, as Mark knew, was outside the walls of Jerusalem. It is simply not possible to conclude that Mark created this parable.

For the same reasons it must be concluded that it is highly improbable that any of Jesus' followers composed the story.[101] The use of the noun "son" is left undeveloped. It does not appear to be a title, as it was most assuredly in the earliest Christian communities. The death of the "son" is against all records of how and where Jesus died. He died on a cross outside the city Jerusalem. The son in the parable dies within the vineyard by means unknown. Jesus' corpse, according to the earliest traditions, was revered and accorded respect by his followers and even others. In the parable the corpse of the son is cast with contempt over the "fence" of the vineyard.

Our conclusion is without reservations: the parable derives ultimately from Jesus himself. If there are any qualms about commencing to reflect on Jesus' understanding of himself found in this quasi-allegorical parable, they pertain to the use of the noun "son" in the story. If Mark added "beloved" to the account, is it not possible that he also added the noun "son"? The answer can be obtained by looking at the other early independent version of the story.

Here is the parable according to the extracanonical Gospel of Thomas:

He [Jesus] said: "A good man[102] had a vineyard. He leased[103] it to tenants so that they might cultivate it, and he might collect (his share of) its fruit from them. He sent his servant so that the tenants might give him (some of) the fruit of the vineyard. They seized his servant (and)[104] they beat him; a little longer and they would have killed him.[105] The servant departed; he[106] told it to his master. His master said: 'Perhaps he did not know them.'[107] He sent another servant; the tenants beat him as well. Then the master sent his son. He said: 'Perhaps they will respect my son.'[108] Since those tenants knew that he was the heir of the vineyard,[109] they seized him; they killed him.[110] He who has ears let him hear."[111]

The noun "son" could not have been added by Mark; it is also in a source independent of Mark.[112] Mark and the compiler of the Gospel of Thomas inherited the noun "son"; Mark then edited it to "beloved son." The noun "son," therefore, like other parts of this parable, derives authentically from Jesus. Now, although there are many questions raised by these two different versions of the parable of the wicked tenant farmers, we can attempt to discern what Jesus had in mind when he composed this parable.

Like the hymn of the Righteous Teacher, the parable is quasi-allegorical. We are not confronted with a simple story about an owner of a vineyard. The owner is surely God, and the vineyard is the well-known symbol for Israel and, more narrowly, Jerusalem, the Holy City of the nation Israel.[113] We saw that the Righteous Teacher had a fondness for the imagery of God planting the eternal planting, or everlasting garden. Previously the prophets had developed the image of the vineyard to symbolize Israel.[114] God had planted and cultivated the vineyard, Israel.

The parable is not a full-blown allegory. The fact that its main features refer to something else does not warrant a search for the meanings of less-essential features. The owner of the vineyard is God. He is called "Lord" (*kyrios*). The vineyard is Israel, even Jerusalem. The ones sent to the vineyard are the prophets and saints of old known from the Old Testament (Hebrew Bible). The fruits required are, of course, the acts of obedience to the Torah. This motif is well developed in the Dead Sea Scrolls, other texts of Early Judaism, and certainly also in much earlier documents.

We have seen that Jesus probably composed this parable. Along with the classical prophets, he referred to God as the owner and cultivator of the vineyard, Israel. He stressed the history of salvation, the suffering of the prophets and those sent[115] to Israel. His proclamations, and the implied exhortations in this parable, called Israel back from sin and to its covenant with God.

Most importantly, Jesus included himself in the review of the history of salvation. He emphasized that last of all God sent his son. What did Jesus intend by this dimension of the quasi allegory? Obviously such words reflect some self-understanding. How and in what ways was Jesus' self-understanding similar to and dissimilar to the Teacher's self-understanding?

A COMPARISON
OF TWO PRE-70 JEWS

Such questions will obviously extend beyond anyone's ability to answer them. My struggle to answer them is arranged under five observations. Three of these are impressively parallel to what we have already learned about the self-understanding of the Righteous Teacher. The last two disclose some significant differences.

At the outset it is helpful to recognize that the setting of the prayer or hymn by the Righteous Teacher reflects a very different time from that assumed by the parable. The Righteous Teacher saw himself as living in the desert removed from the Temple, because illegitimate priests were polluting the holy sanctuary. Unlike the Righteous Teacher, Jesus, living also in Palestine (but not in the desert), knew the pain of occupation by the Romans. The enemies were not fellow Jews; they were the conquering pagans. The land promised to Abraham and his descendants, including Jesus and all his earliest followers, was occupied. The farms were leased, and foreigners (including Herod and his retinue) benefited from the produce of the land. Well-known terms like "land" and "fruit" took on powerful religious, even revolutionary, significance.

Now we can proceed with an attempt to discern Jesus' self-understanding as preserved in the two versions of the parable of the wicked tenant farmers. First, like the Righteous Teacher, Jesus saw himself playing a major part in the economy of God's salvation of his world and people. The Righteous Teacher had a very strong ego and began his hymn with the use of the first person pronoun singular. He is very clear about who he is; the whole hymn is permeated with his celebration of his own role. He is obviously trying to explain and defend his own actual condition and exile from Jerusalem and the Temple cult, in which he had probably played a prominent role.

Comparing him with Jesus clarifies a significant aspect of Jesus' authentic words. He never uses the first person pronoun singular. The parable does move to the climax of the sending of the son, but the latter noun is used in an oblique and undeveloped fashion. Hence, both the Righteous Teacher and Jesus have strong egos and are convinced of their own place in God's schema for history and time, but the Righteous Teacher felt constrained to explain and defend his own status and role in this process.

Second, both the Righteous Teacher and Jesus affirm without any hesitation or qualification their own essential roles in the history of salvation. Jesus sees himself in line with the prophets of old, but he also links himself with the great martyrs. These two were already related by Jesus' time, as we know from the pseudepigraphon called the Lives of the Prophets, which is titled in some manuscripts, the Lives and Deaths of the Prophets.[116] Many of the prophets faced horrible deaths, according to this and other accounts. For example, Jeremiah, one of the prophets who significantly influenced Jesus, was stoned to death, according to the Lives of the Prophets and also 4 Baruch.

Both the Righteous Teacher and Jesus saw their places as firmly established in the history of salvation. Both saw their own lives in continuity with those of the great prophets; hence both probably had something like a prophetic consciousness. Jesus, however, added a significant new dimension: martyrdom.[117]

Third, it is highly significant that both the Righteous Teacher and Jesus shaped their thoughts from beginning to end with the expectation that they were living at the end of all normal time and history. The drama of salvation was almost at its end. The last one sent in both versions of the parable is none other than the "son." Mark's version even has these words: "He sent him to them last (of all, *eschaton*). . . ." There is a slight difference between the Righteous Teacher's looking forward to the growth of the "shoot," which is still in the future—but the very near future—and Jesus' prediction of the coming of the "son," which obviously commenced with his own life. Jesus' eschatology is slightly more "realizing" in this sense.[118]

We now turn to two areas where there is far more difference between the Righteous Teacher and Jesus. The differences already noted are subsumed under the recognition of some similarity.

Fourth, both Jewish teachers held, at least intermittently, to an imminent expectation. In a certain sense each was incorrect.[119] The Righteous Teacher did not participate in the establishment of the final and blessed community. He died long before his community was wiped out by Roman soldiers. His teachings were revered and programmatic for his followers until 68 C.E., when Titus and his troops destroyed Jewish groups in and around Jericho, before ascending to Jerusalem, where they broke through the city's walls and eventually burned the Temple.[120]

Jesus apparently thought he would be martyred. He was correct in that general sense, but he certainly did not think he would be crucified by the Romans. We have no way of knowing how he would have answered this question: What means would be used by the tenant farmers to kill the son? A vineyard is a place in which someone could be hanged, and the farmers may have had swords to behead or pierce someone. While these methods of killing the son are conceivable, it is most likely that the stones lying around in any Palestinian vineyard would be the means used to kill someone. There is reason to assume that Jesus feared he would be stoned by Jews, as Ḥoni, his near contemporary Galilean miracle worker had been, and as Jeremiah had been many centuries earlier.

As we know from Luke 13:31–33 Jesus had been warned early in his life, by Pharisees, that authorities—in this case Herod Antipas—were plotting to kill him. Jesus must have known that he was on a course of possible martyrdom, not only because of his firm conviction that he stood in the continuing history of the prophets but also because of the martyrdom of John the Baptizer, with whom he had early associated himself. Firmly rooted in authentic Jesus traditions, because it contains a false prediction that he would be stoned, is the following saying: "O Jerusalem Jerusalem, she who kills the prophets and stones those sent to her . . ." (Q = Lk 13:34; Mt 23:37).

It is also possible that the following saying[121] preserves an authentic recollection of Jesus' self-understanding: "I must continue my journey, for a prophet must not perish outside Jerusalem" (Lk 13:33).

In contrast to the Righteous Teacher, Jesus feared martyrdom; his expectation, but not that of the Righteous Teacher, came true.

Fifth—and most importantly—each of these two pre-70 Palestinian Jews had a clearly articulated source for his self-understanding. The Righteous Teacher saw meaning in his life because of his organic relation to one elect group, the "sons of light," whom he probably symbolized as the "trees of water." These trees, his own little group of Jews, were chosen by God to establish the shoot of the eternal community, the eschatological garden in which all God's promises would be fulfilled and enjoyed. The Righteous Teacher portrayed this dream as a reality.

Jesus never obtained such assurance or confidence from his group of followers. The disciples, according to our earliest sources, were confused; and some were failures. They never grasped the true meaning of Jesus' teachings. They constantly deserted him and finally left him to die alone.

Jesus' source of confidence and inspiration was only one: God, the Father. In this sense he thought of and referred to himself as the "son"; and so, according to Mark (followed by Mt and Lk), the connection is firmly made with the words of the owner—*kyrios,* "Lord." Of the last one sent to the vineyard, he is made to say: "They will respect my son." The possessive pronoun is powerfully symbolic. The son belongs to God and to him alone. We are left without further insight as to what Jesus might have meant by the reflexive use of the noun "son." Jesus' devotion to God, his obsession with him, and other authentic sayings that show how Jesus was possessed by God indicate the ways in which we should strive to grasp Jesus' self-understanding.

Our research leads to the conclusion that Jesus thought of himself as God's son. Within the Jewish theology that he inherited and in line with his own devotion to God, this term and title denoted a function that was to be performed with the will, power, and grace of God. We would be wise not to venture further with speculations about the precise meaning of sonship in the mind of Jesus. Certainly we must avoid jumping into the use of Greek concepts and vocabulary, as did the Greek fathers, and attempt to equate the substance of God with son.[122]

A more reliable method for understanding Jesus' perception of sonship begins with the Jewish reflections on the concept of the king as God's specially chosen one, his son, as we know especially from Psalm 2:

Let me tell of the decree:
the LORD said to me,
  "You are my son,
  I have fathered you this day."
            (Ps 2:7–8)[123]

A FINAL COMPARISON
OF THE TEACHER AND JESUS

Did Jesus and the Teacher possess a prophetic and eschatological charisma? A careful reading of a hymn in the Dead Sea Scrolls discloses the self-understanding of the Righteous Teacher who founded the Qumran community. A critical analysis of the parable of the wicked tenant farmers reveals the self-understanding of Jesus of Nazareth. In Weberian terms both of these Jews may be understood, in a certain sense at least, as pre-70 Palestinian charismatics who had formative self-knowledge of participating in the continuing history of the prophets and God's movement toward his own.

We have also observed major differences between the Teacher and Jesus. The Teacher left Jerusalem and the Temple, withdrawing to the safety of the desert. On the barren shores of the Dead Sea he felt empowered by God as the gardener of the eternal planting. He was influenced, most likely, by Ezekiel's allegory of the vine in the vineyard which is fruitful because of abundant waters and is then transplanted in a dry land (Ezek 19:10–14).

Jesus went boldly into the heart of the opposition against him. In the assurance that he was God's son, he set his way toward Jerusalem and the Temple. Probably, from years of observing the political climate and the gathering storm that often flashed around him and would wipe away the nation Israel, he thought he was destined to die in the vicinity of Jerusalem. When he composed his parable of the wicked tenant farmers he was also influenced by the great prophets. He probably was influenced by Isaiah's allegory of the vineyard which the Lord dug, planted, and for which he built a watchtower and hewed out a wine vat (Isa 5:1–2). Most likely Jesus had memorized this passage and the following verse (Isa 5:7):

For the vineyard of the LORD of Hosts
Is the House of Israel,

And the seedlings he lovingly tended
Are the men of Judah.
And He hoped for justice,
But behold, injustice;
For equity,
But behold, iniquity![124]

The Dead Sea Scrolls have provided data that help in the search for understanding Jesus' self-understanding.[125]

The dreams of one charismatic were lost until an Arab shepherd boy found scrolls in a Judean cave in 1947. The dreams of the other were preserved and shaped the destiny of Western culture.

Notes

1. Y. Yadin, *The Temple Scroll: The Hidden Law of the Dead Sea Sect* (London, 1985) p. 228.

2. J. Carmignac, *Christ and the Teacher of Righteousness: The Evidence of the Dead Sea Scrolls* (Baltimore, 1962); idem, *Les textes de Qumrân traduits et annotés*, 2 vols. (Paris, 1961, 1963) vol. 1, pp. 129–280. Carmignac concluded that 1QS, 1QSa, 1QSb, 1QH, and 1QM were all composed by the Righteous Teacher. See Carmignac, *Textes*, vol. 2, p. 32. L. H. Schiffman rightly points out that these cannot all have been written by the same person. See Schiffman, *The Eschatological Community of the Dead Sea Scrolls: A Study of the Rule of the Congregation* (SBLMS 38; Atlanta, 1989) p. 74. G. Jeremias, *Der Lehrer der Gerechtigkeit* (SUNT 2; Göttingen, 1963). E. Qimron and J. Strugnell, "An Unpublished Halakhic Letter from Qumran," *The Israel Museum Journal* 4 (1985) 9–12. Qimron and Strugnell, "An Unpublished Halakhic Letter from Qumran," in *Biblical Archaeology Today: Proceedings of the International Congress on Biblical Archaeology* (Jerusalem, April 1984), ed. J. Amitai (Jerusalem, 1985) pp. 400–7. P. Schultz, *Der Autoritätsanspruch des Lehrers der Gerechtigkeit in Qumran* (Meisenheim am Glan, 1974). E. L. Sukenik, *The Dead Sea Scrolls of the Hebrew University* (Jerusalem, 1955 [in Hebrew]) p. 39. Yadin, *The Temple Scroll: The Hidden Law*, p. 87 and esp. p. 228. B. Z. Wacholder presents a maverick opinion: the Temple Scroll (11QTemple), the longest of the Dead Sea Scrolls, is the "precursor of other Qumranic literature." It was composed around 200 B.C.E. by Zadok of CD 4.1 and 5.5 and he is none other than the Righteous Teacher, who sought superiority over Moses. Wacholder, *The*

Dawn of Qumran: The Sectarian Torah and the Teacher of Righteousness (Cincinnati, 1983) esp. pp. 226–29; quotation from p. 203. See also works by A. Dupont-Sommer listed in the following notes.

3. Sukenik, *Dead Sea Scrolls;* G. Vermes, *The Dead Sea Scrolls: Qumran in Perspective* (Cleveland, 1978) p. 145.

4. J. T. Milik, *Ten Years of Discovery in the Wilderness of Judaea,* trans. J. Strugnell (SBT 26; London, 1959) p. 40; H. Ringgren, *The Faith of Qumran: Theology of the Dead Sea Scrolls,* trans. E. T. Sander (Philadelphia, 1963) p. 16. See also J. Daniélou, "The Grandeur and Limits of the Teacher of Righteousness," *The Dead Sea Scrolls and Primitive Christianity,* trans. S. Attanasio (Baltimore, 1963) pp. 80–85.

5. Dupont-Sommer argued that "he unquestionably presents himself in several of the canticles as the leader of the sect of the Covenant: he is the Teacher who teaches, the Father who cares for his children and feeds them, the Source of living waters, the Builder of the Community of the Elect, the Gardener of the eternal Planting. How is it possible to avoid concluding that such a person must be the Teacher of Righteousness himself. . . ." Dupont-Sommer, *The Essene Writings from Qumran,* trans. G. Vermes (Oxford, 1961) p. 200.

6. For a discussion of research prior to 1962, see G. Jeremias, "Das Selbstzeugnis des Lehrers der Gerechtigkeit," *Der Lehrer der Gerechtigkeit,* pp. 167–69.

7. H. Stegemann, *Die Entstehung der Qumrangemeinde* (Bonn, 1971); H.-W. Kuhn, *Enderwartung und gegenwärtiges Heil: Untersuchungen zu den Gemeindeliedern von Qumran* (SUNT 4; Göttingen, 1966); P. von der Osten-Sacken, *Gott und Belial: Traditionsgeschichtliche Untersuchungen zum Dualismus in den Texten aus Qumran* (SUNT 6; Göttingen, 1969); J. Murphy-O'Connor, "The Essenes and Their History," *RB* 81 (1974) 217; P. R. Davies, "Qumran under the Teacher: Period Ia," in *Qumran* (Grand Rapids, 1982) pp. 82–92; J. J. Collins, "The Origin of the Qumran Community: A Review of the Evidence," in *To Touch the Text: Biblical and Related Studies in Honor of Joseph A. Fitzmyer, S.J.,* ed. M. P. Horgan and P. J. Kobelski (New York, 1989) p. 177. Vermes finds this approach to 1QH too conjectural. Vermes, "The Essenes and History," *JJS* 32 (1981) 27. H. Burgmann, *Die Geschichte der Essener von Qumran und "Damaskus"* (QM 5; Krakow, 1990) p. 25.

A distinction needs to be made between trying to recreate the history of the Qumran community on the basis of 1QH and seeking to discern the personal experiences of the Righteous Teacher preserved in his own compositions (the "Lehrerlieder," specifically 1QH 2.1–19; 2.31–39; 3.1–18; 4.5–5.4; 5.5–19, 20–7.5; 7.6–25; 8.4–40). These "Lehrerlieder" were identified and defended by Jeremias in *Der Lehrer der Gerechtigkeit.* See the review of the discussion by P. R. Callaway in "The Personal Experiences of the Teacher: The *Lehrerlieder,*" *The History of the Qumran Community: An Investigation* (JSPS 3; Sheffield, 1988) pp. 185–90. We are presently focusing on 8.4–40 and the self-understanding embedded in these lines.

8. R. Bultmann, *Jesus* (Berlin, 1926; Eng. trans. 1934); idem, *Die Geschichte der*

synoptischen Tradition (Göttingen, 1921; Eng. trans. 1964); *Theologie des Neuen Testaments,* 2 vols. (Tübingen, 1948, 1951; Eng. trans. 1951, 1955). Only the first editions are cited. Obviously, the chasm appeared in the early fifties with the famous lecture among the Bultmannians by E. Käsemann. See Käsemann, "The Problem of the Historical Jesus," *Essays on New Testament Themes* (SBT 41; London, Nashville, 1964) pp. 15–47 [the German dates from 1953]; idem, "Blind Alleys in the 'Jesus of History' Controversy," *New Testament Questions of Today,* trans. W. J. Montague (London, Philadelphia, 1969) pp. 23–65 [the German appeared in 1965]. In the latter publication, Käsemann clarified the purpose of his essay "The Problem of the Historical Jesus": "The purpose of my essay on the historical Jesus was to re-animate the discussion among the circle of Bultmann's pupils and to produce, so far as possible, a certain self-criticism on the part of the master, whose historical skepticism at this point seems to me to be exaggerated and the theological outcome of this skepticism dangerous" (p. 35). I concur fully with Käsemann.

9. Chrys C. Caragounis, *The Son of Man: Vision and Interpretation* (WUNT 38; Tübingen, 1986) p. 242.

10. This point was made long ago by J. C. O'Neill in his "The Silence of Jesus," *NTS* 15 (1969) 153–67. O'Neill suggested that Jesus' silence is conceivably part of an implicit "christology."

11. According to Matthew 16, Jesus accepts the confession and blesses Peter.

12. For bibliographical data, see chapter 1 above, n. 112.

13. E. P. Sanders, *Jesus and Judaism* (Philadelphia, 1985) p. 326.

14. H. Boers, *Who was Jesus? The Historical Jesus and the Synoptic Gospels* (New York, 1989).

15. M. Hengel, *The Charismatic Leader and His Followers,* trans. J. C. G. Greig (Edinburgh, 1981) p. 87.

16. R. Leivestad, "Jesus–Messias–Menschensohn: Die jüdischen Heilands-erwartungen zur Zeit der ersten römischen Kaiser und die Frage nach dem mes-sianischen Selbstbewusstsein Jesu," *ANRW* 11.25.1 (1982) 220–64.

17. This statement is supported by many studies of Jesus' parables.

18. For text and discussion, see J. H. Charlesworth, "Jesus' Concept of God and His Self-Understanding," *Jesus Within Judaism: New Light from Exciting Archae-ological Discoveries* (ABRL 1; New York, 1988) pp. 131–64.

19. M. J. Borg, *Jesus: A New Vision: Spirit, Culture, and the Life of Discipleship* (New York, London, 1987) p. 50. D. Flusser, *Judaism and the Origins of Christianity* (Jerusalem, 1988) pp. 263, 293, 619, 622–23. Flusser's work reveals "Jesus' keen self awareness of his sonship and his close feeling of kinship to his Father" (p. 293). J. D. G. Dunn, *The Evidence for Jesus* (Philadelphia, 1985) pp. 47–50.

20. The exact dates of Hillel are uncertain. P. Rieger dates his time as head ("President") of the Sanhedrin between c. 20 B.C.E. to at least 20 C.E. He then con-cluded that Jesus was most probably a pupil of Hillel. Rieger, *Hillel und Jesus* (Hamburg, 1904) pp. 7, 8, 11. W. P. Rusterholtz contends that Hillel and Jesus "could

have met and held dialogue in the Temple in Jerusalem when Jesus tarried there at the age of twelve. . . ." Rusterholtz, "Hillel and Godson," *Religious Humanism* 20 (1986) 2–7; quotation from p. 2. D. Flusser is convinced that Hillel died before Jesus was born. Flusser, "Hillel's Self-awareness and Jesus," *Immanuel* 4 (1974) 31–36 (reprinted in *Judaism and the Origins of Christianity,* pp. 509–11). Fruitful are the reflections of J. Neusner that some of Jesus' sayings take on meaning only when one studies the debates between Shammaites and Hillelites before 70; see his " 'First Cleanse the Inside,'" *NTS* 22 (1976) 487–95. While the exact dates of Hillel are unknown it is conceivable that he and Jesus were alive at the same time; that does not permit assuming that Jesus conversed with, let alone studied under, Hillel. See the problems in discerning the historicity of Hillel enunciated by Neusner in *The Rabbinic Traditions About the Pharisees Before 70* (2 vols.; Leiden, 1971) part I, pp. 212–302.

21. N. N. Glatzer compared the traditions about Hillel with the Dead Sea Scrolls and came to the conclusion that he may have had some "personal contact" with an Essene and that some of his teachings were directed against the Essenes. Glatzer, "Hillel the Elder in the Light of the Dead Sea Scrolls," in *The Scrolls and the New Testament,* ed. K. Stendahl (New York, 1957) pp. 232–44.

22. See the discussion of the possible relation between Jesus and the Essenes, chapter 1 in this book.

23. For a general review of the history of the Qumran covenanters, see H. H. Rowley, "The History of the Qumran Sect," *BJRL* 49 (1966–67) 203–32; F. M. Cross, "The Early History of the Qumran Community," in *New Directions in Biblical Archaeology,* ed. D. N. Freedman and J. C. Greenfield (Garden City, N.Y., 1969) pp. 3–79; Vermes, "The Essenes and History," *JJS* 32 (1981) 18–31; Murphy-O'Connor, "The Essenes and Their History," *RB* 81 (1974) 215–44; J. H. Charlesworth, "The Origin and Subsequent History of the Authors of the Dead Sea Scrolls: Four Transitional Phases Among the Qumran Essenes," *RQ* 10 (1979–80) 213–33; M. Kister, "Concerning the History of the Sect of the Essenes: Studies on the Animal Apocalypse, Book of Jubilees, and Damascus Covenant" (in Hebrew) *Tarbiz* 56 (1986–87) 1–18; Callaway, *History of the Qumran Community;* Collins, "Origin of the Qumran Community," in *To Touch the Text,* eds. Horgan and Kobelski, pp. 159–78. Also see the pertinent sections of chapter 1 in the present book and the further bibliographical information offered there.

24. H. Stegemann, *Die Entstehung der Qumrangemeinde.*

25. For a sociological study of the early postexilic rivalries among the various priestly groups, see P. Hanson, *The Dawn of Apocalyptic* (Philadelphia, 1975).

26. R. de Vaux, *Archaeology and the Dead Sea Scrolls,* trans. D. Bourke (London, 1973); idem, "Archéologie," DJD 3 (1962) 1–36.

27. Literally, "pursued after."

28. Or, "to confound, confuse"; literally, "to swallow down."

29. The solar calendar was advocated by the groups behind 1 Enoch, Jubilees,

and the Dead Sea Scrolls. The lunar calendar was followed by the establishment in Jerusalem, as we know from the polemics against it in 1 Enoch, many of the Dead Sea Scrolls, and the references in Josephus.

30. See chapter 11 below.

31. Especially petition number 2, which concludes "Blessed are you, O Lord, who resurrects the dead."

32. See the discussion in chapter 1 above.

33. See chapter 11 below.

34. See n. 2 above.

35. See n. 2 above, concerning B. Z. Wacholder.

36. G. Jeremias, *Der Lehrer der Gerechtigkeit,* esp. pp. 249–64.

37. For a philological examination, see J. H. Charlesworth, "An Allegorical and Autobiographical Poem by the *Moreh Haṣ-Ṣedeq* (1QH 8:4–11)," in *Shaʿarei Talmon: Studies in the Bible, Qumran, and the Ancient Near East Presented to Shemaryahu Talmon,* ed. M. Fishbane, E. Tov, with W. W. Fields (in press).

38. Along with most critics I have restored the Hodayoth formula which often begins a hymn.

39. This beth is an example of the *beth essentiae;* see J. H. Charlesworth, "The *Beth Essentiae* and the Permissive Meaning of the Hiphil (Aphel)," in *Of Scribes and Scrolls: Studies on the Hebrew Bible, Intertestamental Judaism, and Christian Origins Presented to John Strugnell on the Occasion of His Sixtieth Birthday,* ed. H. W. Attridge, J. J. Collins, and T. H. Tobin (New York, London, 1990) pp. 67–78.

40. The author, the Righteous Teacher, as G. Jeremias and many others have shown, is meditating on his exile in the desert of Judea. There is no spring or fountain at or near Qumran. The use of water, especially "living water," is highly metaphorical and symbolic of salvific water. This meaning of "living water" is not found in Biblical Hebrew; in the Tanach this term refers to running water.

41. The implication seems clear: the Righteous Teacher portrays, and thinks of himself, as the (source of) water for the trees of life (his followers).

42. Read *wmšqy.* The *waw* and the curved right vertical stroke of the *mem* can be discerned. Literally, "the waterer of" (Hiph. part. cst. sing. of *šqy, šqh*) or "cupbearer of" (noun cst. sing.) the garden; the noun obtains the meaning "irrigation" in latter rabbinics. Sometimes in Qumran Hebrew *yodh* appears in final position for the singular construct state of participles of *Lamedh Yodh* verbs. See Qimron, *The Hebrew of the Dead Sea Scrolls* (HSS 29; Atlanta, 1986) p. 20. Unfortunately, many translators and commentators have misunderstood the meaning of this participle and have therefore missed the autobiographical dimensions of the hymn.

The reading and meaning of *wmšqy* are confirmed by the Gozan inscription (from Tell Fakhariyeh in northern Syria). The date of the inscription is debated (no later than the ninth–eighth century B.C.E.) but it certainly antedates the composition of 1QH in the second century B.C.E. Here is the pertinent Aramaic passage:

*wntn: rʿy * wmšqy: lmt: kln:* (lines 2-3), which means "and the one who gives pasture and who waters (or irrigates) all of the lands." The text is correctly published by S. A. Kaufman in "The Tell Fakhariyeh Inscription," *Maarav* 3 (1982) 137-75, esp. p. 159. The Aramaic text can also be found in J. C. Greenfield and A. Shaffer, "Notes on the Akkadian-Aramaic Bilingual Statue from Tell Fekherye," *Iraq* 45 (1983) 109-16, esp. p. 112. For additional bibliographical data and discussion, see K. Beyer, *Die aramäischen Texte vom Toten Meer* (Göttingen, 1984) p. 26; and J. Huehnergard's book review of the *editio princeps* by A. Abou-Assaf, P. Bordreuil and A. R. Millard in *BASOR* 261 (1986) 91-95. While the inscription is discussed extensively, the meaning of the lines cited is well established.

43. The image of the garden of Eden and of paradise seems to be behind the thought here. Asterisks denote the beginning of a new line.

44. Either the author later develops the concept of the *yaḥad*, "the community," from such seminal reflections and experiences, or he is alluding to this meaning here. The first interpretation seems preferable because of the early date probably to be assigned to this hymn.

45. Literally, "those who keep themselves hidden" (Pual).

46. Note the clear evidence of Qumranic dualism. Here the terms are "the trees of life" (the sons of light) and "the trees of the water" (the sons of darkness). The imagery causes some confusion, and it is not evident why "the trees of the water" should be pejorative. "The trees of life" have access to the water source, and "water" has a very positive salvific meaning in the Qumran Scrolls. Psalm 1:3 lauds the righteous, who are like "a tree planted by streams of water." It is probable that Ezekiel 31 and the allegory of the cedar shaped the imagery. Note in particular this passage: "All this is in order that no trees by the waters may grow to lofty height or set their tops among the clouds, and that no trees that drink water may reach up to them in height; for they are all given over to death, to the nether world among mortal men, with those who go down to the Pit" (Ezek 31:14; RSV).

47. The "mysterious water source" is the Righteous Teacher. This identification is clarified by line 11, in which he refers to "his mystery" not being perceived.

48. As is well known, the word *nṣr* became a highly symbolical term referring to the coming shoot of David who will bring in the promises of God on this earth. This traditional meaning must not be transported into these verses without careful examination of the precise context of this column.

49. Read *wgzʿw* as in 8.8 for *gyzʿw*.

50. Restoration is accepted from J. Licht, *Hodayot Scroll* (Jerusalem, 1957 [in Hebrew]).

51. The technical term *drk*, like *yḥd*, is probably in an early stage of development. It is probable that after the time of the Righteous Teacher this phrase was understood to mean the following: "all transgressors of the Way." For a discussion of "Way" as a self-designation by the Qumran covenanters, see chapter 1 above.

52.   The meaning seems to be that the branches shall be destroyed or impaired by the birds.

53.   Restoration inherited from Licht, *Hodayot Scroll.*

54.   The form is the Hithpoel. The *taw* has assimilated and caused a compensatory lengthening of the vowel.

55.   The implication is that like the sons of darkness, according to 1QS 4, the evil trees will have no hope for survival.

56.   This person is to be identified with the Righteous Teacher. See line 4, in which he sees himself as the "i[rri]gator" of the garden, and the use of the Hiphil in both verbal forms.

57.   This final passage refers to the Righteous Teacher, who was the legitimate heir to the high priesthood in the Jerusalem Temple, but was not honored. He was banished from the Temple, along with his followers, because the mystery revealed to him by God (see 1QpHab 7) was unperceived, except by those loyal to him. The "trees of the water" are the "wicked" priests in Jerusalem; the "trees of life" are his followers, who are "living" because they have the source of life. Many of these thoughts are important background and foreground for the theology developed by the author and redactors of the Gospel of John.

58.   Details must not be pushed to create a full allegory. That would distort the subtlety of the story and pull it out of its historical context, in which authors appreciated the ambiguity of partial allegories.

59.   The conciliatory tone of these lines recalls the tone of 4QMMT. An early date in the history of the Qumran group, perhaps its earliest phase in the desert, is thereby demanded for this hymn. The probability increases that this hymn was composed by the Righteous Teacher; but certainty, of course, is impossible.

60.   The term denotes the early rain that near the end of October breaks the long drought. This rain was seen as an indication of God's love and continuing covenant loyalty. It caused (and still causes today in Jerusalem) rejoicing. Cf. Deut 11:14 and Joel 2:23.

61.   See n. 42 above. I wish to express my appreciation to Loren Stuckenbruck for discussing this important text with me.

62.   Kaufman, "The Tell Fakhariyeh Inscription," *Maarav* 3 (1982) 161. In order not to confuse the readers of the present book, I have not represented the diacriticals.

63.   The Gozan inscription is in Aramaic and Assyrian; it may date from the ninth century B.C.E. Babylonian influence on Qumran theology has been widely recognized.

64.   In some texts the righteous do not eat from the trees in paradise; they are those who are planted in paradise. See especially the Psalms of Solomon and the Odes of Solomon.

65.   My suggestion is not new; it was tendered long ago by Dupont-Sommer; see the popular English edition of his work, *Essene Writings,* p. 228.

66. The Hebrew *mwrh ṣdq* appears, e.g., in CD 1.11; *ywrh hṣdq* is found in CD 6.11. The latter passage has been the center of scholarly debates (see the judicious comments and bibliography cited by J. Carmignac in *Les textes de Qumrân traduits et annotés* [Paris, 1961, 1963] vol. 2, p. 167). On the one hand, Dupont-Sommer (*Essene Writings*, p. 131) was incorrect to claim that CD 6.11 revealed a belief in the return of the Righteous Teacher at "the end of days"; on the other hand, it is obvious that there is a conceptual link between "the Righteous Teacher" and "he who will teach righteousness at the end of days."

67. It is tempting to connect this line (8.8) with the persecution of the Righteous Teacher on the Day of Atonement. This possibility may be more romantic than grounded in exegesis.

68. See the insights and references provided by G. von Rad in *Genesis*, trans. J. H. Marks (Philadelphia, 1961) pp. 75–77.

69. See the discussion by N. M. Sarna in *Understanding Genesis: The Heritage of Biblical Israel* (New York, 1970) pp. 23–28.

70. The threefold agents of salvation—God, the Righteous Teacher, and his followers—are strikingly parallel to John 17 in which God is he who sends, Jesus is he who was sent, and the disciples are they who are sent. As at Qumran, the theme is that they may be one.

71. This means that, despite the initial confusion experienced by Mary Magdalene or Cleopas, the person they eventually recognized was none other than Jesus of Nazareth; only now he was a resurrected person. The earliest Christian writers wisely refused to define the essence of Jesus' resurrected body; it was ontologically similar to but not identical with the crucified one. They refused to explain what they themselves were incapable of comprehending. There is a caveat here for those who attempt to explain too much and exceed the attractive ambiguity of the original documents.

72. For further comments see my "The Foreground of Christian Origins and the Commencement of Jesus Research," and "Jesus, Early Jewish Literature, and Archaeology" in *Jesus' Jewishness: Exploring the Place of Jesus within Judaism*, ed. J. H. Charlesworth (New York, 1991) and "Jesus Research: A Paradigm Shift for New Testament Scholars," *ABR* 38 (1990) 18–32.

73. The Gospel of John reflects Jesus' followers efforts to proclaim him.

74. Sanders in *Jesus and Judaism* contends that he was indicating the imminent destruction of the Temple.

75. The "crowd" is the most dangerous and unstable of social institutions. It has no history and no clear leader. Roman governors learned how to manipulate the crowds (mobs, multitudes) to extract the judgment desired. The governors were in turn frequently ruled and overruled by crowds. As of the present no New Testament scholar has appreciated how paradigmatically significant for the reconstruction of the history of, and for the appreciation of the social dynamics within, Jesus' world are the sociological studies of "crowds." Such study has been known in

sociology for nearly a century. See G. Le Bon, *The Crowd: A Study of the Popular Mind* (London, 1896); E. Canetti, *Crowds and Power,* trans. C. Stewart (New York, 1978).

76. See the discussion in chapter 1 above.

77. The compiler of the Gospel of Thomas did not inherit this parable from Mark or from another of the canonical evangelists, because in Thomas the parable has none of the expansions (redactions) of Mark. Initially it is conceivable that the parable may also have been in a source (other than Mark) known to Matthew and Luke (whether Q or any source), but the only verse in which they agree together against Mark is Matthew 21:38 = Luke 20:14; and these few words can be attributed to numerous causes, for example, the restrictions of the story itself and the need to clarify the narrative.

Luke is clearly dependent on Mark's account of the parable of the wicked tenant farmers. He inherits Mark's redaction: Mark's "beloved son" is found in Luke 20:13, and the Marcan ending (Mk 12:9) is repeated in Luke 20:16. Matthew is obviously dependent on Mark, because he repeats much of Mark 12:10 and 11. Matthew's redactions are clear (Mt 21:41, 43 [in 44 he and Luke may be using another common source]); but what looms as very interesting, in light of the Gospel of Thomas, is the absence of "beloved" son in Matthew.

78. Notable in the Enochian Animal Apocalypse and in 4 Ezra.

79. Stephen's speech is obviously an exception; his long review of the history of salvation is atypical of the *kerygmata* and similar to the Jewish apocalypses. Romans 9–11 is perhaps another exception, as are portions of the Epistle to the Hebrews. All these references indicate that the suggestion should not be pushed.

80. This point, of course, does not mean that Mark or someone prior to him could not have composed it.

81. The principle of dissimilarity—that is, only what cannot be attributed to the Jewishness of Jesus' time—is misleading. It would be absurd to use this criterion to seek to discern Hillel's authentic teachings. It ignores the fact that Jesus was a devout Jew and devoted to the uniqueness of Judaism (far more than Philo or Josephus, which may come as a shock to some readers). It assumes that Jewish sayings known to be those of others and anonymous wisdom sayings were illegitimately attributed to Jesus. This transference could have happened in terms of logic, which is supported by some examples (which are exceptions to a rule); but sociological research has shown that Jesus' sayings were transferred in a Jewish setting that was hostile (polemical) to his followers. They could not survive by ignoring such facts as Peter's denial and Jesus' crucifixion; nor could they clandestinely attribute sayings to Jesus that could possibly be falsified. To be vulnerable to such disproofs would render their incredible claims (that the crucified one had been resurrected) laughable in synagogue and marketplace.

82. Herod the Great spent lavishly, building cities and temples in and out of Palestine (Josephus, *Ant* 15.329), using expensive marble (*Ant* 15.331). He expanded

the Temple (refurbishing it so that it had no rival in the world) and endowed and increased the grandeur of the famous Olympic games (and was then elected "perpetual president of the games"; *Ant* 16.149). To cover such astronomical costs, the Cyprus copper mines given to him by Caesar were not sufficient (*Ant* 16.128), so he brazenly entered David's tomb in search of wealth (even opening the coffins of David and Solomon; *Ant* 16.181). Herod was forced to tax the Palestinians beyond their abilities to pay, eventually in many cases seizing others' wealth for himself and reducing many Jewish landlords to tenant farmers (*Ant* 17.304–9). Property (*chrēma* and *ousia* are the Greek words employed) was seized; in addition to the taxes, "tribute" was imposed "on everyone each year," and these entailed "lavish extra contributions" (*Ant* 16.308).

83. I am convinced that this sweeping generalization still holds, especially for rural Galilee, despite the recent archaeological discoveries that seem to indicate that Galilee was not devastated by the Romans. Surely the portrayal of Galilee as if it were Georgia after Sherman's march to the sea was never attempted by leading scholars.

84. Of course, it is conceivable that some unknown Palestinian Jew created this parable sometime between 30 and 70; but what is conceivable may be far from what is actual. It should not be forgotten that the form is parabolic, and from 26 to 100 the only one within the Jesus Movement who is known to have composed parables was Jesus himself. Sometimes to his followers they were not appropriate but confusing (see Mk 4).

85. M. Avi-Yonah rightly points out that the belief in the dawning of the messianic age is related to the feeling that, unlike their forefathers, the nation "felt like Job; it was being unjustly persecuted." Avi-Yonah, *The Jews Under Roman and Byzantine Rule* (Jerusalem, 1984) p. 8. He attributes this perspective to the time of Herod the Great; it also applies to the time of the evangelists, when some Jews felt that the calamities of 70 could not be attributed to sins (contrast 4 Ezra and esp. 2 Bar); thus, the Jewish Sibyllines portray a quite different picture: the destruction of Pompeii was divine retribution for Roman destruction of Jerusalem. In addition to other major studies of Palestine from 26 to 70, see D. R. Schwartz, *Agrippa I* (Jerusalem, 1987 [in Hebrew]).

86. Within a decade after Jesus' public ministry, the Jesus Movement had spread from Palestine to the west and from rural to urban centers. See W. A. Meeks, *The First Urban Christians: The Social World of the Apostle Paul* (New Haven, London, 1984). Understanding this shift and incorporating it into our attempt to reconstruct the history of the Jesus Movement considerably improve our ability to employ the customary criteria for discerning authentic Jesus traditions.

87. See S. Freyne, *Galilee, Jesus, and the Gospels: Literary Approaches and Historical Investigations* (Philadelphia, 1988) esp. pp. 94–96.

88. See J. H. Charlesworth's articles on "Honi" and "Hanina ben Dosa" in the *Anchor Bible Dictionary.*

89. Hence, it cannot be derived from Mark.

90. Even more so than many of the alleged Q traditions preserved by Matthew and Luke.

91. The tradition is old, real, and symbolic. Vineyards or gardens (recall 1QH 8) were protected by stone or mud-brick walls, or hedges.

92. Literally "and," which can mean "then."

93. Another redundant "and," perhaps indicating the Aramaic *waw* copulative. In Aramaic there are few copulatives; in Greek there are many.

94. Literally "and"; see the preceding notes.

95. The redundant personal pronouns are typical of Aramaic and not Koine Greek.

96. The noun refers back to the owner of the vineyard, namely, God. This word, which means "lord," better reflects Jesus' concept of the lordship of God, the Father, than the evangelists' theology. For Jesus' followers he was "the Lord" (see especially the expansion to the old creedal formula quoted by Paul in Rom 1:4).

97. I am convinced that the parable originally ended here with the question. The evangelist Mark was dissatisfied and added the reference to the impending doom of Jerusalem, a reference that is possible at least as early as 66 (as we know from Josephus's reports of others and his lamentably futile attempts to quell the heat of the rebellion that destroyed Jerusalem. See the forthcoming article by C. Evans, "Predictions of the Destruction of the Herodian Temple in the Pseudepigrapha, Qumran, and Related Texts," *JSP* (in press).

98. See the notes to the translation.

99. Jesus' parable probably ended with a question: "What will the owner of the vineyard do?" The parable of the Good Samaritan, for example, ends with a question. Mark 12:9b–12 are not authentic to Jesus' parable; they were added in the post-Easter community to clarify the appropriate answer.

100. Contrast the editorial expansion by Paul of the old account of the Last Supper; Paul added the last verse of 1 Corinthians 11:23–26. The tradition stressed the celebration of Jesus' life ("in remembrance of me"; cf. vv. 24 and 25); because he was mesmerized by the death of Jesus and struggled with the meaning of the cross, Paul added: "For as often as you eat this bread and drink this cup, the death of the Lord [note the title] you proclaim, until he comes [note the eschatological expectation]." What is impressive is the reserve Mark has shown in recording this parable.

101. The redundancies with the previous section of the chapter are intentional. For decades there has been a mood among New Testament specialists that the burden of proof is upon any who would dare attempt to show that any saying of Jesus is authentic. It is a cliché that we have not one authentic word of Jesus. I find this position uninformed, insensitive to the tendencies in the Gospels (which point not only to the creative energies of the evangelists but also to their reverence for tradition), and oblivious to the personal element in all scientific and historical

research (here I am dependent on Polanyi and Merleau-Ponty).

102. The expansion here in the Gospel of Thomas is noticeable. Mark's "a man" has become "a good man"; such coloring reflects the retelling of the story.

103. Literally, "gave"; does the simple verb reflect Jesus' choice of simple speech? The colorless verb seems to reflect oral speech; a writer might have refined his work.

104. The lack of connectives in the Gospel of Thomas reflects the paucity of connectives in Semitic languages.

105. The style is cryptic, as is often the case in ancient writings.

106. Again, note the lack of a connective.

107. This statement is absurd if it is attributed to the early church. It is full of meaning if we acknowledge Jesus' fondness of irony, rhetoric, and especially humor. Surely an attentive listener would have at least chuckled. The study of Jesus' humor is the subject of another book, and I will not go further into this obvious dimension of Jesus' speech.

108. What kind of a father would be so reckless, after servants had been killed, to send his only son into such a hostile situation? The intent is problematic when attributed to the church; it is understandable in terms of Jesus' love of irony, his conception of mission, and his willingness to continue suffering and perhaps be martyred.

109. As in Mark, the tenant farmers knew the identity of this person now sent to them. They knew the son was the intended heir. Their intent to kill him fits better into the life of Jesus, who was warned about the threats against his life—and the warning came from Pharisees, no less—than into the life of the church, which was becoming divorced from Judaism. An anti-Jewish bias should not be read into this parable.

110. As with the Marcan version, the account here is devoid of details. Are we to think that the son was stoned inside the vineyard? If so, there can be no doubt that this parable derives only from Jesus, who considered that he might be stoned (as was Honi).

111. It is conceivable that the parable ended here and that only the Gospel of Thomas preserves the original ending. The comments appended to the ending of Mark's version indicate that we can work only on what has been left by an editor. The importance of the Gospel of Thomas is clear; we have an indication of what Mark may have omitted.

112. The Coptic word used for "son" in the Gospel of Thomas is *shere*, which is often used to translate *huios*, the Greek noun for "son."

113. See Isaiah 5:1–7, esp. v. 7: "For the vineyard of the Lord of hosts is the house of Israel. . . ."

114. Isaiah 5; Hosea 10; Jeremiah 2; and Ezekiel 19. These passages are linked by an allegorical poem that employs the image of the vineyard.

115.   This aspect is especially emphasized in the version found in the Gospel of Thomas.

116.   For introduction and translation, see *OTP* vol. 2, pp. 379–99.

117.   See also chapter 10 below, "Crucifixion: Archaeology, Jesus, and the Dead Sea Scrolls."

118.   Again, it is imperative not to exaggerate the difference between Jesus' eschatology and the Righteous Teacher's eschatology. See Kuhn, *Enderwartung und gegenwärtiges Heil.* F. Thielman adds to the widely accepted consensus that at Qumran God's purification of his people "has been at least partially realized." Thielman, *From Plight to Solution: A Jewish Framework for Understanding Paul's View of the Law in Galatians and Romans* (SuppNT 61; Leiden, 1989) p. 37.

119.   At a conference at Florida Southern College, M. Borg and R. Horsley argued that Mark 9:1 may not refer to an imminent expectation. Borg considered the passage a product of the church. I am convinced that it derives ultimately from Jesus, although some reworking by Mark is possible. Here is the verse: "Truly, I say to you, there are some standing here who will not taste death until they see that God's rule has come dynamically." Obviously God's rule (the kingdom of God) did not arrive with power in the manner understood—that is, apocalyptically. Accordingly, Matthew and Luke were forced to recast Jesus' saying in significant ways.

120.   According to Josephus, Titus lost control of his troops and the Temple was unintentionally burned. This aspect of Josephus' account seems true to fact, since great treasures were lost to everyone, and Josephus wrote this unflattering account in Rome, under the patronage of the Flavian dynasty (of which Titus was the middle member). Although he lauded Titus throughout his *War* (especially in reconstructing Titus' famous speech and the manner in which he describes how Titus took Gamla in contrast to his father, Vespasian), it is impressive that Josephus depicted this pinnacle moment in the capture of the Temple in a way that makes Titus look incompetent. Josephus wrote the *Jewish War* around 79 C.E., the year Titus became emperor. See M. Stern, "The Date of Composition of *Bellum Judaicum,*" *Proceedings of the Sixth World Congress of Jewish Studies,* ed. A. Shinan (Jerusalem, 1977 [in Hebrew]) vol. 2.

121.   It is preserved only in Luke and is therefore suspect.

122.   One of the most gifted Roman Catholic New Testament experts, J. P. Meier, rightly points out that the parable of the wicked tenant farmers probably preserves authentic Jesus tradition, and he stresses the proper interpretation that "if Jesus did use 'Son' of himself, it must be understood in a functional, salvation-historical sense and not in the ontological sense hammered out in later patristic controversy." Meier, "Jesus," *NJBC,* pp. 1316–28; quotation from p. 1324. See also Meier, "Reflections on Jesus-of-History Research Today," in *Jesus' Jewishness,* ed. Charlesworth, pp. 84–107.

123.   The translation is taken from *TANAKH: A New Translation of THE HOLY SCRIPTURES According to the Traditional Hebrew Text* (Philadelphia, New

York, Jerusalem, 5746=1985). This translation is issued by the Jewish Publication Society.

124. Ibid.

125. The follower of Jesus who composed the Odes of Solomon, probably around 100 C.E., was certainly influenced by Jesus, and perhaps also by the Righteous Teacher. In an autobiographical, and allegorical, poem he mentions that the Lord "has planted me." With the Righteous Teacher he was ruminating creatively on the Eden and paradise traditions (see Ode 11). The Odist is probably influenced in Ode 38 by thoughts in 1QH 6 and 8 and 1QS 8 and 11; and, of course, by much early prophetic traditions. See J. H. Charlesworth, *The Odes of Solomon* (Oxford, 1973; repr., Chico, Calif., 1977).

CHAPTER 6

The Parable of the Unjust Steward: Jesus' Criticism of the Essenes

DAVID FLUSSER*

The Dead Sea Scrolls have made it clear that the Essenes employed as their favorite self-designation "the sons of light." Later, Christians themselves claimed to be the true "sons of light."[1] In the Synoptic Gospels the term "sons of light" appears only in Luke 16:8, in which the reference is not altogether flattering. If this verse reflects Jesus' own words (as I am convinced it does),[2] we cannot be sure that Jesus was denoting his own followers with this appellation. Here I will propose another solution to this problem: When Jesus referred to the "sons of light" in this parable, he did not mean his followers; he was ironically making a reference to the Essenes. A comparison of the parable of the unjust steward (Lk 16:1–9) with the Dead Sea Scrolls will strengthen this thesis. I hope to demonstrate that in this parable Jesus criticized Essene separatism and warned his adherents against such behavior.

I. H. Marshall has summarized the problems that arise when one interprets the parable of the unjust steward:

Few passages in the Gospel can have given rise to so many different interpretations as the parable of the prudent steward. We have in effect

*With the assistance of David M. Freedholm.

176

to deal with three closely linked problems. What was the steward doing? What was the point of the parable, as told by Jesus? What did Luke regard as the point of the parable?

Essentially there are two main interpretations of the steward's actions. The traditional interpretation is that he acted corruptly throughout the story: having wasted his master's goods during his stewardship, he finally proceeded to falsify the accounts of the master's debtors by reducing the amounts owed in order to obtain their good-will. . . . [I]t is not the steward's dishonesty but his foresight in preparing for the future which is commended, and Jesus was prepared to draw lessons (usually by contrast) from the behaviour of sinful men (11:13; cf. 18:6–7).[3]

Recently, several alternative interpretations have been published which propose that the steward's actions were legal and praiseworthy. This fact, according to these interpretations, explains why the lord (or the master) praised the steward.[4]

I do not find it necessary to follow this trend and reject the "traditional interpretation." After all, the steward of the parable is explicitly called a "dishonest steward." Even if the lord of the parable praised this dishonest steward, does this make him any less dishonest? Is his dishonest behavior any less scandalous than the behavior of the "unrighteous judge" in Jesus' parable in Luke 18:1–8?

Rabbinic parables and the parables of Jesus are often characterized by an intended discrepancy between the moral behavior of the characters in the parable and the message of the parable itself (which is intended to be religious and ethical). Thus the dramatic characters in the parables are not characterized as "righteous" or "sinful" but are instead characterized as "clever" (*pkḥym, phronimoi*) or as "foolish" (*tpšym, mōroi*). This tension between an "immoral" example given in the parable and its intended "moral" teaching may have been one of the reasons Jesus liked to speak in parables. They gave him an opportunity to express his understanding of the religious and philosophical paradox of the human condition. It seems he sometimes widened the gap between the dramatic content of the parable and its intended higher meaning in order to stress this paradox and to heighten the initial shock of the parable upon his audience. Parables with this sort of shocking effect appear only in Luke: the importunate friend at midnight (11:5–8), the prodigal son (15:11–32), the dishonest steward (16:1–9), the dishonest judge (18:1–8), and the Pharisee and the publican (18:9–14). The exception is the parable about the laborers in the vineyard, which is preserved only in Matthew

(20:1-16). This may show that, unlike Luke, the other evangelists found these parables too problematic and perverse to include them in their Gospels; they may have feared that such parables could awaken unjustified doubts about the moral integrity of Jesus himself.

In the parable of the unjust steward, Jesus does not admire the righteousness of the dishonest steward (Luke 16:8); he commends only his clever behavior (*phronimōs epoiēsen*). Jesus recommends that his adherents be clever in their daily lives, just as the wicked steward was in his: "For the sons of this world are more clever (*phronimōteroi*) in dealing with their generation that the sons of light." This helps us understand what Jesus meant when he once said: "Behold, I send you as sheep in the midst of wolves; so be clever (*phronimoi*)[5] as serpents and innocent as doves" (Mt 10:16).

Another question that should be asked is whether Luke understood the point of the parable he recorded. It seems that he did not know to whom Jesus referred when he employed the designation "the sons of light." Luke also may have misunderstood the term "mammon of unrighteousness." Luke interpreted this term in light of Jesus' positive evaluation of poverty and his negative approach to wealth. Therefore Luke added to our passage Jesus' saying about the slave of two masters (Lk 16:13), a saying that forms a part of the Sermon on the Mount in Matthew (6:24).[6] Jesus said: "You cannot serve God and mammon." Because the word "mammon" appears both in this saying and in Luke 16:9, Luke added the saying about the slave of two masters to our passage. He not only may have placed this saying in the wrong context but also may have incorrectly interpreted the expression "mammon of unrighteousness" in Luke 16:11 as meaning "the unrighteous mammon." Jesus wanted to say that all wealth is suspected of being unrighteous (Lk 16:13). The final consequence of this development was that Jesus' application of the parable in Luke 16:9 was falsely understood as meaning: "So I say to you, use your worldly wealth to win friends for yourselves."[7]

Before proceeding further let us examine the term "mammon."[8] The word means "wealth." It does not appear in the "Old Testament," but it is the normal word used for wealth during the Second Temple period and also in rabbinic literature. It is an equivalent for the word *hwn*. "Mammon" appears also in the Aramaic Targum on Job from Qumran (on Job 27:17).[9] In the Dead Sea Scrolls, which are written in a classicizing Hebrew, normally the Old Testament word *hwn* appears, but in certain places we find the word "mammon." It is found in a fragment from Cave 1 (1Q27 2.5)[10] from the so-called Book of the Mysteries, while in the next line (2.6) the other word *hwn* appears! Wealth is designated in the Rule of the Community 6.2 by the word "mammon," but in another manuscript of the same passage the word is *hwn*.[11] The reverse situation is found in 1QS 6.25,[12] where the complete manuscript has *hwn*, but in a fragment of the same work and also in a parallel passage from the Damascus Document (14.20) we find the term "mammon." Thus, in the Dead Sea Scrolls the terms *hwn* and *mmwn* are synonymous and interchangeable.

Noting this, let us investigate the meaning of the "wealth of unrighteousness" (Lk 16:9; cf. 16:11) in the ideology of the Essene "sons of light." The Essenes used *mmwn* as a technical term for the wealth of those who did not belong to their exclusive community of the elect. The Essenes believed that God had divided humanity into two opposite camps and that the members of their group were the true "sons of light." Thus, in their view all others were condemned, that is, wicked and sinful "sons of darkness." The Essenes had to separate themselves as far as possible from those outside their community and, of course, also from the wealth of these "sons of darkness." This extreme economic separatism was rooted also in the ritual aspect of their daily life. Their specific ritual purity did not permit them to come in contact with the impure wealth of the outside world. Hence, their high degree of ritual purity was closely linked with Essene dualism. They were obligated "to keep apart from the sons of perdition, to refrain from the unclean wealth of wickedness" (*wlhnzr mhwn hrš'h htm'*, CD 6.14–15).[13] The Essenes not only believed that one became unclean by contact with impure objects and persons, but they also contended that sins pollute ritually: the wicked "defiled themselves in ways of whoredom and the wealth of wickedness" (CD 8.5: *wytgwllw bdrky znwt wbhwn rš'h*).

Another cause for the Essene abstention from the wealth of wickedness was closely related to their militant dualistic eschatology. They believed that the day would come when they would conquer the whole world. Because the date of this war had been preordained by God and had not yet arrived, they were willing to suffer peacefully during the interim in the present wicked social and political order.[14] Because of this perspective, each Essene promised:

> I will not return evil to anybody, with good will I pursue man, for with God rests the judgment of every living being, and he is the one to repay man for his deeds. I will not show jealousy with the spirit of evil and my soul shall not covet wealth of unrighteousness[15] (*hwn hms*) and the

strife of men of perdition I will not handle until the Day of Vengeance. But my anger I will not turn away from the men of iniquity, and I will not be content until He has established judgment. (1QS 10.17–20)

They were to behave passively, peacefully, and even benevolently toward the "sons of darkness," while keeping their hatred of them a secret (1QS 9.21–22). During this interval, they were to wait for the Day of Vengeance, when their abstention from the wealth of unrighteousness would radically change. As noted previously, the "wealth of wickedness" meant the wealth of the surrounding wicked world, and now it becomes clear that here the "wealth of unrighteousness" has the same meaning. This is substantiated by the Habakkuk Pesher, where the Wicked Priest is said to have "robbed and amassed the *wealth of the men of unrighteousness*" (*wygzwl wyqbwṣ hwn 'nšy ḥms*, 1QpHab 8.11).

When the term "wealth" is defined in the Dead Sea Scrolls with a further substantive that has a negative meaning, the whole expression then refers to the wealth of the people outside the Essene community. Every member of the group was commanded to separate himself completely from this kind of wealth.

> So no member shall be united with him (the foreigner) in his work or in his wealth, lest he defile the member with guilty iniquity, but distance shall be kept from him in every matter . . . ; no member shall eat from any of their property nor drink from it, nor take anything from their hands except by payment. . . . For all who are not accounted as in his covenant keep them separate and all that belongs to them . . . and all their deeds are filthiness before him and uncleanness is in all their wealth. (1QS 5.14–20)

The same rule of economic separatism is described in an even more precise manner in the Damascus Document: "And let no man of the covenant of God trade with the sons of perdition except for cash. And let no man make a partnership for trade unless he informs the overseer in the camp and makes a written agreement" (CD 13.14–16).[16] In another passage from the scrolls (1QS 9.8–10) it is clearly said: "And the wealth belonging to men of holiness (*hwn 'nšy/qwdš*) who walk in perfection—their wealth shall not be mingled with the wealth belonging to men of deceit (*hwn 'nšy hrmyh*) who have not cleansed their way to be separated from iniquity and to walk in perfection of way." Here the "wealth belonging to men of holiness" is placed opposite the "wealth belonging to men of deceit" (*hwn 'nšy hrmyh*). No doubt this term is synonymous with the "wealth belonging to men of unrighteousness" (*hwn 'nšy hms*) in 1 QpHab 8.11, the "wealth of unrighteousness" (*hwn hms*) in 1QS 10.19, and the "wealth of wickedness" (*hwn rš'h*) in the Damascus Document 6.15 and 8.5.

All these expressions refer to the same thing, namely, *the wealth of non-covenanters*. The Essene "sons of light" were obliged to separate themselves as far as possible from this wealth of unrighteousness. This attitude was an expression of their concentration on strict dualism and eschatological dreams. It was also connected with their high standard of ritual purity, according to which all other persons and their property were unclean. It is also important to remember that the Essenes, as "paupers of grace," despised wealth and practiced a communism of wealth. Their separatism was so extreme that some of their doctrines were secret. According to Josephus (*War* 2.141) the Essenes were obligated "to conceal nothing from the members of the sect and to report none of their secrets to others, even though tortured to death," or, according to 1QS 9.17, they had "to conceal the counsel of the Law from the men of iniquity."[17]

In the parable of the unjust steward (Lk 16:1-9) there are two technical terms: the "mammon of unrighteousness" and the "sons of light." As mentioned earlier, the term "sons of light" does not appear anywhere else in the Synoptic Gospels. Furthermore, the second term, "the wealth of unrighteousness" has a specific meaning in Essene writings. Thus it is possible to identify the "sons of light" in this parable with the Essenes. Jesus said that "the sons of this world are more clever in dealing with their own generation than the sons of light" (Lk 16:8). This parable then suggests how Jesus interpreted this honorific title which the Essenes applied to themselves. He criticized the "sons of light" by making a paradoxical contrast between them and the "sons of this world." According to a famous rabbinic concept, God concealed the light which he created on the first day from the present world, "but in the world to come it will appear to the pious in all its pristine glory."[18] This explanation of the "sons of light" is absent from the Dead Sea Scrolls, where it is said only that "in the spring of light are the generations of truth and from the well of darkness come the generation of perversity" (1QS 3.19). Jesus either did not agree with or was not acquainted with the Essene meaning of the designation "sons of light." He evaluated it in terms of the rabbinic concept of the primordial light which "is sown for the righteous" (Ps 97:11). The other term in Luke 16:8-9, "the mammon of unrighteousness," is also connected with the Essenes. We have seen that the word mammon is sometimes a substitute for the Hebrew *hwn* in the Dead Sea Scrolls and that both words mean "wealth." We have also seen that in Essene terminology the term "wealth of wickedness" (*hwn hrš'h*) or the "wealth of unrighteousness" (*hwn ḥms*) actually refers to the "wealth of *men* of unrighteousness" (*hwn 'nšy ḥms*) or "wealth of *men* of deceit" (*hwn 'nšy hrmyh*).

The Essene "sons of light" separated themselves from this "wealth of the wicked external world," and any economic contact with others was restricted as far as possible. I suggest that business with this puritanical sect was by no means easy. No member of the sect was permitted to take anything from the hands of the "sons of darkness" except in payment. Recall again CD 13.14-16: "And let no man of the covenant of God trade with the sons of perdition except for cash. And let no man make a partnership for trade unless he informs the overseer in the camp and makes a written agreement." This does not mean that Essene business may not have prospered. Modern Christian separatist sects, who have a similar economic, though less rigid, approach and who also live in a community of wealth, are sometimes very successful in business. Nevertheless, the Essenes constituted more or less small groups. Since Jesus preached a universal love toward sinners, it is likely that he did not approve of Essene economic separatism. Even if there is no extant saying of Jesus criticizing the Essene way of life, one might guess how he would react to their separatism. Fortunately, Luke contains the parable about the dishonest steward. Before the discovery of the Dead Sea Scrolls this parable was an obscure puzzle. Now, we are able to guess at the approximate meaning of Jesus' parable.

When Jesus used the technical term "sons of light," he was making an allusion to the Essenes. We have recognized the fact that the term "mammon of unrighteousness" was an Essene term with a specific meaning. Let us return to the parable itself. The dishonest steward reduced the debts of his master's debtors in order to obtain their goodwill. Often in parables when a reference is made to a man owing a debt to his landlord, the landlord represents God, and the debt denotes human obligation to God. So it is possible that the debtors in our parable signify (among other things) men who had not yet fulfilled their obligations to God. It is not advisable to go too far in this direction because it would weaken or even eliminate the clear purpose of the parable, which pertains to economics. If Jesus was speaking of those who are debtors to God in the parable, this sheds light on why he labeled their debts with the Essene term "mammon of unrighteousness." A simpler explanation would be that Jesus used this technical term because the wealth in the parable became wealth of unrighteousness after the dishonest steward falsified his master's accounts in order to reduce the amounts owed by the debtors.

With a careful reading of Jesus' parable and the words of application that follow it, it becomes clear that the term "wealth of unrighteousness" has not lost its Essene connotation in this context. The usual interpretation of Luke 16:9 attempts to support the idea that Jesus was simply teaching his followers to give alms when he said: "Use your worldly wealth to win friends for yourselves." But even without insight from the Dead Sea Scrolls this explanation would be highly improbable. A recommendation to give alms is not easily recognized as the aim of the parable.[19] Would it actually be necessary to tell a Jewish audience that alms were important? Even to the separatist Essenes, "two things were left to individual discretion: the rendering of assistance and compassion. Members may help the deserving when in need and supply food to the destitute" (Josephus, *War* 2.134). No one would be opposed to the ancient Jewish practice of almsgiving, which was a major characteristic of genuine religious piety—that is, with the exception of the gnostic Jesus in the Gospel of Thomas, who says: "If you give alms, you will do evil to your spirits" (logion 14).

This common understanding of the parable, which linked the main thrust of the illustration to almsgiving, has caused an incorrect translation of Luke 16:9. Jesus did not say: "Make friends for yourselves *by means* of unrighteous mammon," but rather, "Make for yourselves friends *from the* mammon of unrighteousness." In Hebrew it would be *'św lkm ydydym mmmwn hḥms*. As far as I can see, it is impossible to translate the Greek preposition *ek* as "by means of," which expresses agency, though in Hebrew this meaning is possible.[20]

We should not forget two important points. The first is the clear definition of the Essene technical term "wealth of unrighteousness." This expression means "the wealth of men of unrighteousness" and refers to those who did not enter the Essene covenant. The Essene "sons of light" separated themselves from the wealth of the external wicked world. They were even required "to hate all the sons of darkness each according to his guilt in the vengeance of God" (1QS 1.10–11). How could these "sons of light" have made friends for themselves from the wealth of unrighteousness?

The second point that supports this exegesis of the parable is derived from the words of Jesus: "The sons of this world are more clever in dealing with their own generation than the sons of light" (Lk 16:8). The "sons of this world" keep economic contact with others and are even prone to act fraudulently in order to win friends who will show themselves to be helpful in the future. Thus they deal with their own generation in a far more clever way than the "sons of light," who refuse to make friends for themselves from the wealth of unrighteousness. The information furnished by the Dead Sea Scrolls enables us to identify the "sons of light" in Luke 16:8 with the Essenes. At the same time, this evidence compels us to recognize that the two terms in the idiom "friends from the mammon of unrighteousness" are interrelated: these "friends" are nonbelievers who belong to the "wealth of unrighteousness." The "sons of light" did not deal cleverly with these "nonbelievers" but severed their economic ties with them.[21] John the Baptist opposed this idea of a separatist sect in the midst of the Jewish people. Jesus also warned his adherents not to choose the path of sectarian detachment. He viewed the economic separatism of the "sons of light" as a foolish and even dangerous convention. As has already been observed, "no member" of the Qumran community was permitted to "eat from any of their [i.e., the foreigners'] property nor drink from it, nor take anything from their hands except by payment" (1QS 5.16–17). In contrast, Jesus said to those whom he sent into the world: "Whatever house you enter . . . remain in the same house eating and drinking what they provide, for the laborer deserves his wages. . . . Whenever you enter a town, and they receive you, eat what is set before you" (Lk 10:5–8).[22]

The vast difference between the approach to others that Jesus and his disciples practiced and that of the Essenes, who maintained an extreme economic separatism, is very clear. Thus, it is no surprise that Jesus taught his followers not to behave like the "sons of light." Those who wished to follow Jesus were required to live in brotherly love with the outside world and to refrain from isolating themselves from others economically. Jesus' emphasis on maintaining relations with others may have led to his followers having friendships with outsiders, which, in turn, may have led to their acceptance of Jesus' message. This is the purpose of Jesus' application of the parable in vv. 10–12, which, in their present form may have been slightly restyled by Luke.[23]

These explanations form a chain linked together by three arguments *a minore ad maius*. The first argument (Lk 16:10) expresses a general principle:[24] "The man who can be trusted (*hn'mn*) in a small matter can be trusted also in a major one: and the man who is dishonest[25] in a minor matter is dishonest also in a great one." But in Luke 16:10–12 Jesus did not abandon the main theme that he addressed in the parable itself; rather, he enlarged the scope of its message. It may be that Jesus had in mind a specific case of economic contact with nonbelievers, namely, a deposit that had been

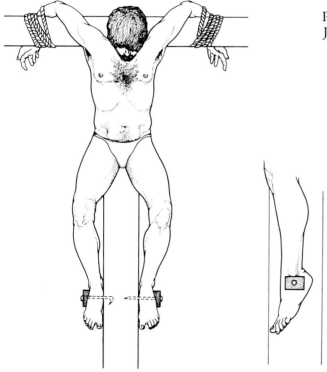

Proposed reconstruction of
Jehohanan's Crucifixion

Crucifixion with legs adjacent according to Dr. Haas

Jehohanan: right calcaneum before reconstruction

Jehohanan: right calcaneum after reconstruction

Cave 4 [courtesy: Charlesworth]

Qumran water channel [courtesy: Bowden]

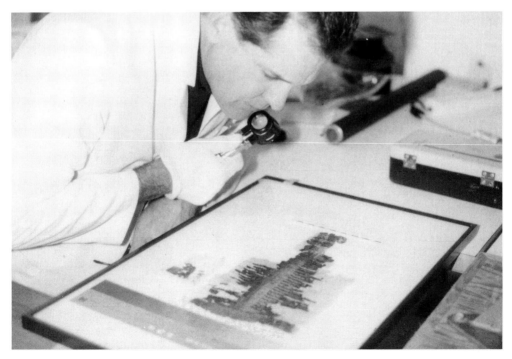

Charlesworth working on the deteriorating Genesis Apocryphon, found in Cave 1
[courtesy: Ken Zuckerman]

Qumran cistern [courtesy: Bowden]

The Copper Scroll (from Cave 3) showing more text thanks to new techniques, equipment, and film [courtesy: Princeton Theological Seminary Dead Sea Scrolls Project and West Semitic Research Project at University of Southern California]

The Temple Scroll (from Cave 11) [courtesy: Israel Department of Antiquities and Museums]

The Rule of the Community (from Cave 1), col.8, which was composed in the second century B.C.E. probably by the Righteous Teacher [courtesy: Israel Department of Antiquities and Museums]

Ruins of Qumran, looking southward from the tower with the scriptorium on the left [courtesy: Charlesworth]

Looking westward from the Dead Sea at the terrace on which the Qumran ruins are situated and the cliffs in the distance where 11 caves have been found from which scrolls and fragments were recovered [courtesy: Charlesworth]

Mount Zion, the southwest corner of Jerusalem. The excavation in which the Essene Gate was found is on the far right, where the wall meets the street [courtesy: R. Riesner]

The Essene Gate on Mount Zion. The white stones are part of a Byzantine gate. The two thresholds are from a gate of Aelia Capitolina (135–330 C.E.). Underneath them are paving stones of the Essene Gate. They were inserted into an earlier Hasmonean wall, perhaps by Herod the Great's workmen [courtesy: R. Riesner]

Jewish ritual bath (*mikweh*) dating from the Herodian period. It is near the Essene Gate and also outside the first-century wall of Jerusalem [courtesy: R. Riesner]

Large ritual baths. The dimensions are unparalleled in Jerusalem. Note the separated stairs [courtesy: R. Riesner]

entrusted to his followers. If this is so, the members of Jesus' movement were then admonished to show themselves trustworthy toward others.

In the famous letter of Pliny the Younger to the emperor Trajan (10.96.7), we find an oath that Christians were to say on Sundays: they swore among other things that they would not betray the trust (of another) and that they would return a deposit when asked for it (... *ne fidem fallerent, ne depositum appellati abnegarent*). Hence, this oath was concerned with being trustworthy with a deposit. The earliest Christian apologist, Aristides of Athens, who delivered his *Apology* to the emperor Hadrian or to Antoninus Pius, also said that Christians were forbidden to appropriate a deposit for themselves.[26] Such a trespass could easily occur in a commercial situation in antiquity; and, therefore, it is quite possible that in his explanation of the parable Jesus also was addressing cases in which his followers would be tempted to be untrustworthy with what belongs to a nonbeliever. In any case, this suggestion fits well with the meaning of Luke 16:10–12.

In order to discover the ties between the parable and the verses that follow in Luke, we will cite the entire passage:

> The man who can be trusted in a small matter (*bdbr qtn*)[27] can be trusted also in a great one. The man who is dishonest in a small matter is also dishonest in a great one. If, then, you have not proved trustworthy with the wealth of unrighteousness,[28] who will trust you with the wealth that is true? And if you have proved untrustworthy with what belongs to another, who will give you what is your own? (Lk 16:10–12)

The three arguments *a minore ad maius* are built in a parallel manner. The "small matter" in the general principle corresponds to the "wealth of unrighteousness" in the second sentence and to that which "belongs to another" in the third. We have seen that the "wealth of unrighteousness" in the context of Essene terminology means all wealth owned by those who are not members of the Essene group. This wealth belongs to another. The parallelism between "the wealth of unrighteousness" in Luke 16:11 and the phrase "what belongs to another" in the following verse, confirms the thesis that the mammon of unrighteousness in Luke 16:9 and 11 refers to the wealth of nonbelievers. Jesus claimed in the parable that the "sons of light" did not behave cleverly when they practiced an economic separatism and did not make friends for themselves from the "wealth of unrighteousness." This is his criticism of the extreme Essene attitude. He asks his followers to remain trustworthy with the "wealth of unrighteousness" which belongs to others. Only in this way will they be able to gain friends among nonbelievers.

In Luke 16:10–12 the "great matter" is defined as "that which is true" and "what is your own." One thing is clear: here Jesus does not refer merely to wealth but also addresses a higher principle. Because the term "that which is true" is unclear and seems to have been coined by Luke (as well as being difficult to retranslate into Hebrew), let us begin with Luke 16:12: "And give you what is your own." The meaning of this clause is somewhat enigmatic. An example of the way it is usually understood is the interpretation of I. H. Marshall:

> The principle is then applied to worldly and heavenly wealth which are equated with small and great responsibilities and (in a further comment) with alien and native wealth respectively. Disciples will not be entrusted with heavenly wealth and responsibilities if they have not already shown themselves faithful over against worldly wealth; cf. the application of this principle to church government in I Tim. 3:5.[29]

Such an interpretation presupposes that the person "who will give you what is your own" is God himself. This would fit the second part of Luke 16:9: "so when it [i.e., the mammon of unrighteousness] fails, they may receive you into the eternal habitations."[30] But this interpretation causes serious difficulties. Would Jesus have spoken about God in such an indefinite fashion: "who will trust you . . ." and "who will give you . . ."?[31] Jesus would never have spoken about God in this less-than-reverent way. Moreover, scholars who accept this common interpretation are aware that Luke 16:10–12 does not actually fit the meaning of the parable. Therefore they are constrained to decide that this passage is "a compilation of related sayings here; they have been added by a compiler to the parable on a basis of a broad community of theme."[32] However, another interpretation of Luke 16:10–12 is possible. It is based on additional material from both Christian and Jewish sources. This explanation is also in line with the very spirit of the parable, whose theme concerns economic contact between believers and nonbelievers.

I suggest that "those who will trust" the followers of Jesus with the wealth that is true and "who will give" them what is their own should be identified with the outside world and not with God. Thus Jesus required his followers to be open-minded to those who are outsiders. In contrast to the Essene "sons of light," they were to make friends for themselves from the wealth of unrighteousness. Jesus' followers were to be trustworthy when they entered into commercial contact with others. The true wealth which they will then receive in recompense is what they received from Jesus and what they have to offer to others. "The harvest is plentiful, but the laborers are few; pray that the lord of the harvest will send out laborers into his harvest!" (Lk 10:2; Mt 9:37–38).

The Essene "sons of light" lived in complete economic communism and opposed any open commercial contact with the outside world. John the Baptist weakened this attitude and abolished its separatist aspect. People came to John and asked, "What then shall we do?" John's reply negated the Essene approach. "He who has two coats, let him share with him who has none; and he who has food, let him do likewise" (Lk 3:10–11). This means that the Essene community of goods—to koinōnikon according to Josephus (*War* 2.122)[33]—received a new meaning in the context of John's message. The community of goods was extended to the external world. This was no longer an economic communism, but in John's preaching it had become a command to his followers to share their own possessions with others.

This new concept was then linked with another idea: if one shares one's material goods with others, then one must share one's spiritual wealth with them as well.[34] This whole complex of concepts appears in a passage from the Two Ways, which is the Jewish source for the early Christian Didache. The Two Ways was composed in a group that was strongly influenced by Essenism. In the Didache this passage is found:

> You shall not turn away the needy, but shall share (*synkoinōnēseis*) everything with your brother, and do not say that it is your own, for if you are sharers (*koinōnoi*) in the immortal, how much more in the things which are mortal? For the Lord's[35] will is that we give to all from the gifts we have received[36] (Did 4:8).[37]

The most important statement in this passage for our discussion is "If you are sharers in the immortal, how much more in the things which are mortal?" As others have noted, this passage is similar in spirit and content to what Paul wrote to the Romans (15:26–27: see also 1Cor 9:11): "For Macedonia and Achaia have been pleased to make some contribution (*koinōnia*) for the poor among the saints of Jerusalem: they were pleased to do it, and indeed they are in debt to them, for if Gentiles have come to share (*ekoinōnēsan*) in their spiritual treasures, they ought also to be of service to them in material treasures." Like the passage from the Didache, this text also teaches that common sharing in spiritual wealth obliges one to be a sharer in material wealth as well.

The affinity between these two passages and Jesus' words in Luke 16:10–12 is obvious. Here we will compare Luke with the Didache:

Luke 16:10-12	*Didache 4:8*
A man who can be trusted in a small matter can be trusted also in a great one.	
(a) If you have not proved trustworthy with the wealth of unrighteousness	how much more (are you sharers) in the things which are mortal,
(b) If you have proved untrustworthy with which belongs to others.	
(a) who will trust you with the wealth which is true?	If you are sharers in the immortal . . .
(b) who will give you what is your own?	

The similarity between the two passages, even in regard to their form, cannot be easily denied. The difference between them is that the order of argumentation has been reversed. In the Didache and in Romans 15:27 the statement is built according to the *argumentum a maiore ad minus*. Luke 16:10–12 is composed of three arguments *a minore ad maius*. Didache 4:8 reads: "If you are sharers in the immortal, how much more in the things which are mortal," and Luke 16:12 is written: "If you have proved untrustworthy with that which belongs to another, who will give you what is your own?" The most important contribution of Didache 4:8 and Romans 15:27 for understanding Luke 16:10–12 is that both texts treat a specific concept connected to a community of goods. At the same time they try to show that there is a necessary connection between a community of goods and a community in the spirit. If one shares in material treasures (or, according to Did 4:8, in things that are mortal), how much more ought one to share in spiritual treasures (or, according to Did 4:8, in the immortal). In Luke 16:10–12 the "small matter" is parallel to the "wealth of unrighteousness" which belongs to others. This corresponds to the material, mortal treasures in the two other texts. The "great matter" is parallel in Luke to the "wealth which is true" and which is "your own." It corresponds to the spiritual treasures which are immortal in the two other sources. In all three texts the arguments are conditional clauses ("If . . .").

I hope now to offer a better interpretation of Luke 16:10–12 and to discover the organic links between these words and the preceding parable of the dishonest steward (Lk 16:1–9). I tried to show that the main aim of the parable was to polemicize against the Essene "sons of light," who restricted themselves to minimal economic ties with the surrounding unrighteous "sons of darkness." Moreover, in Luke 16:10–12 Jesus brings a positive argument to warn his followers against the practice of the Essenes. He rejects the Essene exclusive economic communism and recommends a more broad-minded approach to the surrounding world. The same approach is reflected both in the Jewish Two Ways (Did 4:8) and in Romans 15:27. The Essene concept of a community of goods (*koinōnikon, koinōnia*) receives a new meaning: it is no longer an exclusive communism based on economic separatism but a sharing of property with all. This more broad-minded approach to the world is evident in that Jesus was prone to accept invitations from nonbelievers, and his disciples were reproached because they ate and drank with the tax collectors (Lk 5:30 and parallels).[38] We have seen that "no member" of the Essene sect was to "eat any of their (non-Essene) property nor drink from it, nor take anything from their hands except by payment" (1QS 5.16–17). In contrast to this extreme separatism, Jesus instructed those whom he sent into the world to eat and drink what others would provide, "for the laborer deserves his wages" (Lk 10:5–8). In another passage this command is explained as follows: "You received without paying, give without pay. Take no gold, nor silver, nor copper in your belts, nor bag for your journey, nor two tunics, nor sandals nor a staff; for the laborer deserves his food" (Mt 10:8–10).

This injunction is both similar and dissimilar to the Essene way of life according to Josephus:

On the arrival in any of the sect from elsewhere, all the resources *of the community* are put at their disposal, just as if they were their own; and they enter the houses of men whom they have never seen before as though they were their most intimate friends. Consequently, they carry nothing whatever with them on their journeys, except arms against brigands.[39] In every city there is one of the order expressly appointed to attend strangers, who provides them with raiment and other necessities. . . . There is no buying or selling *among themselves*, but each gives what he has to any in need and receives from him in exchange something useful to himself; they are, moreover, freely permitted to take anything from any of their brothers without making any return. (*War* 2.124–25, 127)

Thus the difference between Jesus' disciples and the Essenes is clear enough. The Essenes lived in an exclusive communism of goods and when they traveled they took nothing with them because in every place an Essene stock supplied their needs for them. Jesus and his disciples accepted the invitation of outsiders. His emissaries ate and drank in the houses of outsiders and accepted what their hosts provided. Therefore, like the Essenes, they did not take anything with them during their mission, "for the laborer deserves his food." The community of goods received a new and broader meaning—that is, a sharing of property with all, "You received without paying, give without pay!"[40]

If I am correct, the message of the parable of the dishonest steward is not complete without Luke 16:10–12. The parable itself teaches that a clever person will make friends for himself from the wealth of unrighteousness. Luke 16:10–12 has certain similarities to a saying of the ancient Chinese sage Lao Tzu: "The sage does not board. Having bestowed all he has to others, he has yet more: having given all he has to others, he is richer still. The way of heaven benefits and does not harm; the way of the sage is bountiful and does not contend" (*Tao Te Ching*, ch. 81).[41] Jesus said among other things: "If you have proved untrustworthy with what belongs to another, who will give you what is your own?" The principal advantage of the comparison between the saying of the ancient Chinese sage and Jesus' words in Luke 16:10–12 is that now it becomes clear that Jesus' words are as deep and meaningful as the saying of the ancient Chinese philosopher. Now it will be difficult to view Luke 16:10–12 as a secondary concoction.

The positive argument in Luke 16:10–12 has two levels—the economic and the spiritual. These levels are interdependent. Economic contact with the "wealth of unrighteousness" belonging to nonbelievers may lead them to believe in Jesus' spiritual message. Then their hearts will be open to the true wealth that is, the message received from Jesus. If they accept this message, they will render it in the same manner: "you received without paying, give without pay" (Mt 10:8)[42] Otherwise the good news would become barren and Jesus' movement would be transformed into a separatist and closed Jewish group, like the Essene "sons of light." Their economic separation was an organic part of a whole dualistic system which required them to hate the "sons of darkness" with a sacred hatred and which led them to produce their own esoteric doctrines of utmost secrecy. It was forbidden for them to report anything of their secrets to others (Josephus, *War* 2.141); they had "to conceal the counsel of the law from the men of iniquity" (1QS 9.17). In contrast, Jesus demanded that his followers love their enemies, and he opposed any doctrinal secrecy. "Nothing is covered that will not be revealed, or hidden that will not be known. What I tell you in the dark, utter in the light; and what you hear whispered, proclaim upon the housetops!" (Mt 10:26–27; Lk 12:2–3). Jesus' message was *open to all.* Thus his followers were taught to make friends for themselves from the "wealth of unrighteousness," because an abstention from economic association with others would inevitably hinder his disciples from sharing their own message of the kingdom of heaven with all peoples. In Jesus' eyes, the dealings of the "sons of light" with their own generation was more foolish than that of the fraudulent "sons of this world."

One of the results of this study is a truism: Jesus knew the Essenes and criticized them precisely in the way which could have been postulated even without knowing that he was referring to them when he employed the term "the sons of light" in the parable of the unjust steward. The discovery of the Dead Sea Scrolls has shed light on this difficult parable. It is to be hoped that this parable has now become less obscure and that we have learned something about Jesus' social and religious views and how they differed drastically from Essene social ideology and practice. This specific case elucidates—in modest measure—a pattern of social trends in religious movements. An indirect consequence of our analysis is that the "sons of light" in Jesus' parable of the unjust steward can be identified directly with the Essenes, who are the authors of the Dead Sea Scrolls.[43]

Notes

1. See D. Flusser, "The Dead Sea Scrolls and Pre-Pauline Christianity," *Scripta Hierosolymitana* 4 (1958) 218–19 and n. 13.

2. Most commentators accept the basic authenticity of this parable (see, e.g., J. Jeremias, *The Parables of Jesus*, trans. S. H. Hooke, New York, 1972 [2d rev. ed.] pp. 45–48), while recognizing that it has undergone later expansion. There has been much disagreement over the boundaries of the original parable; for a summary of

positions taken, see J. A. Fitzmyer, *The Gospel According to Luke X–XXIV* (AB 28A; Garden City, N.Y., 1981) vol. 2, pp. 1094–1104. I suggest that v. 8 was an integral part of the original parable.

3.　I. H. Marshall, *The Gospel of Luke* (NIGTC; Grand Rapids, 1978) p. 614. For his analysis of the whole parable see pp. 614–22; also see his bibliography on p. 617.

4.　For a discussion of these interpretations, see Marshall, *Luke*, pp. 614–17. Also, for a discussion of the interpretation of the term *kyrios* in Luke 16:8, see pp. 619–20.

5.　Here Delitzsch translates correctly '*rwmym* according to Gen 3:1 where in the Greek translation "the serpent" is characterized as *phronimōtatos.*

6.　The author of the so-called Second Epistle of Clement (6:1–6) uses the saying about the slave of two masters in an interesting way. See the recent edition by K. Wengst *Schriften des Urchristentums: Didache, Barnabasbrief, Zweiter Klemensbrief, Schrift an Diognet* (Darmstadt, 1984) vol. 2, pp. 244–45 and p. 271.

7.　This is the translation of the New English Bible (NEB).

8.　See Marshall, *Luke*, p. 621; W. Bauer, W. F. Arndt, and F. W. Gingrich, *A Greek-English Lexicon of the New Testament and Other Early Christian Literature* (Chicago, 1979) p. 490; and J. Licht, *The Rule Scroll* (Jerusalem, 1965 [in Hebrew]) pp. 139, 158–59; see also n. 42 below. Augustine refers to the word "mammon" in the Punic language (*De Serm. Dom. in Monte* 2.14.47): *Lucrum Punice mammon dicitur.* See A. Plummer, *A Critical and Exegetical Commentary on the Gospel According to St. Luke* (ICC; Edinburgh, 1922) p. 385. See also the most recent discussion in G. Vermes, *Jesus and the World of Judaism* (Philadelphia, 1984) p. 79.

9.　See J. A. Fitzmyer and D. J. Harrington, *A Manual of Palestinian Aramaic Texts* (Rome, 1978) p. 20. In Job 27:17 we read: "And the innocent will divide the silver (*ksp*)." The Hebrew word means also "money" and so it was understood both by the Greek Bible and by the author of the Aramaic Targum on Job who translates: "And his money (*wmmwnh*) the true (i.e., the righteous) one will divide."

10.　See DJD 1 (Oxford, 1955) p. 105.

11.　See Licht, *Rule Scroll,* p. 105, *apparatus criticus.*

12.　Ibid., p. 158, *apparatus criticus,* and commentary on p. 159.

13.　See also the fragment from Cave 4, published by J. M. Allegro, DJD 5 (Oxford, 1968) p. 81, no. 183. See also J. Strugnell, "Notes en marge du volume V des 'Discoveries in the Judean Desert of Jordan,'" *RQ* 7 (1970) 260–63.

14.　See esp. 1QS 9.21–25. See also D. Flusser, "A New Sensitivity in Judaism," in *Judaism and the Origins of Christianity* (Jerusalem, 1988) pp. 122–23.

15.　In Luke 16:9 we decided to translate *tou mamōna tēs adikias* by "wealth of unrighteousness" or "the mammon of unrighteousness" in light of the Hebrew idiom *hwn hms.* The Hebrew *hms* is often translated in the Greek Bible by *adikia*, which is the same word that appears in Luke 16:9. The words "my soul shall not covet wealth of unrighteousness" have a parallel in what is referred to by Josephus

(*War* 2.141) as having been said in the oath of Essenes: the Essene swears "to keep his hands from stealing and *his soul* pure from unholy gain." Josephus evidently depoliticized the original meaning of the words. What he writes here is a moral truism, for which a special oath was unnecessary. The same is true in regard to the continuation of the oath, "to abstain from robbery." I venture that Josephus knew the real meaning of the "unholy gain" and that the mention of robbery shows how he understood it.

16.   Josephus (*War* 2.134) also explains that for the Essenes, "presents to relatives are prohibited without leave from the managers." Is this rule also a practical expression of Essene economic separatism?

17.   See Licht, *Rule Scroll,* p. 196.

18.   See L. Ginzberg, *The Legends of the Jews* (Philadelphia, 1947) vol. 1, p. 9. The same term, "sons of this world (or, age)" appears also in Luke 20:34–35: "The sons of this age marry and are given in marriage but those who are accounted worthy to attain to that age . . . neither marry nor are given in marriage."

19.   It is possible that Luke understood the parable of the unjust steward in this way because he placed the saying about the slave of two masters (Lk 16:13) after the parable. The parable can be interpreted as a recommendation of almsgiving only if the debtors are understood as sinners against God. Then the parable would express permission to give alms even to sinners. It is true that the debtors are not conceived of by Jesus as righteous, but it would be very difficult to stress this point too much, as this would destroy the equilibrium of the parable itself.

20.   See Prov 3:9: "Honor the Lord with your wealth," which in Hebrew is *mhwnk.*

21.   A less likely possibility (which does not change the proposed meaning of our pericope) is to connect (as is usually done) the "mammon of unrighteousness" with the verb and to explain the Greek *ek* as a Hebraism (see the preceding note). Then we would paraphrase Jesus' words as follows: "Make friends for yourselves among the nonbelievers by being in commercial contact with their wealth of unrighteousness." Such an interpretation is not impossible per se, but it is difficult to assume that Jesus' hearers would have been able to understand Jesus' words correctly if this were his intention. The words "wealth of unrighteousness" with the Essene connotation of wealth of others is clearer if it is connected with the substantive "friends" than if it is dependent on a preposition meaning "by means of." And we have already said that the verses that follow are restyled by Luke. It would seem that if he had wanted to say "by means of," he would have changed the preposition.

22.   On Luke 10:1–16, see Marshall, *Luke,* pp. 411–12; on our passage, see pp. 419–23. Even those who are prepared to deny that the words quoted in the present study reflect a genuine saying of Jesus cannot deny that he and his disciples accepted invitations from others and ate in their houses and even accepted the hospitality of tax collectors.

23. I do not believe that the changes in Lk 16:10 are so grave as often supposed. It is true that Lk 16:10a resembles 19:17 (and Mt 25:21), but it is very probable that the entire verse (Lk 16:10) is a rabbinic sentence that Jesus hinted at in Lk 19:17 and Mt 25:21. See the rabbinic parallels in H. L. Strack and P. Billerbeck, *Kommentar zum Neuen Testament aus Talmud und Midrasch* (Munich, 1969 [5th ed.]) vol. 1, p. 972; vol. 2, pp. 221–22, 500–1. Especially important is ExR 2:3. See the Soncino English translation, ExR pp. 49–50; a German translation appears in Strack-Billerbeck, *Kommentar,* vol. 1, p. 947, and the Hebrew text appears in A. Shinan, *Midrash Shemot Rabbah* (Jerusalem, 1984) chs. 1–14; pp. 106–7, and see the notes there. The same passage appears also in Tanchuma Ex 7 (not that of Buber).

24. See A. Resch, *Agrapha* (Leipzig, 1906; repr., Darmstadt, 1967) p. 170, Agraphon 126.

25. One cannot be sure that the adjective "dishonest" (*adikos*), which appears twice in Luke 16:10 is original. Luke may have changed the original word because the same Greek adjective (*adikos*) appears also in the following verse (Lk 16:11) in connection with mammon. It is clear that the adjective "dishonest" in v. 10 functions in contrast to "the man who can be trusted" in the preceding verse. In 16:11 Jesus meant "the man who cannot be trusted," or in Hebrew *my šn'mn my š'ynw n'mn.*

26. Aristides. *Apology* 15.4 in J. Geffcken, *Zwei griechische Apologeten* (Leipzig, 1907; repr. Hildesheim, 1970) p. 24, and see the comment on pp. 87–88. The prohibition concerning a deposit appears only in the Syriac translation. The similarity of the whole passage in the *Apology* of Aristides 15.4 to the whole Christian oath in Pliny's letter to Trajan is great.

27. This is the wording in ExR; see n. 23 above.

28. See Lk 16:9. Here in 16:11, the evangelist writes: "the unrighteous mammon."

29. Marshall, *Luke,* p. 622.

30. This phrase has a parallel in the Jewish Pseudo-Philo, *Biblical Antiquities* 19.12 (*Pseudo Philon: Les Antiquités Bibliques,* ed. D. J. Harrington and J. Cazeaux [SC 229; Paris, 1976] pp. 162–63): "You shall dwell in an immortal habitation that is not subject to time" (*habitabitis in habitationem aeternam quae non tenetur in tempore*). 5Ezra 2:11 (*dabo eis tabernacula aeterna, quae praeparaveram illis*) is Christian and is dependent on Lk 16:9. Concerning 5Ezra, see my article "Matthew's 'Verus Israel,'" in *Judaism and the Origins of Christianity,* pp. 561–74.

31. There is also an inherent discrepancy in the Lucan passage itself that I am not able to resolve. In the parable (16:4) the dishonest steward says to himself: "I have decided what to do, so that people may receive me into their houses when I am put out of the stewardship." The houses are those of the debtors, and in the application of the parable (16:9) Jesus speaks about being received "into the eternal habitations." Here, in these parallel words, the subject is God! I have not found any acceptable interpretation that solves this difficulty.

32. Marshall, *Luke,* p. 622.

33.   On the New Testament term *koinōnia* and its Essene background, see the bibliography in Bauer-Arndt-Gingrich, *Greek-English Lexicon,* p. 439. See also M. Wilcox, *The Semitisms of Acts* (Oxford, 1965) pp. 93–100.

34.   This idea could have existed already in the Essene community, although it has not appeared explicitly in the Dead Sea Scrolls that have been published until now. In 1QS 1.12–13 we read only that "all who devote themselves to His truth shall bring all their knowledge and their strength and their wealth into the community of God."

35.   The Didache speaks here about the "Father," but this is a Christian editorial alteration. The Latin translation of the Two Ways retains the "Lord," while the *Apostolic Constitutions* 7.12.5 (ed. F. X. Funk [Paderborn, 1905; repr. Turin, 1962] p. 400) paraphrases the whole last sentence in the following way: "For the common participation of the necessities of life is appointed to all men by *God.*"

36.   Concerning the original place of the last sentence, see Wengst *Schriften des Urchristentums,* pp. 72–73, 95 n. 38. See also the end of the preceding note.

37.   The passage is found also in the apocryphal Epistle of Barnabas 19:8, in the chapters that are an elaboration of the Two Ways. Barnabas changed the original "immortal" and "mortal" (which are attested also in the Latin translation) into "imperishable" and "perishable." See also the *apparatus criticus* in the edition of Wengst *Schriften des Urchristentums,* p. 190.

38.   From the halakic standpoint, the expression "the sinners" does not make sense. It does not appear in Lk 5:30 in two manuscripts, one of them is Codex Bezae. The word crept into the manuscripts of Luke from Mark or Matthew.

39.   In this the Essenes differed from the emissaries of Jesus, who did not even take a staff (Mt 10:10) with them which would have served as a defensive weapon. Mark 6:8 conforms to the Essene prescription according to which Jesus' disciples are commanded, "to take nothing for their journey *except a staff.*" The whole passage in Matthew is more original. This is also confirmed by Lk 22:35–38. When Jesus finally knew that he would be executed as a criminal, he said to his disciples: "Now, let him who has a purse take it, and likewise a bag. And let him who has no (money) at home sell his mantle and buy a sword." This shows that Mt 10:10 is right and that Jesus' disciples did not take protective arms with them previously, as was the custom of Essene emissaries.

40.   On traveling Christian emissaries in the early church, see Didache chs. 11–13 and especially Paul's words in 1Cor 9:1–14. There v. 14 alludes to Jesus' words in Luke 10:7, and they serve as a halakic authority for the economic policy of the early churches: "In the same way the Lord gave instruction that those who preach the gospel should earn their living by the gospel." Among other things Paul says in the same passage (1Cor 9:11): "If we have sown spiritual treasures for you, is it too much if we reap your material treasures?" This verse has the same content and the same grammatical form as Rom 15:27: "For *if* the gentiles have come to share in their *spiritual treasures,* they ought also to be of service to them in *material treasures.*" It

is probable that 1Cor 9:11 is a variant of the more original form in Rom 15:27 and that its wording was adapted to the agricultural metaphor of the preceding verse (1Cor 9:10). Rom 15:27 is also more similar to the Two Ways ("If you are sharers in the immortal, how much more in the things which are mortal?") than is 1Cor 9:11. Thus we are able to follow the history of the concept of the community of wealth in its new meaning from a Jewish source to its two variants in Paul. This concept is evidently reflected also in Jesus' words in Lk 16:10–12, which follow the parable of the unjust steward. When the earliest Jerusalem church became a distinct community, the economic communism there became sharper, possibly under Essene influence; see Acts 2:44–45 and 4:32–37. See also Vermes, *Jesus and the World of Judaism*, pp. 119–20.

41.   Chinese Classics, *Tao Te Ching*, trans. D. C. Lau (Hong Kong, 1982) p. 117. The German translation of R. Wilhelm (Laotse, *Tao Te King* [repr., Cologne, 1982] p. 124) is even nearer to Jesus' words: "Der Berufene häuft keinen Besitz auf. Je mehr er für andere tut, desto mehr besitzt er. Je mehr er anderen gibt, desto mehr hat er. Des Himmels SINN ist fördern, ohne zu schaden. Des Berufenen SINN ist wirken, ohne zu streiten."

42.   The whole passage in Mt 10:5–15 (the commissioning of the twelve) is apparently conformed to Lk 16:10–12! What one receives without paying and gives without paying is the teaching of the Torah; see Strack-Billerbeck, *Kommentar*, vol. 1, pp. 561–63. "Teach the Torah without pay (*ḥnm*) and exact no payment: One is not to receive any material reward for the words of the Torah, for the Holy One, blessed be He, gave the Torah without paying. When you receive money for the teachings of the Torah, you thereby cause the destruction of the whole world." *Massechet Derech Eretz* 3:3, ed. M. Higger (New York, 1935; repr. Jerusalem, 1970) vol. 1, pp. 98–99; Eng. trans. vol. 2, pp. 42–43. See also M. Higger, *Massechtot Zeirot* (repr. Jerusalem, 1970) p. 72 and note on p. 177. For the prehistory of this concept, see Isa 55:1–3 and especially the Targum (ed. J. F. Stenning, pp. 184–85): "Ho every one that wishes to learn, let him come, and learn, and he that has no money; come you, and hear, and learn: come hear and learn, without price and without money (*wl' bmmwn*), instruction that is better than wine and milk. . . ." A fragment from the so-called *Book of the Mysteries* (1Q27), col. 2 (DJD 1, p. 105) is dependent on the passage from Isaiah. The knowledge or the wisdom is acquired, "without wealth and sold without price" (*blw' mḥyr*; see Isa 55:2, even in the same orthography!) and at the same time "it is more worthy than any price" (*wk[wl mḥ]yr lw' yšwh*). The word *mmwn* appears there in line 5.

43.   We have spoken about the Essene community of wealth and its weakened and changed form in semi-Essene circles and in the New Testament. A similar position is reflected in *The Life of Apollonius of Tyana* by Philostratus (4.3), where we read that while Apollonius was in Ephesus he "dealt with the question of a community of wealth (*koinōnia*) and taught that they ought to support (*trephein*) and be supported by one another." Philostratus published his book after 217 C.E.,

and his hero, Apollonius, a Pythagorean philosopher, lived in the first century C.E. The description of the community of wealth is evidently an echo of the economic communism of the early Pythagoreans. See Philostratus, *Das Leben des Apollonios von Tyana,* ed. V. Mumprecht (Munich, 1983) p. 1066. According to Pythagoras, "'Friends have all things in common' and 'Friendship is equality'; indeed, his disciples did put all their possessions into one common stock." Diogenes Laertius, 7.10, Loeb Classical Library, vol. 2, pp. 328–29; see also 8.13; and see Kurt von Fritz, "Pythagoreer," in *Paulys Realencyclopädie der classischen Altertumswissenschaft,* ed. G. Wissowa (Stuttgart, 1963) vol. 24, p. 220. Josephus is aware of the similarity between the early Pythagorean community and the Essenes. He says that the Essenes are "a group which follows a way of life taught to the Greeks by Pythagoras" (*Ant* 15.371).

CHAPTER 7

Jesus, the Primitive Community, and the Essene Quarter of Jerusalem[1]

RAINER RIESNER

THE PRIMITIVE COMMUNITY ON THE SOUTHWEST HILL

Archaeology on the West Hill

The Dormition Abbey is situated on "Mount Zion," the southwest hill of Jerusalem situated just outside the present wall of the Old City. The Abbey was built during the first decade of this century on land acquired by Kaiser Wilhelm II in 1898 from the Turkish sultan. Excavations that preceded its construction yielded the remains of two churches: (1) the Santa Maria in Monte Sion, erected by crusaders in the twelfth century, and (2) Hagia Sion, a huge Byzantine basilica dated to the fourth or fifth century. The Dormition Abbey receives its name from a tradition which locates here the deathbed (*koimēsis, dormitio*) of Mary, the mother of Jesus.

This tradition, along with others associated with Zion[2] (i.e., the Last Supper and Pentecost), appeared to be invalid in 1967 when Kathleen M. Kenyon, the famous English archaeologist, published findings of her excavations in Jerusalem. According to the New Testament, the Last Supper

198

(Mt 26:18; Mk 14:13–16; Lk 22:10) and Pentecost (Acts 1:12–13) took place within the city walls. But Kenyon, on the basis of evidence gathered from the then Jordanian eastern slope of Mount Zion, concluded that this area, first settled under Herod Agrippa I (41–44 C.E.), was actually situated outside the walls during the time of Jesus.[3] Kenyon's work coincided with the year of the Six-Day War between Israel and its Arab neighbors. Once Jerusalem was united under Israeli control, further excavations were made possible on Zion, which had previously been divided by the armistice line. One such area of investigation was the property of the Armenian Church of the Savior (Map 1, F I), which lay just north of the Dormition Abbey and where a late tradition had erroneously located the house of Caiaphas (Mt 26:58; Mk 14:54; Lk 22:54; Jn 18:15).[4] Here the Israeli archaeologist Magen Broshi (1971/1972) unearthed luxurious structures from the time of Herod the Great's reign (37–4 B.C.E.) which were preserved down to the remains of the first floor.[5] There are also excavations from 1979 on (see the section on the Essene Gate below) which show that Kenyon's probings did not provide enough evidence to warrant a conclusion on the matter.

Thus, the earlier work by Frederick J. Bliss and Archibald C. Dickie in 1894/1895 once again merits serious attention. These English archaeologists found a city wall (Map 1, F IV) south of the Dormition Abbey on the property of an Anglican school (today the American Institute of Holy Land Studies) and on Zion's southern slope. This wall was correctly assigned to the period before Jesus,[6] a dating also maintained by August Strobel, a New Testament scholar who now directs the Deutsche Evangelische Institut für Altertumswissenschaft des Heiligen Landes in Jerusalem. Having cautioned against an uncritical acceptance of Kenyon's celebrated theses, Strobel conjectured that whereas in the west the Hasmonean wall (second or first century B.C.E.) intersects with the present Turkish wall (early sixteenth century) of the Old City, its course in the south is identical with the Bliss-Dickie wall.[7] In addition, there is increasing evidence that even the preexilic wall of the eighth or seventh century B.C.E. followed the path of the Hasmonean wall over the Hinnom Valley.[8]

The excavations of Broshi and those of Nahman Avigad[9] in the Jewish quarter of the Old City led to further important results. Their finds revealed that from the destruction of the city by Titus (70 C.E.) until the beginning of large-scale Byzantine building activity in the middle third of the fourth century, Zion was essentially uninhabited. The location of the Legio X Fretensis was assigned to the area of the Citadel and its adjacent Armenian quarter within the wall of the present Old City.[10] "Aelia

Capitolina," the pagan city that the Roman emperor Hadrian had established c. 135 C.E. after the Bar Kochba rebellion, lay to the north of the present King David Street.[11] King David Street runs through a valley, to the south of which stood the first northern wall within the Gennath Gate (*War* 5.142–46). This archaeological picture accords with a statement of Eusebius who, in recounting his visit to Zion at the beginning of the fourth century, says that there he saw "Roman men" (probably veterans of the legion stationed in Aelia) cultivating the fields.[12]

Late Roman Construction

There is one important exception to the lack of colonization on Zion during the late Roman period. From 1949 to 1951, following a Jordanian artillery attack, Joseph Pinkerfeld was able to conduct an investigation of "David's Tomb," the so-called royal tomb[13] located directly under the traditional Roman-Gothic room of the Last Supper.[14] Pinkerfeld's examination revealed that the lowest accessible layers of stone of the south, east, and north walls are attached to a stone floor from the late Roman period.[15] The assignment of the construction to the Aelia Capitolina period is supported also by the appearance of stones in the wall which have been identified as reused ashlars taken from a Herodian structure.[16] The building in question resembles to some extent synagogues of the early centuries of the Common Era.[17] Especially noteworthy is a small adjoining apse, 1.92 m above the floor. In front of the apse today stands a cenotaph from the crusades which both orthodox Jews and uncritical Christian pilgrims regard as the burial site of David. The apse reminds one of Torah niches that have been found in synagogues at Dura-Europos on the Euphrates, Eshtemoa (S. Judea) and Naveh (Batanea).[18] The use of a niche to store Holy Scripture in the period before 70 C.E. can now be verified from excavations at Gamla in Gaulanitis.[19]

Some graffiti, which Pinkerfeld found and Franciscan epigrapher Emmanuele Testa published and interpreted, provide valuable evidence for determining the nature of this construction. The graffiti employ language characteristic of Jewish Christians. The longest inscription, according to Testa,[20] is an allusion to the messianic Psalm 110:1: "O Jesus, Lord of lords, that I might live!" (*IOU IE[SOUS] ZE[SO] KI[RI]E AUTOKRATOROS*). In his Pentecost sermon (Acts 2:34–35), Peter explicitly referred to this passage. The Epistle of James, which may have originated before 62 C.E. within the circle of the "Lord's brother,"[21] apparently indicates (2:2–3) that some Jewish Christians had possession of their own synagogues.[22] Thus, in the period of Aelia Capitolina there must have been such a Jewish-Christian place of worship on the southwest hill of Jerusalem whose history and significance may be illuminated by literary testimony.[23]

The First Meeting Place of the Primitive Church

The "upper room" (*hyperōon*), where the first community was remaining (Acts 1:13: *hou ēsan katamenontes*[24]) after the ascension and where the Pentecost event occurred (Acts 2:1-2), already had an established significance for Luke. Luke seems to represent this center as the prototype for the primitive church's places of worship. The Greek word (*hyperōon*) in the New Testament appears only in Acts and always in contexts that denote a place of worship. According to Acts (9:37, 39) Tabitha, a member of the community of widows in Joppa,[25] was laid in such an upper room after she died. Acts 20:7-8 describes an early Christian meeting for Sunday worship in an upper room at Troas in Asia Minor. This report, given in the first person, specifically observes that "there were many lights" in the room (Acts 20:8). Moreover, inside the "house of Peter" in Capernaum, which was transformed into a house church by the second half of the first century, numerous fragments of oil lamps have been found.[26] Upper rooms had previously acquired some religious significance in the Old Testament (2Kgs 4:10-11: *ʿălîyyâ;* Dan 6:11: *ʿalit,* LXX: *hyperōon*). This is perhaps why, at a later time, they became favorite meeting places for scholars.[27] As shown by a third-century synagogue inscription in Stobi (Dalmatia),[28] even synagogues sometimes had special upper rooms (*hyperōa*).

In connection with the persecution under Herod Agrippa I, Luke introduces (Acts 12:12-14) another meeting place in Jerusalem.[29] The account not only describes the outside (Acts 12:13: a house with its own gateway) but also gives the name of the owner—Mary, the mother of John called Mark (Acts 12:12). Other Christians under the leadership of the "Lord's brother," James, gathered at a different location (Acts 12:17). If Luke's narrative thus far is considered, this other place could only have been the "upper room" at which the presence of Jesus' relatives had been expressly emphasized (Acts 1:13-14). Not until 530 C.E. did a secondary tradition identify the "upper room" with the house of John Mark.[30] Since Luke consciously differentiates between the two places, it is possible, from his common but implicit manner of presentation,[31] to draw the following basic conclusion: Between 41 and 44 C.E. James became the leader of the more conservative Jewish Christians, who were primarily the Aramaic-speaking part of the community (*Hebraioi*; cf. Acts 6:1). John, on the basis of his nickname, Mark, is to be characterized as Greek-speaking (*Hellēnistēs*), while his family, on account of their close ties with Peter, may be described as those who were open to the Gentile mission (Acts 13:5, 13; 15:37).[32] The statements made by Luke should be taken seriously, since he himself was obviously acquainted with Jerusalem.[33] From the first person report in Acts 21:15–18 we learn that he visited the holy city at least once (57 C.E.) and met with James at the meeting place for the strict Jewish Christians. The use of the article before "upper room" in Acts 1:13 implies that Luke himself knew the location of this room.[34]

According to a reliable[35] tradition in Eusebius (*Church History* 3.5.3) and Epiphanius,[36] the Jewish Christian community left the Holy City at the outbreak of the Jewish War (66–70 C.E.) to settle at Pella in the Decapolis. The absence of the Jewish Christians does not appear to have been longer than six or seven years. Evidence for this duration comes from Eutychus, a patriarch of Alexandria in the first half of the tenth century. Relying on earlier sources,[37] he reported that the primitive church of Jerusalem, under the leadership of Simon Bar-Cleophas in the fourth year of Vespasian (72/73 C.E.), returned from the east side of the Jordan to the Holy City and built a church there.[38] This account could be true, since at this time the final resistance of the Zealots was destroyed at Masada,[39] and the political climate in Jerusalem was calm enough by then to make a return understandable. The continuity of place traditions would have been guaranteed by Simon Bar-Cleophas, who himself was a bridge between the time of Jesus and the postapostolic period.[40] As a matter of fact, like James, the "Lord's brother" who led the Jerusalem community until his death in 62 C.E. (see Josephus, *Ant* 20.199–203), Simon was a relative of Jesus.[41]

The statements of the Alexandrian patriarch are supported by a report of Epiphanius, bishop of Salamis (315–403 C.E.). He also passes on interesting information about Jewish Christianity which he attributes to older sources.[42] In the passage cited below he is writing about Hadrian's visit to Jerusalem during his second excursion to the eastern part of the empire in the summer of 130 C.E.:[43]

He found the whole city destroyed and the Temple of the Lord trampled down, except for a few small dwellings such as the small Church of God (*hē tou Theou Ekklēsia mikra*), which lies on the spot where the disciples went into the upper room (*hyperōon*) when they had returned from the Mount of Olives after the ascension of their Savior. Of course it was built on Zion (*Sion*) . . .[44]

This testimony from literature accords well with the archaeological finds at "David's Tomb." The Jewish Christian synagogue, whose remains are preserved, is not identical with the "upper room" of the New Testament but keeps its memory alive.

Naturally the question arises whether or not the Bar Kochba rebellion (132–135 C.E.)[45] and the subsequent establishment of the Roman Aelia Capitolina would have broken the continuity of Christian place traditions. As Eusebius reports, soon after the end of the rebellion there was a Gentile Christian bishop in Aelia named Markus (*Church History* 4.6; 5.12). Yet among the members of the Gentile Christian community there could have been some who had even resided in Jerusalem before 132 C.E.[46] Gentile Christians were also interested in place traditions. For instance, according to Eusebius (*Church History* 6.11,12), Alexander, a friend of Origen and later a bishop in Cappadocia, came to Palestine around 212 C.E. "in order to pray and to investigate the places" (*euchēs kai ton topon historias heneken*). The continuity of Jewish Christian place traditions, therefore, did not simply come to an end.

Moreover, Judah, the last Jewish Christian bishop, outlived the Jerusalem catastrophe by several years, that is, until the eleventh year of the reign of Antoninus Pius (148/149 C.E.).[47] The designation appended to his name, Kuriakos (*kyriakos*), indicates that Judah was from the family of Jesus. This appellative also shows how strongly rooted the Davidic genealogy continued to remain in the consciousness of the Jewish Christian community in Jerusalem. According to Adolf Schlatter, Judah wrote a chronography which contained a report about the so-called tomb of Adam at Golgotha, a tradition known by Julius Africanus (c. 160–240 C.E.) and Origen.[48] This tomb tradition is part of a larger network of legends that were propagated in Jewish Christian writings reminiscent of Essene documents such as the Testament of Adam, the Apocalypse of Adam, the Life of Adam and Eve, and the Syriac Cave of Treasure or Ethiopic Book of Adam.[49] Apparently the writing compiled by Judah played a role in the rediscovery of Golgotha and the tomb of Jesus under the empress Helena (326 C.E.).[50] Thus Jewish Christian place traditions at Jerusalem were known into the early Byzantine period.

According to tradition, Jerusalem is the place where Bishop Judah was martyred.[51] But could it have been possible that a Jewish Christian was living in Jerusalem in 148/149 c.e.? After all, a ban of Hadrian (Eusebius, *Church History* 4.6.3) had forbidden Jews to enter Jerusalem at any time except for the 9th of Ab. But the force of the decree already seems to have been relaxed during the reign of Antoninus Pius (138–161 c.e.);[52] during the period of the Severan emperors (193 c.e. on) at the latest, we know that a Jewish community again existed in Jerusalem.[53] Baruch Lifschitz also assigns the presence of a Jewish Christian group to this period,[54] a supposition that is in fact supported by the outbreak of controversy under Bishop Narcissus (c. 196 c.e.) concerning the observance of Easter on the 14th of Nisan.[55] There are reasons to believe that there was a Jewish Christian minority living in Jerusalem even during the early Byzantine period. It is possible, therefore, that the *hyperōon* outside the city had continued to be in the possession of this minority.[56] Whatever the case, there is still enough evidence to conclude with P. Benoit, the well-known specialist in the archaeology of Jerusalem, that the tradition which locates the first meeting place of the primitive community in Jerusalem on the southwest hill is reliable.[57]

The Tradition of the Last Supper Room

According to the understanding of Luke the "upper room" (*hyperōon*) of Acts 1:13 and the location of the Last Supper are identical,[58] despite the fact that, along with Mark 14:15, he uses the synonym *anagaion*[59] (Lk 22:12) to designate this place. If this identification is correct, then the place tradition of the meeting place for the first post-Easter community would also be the traditional location of the Last Supper. Since the high priest's palace was not situated in the area of the Armenian Church of the Savior near the traditional Last Supper room, but much farther southeast on the grounds of the Church of St. Peter in Gallicantu,[60] this location does not present any difficulties. Nevertheless, there could be reason to doubt that the location of the Last Supper and that of the first primitive community are the same. Not until a fifth-century statement by Hesychius of Jerusalem is there an unmistakable reference that locates the Last Supper on Zion.[61] T. Zahn sought to explain this silence by the rather random character of our sources, which, because of particular interests, often mention only one detail among others of a place tradition.[62] Still a more important explanation has attracted attention in recent years. Igino Grego speaks about a "vow of silence (*congiura di silenzio*)"[63] within the catholic church concerning holy places still in the hand of Jewish Christians during the Byzantine period.

Some comments by Epiphanius refer to an intentional silence concerning Zion traditions of Jewish Christians. While enumerating the holy places in Jerusalem in the year 373 C.E., he consciously omits Zion,[64] but mentions a number of considerably less important sites. In a polemic directed in part against Jewish Christian heresies between 375 and 377 C.E., he says emphatically: "Although the now degraded Mt. Zion was once more important than the place (that is, Golgotha) . . . it is now cut off (*tmētheisa*)."[65] The bishop's mode of expression leaves little doubt that, in his opinion, Zion belonged to heretics. In the time of the pilgrim Egeria (383 C.E.) the institution of the Last Supper was commemorated "*post crucem*,"[66] that is, east of the Golgotha rock. That one would be content with so obvious a makeshift without any mention of the local place tradition[67] is itself an indication that the genuine site was known.

Allusions from before the beginning of the fifth century that the Last Supper took place on Zion are not entirely lacking. Origen (185–253/254 C.E.) apparently knew of the old meeting place of the primitive community "on the summit of the mount," the "visible mountain of the Lord, Zion (*Sion*)."[68] In another passage he seems to suggest that Jesus had the Last Supper with his disciples on this same mountain:

> He taught the disciples . . . , who had received the bread of blessing and eaten the body of the Word and drunk the cup of thanksgiving . . . to go from one hill to the other (*de alto transire in altum*); since the believer can do nothing in the valley, he climbed the Mount of Olives.[69]

This account acquires significance when one considers that the way from the upper part of the city (the west hill) to the Mount of Olives leads through the deep Kidron Valley.[70] When Eusebius writes (c. 315 C.E.) that at Zion "our Savior and Lord stayed and gave many teachings,"[71] he evidently acknowledges the southwest hill not only as the place where the post-Easter community originated but also as the site where Jesus' pre-Easter work transpired. Jerome translates *hyperōon* as well as *anagaion*, which the Old Latin translation rendered with *superiora*, with the term *coenaculum*, since he apparently identified both. Moreover, when he referred to the Spirit's outpouring "in the supper room on Zion (*in coenaculo Sion*)," he was drawing on a tradition he had acquired on a visit (after 385 C.E.) to Jerusalem.[72] *Doctrina Addai*, which originated in Syria near the end of the fourth century, also translates the different words for the upper room with one word ('*ălîthôn*), a rendering that may have been derived from an older pilgrim tradition.[73] Thus, at a much earlier time (see n. 37) the predominant tradition could have been that of Eutychus of Alexandria, according to which Jesus "ate the Passover of the law at the Jewish Easter in the upper room."[74]

The tradition that locates the Last Supper on Zion also has some arguments in its favor, though they are not as strong as those for the first meeting place of the primitive community. R. Pesch writes:

> The history of the Jewish Christians in Jerusalem during the four centuries following the Jewish War (AD 66–70) has not received enough attention. This period began with their flight across the Jordan to Pella, from which they returned to Mt. Zion in the 70's. Has the church handed down reliable testimony about the site of the Last Supper? Investigation of the "Christian Zion" on the west hill of Jerusalem in recent years has strengthened confidence in the tradition.[75]

What follows is a discussion of this research.

THE ESSENE QUARTER OF JERUSALEM

The Period When Qumran Was Uninhabited

The prehistory of the hasidic movement (*ḥăsîdîm, Asidaioi*), from which the Essenes came, goes back to the time of Persian rule.[76] Substantial portions of Enoch literature,[77] the book of Jubilees,[78] and even the oldest form of the Damascus Document[79] were already in existence when the "Righteous Teacher" and a group of followers separated themselves from the rest of Judaism after 152 B.C.E.[80] One must, therefore, always be aware that the Qumran community formed only a small part of the broader Essene movement. Both Philo of Alexandria (*Every Good Man Is Free* 75) and Josephus (*Ant* 18.20), earlier and later contemporaries of the apostles, specify that the number of Essenes was about four thousand. No more than a couple hundred people could have lived at Qumran. The Essene circles shared certain specific convictions such as the observance of the "Old Testament" priestly solar calendar (see the discussion below) but, in matters such as celibacy (Josephus, *War* 2.160) they were divided. In any case, one does well to investigate the possible connection between Essenism and the Palestinian Jesus Movement without limiting the inquiry to the isolated group in the wilderness at Qumran.

Zion was not the only place that went uninhabited for a period of time. The same was also the case with the Essene establishment on the northwest side of the Dead Sea, which we have known about since 1947. R. de Vaux, the excavator of Qumran, originally thought that the settlement had been destroyed by a fire sometime before the massive earthquake in 31 B.C.E. (Josephus, *Ant* 15.121-47; *War* 1.370-80).[81] Later he attributed the destruction to the earthquake and a subsequent fire.[82] It is more likely, however, that the devastation had already occurred, either through the invasion of the Parthians (40/39 B.C.E.)[83] or as a result of the struggle of the Hasmonean Antigonus against Herod the Great (40-37 B.C.E.).[84] Resettlement began between 4 and 1 B.C.E. during the early part of the reign (4 B.C.E.-6 C.E.) of Archelaus (Mt 2:22).[85] It is striking that the period when no one lived at Qumran is covered by the reign of Herod the Great (37-4 B.C.E.). Even more astonishing is that according to Josephus (*Ant* 15.373-78) Herod favored the Essenes. Josephus attributes this preference both to the fulfillment of a prophecy made by Manaemos the Essene that Herod would ascend his throne and to Herod's own hatred of the Hasmoneans. Scholars have raised the possibility that the Essenes inhabited the Holy City during a period when the political climate was in their favor.[86]

Furthermore, it is noteworthy that the resettlement at Qumran turned out to be significantly smaller than the first.[87] Could it be that the group which returned to the wilderness was even more radical and decidedly esoteric than the Essenes who remained in Jerusalem? If this was the case, then we do well to examine arguments based on a remark by Josephus (*Ant* 18.19) according to which at least a few Essenes (perhaps at an isolated spot) after Herod the Great's reign offered sacrifices at the Jerusalem Temple according to their own halakah.[88] Also interesting in this connection is evidence suggesting that those who lived at Qumran during the second phase no longer made use of the Aramaic parts of 1 Enoch that were found there.[89] The oldest portions of these apocalyptic books date back to before the separation in the mid-second century B.C.E. (see n. 77) and, consequently, do not represent Qumran literature as such.

The Essene Gate

More can be said concerning where the Essenes lived in Jerusalem since the reign of Herod the Great. According to the reports of Philo[90] and Josephus (*War* 2.124) and to what is presupposed in the Damascus Document (CD 10.21–23; 12.19–23), we have to expect an Essene settlement. In a description of the western wall of Jerusalem, Josephus points out two pertinent topographical details:

> On the west side it is extended from the same starting point (that is, the Hippicus Tower in the area of the modern-day Citadel) along a piece of land called Bethso until the Gate of the Essenes (*dia de tou Bethso kaloumenou chorou katateinon epi tēn Essēnōn pylēn*), then bent to the south and then ran its course on the other side of the Pool of Siloam. . . . (*War* 5.145)

From Josephus's statement alone it is possible to determine rather exactly the location of the Essene Gate and Bethso. The gate was situated where the so-called "first wall" changed its course from a north-south to a west-east direction.[91]

J. B. Lightfoot and M. J. Lagrange already proposed that the "Gate of the Essenes" implies the existence of an Essene quarter in Jerusalem.[92] Moreover, the eminent authority E. Schürer wrote: "There undoubtedly were Essenes in Jerusalem as well, where they repeatedly appear in history . . . and a gate was named after them . . . presumably because an Essene dwelling was located nearby."[93] Many contemporary scholars have accepted Schürer's judgment, above all O. Michel in the large Tübingen commentary on Josephus.[94]

Are there other traces of this gate, and is there any evidence for an Essene quarter in its vicinity? What comes to mind is the gate that Bliss and Dickie discovered in the southeast corner of the Protestant cemetery and first identified as the Essene Gate.[95] Because of the confusion created by K. Kenyon, it proved necessary to review the dating of this particular site with modern archaeological methodology. The English excavation, however, was left open[96] and one suspects that excavated components of the gate were used in later structures by Arabs. Nevertheless, B. Pixner set about reexcavating the gate, after he published in 1976 a pioneering study concerning the possible Essene quarter on Zion.[97]

In the summer of 1977 the site of the gate was again laid open in its entirety, as is shown by a comparison with older maps.[98] Beginning in 1979 Pixner, with Israeli archaeologist S. Margalit and architect D. Chen, further unearthed the walls on both sides of the gate. The preliminary results can be summarized as follows: The excavation shows a three-tiered gate made up of three superimposed sills, which date back to three different, chronologically successive periods. (1) The ceramic below the lowest sill of the gate (sealed-off pottery) has been examined by experts (Staurislao Loffreda and Benjamin Mazar) and has clearly been dated as Herodian, that is, pottery from the reign of Herod the Great (37–4 B.C.E.) up to 70 C.E. (destruction of Jerusalem). There is therefore no doubt that the lowest sill with flanking stones on both sides belonged to the gate referred to by Josephus Flavius (*War* 5.145) as the "Gate of the Essenes." (2) Also the pottery below the intermediary sill (also sealed-off ceramic) has been examined and the statement of the expert (Renate Rosenthal) ascribes it cautiously to the period of Aelia Capitolina. This sill with a socket for a gate might be the remains of a gate belonging to a wall around Mt. Zion, which the Pilgrim of Bordeaux (333 C.E.) calls the "Murum Sion." (3) The third and uppermost sill belongs most surely to a Byzantine wall built in the middle of the fifth century. The street leading from the gate to the city in northeasterly direction was used throughout the three periods of the gate. So was also the sewage canal running under the street (along its outer edge) and which used to empty itself into the Hinnom Valley a short distance from the gate. Where this canal passes below the gate, it is made of large limestone slabs showing excellent workmanship. It could date back to the time of Herod the Great (B. Mazar). The points of conjunction between the Gate of the Essenes and the Hasmonean wall seem to indicate that sewer and gate were built after a breach had been made into an already existing Hasmonean wall.[99] Thus the assertions of K. Kenyon about the southern expansion of Jerusalem during the New Testament period have proved to be unacceptable.[100]

But how did the name of the gate originate? Is this the place from which the Essenes left the city to reach their settlement at the Dead Sea? This in itself would suggest the presence of a permanent Essene community in Jerusalem. Otherwise such frequent use of the gate, which led to a designation after the Essenes, is inexplicable. In any case, it was common in

Jerusalem topography to have a gate named after the group of people who lived behind it. For example, during the crusades there was a "Pisa Gate" on Zion, named after a settlement of people who had earlier lived in this Italian region.[101]

The finds at the Essene Gate described above, then, are best explained by assuming that an Essene community was established on the southwest hill at the beginning of Herodian rule. Excavations conducted by M. Broshi have shown that the buildings of this area were severely damaged by the earthquake of 31 B.C.E.[102] Broshi's determination could be an added reason for the formation of an Essene settlement. That nothing characteristic of the Essenes was found here (Map 1, F I) does not provide a substantive objection. The area that Pixner has suggested as the place where the Essenes lived lies farther to the south.[103] In contrast to what Broshi found, excavations in 1983/1984 (F V) and 1985 (F VI) unearthed remains of simple dwellings from the period before 70 C.E.

What purpose would there have been for constructing an additional gate on such an ill-suited, steep slope? A reason may be found in the Essenes' apparent theological preference for the city's southwest hill. In a passage of 1 Enoch that goes back to the second century B.C.E.,[104] a "holy mountain" (1En 26:2) is given a topographical description (1En 27:1–4) that could have been a reference to the Mount Zion of today.[105] From this mountain the righteous will see the judgment of the wicked (1En 27:1–4), which will be executed in the Hinnom Valley. Echoes of this motif are present when Jesus designates the eschatological place of judgment and punishment with the Aramaic word *gĕhinnam* (transliterated into the Greek *geenna*).[106] Since the Essenes were extremely wary of cultic impurity, the renowned G. Dalman, on the basis of a statement in the pre-Christian Letter of Aristeas (106), has proposed that they possessed their own entrance to the city.[107] A plausible explanation for this circumstantial evidence may be the construction of an additional gate for pedestrians at such an unfavorable spot. There are still further reasons for supposing that the Essenes formed a community just behind the gate which bore their name.

The Location of Bethso

Josephus mentions a piece of land (*chōros*) called *Bethso*, which he located near the Essene Gate. Early pioneers in the research of Palestine such as E. Robinson and J. Schwarz held the view that the Greek expression, a transliteration of the Aramaic *beth zo'a,* referred to a latrine.[108]

The Temple Scroll (11QTemple), in addition to dealing with the Essene festal calendar and regulations on the holiness of Jerusalem, is above all concerned with describing the eschatological sanctuary. In 1972 Yigael Yadin published an essay in which he pointed to a parallel in the Temple Scroll to Josephus's statement on Bethso.[109] The passage reads as follows:

> And you shall make them a place for a "hand," outside the city, to which they shall go, to the northwest of the city, roofed houses with pits within them, into which excrement will descend, [so that] it will [not] be visible at any distance from the city, three thousand cubits. (11QTemple 46.13–16)[110]

Yadin locates the Bethso area northwest of the Citadel (Map 2), since he interprets the three thousand cubits as minimum distance. But the place he has suggested is only 200 m away from the city[111] and not the minimum 1.5 km, as his interpretation would require. Moreover, this location is incompatible with the statements of Josephus. Yadin contradicted himself when he wrote the following in another publication: "Thus 'the place called Betsoa' and the Essene Gate were both *in the western section* of the city wall and both were *close to each other. . . .*"[112] How can one speak of close proximity when the distance between the gate and Bethso is over 1 km (Map 2)?

Pixner offers another explanation and translation:

> And they shall make themselves a place of the hand outside the city, where they shall go out to in a northwesterly direction from the city, (where they shall make) roofed buildings with pits inside them so that the feces would drop into them and would not be visible to anybody for a distance of three thousand cubits from the city.

Pixner comments:

> The text of the Scroll seems to indicate the direction that would have to be taken after leaving the City rather than the geographical location of the toilets. . . . This matches as closely as possible the topographical situation around the Gate of the Essenes at the time the Scroll was

written. At the time (early Roman Period), we know of no other gate along the western city wall. An Essene leaving the city through this gate and wishing to proceed to the Bethso would turn to the northwest . . . follow somewhere south or north of the present Bishop Gobat School, which stands on the site of a once very imposing tower of the Hasmonean Wall. . . . May I suggest that the distance prescribed both in the *Temple Scroll* and in the *War Scroll* [1QM 7.7] was not to mean the area beyond which, but rather the area within which the latrines had to be placed.[113]

Though Pixner's interpretation of the Temple Scroll passage is philologically at least possible, it seems problematic in view of the prescription of the War Scroll. Because of the difficulties both Pixner and Yadin meet, J. A. Emerton denies every connection between Josephus' Bethso and the law of the Temple Scroll.[114] But even if we grant the problems of interpretation, there are several reasons for retaining this connection: (1) The wording of the Temple Scroll provides the closest philological analogy to the Bethso in the *War* of Josephus. (2) One passage is in an Essene document, the other passage mentions Bethso in close proximity to a "Gate of the Essenes." (3) For his description of the end and turning points of Jerusalem's city walls, of course, Josephus had to choose characteristic topographical features. Could one of the many public toilets in the city serve this purpose? Josephus' description becomes understandable if the Bethso was a very special—that is, an Essene—installation.

Long before the existence of the Temple Scroll was known, scholars such as H. Clementz and G. Dalman located the Bethso area between the Essene Gate and the stone foundation of an immense corner tower (Map 1, T 3) on which stands one of the main buildings of the former Anglican Gobat School.[115] Here, in 1874, on the cliff outside the city wall canal-like installations were found. The English excavator H. Maudslay and the eminent topographer C. R. Conder interpreted the finds as remains of stables.[116] It remains to be seen whether these installations (and perhaps the grooves in the rock which may have signified roof construction) had anything to do with the Essene Bethso.

Originally, Yadin also identified the city exit assumed in the Temple Scroll with the gate excavated by Bliss and considered both to be the Essene Gate mentioned by Josephus. From the proximity of the gate to the latrine he further concluded that the Essene settlement was not situated far from the gate. The argument in itself is plausible but lacks persuasive power on account of where Yadin placed the Bethso. Later Yadin changed his mind and identified the "Gate of the Essenes" with a gate farther to the north (near the southwest corner of the present city wall), apparently to diminish (with little success) the distance between the Essene Gate and Bethso.[117] But this is in conflict with Josephus's description, and the newly proposed gate probably dates only from the time of Aelia Capitolina.

If the Bethso is to be assigned to the grounds of the Episcopal school, then one has a weighty argument in favor of positing an Essene quarter in the southwest corner of Jerusalem. Already before the new excavations, J. Milgrom advanced the following opinion concerning the Essene Gate: "It was probably a small gate or wicket used exclusively by the Essenes to reach their toilets."[118]

A Network of Ritual Baths

Excavations in recent years have increasingly shown how significant ritual washings had become for all pious Jews during the New Testament period. Numerous ritual baths (*mqw'wt*) were found not only in Herodian Jericho, but also in Jerusalem.[119] Qumran possessed an ingenious system of purification baths which were adjusted to the particular needs of the sect.[120] From the presence of ritual baths nothing further about the Essene settlement could be concluded, but the lack thereof would be a serious argument against the presence of an Essene quarter on the southwest hill. However, the grounds south of the Dormition Abbey (Map 1), like those close to the area before the south and southwest wall of the sanctuary,[121] yield a compact network of ritual baths. In a relatively small area within the city wall one finds no fewer than six *miqwā'ôt*. One *miqweh* was only recently discovered (B 1) in excavations (1983/1984) before the entrance to the Dormition Abbey,[122] and another in 1985 on the grounds of the former house of Nigrizia (B 1). One bath (B 2) had already been found at the beginning of this century near the church structure.[123] Two more lie to the southwest (B 3),[124] between the southeast corners[125] (B 4) of the so-called Greek Gardens. Finally, there is one (B 5) that today is covered by a hideous cement roof. The most extensive of all the baths, it was transformed in the Byzantine period into either a hermitage or an underground baptismal chapel.[126] It is the largest bath installation in Jerusalem discovered to date, the size of which suggests that it belonged to a community rather than to private owners.

On the way from the Essene Gate to the possible Bethso, one comes to a double bath, hewn into the rock of the cliff which had earlier supported the wall.[127] We know of only one other possible bath located outside the wall of Jerusalem. Built during the Herodian period, it lies in the vicinity of the upper palace of Herod.[128]

If our placing of Bethso is correct, then the double bath must have been used for ritual cleansings in connection with it. In fact, such washings were practiced by the Essenes after use of the latrine (Josephus, *War* 2.149). As the War Scroll shows, the Essenes considered themselves the eschatological army of God; they therefore applied "Old Testament" passages on holy war to their situation. In addition to this eschatological consciousness, they may have shared the belief that they stood in the tradition of the Rechabites. Such a self-consciousness is indicated by talmudic and Christian sources.[129] It has never been completely disproved that there was a connection between postexilic hasidic groups and the Rechabites from the time of Jeremiah (Jer 35:12–19) and Malchijah Ben-Rechab (Neh 3:14).[130]

The Essenes, under the influence of Deuteronomy (2:14–15; 23:10–15), called their community settlement a "military camp" (*mhnwt*), as the War Scroll (1QM 3.5–6) and the Damascus Document (CD 7.6) attest. The Deuteronomic camp regulations prescribed that a warrior, after nocturnal defilement, had to remain outside the camp for a whole day. He was allowed to return in the evening after a cleansing (Deut 23:11–12). In the same manner, the double bath outside the wall could have served to meet this requirement. In Qumran there is also a large bath installation[131] outside the settlement, which seems to have been directed toward Jerusalem.[132] The following verses (Deut 23:13–15) contain injunctions concerning the construction of latrines outside the camp. This text became the basis for the corresponding instructions given in the Temple Scroll and the War Scroll (1QM 7.6). The double bath outside the city wall provides further evidence for an Essene quarter directly behind the wall. Its water supply, of course, came from cisterns within the walls. Assuming that the double bath was Essene, then the cisterns could only have belonged to Essenes,[133] since according to the Rule of the Community (1QS 5.13) novices were never allowed to touch the ritual bathwater (cf. Josephus, *War* 2.138, 150).

Evidence from the Qumran Scrolls

One of the most puzzling discoveries at Qumran is the so-called Copper Scroll (3Q15), which was found in the third cave in 1952. As a listing of sixty-four treasure hiding places[134] supposedly located in the Holy Land, it became the center of a stormy controversy which has now largely subsided. Against the opinion of the scroll's first publisher, J. T. Milik,[135] more and more scholars have recently advanced the view that the scroll is a genuine document from Qumran and not just a collection of fantastic legends of the late Roman period.[136] According to Pixner, hiding places nos. 3–17 (3Q15 1.6–4.2) are indicative of an Essene community on the southwest hill of Jerusalem.[137]

The War Scroll from Qumran, which was composed near the beginning of the first century C.E., seems to presuppose the existence of an Essene community in the Holy City. This document mentioned (1QM 3.11) the "community from Jerusalem" (*h'dh yrwšlym*). Since in the Damascus Document sexual intercourse was not permitted in Jerusalem (CD 12.1), the community there may have practiced celibacy. Such a way of life is further substantiated by the fact that corresponding regulations of the Temple Scroll (11QTemple 46.13–51.10) include no prescriptions concerning places of purification for wives within the city walls.[138] It would be desirable to be able to evaluate Pixner's thesis on the basis of more extensive excavations on Mount Zion. But it must be admitted that there is enough archaeological data, together with literary testimony, to make an Essene quarter on the southwest hill of Jerusalem probable.[139]

JESUS AND THE ESSENE QUARTER

Disciples from the Essenes?

One of the most striking phenomena of the New Testament is that members of the Essenes are not mentioned alongside the partisans of the Pharisees and Sadducees. They do not appear in any of Jesus' numerous polemical sayings which the Gospels convey. Nevertheless, Jesus must have encountered them, because the wilderness of Qumran was not the only place in which pious Essenes lived (see the Foreword and chapter 1 above).

What kind of relationship existed between Jesus and the Essene circles? Essenes would have rejected Jesus' sovereignty over ritual codes of purity (Mt 15:1–20; Mk 7:1–23) or his table fellowship with tax collectors and other conspicuous sinners. Sayings that prohibited hatred of one's enemy

(Mt 5:43–48; Lk 6:27–36; 1QS 1.10) or allowed one to rescue an animal out of a pit on the Sabbath (Lk 14:5; cf. CD 11.13–17) appear to have been directed against the views of Essenes. On the other hand, some aspects of Jesus' proclamation could be appropriated by the Essenes. Examples include his prohibition of divorce, which he articulated on the basis of the order of creation (Mt 19:4–6; Mk 10:6–9; cf. CD 4.20–21; 11QTemple 57.17–19), and his high regard for celibacy (Mt 19:12; Lk 20:34–36; cf. 1QSb 4.24–26).

The pious Essenes eagerly waited for the eschatological redemption, which in the first century c.e. was apparently intensified by an expectation of a Davidic Messiah.[140] When Jesus claimed to fulfill messianic promises through his work, as his answer to the question of the imprisoned John the Baptist shows (Mt 11:2–6; Lk 7:18–23),[141] at least some Jews of Essene persuasion must have opened themselves to his mission.

Jesus' answer to John the Baptist echoes the prophecy in Isaiah 61, which also was interpreted messianically at Qumran (11QMelch 6–9). The evidently unmarried sisters of Lazarus, Mary and Martha, who lived in Bethany on the Mount of Olives and whose home Jesus frequented as guest (Mt 22:6; Mk 14:3; Jn 11:1–3; cf. Lk 10:38), may be examples of Jesus' supporters who came from Essene circles.[142] According to the Temple Scroll three places east of the Holy City should be isolated for lepers (11QTemple 46.16f). Yadin advanced the view that one of these places was situated near Bethany, since here the house of Simon the leper (Mt 26:6; Mk 14:13) is mentioned.[143] In 1950 a Jewish Christian sanctuary[144] was apparently found in the immediate vicinity of the New Testament Bethany. A shrine to honor Lazarus was attached to it, at the latest, during the early Byzantine period.[145] Originally the sanctuary was a large Jewish ritual bath,[146] which resembles a recently found *miqweh*[147] on the northern side of the Mount of Olives and which also may be compared with baths on Mount Zion.

Just after the discovery of the Qumran Scrolls, noteworthy similarities with the Gospel of John became evident to many scholars.[148] The Scrolls signified a breakthrough in the history-of-religions approach to Johannine thought and language.[149] Much of what some New Testament scholars had attributed to non-Jewish Hellenism or at least diaspora Judaism suddenly acquired substantial parallels in contemporary texts from a predominantly priestly group which did not reside far from Jerusalem. According to its own testimony the tradition of the Johannine Gospel goes back to one of Jesus' disciples (Jn 21:24) who had originally been a supporter of the

Baptizer (Jn 1:35–39), who himself came out of priestly circles (see Lk 1).[150] The Fourth Gospel's particular interest in Jewish baptizing groups[151] and its close affinity with priestly theology[152] are impossible to overlook. Thus the hypotheses of F. M. Braun and R. E. Brown are worthy of consideration.[153] They proposed that there was a connection between Jesus' disciple standing behind the tradition of the Fourth Gospel via John the Baptizer[154] and circles of Essene persuasion. This relationship is also an indication that Jesus' preaching of repentance found a hearing among such groups.

The Last Passover Meal

Questions concerning the calendar and festivals played exceedingly significant roles among the Essenes. At the beginning of the Rule of the Community appears the admonition "not to transgress a single one of all God's words concerning their times and not to move their times forward and not to be late with all their feasts" (1QS 1.13–15). In 1953 A. Jaubert showed that the Qumran community observed a priestly solar calendar of 364 days which already existed in the Old Testament period. This calendar is also exhibited in the book of Jubilees, whose origin is at least closely related to the Essenes.[155] Despite a few controversial matters of detail, this thesis is today considered valid.[156] The Essene orientation to the solar calendar has been confirmed by the Temple Scroll[157] and also by the yet-to-be-published text entitled Some of the Precepts of the Torah (4QMMT). But not only was this system of reckoning observed by the rigid groups of Essenes; it found attention also in wider Jewish circles, such as the Boethusians, the family that temporarily supplied the high priests during the reign of Herod the Great.[158] A recently published Qumran text containing rules (4Q513),[159] when compared with the Mishna tractate Menahot (10.3), reveals further calendrical similarities between the Boethusians and the Essenes, particularly with regard to the omer ceremony.[160] It is also striking that the priestly solar calendar influenced Christian groups of the second and third centuries as well as the Montanists of Asia Minor.[161] Within Montanism, however, this calendrical influence was inherited through Johannine Christianity.[162]

According to the Synoptic Gospels (Mt 26:17–30; Mk 14:12–20; Lk 22:7–20) the Last Supper was a Passover meal. The same is implied by the Fourth Gospel (Jn 13).[163] Despite judicious arguments to the contrary by many exegetes, one must conclude that our sources have preserved the historical situation.[164] In any case, this judgment conflicts with the date of Jesus' crucifixion given in the Fourth Gospel. According to John 18:28 and 19:14 the execution occurred on the 14th of Nisan, one day before the Jewish feast of Unleavened Bread.

Jaubert has attempted to solve this well-known chronological inconsistency with the help of the Essene solar calendar.[165] In this calendar the Passover meal always fell on Tuesday evening to Wednesday. On this calendar date Jesus shared a real Passover meal, which the Synoptics correctly describe as such. Since the 14th of Nisan in the year of Jesus' death (30 c.e.) was a Friday—as all four Gospels also assume (Mt 27:62; Mk 15:42; Lk 23:54–56; Jn 19:31, 42)—the trial of Jesus would have lasted three days. Otherwise, one would have to maintain that the trial took place during an incredibly short time (less than a half day), which hardly seems possible.[166] In fact, however, some texts of the early church present a longer chronology for the passion.[167] The oldest testimony is provided by the Syriac Didascalia (5.12–17). Though the present form of this work dates to the beginning of the third century, the traditions it transmits go back well into the second century.[168]

The main objection brought forth against the thesis of Jaubert has been that the Gospels have no room for a longer passion chronology.[169] Though such is indeed the impression made on an unbiased reader, still more puzzling is the origin of the longer chronology if it is not to be explained by the transmission of any tradition. E. Ruckstuhl, above all, has tried to show that the Gospels do convey traces of a longer trial.[170] In a recent publication, whose point of departure is A. Strobel's important investigation of the trial of Jesus, Ruckstuhl has further observed that all four Gospels, partly for reasons of theological composition, have represented the passion events in abbreviated form.[171] Ruckstuhl's interpretation of the Gospel texts is deserving of serious consideration. If one accepts the possibility that the Jerusalem Essene quarter and the place of the historical Last Supper were situated very close to each other, then there is a further reason to suppose that the Last Supper of Jesus was the Passover meal of the priestly calendar.

The Search for the Location of the Last Supper

Pixner has questioned whether the Synoptic account of the preparation for the Passover meal (Mt 26:17–19; Mk 14:12–17; Lk 22:7–14) allows for hidden indications that Jesus observed it in a primarily Essene environment.[172] In the narrative Jesus sends disciples into the city, where they would recognize a man carrying a pitcher of water and follow him to the place of the Last Supper. Pixner wants to identify this unnamed man as an Essene monk who carried water for ritual cleansings.[173] As a matter of fact, Lagrange, a scholar thoroughly familiar with the Near East and Early Judaism, earlier was surprised to find a description of a man carrying a pitcher of water, which was in complete contrast to the custom.[174] In an argument against the views of many scholars, R. Pesch shows that Mark, at least on the basis of familiar and sometimes unnecessary details, in this passage is probably preserving a "historical record."[175] Moreover, Luke may know an independent, hebraicized tradition with parallel information.[176] The Third Gospel also offers here (see n. 33) a relatively clearer place description. As soon as the disciples entered the city (Lk 22:10), they were told that they would meet the man carrying the water pitcher. By inference, this account suggests a location at the pool of Siloam near the southeast gate of the city, where water was drawn for the feast of Unleavened Bread.[177] A graded street (partly visible near St. Peter in Gallicantu) runs from Siloam up to the supposed area of the Essene quarter. This street was perhaps divided for users with varying degrees of purity,[178] as the Letter of Aristeas assumes (LetAris 105–6). Thus the accounts about the findings of the upper room do not primarily serve to illustrate a miraculous foreknowing. Rather, they point out a familiar arrangement which Jesus could envision in order to eat the Passover according to the law despite the increasingly dangerous situation and a threatened arrest in Jerusalem.[179]

In his study of the Copper Scroll, Pixner indicates that hiding place no. 7 (3Q15 2.3–4), which he locates on Zion, contains a rather striking feature.[180] He renders the text as follows: "In the cave of the laid-out house of Yeshu" (*bm'rt byt hmdhh yšw*).[181] In a variant from Codex Bezae Cantabrigiensis (D; fifth century) which concerns the place of the Last Supper, there is a literal parallel (Lk 22:12D: *oikon estrōmenon*) for the unusual Hebrew expression *bayit hammĕdûkeh*. As its strong harmonizing tendency shows, D as a rule cannot be regarded as a more original text of the Gospels. Occasionally, however, early traditions appear to be preserved therein, such as in the story about working on the Sabbath (Lk 6:4D).[182] In the topographical D variant of Acts 3:11 ("Portico of Solomon" instead of "Beautiful Gate"), memory of an actual place may have been retained.[183] Especially interesting in our context is the peculiar date (*en sabbatō deuteroprōtō*) which the D text, among others, offers for Luke 6:1; here the priestly solar calendar may provide the background by which it is to be understood.[184] At any rate, Semitisms abound in the D text,[185] as well as occasional expressions that closely resemble Qumran ideas.[186] Certainly, one must be very cautious here in drawing any conclusions, because one question raises others. But since the proximity between the room of the Last Supper and the Essene quarter depends more on other arguments, such questions cannot continue to be easily dismissed.

The Primitive Community and the Essene Quarter

G. Lohfink, in a treatise on the trial of Jesus, has offered several considerations that are significant for our inquiry:

> It is remarkable that not a single conflict between Jesus and the Essenes has been transmitted to us. Their community is never once mentioned in the Gospels. Like most of the Pharisees, did they reject Jesus? Or did they observe his manner of life sympathetically despite their differences with him? In a search for factors that led to Jesus' death, one cannot be limited to the Pharisees, Sadducees, high priests, and Herodians. The crucifixion of Jesus was brought about by the indifference of many who were unconcerned with his message and by the hesitation of those who did not want to make a precipitate decision.[187]

The Easter events and the resulting consciousness of the primitive community that the age of salvation had dawned (Acts 2:14–36) must have created a new situation to which those who were undecided needed to respond.[188]

Was there a special mission to Essene circles among the early Christians? K. Schubert attempted to explain the particularly striking parallels between the Qumran writings and the Lucan representation of the primitive community in Jerusalem. He states "that many members of the primitive community were Essenes before they came to believe in Jesus as the Christ."[189] Above all, reference has been made to "the great number of priests"[190] who, according to Acts, "became obedient to the faith" (6:7). Of course the spatial proximity between the *maḥăneh* and the first meeting place of the primitive community is further reason for raising the possibility of mutual influence.

The great scholar of Jewish Christianity J. Daniélou advanced the view that the theological conflicts in the church of the first century can hardly be attributed to Gentile influence; they reflect the diversity among Jewish religious groups.[191] We have explicit information about converted Pharisees, of which Paul is the most obvious example. Paul experienced his conversion as a radical break with his religious past (Phil 3:4–16; Gal 1:11–16); consequently, he was a better witness for what was new in Jesus than some pre-Easter followers. But there were also former Pharisees who even viewed their pre-Christian lives as molded by divine providence and sought, therefore, to integrate their heritage as much as possible into the new community (Acts 15:5). With regard to converts from Essenism, one has to reckon with both attitudes. In any case, the archaeological and historical considerations presented here provide further reason to explore the significance of the converted Essenes in the first days of the primitive community.

Translated by Loren Stuckenbruck

Notes

1. I have already discussed this subject in "Essener und Urkirche in Jerusalem," *BiKi* 40 (1985) 64–76. For reasons of space, the detailed archaeological and historical evidence cannot be given here in its full extent. See R. Riesner, "Das Jerusalemes Essenerviertel und die Urgemeinde," *ANRW* II.26.2 (Berlin, New York, 1991). My special thanks to Professor Otto Betz, who at the University of Tübingen introduced me to the Qumran literature; to Professor Eugen Ruckstuhl (Luzern) and Rev. Dr. Wolfgang Bittner (Fahrwangen, Switzerland), who read the manuscript; and to Father Bargil Pixner, O.S.B., Lecturer in Biblical Archaeology and Topography at the Dormition Abbey (Jerusalem). Since 1979 I have discussed on site the excavations of Mount Zion with Father Pixner.

2. The sources are collected by D. Baldi, *Enchiridion Locorum Sanctorum* (Jerusalem, 1982 [3d ed.]) pp. 471–531, 737–52; B. Bagatti and E. Testa, *Corpus Scriptorum de Ecclesia Matre IV* (SBF.CMa 26; Jerusalem, 1982) pp. 169–87.

3. K. Kenyon, *Jerusalem: Excavating 3000 Years of History* (London, 1967) pp. 155–62.

4. B. Pixner, "Noch Einmal das Prätorium," *ZDPV* 95 (1979) 56–86, esp. 72–74.

5. M. Broshi, "Excavations on Mount Zion: Preliminary Report, 1971–1972,"

IEJ 26 (1976) 81–88; idem, "Excavations in the House of Caiaphas, Mount Zion" in *Jerusalem Revealed: Archaeology in the Holy City 1968*-1974, ed. Y. Yadin (Jerusalem, 1976) pp. 57–60.

6.   F. J. Bliss and A. C. Dickie, *Excavations at Jerusalem* (Jerusalem, 1898) pp. 313–36.

7.   A. Strobel, "Die Südmauer Jerusalems zur Zeit Jesu (Jos Bell 5, 142ff)," in *Josephus-Studien: Festschrift für Otto Michel*, ed. O. Betz, K. Haacker, and M. Hengel (Göttingen, 1974) pp. 344–61.

8.   H. Geva, "The Western Boundary of Jerusalem at the End of the Monarchy," *IEJ* 29 (1979) 84–91; R. Riesner, "Eine vorexilische Mauer auf dem Zionsberg," *BiKi* 44 (1989) 34–36.

9.   N. Avigad, *Discovering Jerusalem* (Jerusalem, Nashville, 1983) pp. 205–7.

10.   See also Josephus, *War* 7.1–2.

11.   H. Geva, "The Camp of the Tenth Legion in Jerusalem: An Archaeological Reconsideration," *IEJ* 34 (1984) 239–54.

12.   Eusebius, *Demonstratio Evangelica* 6.13, ed. I. A. Heinkel (GCS 23) p. 265.

13.   Only since the tenth century has it been supposed, on the basis of a false interpretation of Acts 2:29, that David's tomb must be located on Zion, indeed on the southwest hill of the city (Map 2). See R. Riesner, "More on King David's Tomb," *BAR* 9 (1983) 20, 80–81. This late legend led to the maintenance of the traditional site for the Last Supper during the Muslim period (transformation into a mosque). Today excavations are prohibited because the "Tomb of David" is in the possession of Sephardic Jews and serves as a synagogue.

14.   J. Pinkerfeld, " 'David's Tomb': Notes on the History of the Building (Preliminary Report)," *Fund for the Explorations of Ancient Synagogues Bulletin* 3 (Jerusalem, 1960) pp. 41–43 and pl. IX.

15.   An opposing view, but one without much support, is offered by M. Avi-Yonah, the editor of Pinkerfeld's posthumous excavation report (see n. 14) on construction during the reign of Julian the Apostate (361–363 C.E.) (in the report, see p. 43: Editor's Note). It is highly unlikely that no information would come to us from such an anti-Christian action of the emperor.

16.   B. Pixner, *Das Heilige Land*, 111 nos. 2–3 (Köln, 1979) 7.

17.   B. Bagatti, *The Church from the Circumcision* (SBF.CMi 2; Jerusalem, 1971) pp. 118–21; F. Hüttenmeister and G. Reeg, *Die antiken Synagogen in Israel* (BTAVO B/12; Tübingen, 1977) p. 196. J. Pinkerfeld also identified the building as a synagogue.

18.   The apse of David's Tomb is assigned to the Byzantine basilica Hagia Sion by J. Wilkinson, *Jerusalem as Jesus Knew It* (London, 1978) pp. 168–70; and E. Otto, *Jerusalem: Die Geschichte der Heiligen Stadt* (Stuttgart, 1980) p. 198. But the apse had evidently no function in the Byzantine church. See D. Bahat, *Jerusalem: Selected Plans of Historical Sites and Monumental Buildings* (Jerusalem, 1980) pp. 29–35.

19.   Z. Maoz, "The Synagogue of Gamla and the Typology of Second-Temple

Synagogues," in *Ancient Synagogues Revealed*, ed. L. I. Levine (Jerusalem, 1981) pp. 35–41, esp. p. 38.

20. E. Testa, *Il Simbolismo dei Giudeo-Cristiani* (SBF.CMa 14; Jerusalem, 1962) p. 492. See also Bagatti, *Church from the Circumcision*, p. 120.

21. F. Mussner, *Der Jakobusbrief* (HThK 31/1; Freiburg, 1975 [3d ed.]) pp. 1–8, 237–40; P. Stuhlmacher in *Das Evangelium von der Versöhnung in Christus* (Stuttgart, 1979) pp. 30–33; P. H. Davids, *The Epistle of James* (Exeter, 1982) pp. 2–22; and also J. H. Charlesworth, *The Old Testament Pseudepigrapha and the New Testament: Prolegomena for the Study of Christian Origins* (SNTS Monograph Series 54; Cambridge, 1985) p. 86; J. B. Adamson, *James the Man and His Message* (Grand Rapids, 1989) pp. 3–52.

22. L. Rost, "Archäologische Bemerkungen zu einer Stelle des Jakobusbriefes (Jak. 2,2f)," *PJB* 24 (1933) 53–66; W. Schrage, "*synagoge*," *ThWNT* (Stuttgart, 1964) vol. 7, pp. 798–850, esp. p. 836.

23. See also C. Mommert, "Die Dormitio und das deutsche Grundstück auf dem Zion," *ZDPV* 21 (1898) 149–83; T. Zahn, "Die *Dormitio Sanctae Virginis* und das Haus des Johannes Markus," *NKZ* 10 (1899) 377–429 (also published separately: Leipzig, 1899); F. M. Abel, "La Sainte Sion," in *Jérusalem II: Jérusalem Nouvelle*, ed. L. H. Vincent and F. M. Abel (Paris, 1922) pp. 441–72; E. Power, "Cénacle," *DBSup* (Paris, 1928) vol. 1, cols. 1064–84; C. Kopp, *Die heiligen Stätten der Evangelien* (Regensburg, 1964 [2d ed.]) pp. 378–87; Bagatti, *Church from the Circumcision*, pp. 116–18; B. Pixner, "Sion III–'Nea Sion': Topographische und geschichtliche Untersuchung des Sitzes der Urkirche," *HlL* 111 nos. 2–3 (1979) 3–13; G. Kroll, *Auf den Spuren Jesu* (Leipzig, 1990 [10th ed.]) pp. 312–19; F. Manns, "Le prime generazioni Cristiane della Palestina alla luce degli scavi archeologici e delle fonte letterarie," in *La Terra Santa* (Studi di Archeologia; Rome, 1983) pp. 70–84, esp. pp. 78–83; B. Pixner, "The Apostolic Synagogue on Mount Zion," *BAR* 17 no. 3 (1990) 16–35, 60.

24. G. Schneider, *Die Apostelgeschichte I* (HThK 5/1; Freiburg, 1980) p. 205 n. 62: The periphrastic construction describes a permanent residence.

25. R. Riesner, *Formen gemeinsamen Lebens im Neuen Testament und heute* (ThD 11; Giessen, 1984 [2d ed.]) pp. 24–25. See also Philo, *Hypothetica* (Eusebius, *Praeparatio Evangelica* 8.11, 12).

26. V. Corbo, *The House of Saint Peter at Capernaum: A Preliminary Report* (SBF.CMi 5; Jerusalem, 1972 [2d ed.]) p. 44.

27. H. L. Strack and P. Billerbeck, *Kommentar zum Neuen Testament aus Talmud und Midrasch* (Munich, 1969 [5th ed.]) vol. 2, pp. 594–95. '*alit* is also found in 4QTob 3.10; cf. K. Beyer, *Die aramäischen Texte vom Toten Meer* (Göttingen, 1984) p. 299.

28. J. B. Frey, *Corpus Inscriptionum Judaicarum I* (Rome, 1936) no. 694, lines 17–18.

29. F. F. Bruce, *Men and Movements in the Primitive Church* (Exeter, 1979) p. 88.

30. Theodosius, *De situ terrae sanctae* 7 (Baldi, *Enchiridion*, p. 483). See Kopp, *Stätten der Evangelien*, p. 382; he argues correctly against T. Zahn, *NKZ* 10 (1899) 406–9.

31. Bruce, *Men and Movements*, p. 28.

32. For the Greco-Palestinian John Mark as the author of the second Gospel, see M. Hengel, *Studies in the Gospel of Mark* (London, 1985) pp. 45–53.

33. See M. Hengel, "Luke the Historian and the Geography of Palestine in the Acts of the Apostles," *Between Jesus and Paul* (London, 1983) pp. 97–128, 190–210.

34. F. Mussner, *Apostelgeschichte* (Neue Echter Bibel NT 5; Regensburg, 1984) p. 18.

35. S. Sowers, "The Circumstances and Recollection of the Pella Flight," *ThZ* 26 (1970) 305–20; M. Simon, "La migration à Pella: Légende ou réalité?" *RSR* 60 (1972) 37–54, now in *Le christianisme antique en son contexte religieux* (Scripta varia 2; Tübingen, 1981) pp. 477–94; R. Pritz, "The Historicity of the Pella Tradition," *Nazarene Jewish Christianity* (Jerusalem, Leiden, 1988) pp. 22–27.

36. Epiphanius, *De mensuris et ponderibus* 15 (PG 43, p. 261); *Panarion* 29.7.8, ed. by K. Holl (GCS 25/1; Leipzig, 1915) p. 330; 30.2.7 (ibid., p. 335).

37. Pixner conjectures a source to be the Jewish Christian historian Hegesippus (c. 180 C.E.). Pixner, *HlL* 111 nos. 2–3 (1979) 12. Concerning the credibility of Hegesippus, see B. Gustafson, "Hegesippus' Sources and His Reliability" (TU 78; Berlin, 1961) 227–32.

38. Eutychus, *Annales* (PG 111, col. 985).

39. Josephus, *War* 7.219, 401, 407–9. See also E. M. Smallwood, *The Jews under Roman Rule: From Pompey to Diocletian* (Leiden, 1981 [2d ed.]) pp. 338–39 (nos. 27, 32) and 546–47 against W. Eck, *Senatoren von Vespasian bis Hadrian* (Munich, 1970) pp. 93–111.

40. Concerning this important figure of the early church, see A. Schlatter, *Synagogue und Kirche bis zum Barkochba-Aufstand* (Stuttgart, 1966) pp. 111–18; B. Pixner, "Simeon Bar Kleophas, zweiter Bischof von Jerusalem," in *Heilige im Heiligen Land*, ed. J. G. Plöger (Würzburg, 1982) pp. 300–4.

41. Eusebius, *Church History* 3.11; 32,4–6; 4.22.4.

42. For his sources, see S. Sowers, *ThZ* 26 (1970) 305. Epiphanius's information on Jewish Christianity is collected together with other sources by F. J. Klijn and G. J. Reinink, *Patristic Evidence for Jewish Christian Sects* (NovTSup 36; Leiden, 1973).

43. Concerning the date, see Smallwood, *Jews under Roman Rule*, pp. 431–32. Epiphanius actually offers a wrong date (117 C.E.) but correctly associates the visit with the second excursion (p. 432 n. 16).

44. Epiphanius, *De mensuris et ponderibus* 14 (Baldi, *Enchiridion*, pp. 477–78).

45. On the chronology, see P. Schäfer, *Der Bar Kokhba-Aufstand: Studien zum zweiten jüdischen Krieg gegen Rom* (TSAJ 1; Tübingen, 1981) pp. 10–28.

46. Cf. Eusebius, *Theophania* 3.24 (GCS 11/2, p. 202).

47. Epiphanius, *Panarion* 66.20 (PG 42, col. 61). Schlatter, *Synagoge und Kirche,* p. 144.

48. A. Schlatter, *Der Chronograph aus dem zehnten Jahre Antoninus* (TU 12/1; Leipzig, 1894) pp. 83–86.

49. See P. Riessler, *Altjüdisches Schrifttum ausserhalb der Bibel* (Heidelberg, 1966 [2d ed.] [=1928]) pp. 1311–12; A. Jaubert, "Le calendrier des Jubilés et les jours liturgiques de la semaine," *VT* 7 (1957) 35–61, esp. 52–55; B. Bagatti, *Il Golgota e la Croce: Ricerche storico-archeologiche* (SBF.CMi 21; Jerusalem, 1978) pp. 26–30; G. W. E. Nickelsburg, "Some related Traditions in the Apocalypse of Adam, the Books of Adam and Eve, and in 1 Enoch," in B. Layton, *The Rediscovery of Gnosticism* (Leiden, 1980) vol. 2, pp. 515–39; S. E. Robinson, "The Testament of Adam and the Angelic Liturgy," *RQ* 12 (1985) 105–10.

50. See Schlatter, *Synagoge und Kirche,* pp. 144–53; R. Riesner, "Golgota und die Archäologie," *BiKi* 40 (1985) 21–26; "Golgotha," in *Das Grosse Bibellexikon* I (Wuppertal, Giessen, 1990 [2d ed.]) cols. 480–82.

51. See Schlatter, *Synagoge und Kirche,* pp. 145, 153.

52. See Smallwood, *Jews under Roman Rule,* p. 478.

53. Ibid., pp. 499–500.

54. "Jérusalem sous la domination romaine: Histoire de la ville depuis la conquête de Pompée jusqu'à Constantin (6 a.C.–325 p.C.)," *ANRW* II.8 (Berlin, 1977) pp. 444–89, esp. p. 487. See also S. Safrai, "The Holy Congregation in Jerusalem," *Scripta Hierosolymitana* 23 (1972) 62–78.

55. See Bagatti, *Church from the Circumcision,* p. 10.

56. Ibid., pp. 10–14.

57. P. Benoit, "Le prétoire de Pilate à l'époque byzantine," *RB* 91 (1984) 161–77, esp. 177. Also in recent years, see Kopp, *Stätten der Evangelien,* p. 387; W. Baier, "Coenaculum," in *Bibellexikon,* ed. H. Haag (Einsiedeln, 1982 [3d ed.] [=1968 (2d ed.)]) pp. 299–300; Kroll, *Auf den Spuren Jesu,* pp. 313–14; Otto, *Jerusalem,* p. 186; H. Balz, "*Sion,*" *EWbNT* (Stuttgart, 1983) vol. 3, cols. 588–90, esp. col. 589; E. D. Hunt, *Holy Land Pilgrimage in the Later Roman Empire A.D. 312–460* (Oxford, 1984) p. 2; R. Riesner, "Obergemach," in *Das Grosse Bibellexikon,* vol. 2, cols. 1075–77.

58. See T. Zahn, *Die Apostelgeschichte des Lucas I (Kap. 1–12)* (Leipzig, 1919) pp. 43–45.

59. See W. Bauer, *Wörterbuch zum Neuen Testament* (Berlin, 1963 [6th ed.]) pp. 101, 1666.

60. Cf. E. Power, "Église Saint-Pierre et Maison de Caïphe," *DBSup* (Paris, 1934) vol. 2, cols. 691–756; R. Riesner, "Palast des Hohenpriesters," in *Das Grosse Bibellexikon,* vol. 3, pp. 1109–10.

61. Baldi, *Enchiridion,* pp. 478–81. Concerning the authenticity of locations on Zion given by Hesychius, see M. Aubineau, *Hésychius de Jérusalem ... Homélies Pascales* (SC 187; Paris, 1972) pp. 41, 129–32.

62. Zahn, *NKZ* 10 (1899) 393, 398.

63. Igino Grego, *I Giudeo-Cristiani nel IV Secolo* (Jerusalem, 1982) p. 72.

64. Epiphanius, *Ancoratus* 40 (PG 43, pp. 98–99; ed. by K. Holl in GCS 25/1, p. 50).

65. Epiphanius, *Panarion* 46.5.5, ed. by K. Holl (GCS 25/2; Leipzig, 1922) p. 209.

66. *Peregrinatio Egeriae* 35.1–2 (Baldi, *Enchiridion,* p. 629).

67. In contrast to the opinion of Kopp (*Stätten der Evangelien,* pp. 382–83), neither Theodosius (Baldi, *Enchiridion,* p. 535) nor other pilgrims have misplaced the Last Supper of Jesus in the betrayal grotto at Gethsemane. See Zahn, *NKZ* 10 (1899) 421. Here, on the contrary, a Jewish Christian tradition of one of three special meals of Jesus before the passion (Bethany, Gethsemane, Zion) has survived. See E. Testa, "Les cènes du Seigneur," *Les Dossiers de l'Archéologie* 10 (1975) 98–106.

68. Origen, *Contra Celsum* 5.33 (PG 11, cols. 1229–31; SC 147, pp. 97–99).

69. Origen, *Commentarius in Matthaeum* 86 (on 26:27) (PG 13, col. 1737).

70. B. Bagatti, *The Church from the Gentiles in Palestine* (SBF.CMi 4; Jerusalem, 1971) p. 25.

71. Eusebius, *Demonstratio Evangelica* 1.4 (Baldi, Enchiridion, pp. 476–77).

72. Jerome, *Epistulae* 53.8 (Baldi, *Enchiridion,* pp. 478–79). See also Zahn, *NKZ* 10 (1899) 398–99.

73. Zahn, *NKZ* 10 (1899) 399–400. The text is in A. Vööbus (CSCO 367/68; Louvain, 1975) p. 188.

74. For the text, see Baldi, *Enchiridion,* p. 492. See also Kopp, *Stätten der Evangelien,* p. 38 n. 13.

75. R. Pesch, *Wie Jesus Abendmahl hielt* (Freiburg, 1979 [3d ed.]) pp. 103–4.

76. R. Riesner, *Jesus als Lehrer: Eine Untersuchung zum Ursprung der Evangelien-Überlieferung* (WUNT 2/7; Tübingen, 1988 [3d ed.]) pp. 131–33, 168–70.

77. J. H. Charlesworth in *OTP* vol. 1, pp. 6–8.

78. See J. C. VanderKam, *Textual and Historical Studies in the Book of Jubilees* (HSM 14; Missoula, Mont., 1977) pp. 207–85.

79. See P. R. Davies, *The Damascus Covenant: An Interpretation of the 'Damascus Document'* (JSOTSS 25; Sheffield, 1983).

80. See G. Jeremias, *Der Lehrer der Gerechtigkeit* (SUNT 2; Göttingen, 1963) pp. 36–78.

81. R. de Vaux, "Fouilles au Khirbet Qumrân: Rapport préliminaire sur la deuxième campagne," *RB* 61 (1954) 206–36, esp. 235.

82. R. de Vaux, *Archaeology and the Dead Sea Scrolls,* trans. D. Bourke (London, 1973) pp. 20–23.

83. J. H. Charlesworth, "The Origin and Subsequent History of the Authors of the Dead Sea Scrolls: Four Transitional Phases Among the Qumran Essenes," *RQ* 10 (1980) 213–33, esp. 224–26.

84. See B. Pixner, "Das Essenerquartier in Jerusalem und dessen Einfluss auf die Urkirche," *HlL* 113 nos. 2–3 (1981) 3–14, esp. 4.

85. See de Vaux, *Archaeology*, pp. 33–36. According to E.-M. Laperrousaz, Qumran was abandoned from 61/63 to 24/23 B.C.E. Laperrousaz, *Qoumrân: L'établissement essénien des bords de la mer Morte* (Paris, 1976) pp. 55–56, 184–88. But see de Vaux, *Archaeology*, p. 22 n. 1. His arguments are still valuable also against the recent skepticism of P. R. Callaway, *The History of the Qumran Community: An Investigation* (JSPS 3; Sheffield, 1988) pp. 29–52.

86. Thus, for example, B. C. Daniel, "Nouveaux arguments en faveur de l'identification des Hérodiens et des Esséniens," *RQ* 7 (1970) 397–402, esp. 398; S. Sandmel, *Judaism and Christian Beginnings* (New York, 1978) pp. 165–66; E. Bammel, "Sadduzäer und Sadokiden," *EThL* 57 (1979) 107–15, esp. 113–14; Charlesworth, *RQ* 10 (1980) 227; and Pixner, *HlL* 113 nos. 2–3 (1981) 4.

87. See de Vaux, *Archaeology*, pp. 24–27.

88. See M. J. Lagrange, *Le Judaïsme avant Jésus-Christ* (Paris, 1931) pp. 316–19; M. Black, *The Scrolls and Christian Origins: Studies in the Jewish Background of the New Testament* (New York, 1961; repr. BJS 48; Chico, Calif., 1983) pp. 39–42; E. Ruckstuhl, *Chronology of the Last Days of Jesus: A Critical Study* (New York, 1965) pp. 97–101; J. M. Baumgarten, "The Essenes and the Temple. A Reappraisal," in *Studies in Qumran Law* (SJLA 24; Leiden, 1977) pp. 57–76; M. Delcor, "Is the Temple Scroll a Source of the Herodian Temple?" in *Temple Scroll Studies*, ed. G. F. Brooke (JSPSS 7; Sheffield, 1989) 67–89. Against this view is J. Holland, "A Misleading Statement of the Essene Attitude to the Temple (Josephus, Antiquities, XVIII,I,5,19)," *RQ* 9 (1978) 555–62.

89. See J. T. Milik, *The Books of Enoch: Aramaic Fragments of Qumrân Cave 4* (Oxford, 1976) pp. 59–69.

90. *Every Good Man Is Free* 76; *Hypothetica* in Eusebius, *Praeparatio Evangelica* 8.11.1.

91. See J. Simons, *Jerusalem in the Old Testament* (Leiden, 1952) pp. 279–80; R. Riesner, "Josephus' 'Gate of the Essenes' in Modern Discussion," *ZDPr* 105 (1989) 105–9.

92. J. B. Lightfoot, *Saint Paul's Epistles to the Colossians and Philemon* (London, 1879) p. 94 n. 2; M. J. Lagrange, *Judaïsme avant Jésus-Christ*, p. 317.

93. E. Schürer, *Geschichte des Jüdischen Volkes im Zeitalter Jesu Christi* (Leipzig, 1907 [4th ed.]) vol. 2, pp. 657–58 n. 5. Cf. E. Schürer, *The History of the Jewish People in the Age of Jesus Christ (175 B.C.–A.D. 135)*, ed. G. Vermes et al. (Edinburgh, 1979) vol. 2, p. 563 n. 5.

94. Besides the authors mentioned in n. 86, for example, see also P. Seidensticker, "Die Gemeinschaftsform der religiösen Gruppen des Spätjudentums und der Urkirche," *LA* 9 (1958–59) 94–108, esp. 129–30; M. McNamara, "Were the Magi Essenes?" *IER* 110 (1968) 311 n. 19. O. Michel and O. Bauernfeind eds., *De Bello*

Judaico – Der jüdische Krieg: Griechisch und Deutsch II/1 (Munich, 1963) p. 246 n. 41.

95. F. J. Bliss, "Third Report on the Excavations at Jerusalem," *PEFQS* (1895) pp. 9–25, esp. p. 12. Later they ascribed this gate entirely to the Byzantine period (*Excavations*, pp. 16–20, 323–24) and looked for the Essene Gate a little farther to the north by T 2 (Map 1) *Excavations*, p. 8 n. 1. Already Strobel had expressed doubts concerning this late date. Strobel, "Die Südmauer Jerusalems," 356–58.

96. A photo is found in R. M. Mackowski, *Jerusalem: City of Jesus* (Grand Rapids, 1980) p. 62.

97. B. Pixner, "An Essene Quarter on Mount Zion?" in *Studia Hierosolymitana I: Studi archeologici in onore a Bellarmino Bagatti* (SBF.CMa 22; Jerusalem, 1976) pp. 245–85 (also published separately). There appeared a collection of Pixner's essays, many of them connected with the relationship of Essenism and Early Christianity: B. Pixner, *Wege des Messias und stätten der Urkirche* (Studien für Biblischen Archäologie und Zeitgeschichte 2; Giessen, 1991).

98. Drawn by the German architect T. Sandel, *PEFQS* (1895) 10 and in J. F. Bliss, *Excavations*, after p. 16.

99. B. Pixner, D. Chen, and S. Margalit, "Mount Zion: The 'Gate of the Essenes' Re-excavated," *ZDPV* 105 (1989) 85–95 and plates 8–16; B. Pixner, "The History of the 'Essene Gate' Area," *ZDPV* 105 (1989) 96–104.

100. See already M. Avi-Yonah in *Encyclopaedia of Archaeological Excavations in the Holy Land* (Jerusalem, 1976) vol. 2, pp. 599–603.

101. A reference from Dr. Brian J. Capper. See M. Avi-Yonah, *A History of the Holy Land* (London, 1969) pp. 230–31.

102. M. Broshi, "Excavations in the House of Caiaphas," pp. 57–58.

103. See also *Student Map Manual: Historical Geography of the Bible Lands*, ed. J. Monson (Jerusalem, 1979) section 14-2, against the view of B. Schwank, "Neue Funde in Nabatäerstädten und ihre Bedeutung für die neutestamentliche Exegese," *NTS* 29 (1983) 429–35, esp. 432.

104. See L. Rost, *Einleitung in die alttestamentlichen Apokryphen und Pseudepigraphen* (Heidelberg, 1979 [2d ed.]) p. 104; and Beyer, *Texte vom Toten Meer*, pp. 225–31.

105. See G. Beer in *Die Apokryphen und Pseudepigraphen des Alten Testaments*, ed. E. Kautzsch (Darmstadt, 1975 [4th ed.]) vol. 2, pp. 254–55.

106. Mt 5:22, 29, 30; 10:28; 18:9; 23:15, 33; Mk 9:43; Lk 12:5; in the remainder of the New Testament only – but hardly by chance – in Jas 3:6 (see n. 21 above).

107. G. Dalman, *Jerusalem und sein Gelände* (BFChTh 2/19; Gütersloh, 1930) pp. 86–87.

108. E. Robinson, *Biblical Researches in Palestine, Mount Sinai and Arabia Petraea I* (London, 1841) p. 474 n. 1; J. Schwarz, *Das heilige Land nach seiner ehemaligen und jetzigen geographischen Beschaffenheit* (rev. I. Schwarz) (Frankfurt am Main, 1852) p. 206; Hebrew original, *Tevu'ot ha-'Arez* (Jerusalem, 1845) p. 334. Concerning Joseph Schwarz, see Y. Ben-Arieh, *The Rediscovery of the Holy Land in*

the Nineteenth Century (Jerusalem, 1983 [2d ed.]) pp. 104–7.

109. Y. Yadin, "The Gate of the Essenes and the Temple Scroll," *Qadmoniot* 5 (1972) 129–30 [in Hebrew]. Translated in *Jerusalem Revealed*, ed. Yadin, pp. 90–91.

110. Y. Yadin, *The Temple Scroll II: Text and Commentary* (Jerusalem, 1983) pp. 99–100. The Hebrew edition appeared in 1977.

111. See the map in *Jerusalem Revealed*, p. 90.

112. Y. Yadin, *The Temple Scroll: The Hidden Law of the Dead Sea Sect* (London, 1985) p. 180 (emphasis added).

113. Pixner, "Essene Quarter," 255–57.

114. J. A. Emerton, "A Consideration of two Recent Theories about Bethso in Josephus's Description of Jerusalem and a Passage in the Temple Scroll," in *Text and Context: Old Testament and Semitic Studies for F. C. Fensham*, ed. W. Claassen (JSOTSS 48; Sheffield, 1988) pp. 93–104. Against Emerton and other critics of the theory of an Essene Quarter in Jerusalem with close proximity to the primitive community, see R. Riesner, "Das Jerusalemer Essenerviertel — Antwort auf einige Einwände," in *Qumranica Mogilanensia 4: A Festschrift in Honour of Józef Tadeusz Milik*, ed. Z. J. Kapera (Krakow [forthcoming]).

115. See the map of F. Spiess in H. Clementz, *Flavius Josephus: Geschichte des Jüdischen Krieges* (Cologne o.J., 1900) after p. 695; and the map of W. Goering in Dalman, *Jerusalem*, after p. 390.

116. C. R. Conder, "The Rock Scarp of Zion," *PEFQS* (1877) 81–89, esp. 84 and map after 82.

117. Yadin, *The Temple Scroll: The Hidden Law*, p. 181.

118. J. Milgrom, "The Temple Scroll," *BA* 41 (1978) 105–20, esp. 117.

119. See E. Netzer, "Ancient Ritual Baths (*miqvaot*) in Jericho," in *The Jerusalem Cathedra*, ed. L. I. Levine (Jerusalem, Detroit, 1982) vol. 2, pp. 106–19; N. Avigad, *Discovering Jerusalem*, pp. 139–43.

120. See A. Strobel, "Die Wasseranlagen der *Hirbet Qumrân*: Versuch einer Deutung," *ZDPV* 88 (1972) 55–86; B. G. Wood, "To Dip or Sprinkle? The Qumran Cisterns in Perspective," *BASOR* 256 (1984) 45–60.

121. See the index map of R. Reich, "Mishna, Sheqalim 8,2, and the Archaeological Evidence" [in Hebrew], in *Jerusalem in the Second Temple Period*, ed. A. Oppenheimer et al. (Jerusalem, 1980) pp. 225–56, esp. 228.

122. See E. Eisenberg, "Church of the Dormition," in *Excavations and Surveys in Israel 1984* (Jerusalem, 1985) vol. 3, p. 47.

123. See H. Renard, "Die Marienkirchen auf dem Berg Sion in ihrem Zusammenhang mit dem Abendmahlssaale," *HlL* 44 (1900) 3–23, esp. 16, 18.

124. See Pixner, "Essene Quarter," pp. 271–73.

125. See F. J. Bliss, "Second Report on the Excavations at Jerusalem," *PEFQS* (1894) 243–61, esp. 255–56.

126. See F. M. Abel, "Petites découvertes au Quartier du Cénacle à Jérusalem," *RB* 8 (1911) 119–25, esp. 122–24.

127. See Pixner, "Essene Quarter," pp. 269–71; Reich, "Mishna," pp. 239–40.

128. See H. Geva, "Excavations in the Citadel of Jerusalem, 1979–1980, Preliminary Report," *IEJ* 33 (1983) 55–67, esp. 61–62. Josephus (*War* 2.112–13; cf. *Ant* 12.345–48) presupposes Essenes at the court of Archelaus. See M. McNamara, "Were the Magi Essenes?" *IER* 110 (1968) 305–28, esp. 308–9. With Manaen in Acts 13:1 we perhaps know an Essene in the service of Herod Antipas. See A. Zimmermann, *Die Urchristlichen Lehrer* (WUNT 2/12; Tübingen, 1988 [2d ed.]) pp. 130–32. Did the *miqweh* serve such pious ones outside Herod's palace?

129. See y.Ta'an 4.2 (68a); GenR 98:13: the Essene R. Jose b. Halaphta as descendant of the Rechabites. See further N. I. Weinstein, *Beiträge zur Geschichte der Essäer* (Vienna, 1892) pp. 12–21; H. J. Schoeps, *Theologie und Geschichte des Judenchristentums* (Tübingen, 1949) pp. 247–55. For Christian sources, see Nilus von Ankyra, *Tractatus de monastica exercitatione* 3 in A. Adam (rev. by C. Burchard), "Antike Berichte über die Essener," *KLT* 182 (Berlin, 1972 [2d ed.]) p. 57; *Suda*, E 3123 (ibid., p. 59). According to Hegesippus (Eusebius, *Church History* 2.23.14) a "priest from the family of Rechab," when James was martyred, joined the cause of the party of "the Lord's brother." For consideration in this connection would also be the History of the Rechabites, which in addition to Christian parts also contains a Jewish core (chs. 3–15a) originally written in a Semitic language. See J. H. Charlesworth, *The Pseudepigrapha and Modern Research with a Supplement* (SCS 7; Chico, Calif., 1981 [2d ed.]) pp. 223–28. The HistRech also exhibits noteworthy parallels to the Qumran writings. See J. C. Picard, "L'Histoire des Bienheureux du Temps de Jérémie en la Narration de Zosime: arrière-plan historique et mythique," in *Pseudépigraphes de l'Ancien Testament et manuscrits de la Mer Morte*, ed. M. Philonenko (CRHPhR 41; Paris, 1967) pp. 27–43. See also A. Strobel, *ZDPV* 88 (1972) 81, 84–85.

130. See H. Kraft, *Die Entstehung des Christentums* (Darmstadt, 1981) pp. 7–8.

131. See de Vaux, *Archaeology*, p. 9 and pl. XXXIX (locus 138).

132. See Strobel, *ZDPV* 88 (1972) 57–58, 70.

133. See Pixner, *HlL* 113 nos. 2–3 (1981) 8.

134. See H. Bardtke, "Qumran und seine Probleme," *ThR* 33 (1968) 185–236, esp. 185–204.

135. DJD 3 (Oxford, 1962) pp. 199–302.

136. D. Dimant, "Qumran Sectarian Literature," in *Jewish Writings of the Second Temple Period*, ed. M. E. Stone (CRINT 2.2; Assen, Philadelphia, 1984) pp. 483–550, esp. 488. The authenticity of 3Q15 is also argued in a dissertation by D. Wilmot (University of Chicago, 1985). See N. Golb, "Who Hid the Dead Sea Scrolls?" *BA* 48 (1985) 68–82, esp. 82 n. 4. See also Y. Thorion, "Beiträge zur Erforschung der Sprache der Kupferrolle," *RQ* 12 (1986) 163–76; A. Wolters, "Notes on the Copper Scroll (3Q15)," *RQ* 12 (1987) 589–96; and G. Stemberger, *Pharisäer, Sadduzäer, Essener* (SBS 144; Stuttgart, 1991) pp. 123–24.

137. B. Pixner, "Unravelling the Copper Scroll Code: A Study on the Topography of 3Q15," *RQ* 11 (1983) 323–65.

138. See Y. Yadin, *Temple Scroll I*, pp. 288–89; J. Milgrom, "Studies in the Temple Scroll," *JBL* 97 (1978) 501–23, esp. 517.

139. The views of B. Pixner were adopted by, among others, Y. Eldar, "An Essene Quarter on Mount Zion?" *CNfI* 26 (1976) 53–54; S. Goransson, "On the Hypothesis that Essenes Lived on Mt. Carmel," *RQ* 9 (1978) 563–67, esp. 564; Pesch, *Abendmahl*, p. 104; Mackowski, *Jerusalem*, pp. 62–66; G. Cornfeld, *The Historical Jesus* (New York, 1982) pp. 33–38; *Josephus: The Jewish War*, ed. G. Cornfeld, B. Mazar, and P. L. Maier (Grand Rapids, 1982) pp. 336, 339; O. Michel, *Das Zeugnis des Neuen Testaments von der Gemeinde* (Giessen, 1983 [2d ed.]) p. 116; F. Manns, "Le prime generazioni Cristiane" 84; F. Heyer, *Kirchengeschichte des Heiligen Landes* (Stuttgart, 1984) pp. 14–15, 260; E. Ruckstuhl, "Der Jünger, den Jesus liebte," *BiKi* 40 (1985) 77–83, esp. 82–83; J. A. T. Robinson, *The Priority of John* (London, 1985) pp. 64–67; E. E. Ellis, "Traditions in the Pastoral Epistles," in *Early Jewish and Christian Exegesis*, ed. C. A. Evans (Atlanta, 1987) pp. 237–53, esp. 241–42 n. 29; and Hengel, "Der vorchristliche Paulus," *ThBeitr* 21 (1990) 174–95, esp. 185–86.

140. See A. Caquot, "Le messianisme qumrânian," in *Qumrân: Sa piété, sa théologie et son milieu*, ed. M. Delcor (BETL 46; Paris, Leuven, 1978) pp. 231–47.

141. Concerning the historicity of John the Baptist's inquiry, see W. G. Kümmel, *Jesu Antwort an Johannes den Täufer* (Wiesbaden, 1974); Riesner, *Jesus als Lehrer*, pp. 299–301; idem, "Johannes der Täufer auf Machärus," *BiKi* 39 (1984) 176.

142. Ruckstuhl, *Chronology*, p. 123; W. Pesch, "Lazarus, Maria und Martha," in *Heilige im Heiligen Land*, ed. Plöger, pp. 205–8, esp. pp. 205–6.

143. Yadin, *Temple Scroll I*, p. 305. O. Betz agrees with him ("Die Bedeutung der Qumranschriften für die Evangelien des Neuen Testaments," *BiKi* 40 (1985) 54–64, esp. 63 n. 20. Now in *Jesus der Messias Israels: Aufsätze zur biblischen Theologie* (WUNT 1/42; Tübingen, 1987) pp. 318–32, esp. 332 n. 20.

144. Testa, *Les Dossiers de l'Archéologie* 10 (1975) 105–6. See also n. 67 above.

145. P. Benoit and M. É. Boismard, "Un ancien sanctuaire chrétien à Béthanie," *RB* 58 (1951) 200–51.

146. Reich, "Mishna," pp. 253–55.

147. R. Reich, "A *miqweh* at 'Isawiya near Jerusalem," *IEJ* 34 (1984) 220–23.

148. See especially *John and the Dead Sea Scrolls*, ed. J. H. Charlesworth (New York, 1990), as well as J. Roloff, "Der johanneische 'Lieblingsjünger' und der 'Lehrer der Gerechtigkeit,'" *NTS* 15 (1968–69) 129–51.

149. J. A. T. Robinson, *Priority of John*, pp. 36–45.

150. Ruckstuhl, *BiKi* 40 (1985) 77–78.

151. C. Perrot, *Jésus et l'histoire* (Paris, 1979) pp. 99–166.

152. O. Cullmann, *Der johanneische Kreis: Zur Ursprung des Johannes-*

Evangeliums (Tübingen, 1975) pp. 41–60, 89–98; J. A. T. Robinson, *Priority of John*, pp. 63–67, 171–79.

153. F. M. Braun, "L'arrière-fond judaïque du quatrième évangile et la Communauté de l'Alliance," *RB* 62 (1955) 5–44, esp. 42–44; R. E. Brown, "The Qumran Scrolls and the Johannine Gospel and Epistles," in *The Scrolls and the New Testament*, ed. K. Stendahl (New York, 1957), pp. 183–207, 282–91.

154. Concerning John the Baptist and Qumran, see C. H. H. Scobie, *John the Baptist* (London, 1964) pp. 33–40; idem, "John the Baptist," in *The Scrolls and Christianity*, ed. M. Black (London, 1969) pp. 58–69, 112–13. Further bibliography is in Riesner, *Jesus als Lehrer*, pp. 292–93.

155. A. Jaubert, "Le calendrier des Jubilés et de la secte de Qumrân: Ses origines bibliques," *VT* 3 (1953) 250–64.

156. See J. C. Vanderkam, "The Origin, Character and Early History of the 364-Day Calendar: A Reassessment of Jaubert's Hypotheses," *CBQ* 41 (1979) 390–411. A good introduction to the calendar is offered in Ruckstuhl, *Chronology*, pp. 72–113. See the literature cited in J. A. Fitzmyer, *The Dead Sea Scrolls: Major Publications and Tools for Study* (SBL Sources for Biblical Study 20; Atlanta, 1990 [rev. ed.]) pp. 80–86.

157. See Y. Yadin, *The Temple Scroll I*, pp. 89–136.

158. See Ruckstuhl, *Chronology*.

159. M. Baillet, DJD 7 (Oxford, 1982) pp. 287–95.

160. See J. M. Baumgarten, "Halakhic Polemics in a New Fragment from Qumran Cave 4," in *Biblical Archaeology Today: Proceedings of the International Congress on Biblical Archaeology (Jerusalem, April 1984)*, ed. J. Amitai (Jerusalem, 1985) pp. 390–99, esp. pp. 396–97. See also B. Z. Wacholder, *The Dawn of Qumran: The Sectarian Torah and the Teacher of Righteousness* (MHUC 8; Cincinnati, 1983) pp. 160–67; and E. Qimron and J. Strugnell, "An Unpublished Halakhic Letter from Qumran," *The Israel Museum Journal* 4 (1985) 9–11.

161. See A. Strobel, *Ursprung und Geschichte des frühchristlichen Osterkalenders* (TU 121; Berlin, 1977) esp. pp. 167–224.

162. See J. Daniélou, *Geschichte der Kirche I: Von der Gründung der Kirche bis zu Gregor dem Grossen* (Einsiedeln, 1963) p. 122.

163. See J. Jeremias, *The Eucharistic Words of Jesus* (London, 1966) pp. 15–88.

164. In addition to the work by J. Jeremias mentioned in the preceding note, see R. Pesch, *Das Markusevangelium (Kommentar zu Kap. 8,27–16,20)* (HThK 2/2; Freiburg, 1980 [2d ed.]) vol. 2, pp. 340–77; idem, "Das Evangelium in Jerusalem: Mk 14,12–26 als ältestes Überlieferungsgut der Gemeinde," in *Evangelium*, pp. 113–55.

165. A. Jaubert, "La date de la dernière cène," *RHR* 146 (1954) 140–73. The most important is *The Date of the Last Supper* (Staten Island, 1965); "Jésus et le calendrier de Qumrân," *NTS* 7 (1960–61) 1–30; "Le mercredi où Jésus fut livré," *NTS* 14 (1967–68) 145–64; "The Calendar of Qumran and the Passion Narrative in John," in *John and the Dead Sea Scrolls*, ed. Charlesworth, pp. 62–75.

166. See Strobel, *Ursprung und Geschichte*, pp. 70–121.

167. See also Ruckstuhl, *Chronology*, pp. 32–35.

168. Ibid., pp. 56–72.

169. See, among others, P. Benoit, "La date de la cène," *RB* 65 (1958) 590–94; J. Blinzler, "Qumran-Kalender und Passionschronologie," *ZNW* 49 (1958) 238–51.

170. Ruckstuhl, *Chronology*, pp. 35–55.

171. E. Ruckstuhl, "Zur Chronologie der Leidengeschichte Jesu," *SNTU* 10 (1985) 27–61; 11 (1986) 97–129. Also in Ruckstuhl, *Jesus im Horizont der Evangelien* (SBANT 3; Stuttgart, 1988) pp. 101–84 (with an appendix, pp. 177–84). A. Strobel, *Die Stunde der Wahrheit: Untersuchungen zum Strafverfahren gegen Jesu* (WUNT 1/21; Tübingen, 1980).

172. See Pixner, "Essene Quarter," p. 277.

173. B. Pixner, *HlL* 113 nos. 2–3 (1981) 12–14.

174. M.-J. Lagrange, *Évangile selon Saint Marc* (Paris, 1929) p. 373.

175. R. Pesch, *Markusevangelium*, vol. 2, pp. 340–45.

176. Riesner, *Jesus als Lehrer*, p. 255.

177. Kroll, *Auf den Spuren Jesu*, p. 312.

178. See R. Riesner in *Das Grosse Bibellexikon*, vol. 3, col. 1110 (but here without the Essene connection).

179. Thus (but without the Essene connection), for example, also E. E. Ellis, *The Gospel of Luke* (London, 1974 [2d ed.]) p. 252; and I. H. Marshall, *The Gospel of Luke* (Exeter, 1978) p. 798.

180. Pixner, *RQ* 11 (1983) 344–46 n. 11.

181. The reading and separation of the last two words are contested. J. T. Milik (DJD 3, p. 286), followed by B. J. Luria (*Megillat han-Nehoshet mem-Midbar Yehuda* [Jerusalem, 1963] p. 68) reads: *hmrh hyšn*. But it is just as possible, with J. M. Allegro (*The Treasure of the Copper Scroll* [London, 1960] p. 35) to render the third letter as a *daleth*. Either the fourth letter looks more like the usual *heth* of the writer, or all three authors detect it as the third last letter in the same cache (3Q15 2.4). The separation of the words proposed by Pixner is at least as possible as that of the other three (cf. DJD 3, plate L). Concerning the final letter, Milik adds that it resembles more a *waw* than a *nun* (DJD 3, p. 286).

182. J. Jeremias, *Unbekannte Jesusworte* (rev. by O. Hofius) (Gütersloh, 1963 [3d ed.]) pp. 61–64.

183. F. F. Bruce, *The Acts of the Apostles* (London, 1970) pp. 106–7.

184. J. P. Audet, "Jésus et le 'Calendrier sacerdotal ancien': Autor d'une variante de Luc 6,1," *ScE* 10 (1958) 361–83.

185. M. Black, *An Aramaic Approach to the Gospels and Acts* (Oxford, 1967 [3d ed.]) pp. 277–78.

186. E. Ferguson, "Qumran and Codex 'D,' " *RQ* 8 (1972) 75–80.

187. G. Lohfink, *Der letzte Tag Jesu: Die Ereignisse der Passion* (Freiburg, 1982) p. 23.

188. J. O'Callaghan advocated the thesis that 7Q fragments of the New Testament are also to be found. The proposal has met with little approval. O'Callaghan, "Papiros neotestamentarios en la cueva 7 de Qumrân," *Bib* 53 (1972) 91–100 (Eng. trans. *JBL* 91 [1972] Supplement, pp. 1–14). See Fitzmyer, *Dead Sea Scrolls,* pp. 168–72. C. P. Thiede has now introduced somewhat new arguments in favor of identifying 7Q5 with Mk 6:52–53. Thiede, "7Q—Eine Rückkehr zu den neutestamentlichen Papyrusfragmenten in der siebten Höhle von Qumran," *Bib* 65 (1984) 538–59. Thiede attempts to substantiate his opinion by providing a detailed account in *Die älteste Evangelien-Handschrift?: Das Markus-Fragment von Qumran und die Anfänge der schriftlichen Überlieferung des Neuen Testaments* (Wuppertal, 1990 [2d ed.]). For an expanded English translation, see Thiede, *The Earliest Gospel Manuscript and Its Significance for New Testament Studies* (Exeter, 1991). Critical responses to Thiede's thesis are given by C. Focant, "Un fragment du second évangile à Qumrân: 7Q5=Mc 6,52–53?" *RThL* 16 (1985) 447–54; H.-U. Rosenbaum, "Cave 7Q5! Gegen die erneute Inanspruchnahme des Qumran-Fragments 7Q5 als Bruchstück der ältesten Evangelien-Handschrift," *BZ* 31 (1987) 189–205. A strong supporter of Thiede is F. Rohrhirsch, *Markus in Qumran? Eine Auseinandersetzung mit den Argumenten für und gegen das Fragment 7Q5 mit Hilfe des methodischen Fallibilismusprinzips* (Wuppertal, 1990). For the moment, however, the questions concerning the relationship between the Jerusalem Essene quarter and the primitive community and the identification of the 7Q fragments should be treated as two separated subjects.

189. K. Schubert, *Die Qumran-Essener: Texte der Schriftrollen und Lebensbild der Gemeinde* (UTB 224; Munich, Basel, 1973) p. 130.

190. Thus C. Spicq, "L'épître aux Hébreux: Apollos, Jean-Baptiste, les Hellénistes et Qumrân," *RQ* 1 (1958–59) 365–90. Further bibliography is provided by H. Braun, *Qumran und das Neue Testament* (Tübingen, 1966) vol. 1, pp. 153–54.

191. Daniélou, *Geschichte der Kirche,* vol. 1, p. 45.

CHAPTER 8

Opposition to the Temple: Jesus and the Dead Sea Scrolls

CRAIG A. EVANS

However Jesus' action in the Temple is understood, most interpreters believe that it was a major factor in the chain of events that resulted in his crucifixion.[1] This action should also help us to understand a principal element in Jesus' teaching. Just what did he think of the Temple establishment? Was he opposed to it? And, if he was, on what grounds? Were other groups or individuals opposed to or critical of the Temple establishment? Obviously one such group that was very critical of the religious authorities of its time was the Qumran community, whose members were in all likelihood known as the Essenes (see Foreword and chapter 1 above). How did Jesus' views compare to those of this group? It is to these questions, at least certain aspects of them, that the present essay addresses itself.

Although the following subsection is concerned with criticisms of the Temple establishment, it should be stated at the outset that the overall Jewish view of the Temple as a divinely given institution was undoubtedly positive. Great quantities of money, whether from the annual half-shekel tax or from the various tithes and offerings, poured into the Temple's coffers, making it one of the wealthiest institutions in the ancient world. This could never have been the case had the Temple itself, the sacrificial system, or the priesthood been widely distrusted, held in contempt, or viewed as an inferior form of religious expression. But there is, nevertheless, significant evidence of criticism, some sharp and bitter; and this criticism is widespread and amply attested. I believe that Jews of the first century made a distinction between the Temple as an ideal, divinely given and divinely directed, and the Temple as it actually functioned. Almost all of the criticism derives from Palestinian, not diaspora, sources. This clearly suggests that those who came into close and frequent contact were the most critical. But the critics believed in the Temple; and I think that it was this belief and the commitment that arose from it that prompted their criticisms and longings for reform. At the heart of much of this belief was the conviction that the restoration of Israel could be realized only if Israel's religion was pure; and the religion of Israel could hardly be pure if things were amiss in the Temple.

CRITICISMS OF
THE FIRST-CENTURY TEMPLE

It was only natural, if not tragic, that one of the consequences of the rift between Early Judaism and Christianity was polemic. Christians were viewed as heretics; Jews as obdurate apostates. Given this unfortunate state of affairs, what each says of the other, especially if in a critical context, needs to be assessed very carefully. If the Gospels portray Jesus as critical of the Temple establishment, there is always the danger that the portrait reveals more of the early church and its quarrels with the synagogue than it does of Jesus and his contemporaries. It is therefore plainly evident that a survey of the evidence outside of the New Testament and early Christian sources is essential for any reconstruction of first-century Jewish attitudes toward the Temple establishment. When such a survey is complete, we shall be in a much better position to assess the nature of the polemic found in the Christian sources, as well as in Essene sources.

Josephus

Josephus tells us of the Temple's great wealth (*War* 5.222–24; 5.210–11; *Ant* 14.110; 15.395) and of the political power of the ruling priests, especially the high priest (*Apion* 2.185–87; 2.194). Although not intending to impugn them, he also tells us that during the 50s and 60s the ruling priests committed acts of theft, violence, and bribery (*Ant* 20.181, 206–7). Several of these crimes are reported in rabbinic writings, but in these the crimes are not limited to the 50s and 60s.

Pseudepigrapha

Several post-70 C.E. texts assert that it was because of Israel's sin that the Herodian Temple was destroyed (esp. LadJac 5:8–9; ApAb 17:7; Pseudo-Philo 19.6–7; 4Bar 1:1, 8; 4:4–5; SibOr 4.115–18). Two of these apparently indict the priesthood itself. An interpolation in the Life of Adam and Eve (in several manuscripts following 29:3) reads: "and again they will build a house of God, and the latest house of God shall be exalted more highly than before. And once again iniquity will surpass equity" (late first century C.E.).[2] Lack of equity in connection with the Temple probably refers to unfair and oppressive taxation and Temple polity. Lamenting the fate of Jerusalem, Baruch says: "You, priests, take the keys of the sanctuary, and cast them to the highest heaven, and give them to the Lord and say, 'Guard your house yourself, because, behold, we have been found to be false stewards'" (2Bar 10:18).[3] Although ostensibly describing the destruction of the First Temple, the author of this early second-century pseudepigraphon is describing the destruction of the Second Temple in 70 C.E. (see 2Bar 1:4; 32:2–4).[4] It is significant that the priests are characterized as "false stewards," a characterization that coheres with some of Jesus' parables (see Mt 24:45–51 and parallels; Mk 12:1–9 and parallels; Lk 16:1–8).

Although some have argued for a Maccabean date for the Testament of Moses, the allusions to Herod and his successors in chapter 6 have led most scholars to conclude that this work was written sometime in the first century.[5] R. H. Charles dated the writing to just prior to 30 C.E., a conclusion with which J. Priest agrees.[6] Chapter 5 describes the corruption of the Hasmonean priests; chapter 6 describes the oppression of Herod the Great (for thirty-four years; see v. 6); and chapter 7 apparently describes the priesthood of the first century C.E. The fragmentary chapter reads:

When this has taken place, the times will quickly come to an end. [. . .] Then will rule destructive and godless men, who represent themselves as being righteous, but who will (in fact) arouse their inner wrath, for they will be deceitful men, pleasing only themselves, false in every way imaginable, (such as) loving feasts at any hour of the day— devouring, gluttonous.

[Seven-line lacuna] But really they consume the goods of the (poor), saying their acts are according to justice, (while in fact they are simply) exterminators, deceitfully seeking to conceal themselves so that they will not be known as completely godless because of their criminal deeds (committed) all the day long, saying, "We shall have feasts, even luxurious winings and dinings. Indeed, we shall behave ourselves as princes." They, with hand and mind, touch impure things, yet their mouths will speak enormous things, and they will even say, "Do not touch me, lest you pollute me in the position I occupy. . . ."[7]

The passage is clearly directed against a wealthy and powerful priestly aristocracy. Since the passage apparently follows the demise of Herod's sons, the setting of this apocalyptic vision must be the first century C.E., and probably sometime in the 30s. If this is indeed the case, then what we have here is pre-70 evidence—possibly from the very time of Jesus—of the belief that the priestly aristocracy was corrupt.

Targumim

The so-called Targum Jonathan to the Prophets contains criticisms of the first-century priesthood.[8] 1 Samuel speaks of "robbing" God's sacrifices (2:17, 29). In Isaiah the Temple establishment is threatened with destruction (5:1–7) and is accused of having forsaken God's service (17:11) and feasts (24:5). The high priest is called the "foolish master of Israel" (28:1). In Jeremiah the priests are called "thieves" (7:9), "robbers of money" (8:10), and "robbers of wealth" (6:13), who have "stolen their ways" (23:11).

Rabbinic Literature

Similar criticisms, only fuller and more explicit, appear in the rabbinic writings. On one occasion R. Simeon ben Gamaliel (c. 10–80 C.E.) vigorously protested because the price of a pair of doves had been raised to one gold denar, a price some twenty-five times the proper charge (m.Ker 1:7).

It should be remembered that the dove was the poor man's sacrifice (Lev 5:7; 12:8). Such a charge would be bitterly resented. In this instance, however, Simeon's protest apparently brought about an immediate reduction in the charge. There is also a Tannaitic tradition claiming that the family of Annas did not tithe their produce, and for this reason their property was destroyed three years before the rest of Israel. Their refusal to tithe was apparently based on an exegesis of Deuteronomy 14:22–23, an exegesis for which the rabbis had little sympathy (SifDeut 105 [on 14:22]). A similar tradition is found in y.Pe'a 1:6 and b.B.Meṣ 88a–b. It is possible that the addition in the Targum to Isaiah 5:10 ("because of the sin that they did not give the tithes") alludes to this failure to tithe. Apparently the high priestly families profited in ways that the rabbis considered at best questionable (m.Sheq 4:3–4) and at other times clearly oppressive (SifDeut 357 [on 34:1, 3]; Mek., Amalek 2 83–87).[9]

The Tannaitic rabbis also preserve traditions, in part corroborated by Josephus (as noted above), that the office of high priest was often secured through bribery. Commenting on Leviticus 16:3 ("with this shall Aaron come"), R. Berekiah (second century c.e.) is reported to have said:

> But the verse [i.e., Lev 16:3] does not apply to the Second Temple [as it does to the First Temple], because in its time the priests used to outbid one another for the office of High Priest, so that there were eighty high priests who served (in disorderly succession) in the Temple. Hence the first part of the verse, "The fear of the Lord prolongs days" (Prov 10:27a), applies to the priests of the First Temple, and the conclusion of the verse, "the years of the wicked shall be shortened" (Prov 10:27b), applies to the priests of the Second Temple. (PR 47:4)[10]

The same tradition also appears in Wayyiqra Rabbah 21:9 (on 16:3), with a slight variation: "In the Second Temple, however, because they used to obtain the office of High Priest for money, or, as some say, because they used to kill each other by means of witchcraft. . . ."[11] It is likely that this tradition particularly has in mind the Herodian and Roman periods, for some twenty-eight high priests (only two of which were from families that had any legitimate claim) held office in little more than one century (from 37 b.c.e. to 70 c.e.).

In the Tosephta and Talmuds there are complaints of corruption and oppression among the ruling priests. It is claimed that the high priests took more than what was lawfully required. This is seen in a discussion of the distribution of the hides of the sacrificed animals:

> At first did they bring the hides of holy things to the room of *bet hap-parvah* and divide them in the evening to each [priestly] household which served on that day. But the powerful men of the priesthood would come and take them by force. They ordained that they should divide it on Fridays to each and every watch. But still did violent men of the priesthood come and take it away by force.... Beams of syca-more were in Jericho. And strong-fisted men would come and take them by force. (t.Men 13:18–19; cf. t.Zeb 11:16–17; b.Pes 57a)[12]

Apparently the ruling priests (i.e., the "powerful men of the priest-hood") were stealing the tithes (hides, in this case) to which the lower-ranking priests were entitled.[13] Because of this practice, it was not long "before the priests covered the face of the entire porch [of the Temple] with golden trays, a hundred by a hundred [handbreadths], with the thickness of a golden denar" (t.Men 13:18–19; cf. b.Pes 57a: "they covered the whole Temple with gold plaques a cubit square of the thickness of a gold denar"; m.Sheq 4:4: "What did they do with the surplus of the heave offering? Golden plating for bedecking the Holy of Holies").[14]

The four principal high priestly families are remembered for their violence and oppression:

> Concerning these and people like them . . . did Abba Saul ben Bithnith [first century C.E.] and Abba Joseph ben Johanan [first century C.E.?] of Jerusalem say, "Woe is me because of the house of Boethus. Woe is me because of their staves. Woe is me because of the house of Kathros. Woe is me because of their pen. Woe is me because of the house of Hanin [=the family of Annas; cf. John 18:13]. Woe is me because of their whispering. Woe is me because of the house of Ishmael ben Phabi. For they are high priests, and their sons [are] treasurers, and their sons-in-law [are] supervisors, and their servants come and beat us with staves." (t.Men 13:21; cf. b.Pes 57a; see also t.Zeb 11:16–17; y.Ma'as. Sh. 5:15)[15]

It is not likely that this rabbinic tradition has in mind only the excesses that took place in the years immediately preceding the war with Rome. The woes are pronounced against three of the principal families that served throughout the first century. The rabbis were also critical of the politics behind the appointment of the high priests. "When [unacceptable] kings became many, they ordained the practice of regularly appointing priests, and they appointed high priests every single year" (t.Yoma 1:7; cf. PR 47:4).[16] The passage goes on to describe the cultic violations and resulting death of one of the high priests from the family of Boethus (1:8). Moreover, the gold plaques that covered the Temple may be related to the plates of gold that Josephus describes (*War* 5.222; cf. m.Sheq 4:4). It is likely that the profiteering and extortion that resulted in the accumulation of so much gold took years and perhaps had something to do with the refurbishing of the Temple that continued throughout most of the first century.

According to the Tosephta tractate considered above, because of the greed and hatred of the powerful priestly families, the Second Temple was destroyed:

> As to Jerusalem's first building, on what account was it destroyed? Because of idolatry and licentiousness and bloodshed which was in it. But [as to] the latter building we know that they devoted themselves to Torah and were meticulous about tithes. On what account did they go into exile? *Because they love money* and hate one another. (t.Men 13:22; my emphasis)[17]

Whereas hating one another could refer to the bloody fighting between the rebel factions during the war, loving money undoubtedly refers to the greed of the high priestly families. Finally, echoing first-century tradition already cited, a rabbinic tradition reads:

> This verse [Zech 11:1] refers to the high priests who were in the Temple, who took their keys in their hands and threw them up to the sky, saying to the Holy One, blessed be He, "Master of the Universe, here are your keys which you handed over to us, for we have not been trustworthy stewards to do the King's work and to eat of the King's table." (ARN A 4; see also B 7)[18]

THE TEMPLE ACCORDING TO JESUS AND THE DEAD SEA SCROLLS

Priestly matters were of great interest to the Essenes. The community had its own "priests" (1QS 1.18, 21; 2.1, 19; 6.4, 5, 8, 19; CD 3.21–4.2; 7.1;

9.13, 15; 13.2, 5, 6; 16.14), whose names were inscribed in some sort of registry (1QS 7.2). The priests were called the "sons of Zadok" (1QS 5.2; cf. 9.14; CD 4.1; 1QSb 3.22), in deliberate contrast to the priests of the Hasmonean, Herodian, and Roman periods, almost none of whom were descendants of Zadok. The longest scroll found at Qumran (11QTemple) is devoted to the details of proper Temple service, whenever the community should gain control of the Temple. Twelve men and three priests made up the Council of the Community (1QS 8.1). Every member of the community is to be "counted by name: the priests first, and the Levites second, and the sons of Israel third, and the proselytes fourth" (CD 14.3–6). Finally, the priests were to play an important role in the final eschatological battle (1QM 2.1; 7.10; 13.1–16, where priests bless Israel and curse Belial; 15.4; 16.4, where priests sound the battle call; 16.9, where priests sound trumpets).

For all of the interest in the roles of the chief priest, ruling priests, and priests, it is somewhat passing strange that there is relatively little interest, at least so far as the published materials indicate, in the Jerusalem Temple itself. Even with the added testimony of Josephus, our information regarding Qumran's attitude toward the Temple establishment is scanty. Nevertheless, there are several noteworthy parallels that place Jesus in the spectrum of first-century Palestinian Judaism within proximity of the sectarians whose writings have been found near the Dead Sea and who are called Essenes by Josephus and Philo. The Gospels attribute to Jesus some critical remarks regarding the Temple establishment that in some significant ways parallel the views expressed in the Dead Sea Scrolls. Let us consider the following common points.

Oppression of the Poor

In the Qumran commentary on Habakkuk, Jerusalem's high priest is called the "Wicked Priest" (1QpHab 1.3; 8.9; 9.9; 11.4). In a few places he is accused of robbing the people, including the poor (1QpHab 8.12; 9.5; 10.1; 12.10; cf. CD 6.16), and of amassing wealth (1QpHab 8.8–12; 9.4–5; cf. CD 6.15). Similarly, 4QpNah 1.11 refers to "riches that he [the Wicked Priest?] heaped up in the Temple of Jerusalem." It is likely, however, that the Wicked Priest referred to in these commentaries originally was one of the Hasmonean priest-kings (see 1QpHab 8.8–11). Therefore, one might assume that the Habakkuk commentary does not represent the views of the

Qumran community and the Essenes in general in the time of Jesus. But I cannot agree with such an assumption. Admittedly, the Wicked Priest of this pesher originally had nothing to do with Caiaphas, or any other high priest of the first century, but I suspect that Qumran's critical views of the high priesthood in Jesus' time were essentially the same as those of the earlier generation. One reason for this suspicion rests on the eschatological orientation of the Qumran community in general and of the Habakkuk Pesher in particular. According to 1QpHab 7.1–2 the events described were to happen in the "last generation." In light of the fact that every generation of the covenanters of Qumran believed that theirs was the final generation, it is probable that every Jerusalem high priest was identified, at least potentially, as the "Wicked Priest."

Apparently Jesus also viewed the Temple establishment, particularly the ruling priests, as an oppressor of the poor. He regarded the corban tradition as potentially contrary to the commandment that enjoins support and honor for one's parents Mk 7:9–13; cf. Ex 20:12). These vows usually had to do with goods dedicated to the Temple. Jesus warned of the scribes "who devour widows' houses" (Mk 12:38–40). Economic oppression, evidently in the name of religion, is clearly in view. As is observed by the context, the Marcan evangelist evidently thought that these [Sadducean?] scribes had something to do with the Temple establishment. In the next pericope (Mk 12:41–44) Jesus' comment concerning the widow who threw her penny into the Temple treasury was probably originally a word of lament, not of praise. That is, he lamented the fact that the Temple had become an economic burden to the poor and not the source of relief that it should have been (cf. CD 6.21, where the Temple establishment is criticized for not supporting "the hand of the needy, the poor, and the stranger"). In many of Jesus' sayings there is clear evidence of a bias in favor of the poor and of warning for the rich (Mt 5:3; 6:19–34; Mk 10:17–22, 23–31; Lk 6:24–26; 12:15–21; 14:12–14, 15–24; 16:19–25; 19:1–9).

Temple Tax Controversy

There are two questions concerning taxation that were put to Jesus, and both had to do with the Temple. The first, and more obvious, had to do with the half-shekel Temple tax that every adult Jewish male had to pay annually: "Does not your teacher pay the tax?" (Mt 17:24–27). Although Peter answered in the affirmative, Jesus' position was not so simple.

Whether or not one regards v. 27 as a later quietist accommodation to the Roman Empire,[19] it nevertheless is unable to efface the point in Jesus' answer in the preceding verse: "The sons are free." Not only is Jesus implying that the Temple tax is invalid; the rhetorical question put to Peter in v. 25 suggests that this tax is similar to the various taxes and tributes imposed by the "kings of the earth." If the ruling priests viewed all Israelites as sons of God, they would not impose on them taxation, as though they were servants or foreigners.

There is evidence that the Qumran covenanters also had misgivings about the Temple tax. According to 4Q159 2.6–8: "as for the half-[shekel, the offering to the Lord] which they gave, each man as a ransom for his soul: only one [time] shall he give it all his days."[20] This assertion is in all probability polemical.[21] Contrary to the Temple establishment, which expected the tax to be paid every year, Qumran understood Ex 30:13 as commanding the tax to be paid only *once* in one's lifetime. What undoubtedly exacerbated the situation was the priests' claim of exemption from the half-shekel tax, an exemption that Johanan ben Zakkai (first century C.E.) explicitly condemned: "If a priest did not pay the shekel he committed sin; but the priests used to expound this scripture [i.e., Lev 6:23] to their advantage . . ." (m.Sheq 1:4).[22] It was "in the interests of peace" that no one insisted that the priests pay the tax. This statement probably alludes to the violence sometimes suffered by those who opposed the ruling priests. R. A. Horsley avers that the "half-shekel tax was almost certainly a late development in Second Temple times, and its payment was controversial at the time of Jesus."[23]

Obviously the half-shekel Temple tax was to be paid to the Temple. But even Roman taxation was ultimately collected by the Temple establishment, a fact not often appreciated in Gospel studies.[24] The question put to Jesus concerning Roman taxation (Mk 12:13–17) had as much to do with the Temple establishment as it had to do with the Roman government. It is not surprising, therefore, that the Marcan evangelist places this pericope in the larger context of Jesus in conflict with the religious authorities of his day. Jesus' answer, "Render to Caesar the things that are Caesar's, and to God the things that are God's" (v. 17), has sometimes been understood as acquiescence to Roman authority (as seen, e.g., in Rom 13:7; 1Pet 2:13–17). But if that had been what he meant, his answer would surely have been very disappointing to most of his loyal following. According to another interpretation, Jesus may have been implying that since from a Jewish point of view everything belongs to God, Caesar is to receive his due: nothing.[25] If such was indeed what he meant, then this could explain the charge later brought against Jesus: "We found this man perverting our nation, and forbidding us to give tribute to Caesar, and saying that he himself is Christ a king" (Lk 23:2).

But why does Jesus make an issue of the image and inscription on the coin? Neither of the aforementioned interpretations takes this aspect adequately into account. It is possible that he intends to point out the most offensive features of the Roman denarius (the image, which contravenes Ex 20:4, and the inscription, which contravenes Ex 20:3 in that the emperor has claimed semidivine status), the medium by which Roman taxes were to be paid, implying that no pious Jew would want to possess such money. If this is all that Caesar wants, then by all means give it to him. This interpretation finds an interesting parallel in the Essenes. According to Hippolytus (*Refutation* 9.26) some Essenes would not even touch a Roman coin that bore the image and inscription of Caesar. This may very well have been Jesus' point.[26] Perhaps for this reason, and not simply because of poverty, Jesus did not possess a denarius for the object lesson; it had to be produced by his interlocutors!

Ritual Purity

The Essenes were very concerned with ritual purity, especially with regard to the Temple: "And whoever enters the House of Prostration [probably the Temple], let him not enter in a state of uncleanness; let him wash himself" (CD 11.21–22). Jesus too was evidently concerned that his disciples approach the altar in the right spirit: "So if you are offering your gift at the altar, and there remember that your brother has something against you, leave your gift there before the altar and go; first be reconciled to your brother, and then come and offer your gift" (Mt 5:23–24). But the Essenes' concern with ritual purity was a major factor in their break with the Temple establishment. According to Josephus, "the purification rites to which [the Essenes] are accustomed are different. For this reason, they are excluded from the common enclosure" (*Ant* 18.19). These differences no doubt reflected points over which the Essenes differed sharply with the Temple establishment. What were some of these points of difference? The exhortations in CD 6.11–7.6 imply that the "sons of the Pit" (apparently a reference to the priests of Jerusalem) did not always correctly "distinguish between the unclean and the clean" and the "sacred and profane," or "observe the Sabbath day according to its exact tenor, and the feasts, and the Day of Fasting" (cf. CD 11.18–12.2).[27] There are many indications that the Essenes expected someday to purify the Temple and restore the sacrificial system as they understood it (e.g., 1QS 6.2–5; 8.4–10; 9.4–5; 1QM 2.1–6; 4QpPs 37 3.11; cf. 5QJN ar; 11QTemple).[28]

Jesus' action in the Temple (Mk 11:15–17), traditionally understood as some sort of "cleansing," may have paralleled the Essenes' hope for a purified Temple. But recently this action has been interpreted as a prophetic gesture in which Jesus threatened to destroy the Herodian Temple and replace it with the Temple of the Messianic Age.[29] This interpretation, however, comes to grief at several points,[30] for most of the pericope simply does not cohere with this proposal. Prohibiting people from carrying "anything through the Temple" (v. 16) and the allusion to Jeremiah 7:11 ("den of robbers," v. 17) suggest that Jesus strongly objected to certain aspects of Temple practice and polity.[31] As the evidence surveyed above makes abundantly clear, the first-century Temple establishment was widely viewed as corrupt and oppressive. Although Jesus may have warned of future destruction (Mk 13:2), which would explain the accusations brought against him (Mk 14:58; Acts 6:14), his action may very well have been a protest, modeled somewhat after the examples of the classical prophets, such as Jeremiah. But Jesus' protest apparently was directed not against the sacrifices but against the trafficking in sacrificial animals. There is no indication that he regarded the animals as unclean or the sacrifices as improper. Therefore, whereas Jesus also criticized Temple polity, his criticism seems to have been different from that of the Essenes and the Dead Sea Scrolls. Jesus' complaint seems to have been limited to the activity of buying and selling. But there was nothing inappropriate about buying and selling, which included, of course, the changing of money. Jesus' complaint may have been prompted by overcharging,[32] or possibly by the presence of the vendors in the Temple precincts, which may have been a recent innovation on the part of Caiaphas.[33]

Spiritual Offerings

Jesus and the Essenes apparently had more in common in their articulation of and apparent preference for spiritual offerings. According to Josephus, because the Essenes had been excluded from the Temple, owing to their distinctive rites, "they offered their sacrifices among themselves"

(*Ant* 18.19). But what form did these sacrifices take? It has been suggested that they offered animal sacrifice at Qumran.[34] But no altar has been found, and the small stone cube unearthed by S. H. Steckoll could hardly have been one.[35] It is possible that some of the Essenes did attempt to offer sacrifices at the Jerusalem Temple, taking care to avoid contact with those whom they regarded as ritually impure.[36] But the Dead Sea Scrolls seem to suggest that the Qumran group, while awaiting eventual restoration and control of the Temple, believed that its duty was to offer up spiritual offerings. Such an idea is expressed in 1QS 9.3–5:

> They shall expiate guilty rebellion and sinful infidelity . . . without the flesh of burnt offering and the fat of sacrifice, but the offering of the lips in accordance with the Law will be as an agreeable odor of righteousness, and perfection of way shall be as the voluntary gift of a delectable oblation.[37]

Elsewhere the community itself is described as an "expiation for the earth" (1QS 8.10). Perhaps this is what lies behind Philo's comment that the Essenes "are men utterly dedicated to the service of God; they do not offer animal sacrifice, judging it more fitting to render their minds truly holy" (Philo, *Every Good Man Is Free* 75).

Jesus' use of Hosea 6:6 ("I desire mercy, and not sacrifice") affords an interesting and instructive parallel. The prophetic utterance occurs in two passages in Matthew, which represent expansions of material taken from Mark. In the first passage Hosea is cited in defense of Jesus' fellowship with "tax collectors and sinners" (Mt 9:10–13; cf. Mk 2:15–17), thus implying that mercy fulfills the law. In the second passage it augments Jesus' argument justifying the disciples' plucking of grain on the Sabbath (Mt 12:1–8; cf. Mk 2:23–26).

Although clearly representing Matthean interpolations, these verbatim citations of Hosea 6:6 probably originated with Jesus.[38] They seem to cohere with the whole tenor of his ministry. But it is a theme that, with the exception of the Fourth Gospel (and even here it is quite limited), finds no expression in the New Testament. Indeed, the Matthean and Lucan evangelists hold the Temple in high regard. These considerations tell in favor of the authenticity of the tradition. But if the Matthean contexts are secondary, what did Hosea 6:6 originally mean in Jesus' teaching? Obviously the critical sentiment expressed by Hosea could find many applications, with Matthew finding two as likely as any. I suspect that the passage that comes closest to Jesus' original application is Mark 12:28–34, in which Hosea 6:6 and related texts are alluded to (1Sam 15:22; Mic 6:6–8). In this passage Jesus cites the great commandments of love for God and for one's neighbor (Deut 6:45; Lev 19:18). Approving this answer, the scribe responds (vv. 32–34):

> You are right, Teacher; you have truly said that he is one, and there is no other but him; and to love him with all the heart, and with all the understanding, and with all the strength, and to love one's neighbor as oneself, is much more than all whole burnt offerings and sacrifices.

Again, this tradition is probably authentic, for had the early church invented it, why not give Jesus credit for saying it? Moreover, the fact that it was spoken by "one of the scribes" and not by Jesus could explain why the tradition was not preserved by Matthew or Luke. This tradition coheres well with the Matthean interpolations. Together they illustrate Jesus' assessment of the comparative relation between the ethical and cultic aspects of Jewish faith: Love of God and of neighbor is better than burnt offerings and sacrifices and, if lived out in one's life, fulfills the word of God through Hosea: "I desire mercy, and not sacrifice."

A Spiritual Temple

Although the Essenes hoped someday to gain control of the Temple and to practice the cultus as they believed it should be practiced, they evidently understood their community (*yaḥad*), perhaps in the interim, as constituting a sort of spiritual temple.

> The Council of the Community shall be established in truth as an everlasting planting. It is the House of holiness for Israel and the Company of infinite holiness for Aaron . . . appointed to offer expiation for the earth. . . . It is the tried wall, the precious corner-stone. (1QS 8.5–7)[39]

There is another related passage that presents some difficulties:

> This is the House which [will be built at the e]nd of days. . . . It is the House into which will enter [neither the ungodly nor the defiled], ever . . . but they that are called saints. Yah[w]eh [will reign (there) for]

ever; He will appear above it constantly, and strangers will lay it waste no more as they formerly laid waste the sanctua[ry of I]srael because of their sin. And He has commanded a sanctuary (made by the hands) of men to be built for Himself, that there they may send up, like the smoke of incense, the works of the Law. (4QFlor 1.2–7)[40]

Does this passage speak of a physical temple, such as the Solomonic Temple that was "laid waste"? Or does it speak of a spiritual house in contrast to the Solomonic, or of both? Dupont-Sommer assumes that the passage is speaking of a physical temple to come. That is why he inserts the parenthetic "made by the hands." But these words are not found in the text. Surely the idea of "works of the law" being sent up "like smoke of incense" requires us to understand the "house of men" as something spiritual. This does not, of course, contradict the idea that the Essenes would someday occupy the physical Temple, perhaps one divinely rebuilt (see 11QTemple 29.9–10). However 4QFlorilegium is to be understood, it is clear that the Essenes spoke of spiritual offerings and sacrifices as substitutions for literal offerings and sacrifices.

There are several texts in the New Testament that bear significant relationship to this idea. Three of these texts are presented as the words of Jesus on the subject. The first passage, whose authenticity can scarcely be doubted, tells us that Jesus was accused of saying: "I will destroy this Temple that is made with hands, and in three days I will build another, not made with hands" (Mk 14:58). Since it is not likely that the early church would invent such a potentially embarrassing and confusing saying, many think that it represents something that Jesus actually said.[41] If so, then Jesus must have taught something to the effect that he and his followers made up some sort of community in which true worship could take place. Elsewhere Jesus is reported to have said, "Something greater than the Temple is here" (Mt 12:6). Was he referring to himself as that greater something? He may have been, since he implies that he is also greater than Jonah and greater than Solomon (cf. Mt 12:41–42; Lk 11:31–32). In the more theologically advanced Fourth Gospel, Jesus is presented not simply as one greater than the Temple but as the temple itself, something that was understood in the light of Easter (Jn 2:19–21). Paul extends the metaphor to include the Christian community as a whole: "We are the temple of the living God" (2Cor 6:16; cf. 1Cor 6:19: "Your body is a temple of the Holy Spirit within you"). The metaphor, with all of its symbolic potential, is extended still further by the author of 1 Peter: "Come to him that living stone . . . and like living stones be yourselves built into a spiritual house, to be a holy priest-hood, to offer spiritual sacrifices acceptable to God through Jesus Christ" (1Pet 2:4–5).[42]

CONCLUSION

Both Jesus and the Essenes anticipated an eschatological restoration of Israel. Both apparently believed that some sort of national purification was necessary. Although critical of the Temple establishment, Jesus and the Essenes were committed to Israel and to the nation's restoration. In no wise does Jesus' criticism lay a foundation for the condemnation of Judaism or the Jewish people. Jesus' criticisms were motivated by a deep desire for Israel's best, a hope that Israel would someday attain to its God-given destiny. Part of this hope was the anticipation of the day when the Temple Mount would become a place of prayer for all the nations. Jesus feared that if the nation did not significantly alter its policies, it would instead become a place of trampling under the feet of the nations. His criticisms of the Temple establishment must be seen in this light.

Notes

1. See E. P. Sanders, *Jesus and Judaism* (Philadelphia, 1985) pp. 61–76.
2. Translation from M. D. Johnson, "Life of Adam and Eve," in *OTP,* vol. 2, p. 270 n. 29b.
3. Translation from A. F. J. Klijn, "2 (Syriac Apocalypse of) Baruch," in *OTP,* vol. 1, p. 624. There were literal keys of the Temple (see Josephus, *Apion* 2.108), but they also had taken on a symbolic value (see also Mt 16:19; Rev 3:7). Further references are considered below.
4. Klijn, "2 Baruch," *OTP,* vol. 1, pp. 615–18.
5. The allusions are obvious. According to 6:2–6a, a "rash and perverse" man [Herod] will rule "for thirty-four years." According to 6:7, Herod "will beget heirs [Archelaus, Herod Antipas, Philip] who will reign after him for shorter periods of time." These heirs will be subdued by a "powerful king of the West," that is, Rome (6:8).

6. R. H. Charles, *The Assumption of Moses* (London, 1897) pp. lv–lviii; J. Priest, "Testament of Moses," in *OTP,* vol. 1, pp. 920–21. Even if a Maccabean date is retained, chs. 6–7 would have to be understood as a later, probably first-century, interpolation.

7. Translation from Priest, "Testament of Moses," *OTP,* vol. 1, p. 930.

8. On the presence of first-century traditions in this targum, see D. J. Harrington and A. J. Saldarini, *Targum Jonathan of the Former Prophets* (Aramaic Bible 10; Wilmington, 1987) p. 13; B. D. Chilton, *The Isaiah Targum* (Aramaic Bible 11; Wilmington, 1987) pp. 55–57 (and notes); and R. Hayward, *The Targum of Jeremiah* (Aramaic Bible 12; Wilmington, 1987) pp. 37–38.

9. See R. Hammer, *Sifre: A Tannaitic Commentary on the Book of Deuteronomy* (Yale Judaica 24; New Haven, London, 1986) pp. 378 (and n. 4, p. 512), 380. Employing wordplay, "Gilead" (Deut 34:1) is understood as a reference to Jerusalem; "Zoar" (34:3) is understood as a reference to the oppressive establishment in Israel.

10. Translation based on W. G. Braude, *Pesikta Rabbati* (2 vols.; Yale Judaica 18; New Haven, London, 1968) vol. 2, p. 808.

11. Translation based on J. J. Slotki, *Midrash Rabbah: Leviticus* (London, New York, 1983) p. 272. In this version R. Aha (third century C.E.) is given credit for the interpretation of Prov 10:27.

12. Translation from J. Neusner, *The Tosefta* (6 vols.; New York, 1977–81) vol. 5, p. 161.

13. It is probably against this inequity that t.Yoma 1:5 speaks: "But in the case of Holy Things . . . the High Priest and the ordinary priest are the same: each receives an equal portion." Translation based on Neusner, *Tosefta,* vol. 2, p. 186. Although the laws of the Pentateuch did not, with regard to the offerings and tithes, favor the ruling priests over the lower-ranking priests, from the time of Roman control the ruling priests had such control (Josephus, *Ant* 14.202–3 [44 B.C.E.]).

14. Translation from Neusner, *Tosefta,* vol. 5, p. 161. The talmudic quotation is from H. Freedman, "Pesahim," in *The Babylonian Talmud,* ed. I. Epstein (17 vols.; London, 1935–45) vol. 3, p. 284; the mishnaic quotation is from H. Danby, *The Mishnah* (Oxford, 1933) p. 156.

15. Translation based on Neusner, *Tosefta,* vol. 5, pp. 161–62. The reading is modified slightly in light of the parallel passage in b.Pes 57a.

16. Translation from Neusner, *Tosefta,* vol. 2, p. 187. Tosephta's statement is hyperbolic. High priests were not appointed "every single year" (cf. Jn 18:13). Some served less than a year, but most served for more than a year.

17. Translation from Neusner, *Tosefta,* vol. 5, p. 162.

18. Translation based on J. Goldin, *The Fathers According to Rabbi Nathan* (Yale Judaica 10; New Haven, London, 1955) p. 37. This tradition is at times applied to the destruction of the First Temple; see b.Ta'an 29a; LevR 19:6 (on 15:25). It

should be noted that comparison between the two Temples, their destructions, and the ensuing exiles is not rare in the Targums and writings of the rabbis (see TargIsa 51:19; TargEzek 24:6; TargPs.-J. Gen 45:15; t.Men 13:22; b.Ta'an 28b–29a; PR 47:4).

19.   So D. E. Oakman, *Jesus and the Economic Questions of His Day* (Lewiston, Queenston, 1986) p. 172 n. 30.

20.   J. M. Allegro, "An Unpublished Fragment of Essene Halakhah (4Q Ordinances)," *JSS* 6 (1961) 71–73; J. Liver, "The Half-Shekel in the Scrolls of the Judaean Desert Sect," *Tarbiz* 31 (1961–62) 18–22.

21.   W. Horbury, "The Temple Tax," in *Jesus and the Politics of His Day*, ed. E. Bammel and C. F. D. Moule (Cambridge, 1984) p. 279.

22.   Translation based on Danby, *Mishnah*, p. 152.

23.   R. A. Horsley, *Jesus and the Spiral of Violence: Popular Jewish Resistance in Roman Palestine* (San Francisco, 1987). pp. 280 and 345 n. 7. See also S. Freyne, *Galilee from Alexander the Great to Hadrian* (Wilmington, 1980) pp. 277–81; Horbury, "Temple Tax," pp. 265–86.

24.   See R. A. Horsley, "High Priests and the Politics of Roman Palestine," *JSJ* 17 (1986) 23–55, esp. 30–31.

25.   S. G. F. Brandon, *Jesus and the Zealots* (New York, 1967) pp. 345–47.

26.   F. F. Bruce, "Render to Caesar," in *Jesus and the Politics of His Day*, ed. Bammel and Moule, pp. 249–63, esp. 259.

27.   Translations based on A. Dupont-Sommer, *The Essene Writings from Qumran*, trans. G. Vermes (Gloucester, 1973) p. 132.

28.   Y. Yadin, *The Scroll of the War of the Sons of Light against the Sons of Darkness* (Oxford, 1962; Hebrew original, 1957) pp. 198–201.

29.   Sanders, *Jesus and Judaism*, pp. 61–76.

30.   See M. D. Hooker, "Traditions about the Temple in the Sayings of Jesus," *BJRL* 70 (1988) 7–19; C. A. Evans, "Jesus' Action in the Temple: Cleansing or Portent of Destruction?" *CBQ* 51 (1989) 237–70; idem, "Jesus' Action in the Temple and Evidence of Corruption in the First-Century Temple," *SBL 1989 Seminar Papers*, ed. D. J. Lull (Atlanta, 1989) pp. 522–39).

31.   Not surprisingly, Sanders finds it necessary to dismiss vv. 16–17 as inauthentic (*Jesus and Judaism*, pp. 66, 364).

32.   According to m.Ker 1:7 the first-century ruling priests charged twenty-five times the customary price for a pair of doves.

33.   V. Eppstein, "The Historicity of the Cleansing of the Temple," *ZNW* 55 (1964) 42–58.

34.   F. M. Cross, *The Ancient Library of Qumran and Modern Biblical Studies* (repr., Grand Rapids, 1980) p. 102.

35.   S. H. Steckoll, "The Qumran Sect in Relation to the Temple of Leontopolis," *RQ* 6 (1967–69) 55–69, esp. 57.

36.   So T. S. Beall, *Josephus' Description of the Essenes Illustrated by the Dead Sea Scrolls* (SNTS Monograph Series 58; Cambridge, 1988) p. 119.

37. Dupont-Sommer, *Essene Writings*, p. 93 and n. 1.

38. Indeed, R. Bultmann, in reference to this and other passages, concedes that "this or that scripture which the Church used, was [possibly] also used by Jesus in his struggle." Bultmann, *The History of the Synoptic Tradition* (Oxford, 1972) p. 49.

39. Dupont-Sommer, *Essene Writings*, p. 91.

40. Ibid., 311–12; G. Vermes, *The Dead Sea Scrolls in English* (New York, 1975 [2d ed.]) p. 246.

41. Sanders, *Jesus and Judaism*, pp. 61, 364 nn. 2–3.

42. For a recent survey of the question, see I. H. Marshall, "Church and Temple in the New Testament," *TynBul* 40 (1989) 203–22.

CHAPTER 9

Jesus, Table-Fellowship, and Qumran

JAMES D. G. DUNN

There can be no question about the importance of the meal table as a focus of religious and social significance in the ancient Near East. J. Jeremias expresses the point well:

> to invite a man to a meal was an honour. It was an offer of peace, trust, brotherhood and forgiveness; in short, sharing a table meant sharing life.[1] . . . In Judaism in particular, table-fellowship means fellowship before God, for the eating of a piece of broken bread by everyone who shares in the meal brings out the fact that they all have a share in the blessing which the master of the house had spoken over the unbroken bread.[2]

This, what we might call the sacredness of the meal table, is often lost sight of in a Christianity where the link between sacrament and meal has been long broken and the heightened sacredness of the sacrament has resulted in a diminished religious significance for the ordinary meal. Nor is it sufficient to focus that significance in food taboos and dietary laws, much as a social anthropological perspective sharpens our awareness of dimensions we might otherwise have missed or disparaged.[3] It is much more, as Jeremias noted, that in the sharing of everyday food that is blessed before God human relationships can become an expression of the more fundamental divine–human relationship. The ideal had long since been characterized in the Greek legend of Philemon and Baucis (Ovid, *Metamorphosis* 8.613–70) and in Judaism particularly in the story of Abraham's entertaining the three heavenly visitors in Genesis 18 (Philo, *Abr.* 107–14; Josephus, *Ant* 1.196; Heb. 13:2; 1 Clem 10.7).[4] It is against this background that any discussion of Jesus' practice of table-fellowship has to be set.

JESUS AND TABLE-FELLOWSHIP

The significance of table-fellowship in the ministry of Jesus has also been recognized in recent years. It is obvious from the Gospel traditions that much of Jesus' ministry took place in the context of the meal table. He is remembered as one who often was a guest at another's table (Mk 2:15–16 pars.; 14:3 par.; Lk 7:36; 10:39; 11:37; 14:1; 19:5–7), and he seems to have acted as host on a number of occasions (Lk 15:2; Mk 14:22–23 pars.; cf. Mk 6:41 pars.; Lk 24:30–31).[5] Evidently guest friendship as expressed in the shared meal was so much a feature of Jesus' ministry that it was regarded as something notorious. Fasting was typical of other religious groups, but not of the group around Jesus (Mk 2:18–19 pars.). In contrast to John the Baptist's asceticism, Jesus' enjoyment of the table was almost proverbial: "Behold, a glutton and a drunkard" (Mt 11:19//Lk 7:34). The accounts of the meal(s) in the desert (Mk 6:30–44 pars.; Mk 8:1–10 par.)[6] and of the Last Supper (Mk 14:17–25 pars.) are best seen against this background. Against the same background Mark's repeated note that at times the demands on Jesus were so intense that he had no time even to eat (Mk 3:20; 6:31) gains an added poignancy, as do the Lucan accounts of renewed table-fellowship after Jesus' resurrection (Lk 24:30; Acts 1:4). According to Luke, Jesus also commended the model of itinerancy dependent on table hospitality to his disciples (Lk 10:7–8). Although Luke has chosen to highlight this feature of Jesus' ministry, the motif is sufficiently well rooted in the Synoptic tradition as a whole. The probability is that much of Jesus' remembered teaching began as "table talk" (Mk 2:17; 14:6–9; Lk 7:36–50; 10:39; 11:39–41; 14:1–24; cf. Mk 6:34).

The meal was also a feature of Jesus' *teaching*, particularly the wedding banquet with all its eschatological overtones of God's final acceptance (Mk

2:19 pars.; Mt 22:1–14; 25:10; Lk 14:16–24; 22:30).[7] Hence, the power of the parable of the prodigal son: the welcome back to the table of celebration marks the son's acceptance as "son," the transition from death back to life again (Lk 15:23–24, 32). Hence too the seriousness of the warning in Luke 13:26–27 – to have participated in table-fellowship with Jesus is no guarantee of final salvation – and the significance of Matthew 8:11–12//Luke 13:28–29 (also Lk 12:35–37). Not least in importance is the fact that Jesus saw it as desirable that contemporary practice of table-fellowship should be determined by (and thus foreshadow) the eschatalogical banquet in character (Lk 14:13, 21).

Particularly noticeable is the extent to which Jesus' practice of table-fellowship is remembered in the Synoptic tradition as a focus of controversy. The fact that he ate with tax collectors and sinners was evidently a cause of offense (Mk 2:16 pars.; Mt 11:19//Lk 7:34; Lk 15:2; 19:7). The Marcan and Matthean traditions also record that the table practice of his group called forth critical comment by its failure to observe purity ritual (Mk 7:1–5; Mt 15:1–2, 20). It will be no accident then that both evangelists immediately present the story of the Syrophoenician woman; it too turns very neatly on the limits and significance of table etiquette as expressing much more profound issues of mutual acceptance and of human acceptability to God (Mk 7:24–30//Mt 15:21–28). Gentile inferiority ("dogs") to the privileged covenant relationship of Israel is characterized precisely by their unacceptability at the meal table of the chosen ("children"); cf. again Mt 8:11–12//Lk 13:28–29).[8]

The picture provided by the Synoptics of this dimension of Jesus' ministry is therefore clear and is consistent across all four strands of the Synoptic tradition (Mk, Q, M, L).[9] If we were to summarize the evidence documented above it would be in terms of the coherence between Jesus' teaching and his own life-style. Jesus evidently saw the fellowship of the meal table as an expression of life under the rule of God (particularly Mt 22:2; 25:1); in his own social relationships he sought to live in accordance with his vision of the kingdom (cf. particularly Lk 6:20 with 14:13, 21). It was this lived-out vision of acceptability before God as expressed in table-fellowship which, according to the Synoptics, was one of the major causes of complaint against Jesus among some of his contemporaries.[10]

We should also note that the Synoptic tradition is consistent in attributing such criticism to some Pharisees in particular (but certainly not all Pharisees). The picture just sketched does not actually depend on such specific identification, but though many of the references to Pharisees in the Synoptic tradition are clearly redactional,[11] on this point the testimony is unanimous (Mk 2:16 pars.; 7:1). In filling out the context of Jesus' table-fellowship, therefore, we must look more closely at what lies behind this element in the tradition.

A FOCUS OF CONTROVERSY
WITH PHARISEES

The Synoptic picture of Jesus' table-fellowship as something that drew fire from Pharisees has been brought into sharper focus in recent years by the work of J. Neusner. As is now well known, Neusner's study of rabbinic traditions specifically attributed to the period before 70 C.E. has produced a striking conclusion:

> Of the 341 individual Houses' legal pericopae, no fewer than 229, approximately 67 percent of the whole, directly or indirectly concern table-fellowship. . . . The Houses' laws of ritual cleanness apply in the main to the ritual cleanness of food, and of people, dishes, and implements involved in its preparation. Pharisaic laws regarding Sabbath and festivals, moreover, involve in large measure the preparation and preservation of food.[12]

Neusner also draws out two points of particular interest to this inquiry. First, that this concern to maintain ritual purity in respect of the meal table was a primary expression of Pharisees' desire to live as though they were serving as priests in the Temple—to regard, we might say, the whole land as sharing the sanctity of the Temple and thus requiring the same degree of holiness as for the Temple priest. Second, that this concern did not focus on special or ritual meals, but came to expression in all meals; it was precisely in their daily life, in the daily meal table, that the test of their priestlike dedication would be proved.

The importance of Neusner's work at this point is twofold: (1) It confirms the initial assumption that the daily meal table had a significance at the time of Jesus which was much richer and deeper than typical Christian practice today. (2) It confirms in a striking way the picture of the gospels, that table-fellowship would probably have been a sensitive issue between

Jesus and many of the Pharisees. This is perhaps the most significant feature of Neusner's work: Not only has he pioneered the critical analysis of the rabbinic traditions—enabling us to gain a firmer "fix" on those traditions which go back to the pre-70 period[13]—but, he has also demonstrated that the Synoptic Gospel tradition is to be regarded and used as a more valuable source for our knowledge of pre-70 *Judaism* than most of his Jewish colleagues have hitherto acknowledged.[14]

Neusner's conclusions, however, have recently come under heavy fire from E. P. Sanders.[15] Sanders's argument has two major prongs. (1) The sayings specifically attributed to the period before 70 cannot be regarded as particularly characteristic of that period, since there are numerous anonymous laws which were equally characteristic of the same period.[16] And while concern regarding the purity of the meal table can be attributed to the *haberim* (associates), it cannot be assumed that all Pharisees were *haberim*.[17] In other words, Sanders calls into question whether there was more than a small group who at the time of Jesus sought to maintain such a degree of purity at the meal table as Neusner has pointed to.

(2) Having called into question the significance of the pre-70 rabbinic traditions, Sanders also diminishes the historical value of the Synoptic tradition which seems to mesh into the former so well, specifically, the Synoptic attestation that Jesus' meal table practice aroused criticism from Pharisees. In particular, he notes the confusion between impurity and sin. Impurity merely debarred from participation in the Temple cult for the duration of the impurity; it did not constitute anyone a sinner. And since impurity only related to the Temple cult, it would not be a cause for comment outside the Temple; lack of concern for purity outside the Temple simply showed that one was not a *haber*. What Jesus was criticized for was association with *sinners*—that is, people who were generally regarded as "wicked" or "traitors." To make purity and table-fellowship the focal points of debate, therefore, is to trivialize the charges against Jesus.[18] In fact, Sanders finds no evidence of substantial conflict between Jesus and the Pharisees in respect of food and purity laws, and traditions like Mark 7:1–23 must, in his view, be discounted as later retrojections into the Synoptic tradition.[19]

I have offered a fuller critique of Sanders elsewhere,[20] and so can focus more briefly on the main points that bear upon the present discussion. (1) Although Sanders dismisses much of the Synoptic tradition as good evidence for Jesus' ministry itself, so far as it bears on the topic of our interest, he does not dispute the basic facts outlined above in "Jesus and

Table-Fellowship": that Jesus was notorious for his acceptance of "sinners," that he did eat with "tax collectors and sinners," and that he probably saw this as an expression of his understanding of the kingdom and of who would be members of it.[21] He doubts whether this aspect of Jesus' ministry had a lasting impact on Jesus' followers. But the important point for us is his confirmation, as a historian, of this dimension of Jesus' historical ministry. What then of the more specific issue of whether Jesus was in fact criticized by Pharisees, and if so on what grounds?

(2) Despite Sanders, it must be significant that those who passed down the rabbinic traditions from the pre-70 period chose to retain the attribution of so many of them to that period. At the very least it indicates that the purity of table-fellowship was recalled as a particular concern of the pre-70 predecessors of the rabbis. And even if Pharisees and *ḥaberim* are not to be completely identified, the latter almost certainly constituted a significant proportion of the former,[22] so that once again the conclusion is probably sound that the purity of the meal table was a very active concern among many or most of Jesus' Pharisaic contemporaries.

(3) Sanders completely ignores the fact that the term "sinners" had a well-established factional use within the Judaism of the time. The clear testimony of the Jewish literature which dates to the two hundred years between the Maccabean revolt and Jesus is that Judaism was fairly riven with factions. Prominent among the factional terms was the description "sinners." The factions represented by such documents as 1 Enoch (1–5 and 81–82) or the Psalms of Solomon, or the sectarian scrolls from Qumran, clearly saw themselves as "the righteous" and condemned those outside or opposed to their factions as "sinners" (e.g., 1En 1:1, 7–9; 5:6–7; 82:4–7; PssSol 3; 13; 15; CD 1.13–21; 1QH 2.8–19). The point, of course, is that the term "sinners" was being used *by Jews* of *fellow Jews,* and being used to designate what was regarded by the members of the faction as unacceptable conduct for a devout Jew.[23] This is precisely the position reflected in the Synoptic tradition, where it is the Pharisees who are depicted as condemning those whose conduct they counted unacceptable for a righteous Jew. In short, within the context of late Second Temple Judaism, it is wholly to be expected that Pharisees would characterize those who were outside their circle and who disputed their understanding of what righteousness involved and required as "sinners."

(4) Added to this firm historical data is the sociological probability that such factions would draw clear boundaries around themselves, to mark off

the righteous from the sinners, and that the boundaries would most probably have ritual expression. For example, in the case of Jubilees and 1 Enoch, we know that the correct dating of the feasts was regarded as a crucial boundary issue (Jub 6:32–35); 1En 82:4–7).[24] Into this background the historical Pharisees fit well. The very name "Pharisees" (probably a nickname="separated ones")[25] indicates a desire for social distinctiveness. And one of the areas in which ritual could safeguard that distinctiveness where it might be most threatened by careless conduct would be the food used in a meal and its preparation. Despite his concern to evaluate the Synoptic data as a historian, Sanders has ignored these important dimensions of the historical context.

(5) Finally, we may simply note that the Synoptic traditions cannot be dated after 70 C.E. with any probability.[26] The traditions on which Mark draws in chapters 2 and 7 must certainly be dated at the very least to the period before 70. They therefore provide the confirmation that Neusner found in them for a pre-70 group of Pharisees who regarded table-fellowship as very important and who criticized the followers of Jesus for their slackness in this respect. It is not necessary to hypothesize outright conflict between Jesus or his disciples and all Pharisees (on the contrary, Lk 7:36; 11:37; 14:1). All that is required for the Synoptic tradition to make good historical sense is that at least some Pharisees felt their own understanding and practice of covenant loyalty to be called into question and in some degree threatened by the life-style and message of Jesus. That would be quite sufficient to explain the kind of criticism and complaint attested in Mark (chs. 2, 7).

In short, Sanders's challenge to the mutually reinforcing picture drawn by Neusner's analysis of the pre-70 rabbinic traditions and by the Synoptic traditions must be judged to have failed. Table-fellowship was at the heart of many Pharisees' self-identity; for them Sirach's counsel, "Let *righteous* men be your table companions," would be a basic rule of life.[27] A practice of table-fellowship that rode roughshod over and called into sharp question the deeply held convictions of these Pharisees was liable to trigger a strong reaction on the part of at least some of them. Jesus' table-fellowship seems to have been just such and was evidently perceived by at least some Pharisees as a threat to their ritually expressed and maintained boundaries.[28]

It is within this context that the question of table-fellowship as understood and practiced at Qumran comes into focus.

QUMRAN AND TABLE-FELLOWSHIP

The importance of the common meal for the Essenes is also beyond dispute. It was a familiar feature of Essene life long before the discovery of the Dead Sea Scrolls, since both Philo and Josephus draw attention to it. Philo comments on how developed was the common life of the Essenes in this respect:

> They all have a single treasury and common disbursements; their clothes are held in common and also their food through their institution of public meals. In no other community can we find the custom of sharing roof, life and board more firmly established in actual practice. (Philo, *Every Good Man Is Free* 86; LCL)

In Josephus the fullest description of the Essenes comes in *War* 2.119–61. He describes their daily meal:

> After this purification[29] . . . they repair to the refectory, as to some sacred shrine (*eis hagion ti temenos*). When they have taken their seats in silence, the baker serves out the loaves in order, and the cook sets before each one plate with a single course. Before meat the priest says a grace, and none may partake until after the prayer. When breakfast is ended, he pronounces a further grace; thus at the beginning and at the close they do homage to God as the bountiful giver of life. Then laying aside their raiment, as holy vestments, they again betake themselves to their labors until the evening. On their return they sup in like manner. . . . No clamor or disturbance ever pollutes their dwelling. . . . To persons outside the silence of those within appears like some awful mystery. . . . (*War* 2.129–33; LCL)

Later on Josephus describes the probationary period for the novice: after one year he is permitted "to share the purer kind of holy water," but he is "not yet received into the meetings of the community." After a further two years, if found worthy, he is "enrolled in the society. But before he may touch the common food (*tēs koinēs trophēs*), he is made to swear tremendous oaths" (*War* 2.138–39; LCL). Still later Josephus notes that even the expelled member still bound by his oath was "not at liberty to partake of other men's food" and so often died of starvation (*War* 2.143), and that during the war against the Romans the Essenes resolutely refused "to blaspheme their lawgiver or to eat some forbidden thing," despite horrendous torture (*War* 2.152; LCL).

The picture provided by Philo and Josephus received fairly detailed confirmation from the Dead Sea Scrolls, confirming beyond a reasonable doubt that the Rule of the Community (1QS) in particular is an Essene document. We may note especially 1QS 6.2, 4–5:

> They shall eat in common. . . . And when the table has been prepared for eating, and the new wine for drinking, the Priest shall be the first to stretch out his hand to bless the first-fruits of the bread and the new wine.[30]

The subsequent descriptions of the hierarchical character of the seating in their assemblies (6.8–9) matches Philo (*Every Good Man Is Free* 81; cf. Josephus, *War* 2.150), and that of the orderly manner of their spoken contributions (6.10–11) matches Josephus (*War* 2.132). Most striking of all, the stages of novitiate are more or less just as Josephus described: a one-year's probation before the would-be member may "touch the purity of the Many"; but "he shall not touch the drink of the Many until he has completed a second year among the men of the community" (1QS 6.16–17, 20–21).[31]

It is clear from all this that the meal table was regarded by the Essenes as of particular significance; it was a feature of their common life recognized by others. Like (many of) the Pharisees, the Essenes clearly believed that the character and purity of the daily meal table were an expression of and indeed a test case for their devotion to the covenant as understood within the community. The purity rule governing their table-fellowship obviously functioned as a boundary around the community—indeed as an inner boundary, requiring not just separation from "the men of falsehood" and devotion to the covenant (1QS 5.10–11) but also a still stricter observance of purity rules than among the *haberim*.[32] Whatever the precise distinction between "the purity of the many" and "the drink of the many,"[33] it is clear that full participation in the common meal was reserved for the full members alone ("the Many"). Acceptance into table-fellowship was the final hurdle by surmounting which the novice became one of "the Many."

Particularly interesting is 1QSa, the Rule of the Congregation "in the last days" (1QSa 1.1). The interest for us is in two points. First, the community was expected to function in "the last days" in the same way as it always had, even when the Messiah of Israel was among them.

[When] they shall gather for the common [tab]le, to eat and [to drink] new wine, when the common table shall be set for eating and the new wine [poured] for drinking, let no man extend his hand over the first-fruits of bread and wine before the Priest; for [it is he] who shall bless the first-fruits of bread and wine, and shall be the first [to extend] his hand over the bread. Thereafter the Messiah of Israel shall extend his hand over the bread. . . . (1QSa 2.17–21)[34]

At this point the parallel with Jesus' table-fellowship becomes obvious. As with Jesus, so also with the Essenes, the current practice of table-fellowship seems to have been seen as an expression and a foretaste of the fellowship of the future age.[35] For both groups the meal table was an eschatological symbol, an enacted conviction, commitment, and promise.

The other noteworthy feature of 1QSa is the list of those whom the community excluded from its assembly, that is, from the community of the last days, including by clear implication the common meal—an exclusions policy presumably already enacted in the life of the community at the time of Jesus.

[3]No man smitten with any [4]human uncleanness shall *enter* the assembly of God. . . . [5]No man smitten in his flesh, or *paralysed in his feet or* [6]*hands*, or *lame (psh)*, or *blind ('wr)*, or deaf, or dumb, or smitten in his flesh with a visible *blemish (mwm)* . . . for the angels of holiness are [with] their [congregation] . . . let him not *enter* among [the congregation], for he is smitten. (1QSa 2.3–10)[36]

The passage is obviously based on Lev 21:17–24:[37]

[17]Say to Aaron, None of your descendants throughout their generations who has a *blemish (mwm)* may *approach* to offer the bread of his God. [18]For no one who has a *blemish* shall *draw near,* a man *blind ('wr)* or *lame (psh),* . . . [19]or a man who has an *injured foot* or an *injured hand.* . . . (Lev 21:17–21)

Once again the significance is obvious: the Essenes saw themselves as a priestly community who regarded the purity regulations governing priestly service as binding on their community.[38] Here a close parallel with (many of) the Pharisees is evident: both groups sought to maintain in their daily meals a level of purity required for the Temple and its service. In the case of the Essenes, however, particularly in the closed community at

Qumran,[39] the purity norms and boundaries were intensified, and the purity of the community more tightly controlled and safeguarded.

A final point worthy of note is how frequently the Dead Sea Scrolls make a point of listing who is excluded from the community by virtue of physical defect. As well as 1QSa 2.3–10 cited above, we may add the following texts:

> [4]No man who is *lame* (*psh*), or *blind* ('*wr*), or crippled (*hgr*), or afflicted with a lasting bodily *blemish* (*mwm*), or smitten with a bodily impurity, [5]none of these shall march out to war with them . . . [6]. . . for the holy angels shall be with their hosts. (1QM 7.4–6)[40]

> Fools, madmen, simpletons, and imbeciles, the *blind* (literally, those who, being weak of eye, cannot see), the *maimed* (*hgr*), the *lame*, the deaf, and minors, none of these may *enter* the midst of the community, for the holy angels (are in the midst of it). (4QCD[b])[41]

> No *blind* people may enter it (the holy city and the sanctuary) all their days lest they defile the city in whose midst I dwell, for I YHWH, dwell amongst the sons of Israel for ever and eternally. (11QTemple 45.12–14)[42]

With these passages is confirmed the twin logic of Essene purity emphasis: the community saw itself as representing and maintaining the purity of the Temple, a community in whose midst God and his holy angels could dwell. Moreover, the emphasis on exclusion of all impurity, including physical blemish, was so consistently maintained that it would probably be well known outside the community.

Since this was evidently a matter of major concern for the Qumran meal table and may have been well known as such, and since Jesus seems to have reacted against the somewhat similar concerns lived out by (many) Pharisees, the remaining question is whether Jesus also knew of and reacted against the Essene practice of exclusive table-fellowship as well.

LUKE 14:13, 21 – A CRITIQUE OF QUMRAN?

Only one passage provides support for the suggestion that Jesus did indeed know of and react critically to the practice of table-fellowship which evidently characterized the Qumran community. The passage is Luke 14:12–21, which reads as follows:

> [12]Jesus said to the one who had invited him, "When you give a dinner or banquet, do not invite your friends, or your brothers, or your relatives, or your rich neighbors, lest they too invite you in return, and you are repaid. [13]But when you give a feast, invite the poor (*ptōchous*), the *maimed* (*anapeirous*), the *lame* (*chōlous*), the *blind* (*typhlous*); [14]and you will be blessed, because they cannot repay you . . ." [21] . . . Then the householder was angry and said to his servant, "Go out quickly into the streets and lanes of the city and bring in the poor and the *maimed* and the *blind* and the *lame*" (*tous ptōchous kai anapeirous kai typhlous kai chōlous eisagage*).

The (contrasting) parallel between Luke 14 and 1QSa 2 has, of course, been recognized,[43] but these were only brief references. The possibility that Jesus actually had Qumran teaching and practice in mind deserves closer and more careful scrutiny.

Two points of significance emerge immediately. First, the point already noted, that the conjunction of 1QS 6.4–5 with 1QSa 2.17–21 is paralleled by the conjunction of Luke 14:13 with 14:21. In both cases there was an explicit intention that the practice of table-fellowship in the present should be determined by and express already the eschatological experience of covenant fellowship—community at table as it should be, as God intended it to be. Second, the clear implication of Luke 14:12–24 that Jesus' vision and recommendation would be surprising to contemporary etiquette and probably to some extent offensive to religious sensibilities. These observations suggest that the Jesus tradition was formulated in opposition to an alternative practice and vision, such as we see in the Dead Sea Scrolls. But whether we can say more than that depends heavily on a comparison of the two sets of lists cited previously. Those explicitly excluded according to the Dead Sea Scrolls from the meals of the community (especially from the common meal) include those specifically named in the Jesus tradition as the ones who should be invited to table-fellowship.

In comparison with the list of four groups in Luke 14, of course, the Dead Sea Scrolls lists (and Lev 21) are more extensive and more varied. But a close parallel is immediately evident in the case of two elements: the "lame" and the "blind." *Chōlos* is the unvarying Septuagintal translation of the Hebrew *psh,* and *typhlos* likewise of *'wr.* The association of the two categories, however, is fairly common in the Old Testament; apart from Leviticus 21:18, there are Deuteronomy 15:21 and Malachi 1:8 (in reference to sacrifice); 2 Samuel 5:6, 8, 9 and Job 29:15 (linked with "the poor" in a description of Job's righteousness); and Isaiah 35:5–6 (a description of eschatological blessing. In the New Testament, apart from Luke 14:13, 21, we can list Matthew 11:5//Luke 7:22 (reference to Isa 35:5–6); Matthew 15:30–31 and 21:14 (further descriptions of Jesus' healing ministry); and John 5:3. Consequently, the association of the two categories, the *lame* and the *blind*, cannot be said to demonstrate a specific or distinctive link between Luke 14 and the Qumran texts. Nevertheless, it may well be significant that in the various Dead Sea Scrolls lists it is these two categories which appear most regularly. If Jesus had compared or contrasted his position with Qumran, he would most probably have included some mention of the lame and the blind.

Working backwards in the Luke 14 lists, the second category is *anapeirous*, "the crippled." *Anapeiros* is a variant form of *anapēros*; the former is attested also in the Septuagint manuscripts of Tobit 14:2 (*anapeiros tois ophthalmois*, "a defect of the eyes" or "an affliction of the eyes") and 2 Maccabees 8:24 (*tois melesin anapeirous*, "the wretchedly wounded"), but the more common literary usage is *anapēros*,[44] which has a more general sense, denoting physical disability of an unspecific kind. A better translation, therefore, would probably be "disabled" or "seriously disabled," rather than the too-specific "crippled" and the somewhat emotive "maimed." The point, however, is that *anapeiros* would naturally offer itself as an appropriate equivalent to Hebrew *ḥgr* (cf. above 1QM 7.4 "crippled"; 4QCD[b] "maimed") or possible also *mwm*, "blemish" (Lev 21:17–18; 1QSa 2.5; 1QM 7.4)—since physical impairment is clearly in view in the Dead Sea Scroll texts at least—or indeed as a general word to embrace a range of physical disabilities such as featured in the Qumran texts.[45] In other words, behind Luke 14:13, 21 at this point may well lie a word that recalled or specifically alluded to the list of disabilities which Qumran was known to exclude from its community; Luke or his source saw *anapeiros* as the obvious Greek equivalent.[46]

This means that three out of the four items in the Luke 14 list are closely matched by items in the typical Dead Sea Scroll lists. But what about the other item—the "poor"—which appears first on Luke's list? It is obvious that "the poor" do not feature in any of the other lists (Leviticus, Dead Sea Scrolls, Qumran), although it may be significant that Diogenes Laertius cites Diogenes redefining "the disabled" not as the deaf or blind but as "those who have no wallet" (see above). More immediately to the point, however, is the fact that "the poor" feature prominently in both Jesus' and the Essenes' teaching. In the Synoptic tradition Jesus' concern for the poor is quite marked (Mk 10:21 pars.; 12:42–43 par.; Lk 6:20//Mt 5:3; Mt 11:5//Lk 7:22; Lk 4:18; 14:13, 21; 16:19–31; 19:8). In the Dead Sea Scrolls "the poor" seems to have been a favorite self-designation for the sect itself (1QpHab 12.2–10; 1QM 11.9, 13; 13.14; 1QH 5.22; 4QpPs 37 1.9; 2.10 [= "the congregation of the poor"]; cf. in the singular 1QH 2.32; 3.25; 5.16, 18)[47] with only the Damascus Document (6.21 and 14.14) using it in the more common sense. Moreover, in 4QpPs 37 1.9 the motif of the messianic banquet appears in the same context.

May it be then that we should see in the Lucan inclusion of "the poor" a further allusion to the belief and practices of Qumran? Clearly, the Qumran community delighted in the self-designation "the poor." "The poor" designated the community in assembly, at the communal meal, and at the eschatological banquet. "The poor" designated their scrupulous exclusiveness from the disabled, the lame, and the blind.

Jesus, in contrast, was remembered as one who had been very open to the actual poor, the very much wider circle of those living at or below subsistence level. Jesus linked the poor equally with the disabled, the lame, and the blind, as special objects of God's favor. The contrast was evident: A self-styled "poor" who lived by a scrupulous understanding of what and who were acceptable to God contrasts impressively with a Jesus who lived by an understanding of God's grace as open precisely to those excluded by Qumran. Whether it was Jesus himself who formulated it (as is quite possible), or the Lucan tradition (with its special interest in the poor), the contrast was too inviting to remain unformulated. In the Palestinian Jesus movement the table of God was open to *all* the poor, and not least to the disabled, the lame, and the blind—those specifically excluded by the self-styled "poor" of Qumran.

CONCLUSIONS

We can summarize our findings very straightforwardly.

(1) Table-fellowship was an important expression of the teaching and practice of Jesus, Pharisaic *ḥaberim,* and the Qumran covenanters. It

expressed their understanding of communion with God, of the company of the kingdom, an eschatological ideal to be prepared for and lived out now.

(2) For Pharisee and Qumran Essene the measure of acceptability of such table-fellowship to God was the unacceptability at such table-fellowship of those whose attitude or actions showed them to be "sinners." In contrast, Jesus ignored, resisted, and even denounced such measuring of acceptability. His table-fellowship was notable for its *acceptance* of the "sinner" and tax collector. This brought him into controversy with at least some Pharisees, a controversy whose traces are still clear in the Gospel traditions.

(3) Cumulatively, it is likely that Jesus' table-fellowship would also be seen as a point of comparison and contrast with the Essene common meal—particularly as the Qumran practice and measure of acceptability were even more tightly drawn than those of the Pharisees, excluding not just "sinners" but also those physically blemished. This likelihood becomes a firm probability when the close degree of parallel between Luke 14:13, 21 and the list of those excluded from the Qumran messianic banquet is recognized. Jesus was probably aware of the strictness of the Qumran ideal and, on at least one occasion, deliberately spoke out against it. Those whom God counted acceptable were not so much the self-styled "poor" as those who actually were poor, together with the disabled, the lame, and the blind—the very ones excluded by the Qumran ideal.

In short, Jesus' table-fellowship must be seen as both a protest against a religious zeal that is judgmental and exclusive and as a lived-out expression of the openness of God's grace.

Notes

1. The story is told of Lawrence of Arabia, who on one occasion was fleeing for his life across the desert from the Turks. As he fled he encountered a bedouin family who had just made camp at an oasis. Invited to partake of their meal, Lawrence had scarcely dipped his hand in the communal dish when he revealed to them his plight. Without more ado his hosts struck camp and took Lawrence with them. He had eaten with them. They were one with him. Regrettably I have been unable to track down the source of this story.

2. J. Jeremias, *New Testament Theology, Vol. 1, The Proclamation of Jesus* (London, 1971) p. 115. He cites appropriately 2Kgs 25:27–30 (par. Jer 52:31–34) and Josephus, *Ant* 19.321. See also O. Hofius, *Jesu Tischgemeinschaft mit den Sündern* (Stuttgart, 1967) pp. 9–13; I. H. Marshall, *Last Supper and Lord's Supper* (Exeter, 1980) pp. 18–20; X. Léon-Dufour, *Sharing the Eucharistic Bread* (Mawah, N.J., 1987) pp. 35–38.

3. The work of M. Douglas has been particularly important here: *Purity and Danger: An Analysis of the Concepts of Pollution and Taboo* (London, 1966).

4. Also Job (Job 31:32; T Job 10:1–3; 25:5; 53:3). See further G. Stählin, *TDNT,* vol. 5, pp. 17–20; Strack-Billerbeck, *Kommentar,* vol. 1, pp. 588–89; vol. 4, pp. 565–71.

5. If Mk 2:15–17 was formed independently before being incorporated into the sequence of controversy stories, the house would be most naturally understood as Jesus' own house (as also 2:1); see, e.g., V. Taylor, *The Gospel According to St. Mark* (New York, 1966) p. 204; J. Jeremias, *The Parables of Jesus* (London, 1963) p. 227 n. 92; Hofius, *Tischgemeinschaft,* p. 29 n. 42.

6. Even if the two accounts are doublets (see, e.g., J. Gnilka, *Das Evangelium nach Markus I (Mk 1-8.26)* [Neubirke, 1978] pp. 25–26), the fact that the tradition had so developed and diverged indicates that it was a story much retold.

7. No doubt in echo of such scriptural passages as Isa 25:6; 54:4–8; 62:4–5; and Hos 2:16–20. See also M. Trautmann, *Zeichenhafte Handlungen Jesu: Ein Beitrag zur Frage nach dem geschichtlichen Jesu* (Würzburg, 1980) pp. 161–62, and those cited there.

8. See, e.g., Taylor, *Mark,* p. 350; Gnilka, *Markus,* pp. 292–93.

9. M=material peculiar to Matthew. L=material peculiar to Luke. I do not envisage M and L as written sources.

10. Others who emphasize the importance of table-fellowship in Jesus' ministry include Hofius, *Tischgemeinschaft,* pp. 16–20; N. Perrin, *Rediscovering the Teachings of Jesus* (London, 1967) pp. 102–8; B. F. Meyer, *The Aims of Jesus* (London, 1979) pp. 158–62; J. Riches, *Jesus and the Transformation of Judaism* (London, 1980) pp. 104–6; M. Trautmann, *Zeichenhafte Handlungen Jesu,* pp. 160–64; M. J. Borg, *Conflict, Holiness and Politics in the Teachings of Jesus* (New York, Toronto, 1984) pp. 73–121; R. Horsley, *Jesus and the Spiral of Violence: Popular Jewish Resistance in Roman Palestine* (San Francisco, 1987) pp. 178–80; P. Stuhlmacher, *Jesus von Nazareth—Christus des Glaubens* (Stuttgart, 1988) p. 49.

11. E.g., Mt 3:7; 12:24, 38; 21:45; 22:34, though secondary redaction and sound historical information need not, of course, be mutually exclusive categories.

12. J. Neusner, *From Politics to Piety* (Englewood Cliffs, 1973) p. 86, being a more popular statement of his *The Rabbinic Traditions About the Pharisees Before 70* (2 vols.; Leiden, 1971).

13. It is worth recalling at this point the warnings, e.g., of P. Alexander, "Rabbinic Judaism and the New Testament," *ZNW* 74 (1983) 237–46.

14. See G. Vermes, "Jewish Literature and New Testament Exegesis: Reflections on Methodology," *Essays in Honour of Yigael Yadin, JJS* 33 (1982) 361–76; reprinted in *Jesus and the World of Judaism* (London, 1983) pp. 74–88.

15. E. P. Sanders, *Jesus and Judaism* (Philadelphia, 1985).

16. Ibid., p. 388 n. 59.

17. Ibid., pp. 187–88.

18. Ibid., pp. 177–87.

19. Ibid., pp. 264–67.

20. J. D. G. Dunn, "Pharisees, Sinners and Jesus," in *The Social World of Formative Christianity and Judaism,* ed. P. Borgen, J. Neusner et al. (Philadelphia, 1988) pp. 264–89; repr. in my *Jesus, Paul and the Law* (London, 1990) ch. 3.

21. Sanders, *Jesus and Judaism,* pp. 206–9.

22. "Before 70, there was probably an appreciable overlap between Pharisees and *haberim*." Sanders, *Jesus and Judaism,* p. 187.

23. We need not identify the authors or communities behind these documents, to which we could add Jubilees and the Testament of Moses. The point is the clear intra-Jewish, factional character of the charges made. Insofar as opponents can be identified, most would accept that the likely targets of the Qumran and Testament of Moses attacks are the Pharisees themselves! Particularly noteworthy is the fact that the eating habits of these opponents are at the very center of the no doubt highly biased attack of TMos 7.

24. In Jubilees, cf. particularly 6:35 and 22:16: to celebrate a feast on the wrong date was to "forget the feasts of the covenant and walk according to the feasts of the Gentiles" (6:35); separation from the Gentiles meant in particular not eating with them (22:16).

25. E. Schürer, *The History of the Jewish People in the Age of Jesus Christ (175 B.C.–A.D. 135),* ed. G. Vermes et al. (Edinburgh, 1979) vol. 2, pp. 396–98.

26. Most scholars continue to date Mark to the period 64–70 c.e.; see W. G. Kümmel, *Introduction to the New Testament* (London, 1975 [rev. ed.]) p. 98.

27. Hofius, *Tischgemeinschaft,* p. 16.

28. See particularly Borg, *Conflict,* pp. 73–143.

29. "The obligation to take a ritual bath, instead of merely washing the hands, implies that the Essene meal was endowed with a sacred character." Schürer, *History,* vol. 2, p. 569 n. 44.

30. Translation from G. Vermes, *The Dead Sea Scrolls in English* (London, New York, 1987).

31. See further K. G. Kuhn, "The Lord's Supper and the Communal Meal at Qumran" in *The Scrolls and the New Testament,* ed. K. Stendahl (London, 1958) pp. 67–70.

32. Given the degree of antagonism that seems to have been cherished at Qumran against the Pharisees (above n. 23), it is more than a little surprising that

J. Jeremias should use the Dead Sea Scrolls to illustrate Pharisaic practice. Jeremias, *Jerusalem in the Time of Jesus* (London, 1969) pp. 259–62.

33.   See further A. R. C. Leaney, *The Rule of Qumran and its Meaning* (London, 1966) pp. 191–95; G. Vermes, *The Dead Sea Scrolls: Qumran in Perspective* (London, 1977) pp. 95–96; M. Newton, *The Concept of Purity at Qumran and in the Letters of Paul* (SNTS Monograph Series 53; Cambridge, 1985) pp. 10–26.

34.   Translation from Vermes, *Dead Sea Scrolls in English.* See 1QS 6.4–5 cited above.

35.   M. Black, *The Scrolls and Christian Origins* (London, 1961) pp. 109–11; Vermes, *The Dead Sea Scrolls: Qumran in Perspective,* p. 182; questioned by Marshall, *Last Supper,* p. 26.

36.   Translation from Vermes, *Dead Sea Scrolls in English.*

37.   J. A. Fitzmyer, "A Feature of Qumran Angelology and the Angels of 1 Cor 11.10," in *Essays on the Semantic Background of the New Testament* (London, 1971) pp. 198–99.

38.   See further B. Gärtner, *The Temple and the Community in Qumran and the New Testament* (SNTS Monograph Series 1; Cambridge, 1965) chs. 2 and 3; Newton, *Concept of Purity,* ch. 2, esp. pp. 34–36.

39.   I have left the question of other Essene communities open; but since Qumran is the only obvious example known to us in any detail, the issues can be posed most simply and most sharply by reference to it as such. See the Foreword and chapter 1 above.

40.   Translation from Vermes, *Dead Sea Scrolls in English.*

41.   Reference and translation from J. T. Milik, *Ten Years of Discovery in the Wilderness of Judaea,* trans. J. Strugnell (SBT 26; London, 1959) p. 114.

42.   J. Maier, *The Temple Scroll* trans. R. T. White (JSOTSS 34; Sheffield, 1985) p. 41.

43.   D. Barthélemy and J. T. Milik, DJD 1 (Oxford, 1955) p. 117; F. M. Cross, *The Ancient Library of Qumran and Modern Biblical Studies* (London, 1958) p. 179: "It is difficult to suppose that the parable is not told in conscious reaction to sectarian doctrine" (n. 89)—though Cross' translation of 1QSa 2.11, 13 as "the men of the name who are invited to the festival" (to bring out the parallel with Luke 14:21) was rather tendentious. M. Burrows was less confident: "No specific reference to the Qumran sect in particular is indicated, but the contrast between its attitude and that of Jesus is unmistakeable." Burrows, *More Light on the Dead Sea Scrolls* (London, 1958) p. 91. Cf. A. Vögtle, *Das öffentliche Wirken Jesu auf dem Hintergrund der Qumranbewegung* (Freiburger Universitätsreden N.F. 27; Freiburg, 1958) pp. 12–13.

44.   The same passage is cited in Eusebius, *Praeparatio Evangelica* 13.8.3. A brief examination of the TLG texts quickly shows how natural it was for *anapēros* to be associated with *chōlos* and *typhlos:* Plato, *Crito* 53a (*ē hoi chōloi te kai typhloi kai hoi alloi anapēroi,* ". . . than the lame and the blind and the other cripples"); Aristotle,

Historia Animalium 585b (*ginontai de kai ex anapērōn anapēroi, hoion ek chōlōn chōloi kai typhlon typhloi*, ". . . the crippled give rise to the crippled; such as is lame to the lame, the blind to the blind"); Diogenes Laertius, *Vit.* 6.33 (*anapērous elegen ou tous kōphous kai typhlous, alla tous me echontas pēran*, ". . . the deaf and the blind should not be said to be crippled, rather he who has no money bag"). See also Plutarch, *Regum* 194C; Galen, *De usu partium* 3.237; and Clement of Alexandria, *Protrepticus* 10.105.

45. *Kyllos* ("crippled, deformed") is used in a similar unspecific way and in close association with *chōlos* and *typhlos* in Mt 15:30–31, but it is not as widely attested as *anapēros*, which was almost certainly better known to Luke.

46. I use "equivalent" deliberately since more than translation as such may be involved.

47. We need not speak of a title as such, but in some texts at least the group behind these texts clearly identified themselves with "the poor" of the biblical tradition; see further A. Dupont-Sommer, *The Essene Writings from Qumran*, trans. G. Vermes (Oxford, 1961) ad loc.; E. Bammel, *ptōchos*, *TDNT* vol. 6, p. 897; L. E. Keck, " 'The Poor among the Saints' in Jewish Christianity at Qumran," *ZNW* 57 (1966) 54–78.

CHAPTER 10

CRUCIFIXION: *Archaeology, Jesus, and the Dead Sea Scrolls*

JOE ZIAS AND JAMES H. CHARLESWORTH

The Righteous Teacher had been martyred, perhaps crucified, and his followers thought that he would be resurrected as the Messiah. The Dead Sea Scrolls thus reveal a "pre-Christian" Christ martyr cult. This interpretation of some passages in the Dead Sea Scrolls has been disseminated for decades among popular and even scholarly publications. It was introduced in the early 1950s and continues to appear until today. Some excellent scholars have assumed that certain elements in the picture are built on meticulous and insightful research. Obviously such claims merit attention.

Did the Righteous Teacher suffer crucifixion? Did his followers think he was messianic and perhaps would return as the Messiah? Was he then something like a crucified Messiah before the birth of Jesus?

In the following chapter an attempt will be made to answer these questions, by inquiring whether "crucifixion" or "to crucify" appears in the Dead Sea Scrolls and examining the archaeological evidence of crucifixion in Palestine before 70 C.E. Human remains of one crucified have been found, and we will learn what anthropologists can discern from the bones. These textual, historical, archaeological, and anthropological studies may shed light on Jesus' crucifixion.

THE CLAIM

One of the pioneers of Qumran research, A. Dupont-Sommer, concluded in 1950 that the Righteous Teacher had suffered martyrdom at the hands of his archenemy, a priest in the Jerusalem Temple called "the Wicked Priest."[1] Dupont-Sommer's interpretation of the Dead Sea Scrolls (esp. 1QpHab, 1QH, 4QpPs37) led him to claim: "In fact, the Qumran documents frequently mention a bloody persecution which raged against the sect, a persecution 'by the sword,' in the course of which the Teacher of Righteousness was finally arrested, judged, maltreated and very probably put to death."[2] Dupont-Sommer's opinion is clear, as he revealed later in the same chapter on the Righteous Teacher: "We know from the *Commentary on Habakkuk* that the Teacher was persecuted by the 'Wicked Priest,' ill-treated and executed.[3] This contention is not only a claim of the 1950s; Dupont-Sommer, for example, continued to make this claim until his death.[4]

John Allegro, the first British scholar to be selected to the international team to publish the Dead Sea Scrolls, claimed sensationally in the 1950s over the BBC that the Righteous Teacher had not only been martyred but was even crucified. He first published this hypothesis in 1956.[5] He reiterated the fantastic hypothesis as late as 1986. According to Allegro, the Righteous Teacher was crucified along with many other Jews by Alexander Janneus in the early decades of the first century B.C.E. As if this claim were not sufficiently astounding, Allegro interjected that the execution of the Righteous Teacher eventually led his followers, upon "later reflection," to think "that the historic Teacher of Righteousness, the Priest, the Law Interpreter, would reappear at the End-time as the Messiah, that second Joshua/Jesus who was to lead his people to the New Jerusalem."[6]

THE TEXTS: CRUCIFIXION
AND THE RIGHTEOUS TEACHER

Is there any semblance of truth in such claims? Let us turn to the Habakkuk Pesher to examine the text and context.[7] Four passages have been cited to substantiate the claim that the Righteous Teacher had been martyred or crucified: 1QpHab 2.7–8, 8.16–17; 9.1–2; and 9.9–12. Here are those sections of the Habakkuk Pesher, according to a reliable edition:[8]

> They are the ruthless [ones of the coven]ant who will not believe when they hear all that is going to co[me up]on the last generation from the mouth of the priest into [whose heart] God put [understandi]ng to interpret all the words of his servants the prophets by [whose] hand God enumerated all that is going to come upon his people and up[on his congregation.] (1QpHab 2.6–10)

All would agree that this passage refers to the Righteous Teacher. Some persecution of him and his followers may be implied but is not evident. There is certainly no mention of martyrdom and obviously no crucifixion.

Here is the second excerpt:

> The in[terpretation of the passage] concerns the priest, who rebelled [and trans]gressed the statutes of [God, plundering many peoples, but they will pl]under him *l*[. . .]. (1QpHab 8.16–17)

What is meant by "plundering" is unclear. Dupont-Sommer filled in the lacuna in line 17 with these words: "the precepts [of God and persecuted the Teacher of righteousness. . . .]."[9] According to this restoration the Righteous Teacher was persecuted by the Wicked Priest. Without doubt, however, texts should be restored according to other ancient sources and not according to a subjective hypothesis. We have not yet found any evidence of martyrdom and clearly no crucifixion.

The third passage is as follows:

> And horrors of evil diseases were at work in him, and acts of vengeance on his decaying flesh. (1QpHab 9.1–2)

This difficult passage surely refers to some suffering. What is the relation between the diseases and "vengeance"? Are both expressions referring to the same phenomenon, that is, the sickness of the Righteous Teacher? Or are two different afflictions implied? Dupont-Sommer rejected the meaning "diseases" and rendered the passage as follows: ". . . and evil profaners committed horrors upon him and vengeance upon his body of flesh." This interpretation does not sufficiently represent the context, which clearly refers to the punishment to be inflicted on the one who has "plundered many

nations," that is, obviously "the Wicked Priest." Most translators rightly disagree
with Dupont-Sommer's rendering. For example, Dupont-Sommer's protégé,
Professor Geza Vermes of Oxford, defended the following translation: "And
they inflicted horrors of evil diseases and took vengeance upon his body
of flesh."[10] At best we are left only with a slight possibility that the
Righteous Teacher was persecuted. In summation, there is no evidence of
martyrdom and certainly none of crucifixion.

The final passage reads as follows:

> The interpretation of it concerns the [W]icked Priest, whom—because
> of wrong done to the Teacher of Righteousness and his partisans—God
> gave into the hand of his enemies to humble him with disease for annihi-
> lation in despair, beca[u]se he had acted wickedly against his chosen ones.
> (1QpHab 9.9–12)

This passage indicates that some wrongs were done to the Righteous
Teacher, but it is far from clear what they might be. Although it seems that
the Wicked Priest persecuted the Righteous Teacher, it is not clear what
actually happened.[11] As in the previous passage, the final lines of this
excerpt refer to the pains and probable death suffered by the Wicked Priest
(not the Righteous Teacher).[12]

Passages in the Thanksgiving Hymns may derive from the Righteous
Teacher.[13] Some of them do suggest that he may have suffered some persecution and perhaps some bodily harm; but it is uncertain from whom he may
have suffered these injuries. They may well be metaphorical in light of
generic laments in the Davidic Psalms. No hymn clearly states that the
author, whoever he may be, was martyred; there is no mention of crucifixion in these hymns.

We find no evidence in the Dead Sea Scrolls that the Righteous Teacher
was martyred or persecuted. As R. B. Y. Scott stated in 1956, there is no
"unambiguous statement that he [the Righteous Teacher] was put to
death."[14] In 1957, J. T. Milik wrote these definitive words:

> To sum up, in no place do the texts speak of, nor [sic] presuppose, a
> violent death of the Teacher of Righteousness; they rather favor the
> hypothesis that he died naturally. Moreover, whatever the historical
> truth may have been, the fact and manner of the Teacher's death had
> for the Essenes no theological nor [sic] soteriological significance

analogous to that seen by the early Church in the death of Jesus of Nazareth.[15]

In 1958 Cardinal Jean Daniélou rightly quipped that the sections of the Habakkuk Pesher excerpted above do "not entail the specific description of one being tortured and put to death. Hence, use of the word 'Passion' here is incorrect."[16] F. M. Cross, also in 1958, warned that we "do not know the time or circumstance of the Righteous Teacher's death."[17] Vermes wisely and cautiously concludes that "we neither know who the founder of the Essenes was, nor how, nor where, nor when he died."[18]

It is surprising that the notion that the Righteous Teacher was martyred continues to linger in publications.[19] R. de Vaux rightly stated that not one of the Dead Sea Scrolls makes "any allusion, even remotely, to his 'crucifixion.'"[20] When the Qumran group was taking shape and during its early years in exile, the Righteous Teacher was persecuted. That interpretation remains valid.[21]

The idea that the Righteous Teacher was martyred was promulgated when the Dead Sea Scrolls were erroneously read in terms of the Bible, especially the New Testament. The Qumran texts and the history of the Qumran community have too often been interpreted in light of Christian words and concepts. As a result, the life and teachings of Jesus and Paul often influenced the interpretation of these Jewish texts. The community is still popularly called a "monastery."

THE TEXTS: "TO CRUCIFY" IN THE DEAD SEA SCROLLS

Even though it is clear that the Righteous Teacher was not crucified, we may consider the possibility that crucifixion is mentioned in the Dead Sea Scrolls. Terms denoting "crucifixion" were not found in any of the documents from Cave 1, but the Nahum Pesher from Cave 4 mentions an episode during the time of the struggles against the Seleucid king named Demetrius III Eukairos (95–75 B.C.E.). Significant is the document's reference to the Lion of Wrath who "would hang men up alive" and the reference to "one hanged alive upon the tree" (4QpNah frags. 3–4 col. i lines 6–7). This "hanging" (*tlh*) probably refers to crucifixion.[22] Without any doubt the author is referring to Alexander Janneus's diabolical actions in Jerusalem. After Demetrius left Palestine, Alexander Janneus crucified eight hundred Jewish rebels (probably most were Pharisees; *Ant* 13).

Column 64 of the Temple Scroll also contains the verb *tlh*.[23] It refers to crucifixion, as the editor of this text surmised from the beginning.[24] Here is the translation:

> If a man informs against his people, and delivers his people up to a foreign nation, and does harm to his people, you shall hang him on the tree, and he shall die. On the evidence of two witnesses and on the evidence of three witnesses he shall be put to death, and they shall hang him on the tree. And if a man has committed a crim[e] punishable by death, and had defected into the midst of the nations, and has cursed his people [and] the children of Israel, you shall hang him on the tree, and he shall die. And their body shall not remain upon the tree all night, but you shall bury them the same day, for those hanged on the tree are accursed by God and men; you shall not defile the land which I give you for an inheritance. (11QTemple 64.6–13)[25]

Obviously *tlh* denotes some form of crucifixion.[26] The man is hung on the tree (a noun interchangeable with cross).[27] It is possible that the Temple Scroll and the Nahum Pesher independently refer to the crucifixion of Jews, probably Pharisees, by Alexander Janneus. The Jews who were crucified had enlisted the military assistance of a non-Jew, Demetrius, and could therefore be charged with high treason. In the minds of many Jews, Alexander Janneus's actions were unjust, grotesque, and unforgivable.

Apparently not only men but also women were crucified before the time of Jesus.[30] About the time of Alexander Janneus eighty women were "hanged," probably crucified (Aramaic *ṣlb*;[29] Hebrew *tlh*), near Ashkelon by Simon b. Shetah.[30] Rabbinic legislation that disallows crucifixion as a means of execution[31] should not be allowed to mask the fact that during the time of Jesus the Romans employed this means of execution in Palestine for robbers, revolutionaries, and insurrectionists;[32] that Antiochus Epiphanes crucified Jews during the Maccabean revolt (*Ant* 12.256); and especially that Jews in power crucified other Jews.[33] Crucifixion in ancient Palestine had a long history. Its exact origins are unknown, but it may have been brought to Palestine during Persian times. It was abolished finally in the west by Constantine in the fourth century.[34] Cicero's characterization of crucifixion as a "plague" eventually won out over the view that regarded it as a form of entertainment.[35]

The Dead Sea Scrolls reflect crucifixions in Palestine before the time of Jesus. We know that from the time of Herod the Great until the destruction of Jerusalem in 70 C.E. the Romans crucified thousands in Palestine.[36] During the riots after the death of Herod in 4 B.C.E., Quintilius Varus crucified two thousand rebellious Jews (Josephus, *Ant* 17.295). Jesus was crucified with two others around 30 C.E., and there is no evidence that this action by Pilate was unique. Later, about 52 C.E., we learn from Josephus that Tiberius Julius Alexander condemned two Jewish rebels to be crucified (*Ant* 20.102). We have documentary evidence of numerous sporadic crucifixions until the late 60s, when Titus built a wall around Jerusalem and then crucified five hundred Jews a day on it (Josephus, *War* 5.449–51).

ARCHAEOLOGY AND ANTHROPOLOGY

Thus far we have considered only the literary evidence of crucifixion in Palestine before 70 C.E. Despite the fact that we clearly know about thousands of crucifixions in the ancient Near East, we have archaeological evidence of only one person.

In 1968 Israeli archaeologists discovered a tomb complex in one of the suburbs north of Jerusalem which was a Jewish burial ground during the late Second Temple period.[37] Subsequent analysis of the bones in one of the ossuaries revealed the remains of a male whose right heel bone (*calcaneum*) had been pierced by an iron nail (see Illus. 3-4). Because its distal end was bent backwards, the nail was not removed from the heel after death.

The original publication of the anthropological findings in 1970 by N. Haas was severely flawed, in part because of the haste in which the remains were reburied to satisfy conservative religious authorities.[38] A reappraisal of the evidence was demanded. It was conducted in 1985 and attempted to remove the errors contained in the original article.[39] This reappraisal was based on minute examinations of the bones before they were reburied. New photographs, casts, and radiographs were taken. A partial summary of the results is as follows:

1. The length of the nail was 11.5 cm and not 17–18 cm as described by Haas. This means that it would be anatomically impossible to secure both feet with a single nail, as Haas assumed in his reconstruction of the crucifixion (see Illus. 1).

2.   Haas's assertion that a portion of the left heel bone (*sustentaculum tali*) adhered to the right heel bone was disproved by radiological examination. No portion of the left heel (*calcaneum*) was found in relation to the right.

3.   Haas claimed that "there was no evidence of intrusion of a third individual" in the ossuary. We found, however, that interred in the ossuary with the remains of Jehohanan was not only a second adult, possibly male, but also the remains of a child who was three to four years old at the time of death. The finding of a second male corresponds to the inscription on the ossuary: "Jehohanan and Jehohanan ben (son of) Jehohanan." There is now no doubt that the son was buried with the father, which was a common Jewish practice during the Second Temple period.

4.   Our reappraisal showed no evidence of nails penetrating the wrist or forearm. The indentation that Haas interpreted as evidence of nailing was in our estimation nontraumatic in origin. The tiny mar in the wrist bone resulted from contact with other remains in the crowded ossuary. Similar indentations were found on other parts of the postcranial skeleton.

5.   The fragment from a plaque beneath the head of the nail was originally published as being from pistacia or acacia wood. Subsequent analysis by botanists from the Hebrew University identified the wood as being from neither. It is from an olive tree.

6.   Evidence among the skeletal remains indicating postmortem amputation of the feet as Haas asserted was not evident. Therefore, his belief that a final *coup de grace* was administered to the lower limb of the individual is, in our estimation, inconclusive. The numerous breaks in the lower limb were not related to the crucifixion process, but rather to the passage of time.

7.   Haas erred in his interpretation that the victim suffered from a palatal cleft. The radiographs were reviewed by six specialists from the Johns Hopkins University School of Medicine. They concurred that there is no radiological evidence that the individual suffered from this defect. Thus, the attempt at facial reconstruction in the original report by Haas is without medical support.

8.   Haas's attempt at reconstructing the crucifixion (Illus. 1) is anatomically impossible on the basis of the available skeletal evidence. The nail penetrated the right heel bone laterally, whereas in his reconstruction, he shows the nail penetrating the left heel.

Cause of Death

There have been numerous attempts since the 1920s to explain the medical cause of death via the process of crucifixion. Methodologically, most attempts have fallen prey to the fourteenth-century Shroud of Turin, which was purported to be the burial shroud of Christ. As a result, most of these findings must be viewed with a healthy dose of skepticism. Many biblical scholars would probably judge the article in the prestigious *Journal of the American Medical Association* (1986) entitled "On the Physical Death of Jesus Christ"[40] as inappropriate for a journal of scientific inquiry. Such arguments are virtually analogous to a palaeoanthropologist using a literal reading of the Genesis creation story as the basis for the reconstruction of human origins.

The earliest study of what must be regarded as a poorly described and documented form of capital punishment was done in 1925 by A. A. Le Bec, who proposed the asphyxiation theory.[41] This theory hypothesized that with the arms suspended overhead, the two sets of muscles used for breathing (the diaphragm and the intercostals) would eventually weaken, leading to the eventual suffocation of the victim.

The French physician P. Barbet, in his well-known book *A Doctor at Calvary* (1953), supported Le Bec's theory by eyewitness accounts of European prisoners of war who were hung by their wrists with their feet weighted.[42] Death occurred in a span of six to ten minutes, apparently by suffocation, as described clinically by Barbet.[43]

Barbet also tested the hypothesis that victims were crucified through the palms of the hand and found this untenable. By affixing weights to cadavers he found that the maximum weight which the nailed palms could support was forty kilograms (approximately 88 pounds), hardly the normal weight for an adult. He then experimented on freshly amputated arms from cadavers on which he placed the nail between the ulna and radius, adjacent to the wrist. This area, he contended, would fully support an adult nailed to an upright cross.[44]

Recent research by an American physician, F. Zugibe, challenged the earlier studies of Le Bec and Barbet.[45] Dr. Zugibe agreed that while death by asphyxiation is the probable cause of death when the victim is suspended by his hands, it is no longer tenable when the arms are positioned perpendicular to the torso. To test this hypothesis, Dr. Zugibe suspended student volunteers with special foot and hand supports from a conventional T-shaped cross and monitored their physiological response. According to Dr. Zugibe, the critical issue involved here is the angle of the victim's arms

to the upright. If the arms were outstretched, there was no evidence what-
soever of breathing difficulty despite their suspension, which ranged from
five to forty-five minutes. On the basis of these experiments, Dr. Zugibe
concluded that hypovolemic shock, which is brought on by the traumatic
shock of crucifixion, is the cause of death.

While Zugibe's conclusions are probably medically accurate, his
research design is biased on two accounts. First, he assumes a priori that all
victims were nailed to the cross in the traditional manner as depicted by
religious art. Thus he ignores two of the three people in the crucifixion
scene (the good and the bad thief), whose hands are usually depicted as tied
to the cross, a method that may well have been the case in antiquity. Had
he conducted experiments with volunteers tied to the cross in the "arms
over the crossbar manner," the results may have been significantly different.
Second, Dr. Zugibe, like his predecessors, fell prey to believing in the
authenticity of the Shroud of Turin, which he utilized to interpret his
findings and subsequent conclusions.

While medical investigators have in good faith tried to determine the
cause of death of an individual that was crucified nearly two thousand years
ago, they unwittingly, partially through their reliance on the Shroud of
Turin, present an explanation that is more hypothetical than historical. As
a result, much of what has been written falls into the category of pseudo-
scientific forensic mythology.

Reconstruction

Anthropological interpretation of past historical processes is often
hampered to a large extent by the limited data available. One's assessment,
consequently, must not be limited to the skeletal remains. One must take
into account the literary sources from the Roman period, and these, as is
well known, contain numerous references to crucifixion.[46] Unfortunately,
however, the literary evidence provides few exact details about how the
condemned were affixed to the cross. The remains of Jehoḥanan also provide only limited data to help recreate the manner of his crucifixion; we
are forced to work from only one right *calcaneum* (heel bone), which was
pierced by an 11.5 cm iron nail with traces of wood at both ends.

In reconstructing the crucifixion, we have used the available osteo-
logical evidence in conjunction with observations by Haas, Barbet, and the
ancient historical sources. According to these sources, the condemned man

never carried the complete cross, as is commonly believed; instead, only the crossbar was carried. The upright beam was set in a permanent place where it was used for subsequent executions.

We know from Josephus that during the first century C.E. wood was so scarce around Jerusalem that the Romans were forced to travel ten miles outside the city to secure timber for their siege machinery (*War* 5.522–23). From this one account we can reasonably assume that the scarcity of wood may have affected the economics of crucifixion, so that the horizontal bar as well as the vertical beam may have been used repeatedly. Thus the lack of traumatic injury to the forearm and metacarpals of the hand seems to suggest that the arms of the condemned were *tied* rather than nailed to the cross. There is ample literary and artistic evidence for the use of ropes rather than nails to secure the condemned to the cross.[47]

In Egypt, where according to one source crucifixion originated, the victim was not nailed but tied.[48] The fact that crucifixion was a common form of capital punishment in the ancient world and that only one archaeological find provides evidence for it may further suggest that tying the victim to the cross was the preferred mode of crucifixion. If this supposition is correct, it becomes obvious why there is virtually no archaeological evidence of crucifixion; such an execution would leave no traumatic effect on the skeleton.

How were Jehohanan's lower limbs attached to the upright beam? The evidence suggests that the most logical reconstruction would have the condemned man straddling the upright with each foot nailed laterally to the cross (Illus. 2). This open position presumably provides the reason why the executioners chose to place the nail in the largest bone of the foot, the *calcaneum*. The olive wood plaque, the remains of which were found beneath the nail head, may have been intended to prevent the condemned man from pulling his feet free from the nail by enlarging the diameter of the head of the nail.

This theoretical reconstruction may also provide an answer to why the distal end of the nail was bent downward. After affixing the right foot to the vertical beam in the manner described above, the nail, as Haas and Kuhn suggested, may have accidentally struck a knot in the wood, which bent the nail downward.[49] Once the body was removed from the cross, albeit with some difficulty in removing the right leg, the condemned man's family would have found it impossible to remove the bent nail without completely destroying the heel bone. Their reluctance to inflict further postmortem damage to the body left for us the undeniable evidence of crucifixion.

How does this discussion help us understand the Gospel accounts of Jesus' death? Obviously, it is impossible to conclude that Jesus and Jehohanan were crucified in exactly the same manner. We are presented, however, with data and reflections that will inform speculations and reconstructions.

The ways in which people were crucified in the Roman period were many and diverse, particularly during the revolt against Rome of 66 to 70 C.E. Josephus reported on numerous crucifixions just outside the walls of Jerusalem. In one account he mentioned that Roman soldiers

> out of the wrath and hatred they bore the Jews, nailed those they caught, one after one way, and another after another, to the crosses, by way of jest; when their multitude was so great that room was wanting for the crosses, and crosses wanting for the bodies. (*War* 5.460)[50]

The ossuary that preserved the remains of Jehohanan probably did not preserve one of these unfortunate victims of Roman cruelty. Jehohanan was crucified closer to the time of Jesus' own crucifixion.

Finally, let us return to the issues raised by the appearance of *tlh* in the Dead Sea Scrolls. Scholars have wrestled with this verb often presupposing that crucifixion was by means of nailing a victim to wood. Now, we learn from anthropological examinations of the bones of Jehohanan that he was "hung" by his arms from a horizontal bar or a tree. Any remaining problems with translating *tlh* to denote crucifixion should now be removed.

CONCLUSIONS

Our examination of the Dead Sea Scrolls and of the remains at Giv'at ha-Mivtar leads to the following conclusions: (1) There is no evidence that the Righteous Teacher suffered martyrdom or crucifixion. (2) He certainly was in some ways a precursor of Jesus,[51] but he was not crucified; and surely he was not revered as a crucified Messiah. (3) The verb "to crucify" appears in the Dead Sea Scrolls (4QpNah, 11QTemple). (4) Archaeologists have found the remains of a crucified man just north of the city limits of Jerusalem. They have discerned that he was crucified, like Jesus, near Jerusalem sometime in the first half of the first century C.E. (5) On the side of the ossuary we learn the name of the crucified man; he was called "Jeho-ḥanan." (6) Anthropologists have suggested that a careful study of the bones may indicate how the man was crucified, and we can speculate how he may have died. (7) Cumulatively, these studies shed some light on the crucifixion of Jesus by presenting palpable proof of crucifixion in first-century Palestine, by reminding us that thousands of Jews were crucified, by indicating that more than one means of crucifixion was utilized, by demon-strating that at times hands could be tied but feet nailed to the wooden cross, and by forcing us to imagine the horrific suffering deliberately caused by such an execution.

Notes

1. A. Dupont-Sommer was gifted and prolific. From 1949 to 1960 he issued forty-five "principal publications" on the Dead Sea Scrolls; see his *The Essene Writings from Qumran,* trans. G. Vermes (Cleveland, New York, 1962; reprinted numerous times; the French original has seen four editions and has also been reissued as recently as 1980) pp. 413–16. He contributed significantly to our understanding of the Dead Sea Scrolls and was one of the first to argue that they should be identified with the Essenes. His translation in many ways is still valuable. He was *directeur d'études* at the Ecole des Hautes Etudes, professor at the Sorbonne, and president of the Institut d'Études Sémitiques of the University of Paris.

2. Dupont-Sommer, *Essene Writings,* p. 360. Earlier he went even further, claiming that the Righteous Teacher was not only martyred but also "without doubt a divine being." See Dupont-Sommer, *Aperçus préliminaires sur les manuscrits de la Mer Morte* (Paris, 1950; Eng. trans. Oxford, New York, 1952) p. 47.

3. Dupont-Sommer, *Essene Writings,* p. 364.

4. Dupont-Sommer, *Les Écrits Esséniens découverts près de la Mer Morte* (Paris, 1980 [4th ed.]) pp. 276–77, 369–79.

5. J. M. Allegro, in *Time* (February 6, 1956) 37; see also Allegro, *The Dead Sea Scrolls and the Origins of Christianity* (New York, 1957) pp. 95, 99–100.

6. J. M. Allegro, "Jesus and Qumran: The Dead Sea Scrolls," in *Jesus in History and Myth,* ed. R. J. Hoffmann and G. A. Larue (Buffalo, N.Y., 1986) pp. 89–96; quotation from p. 96.

7. Dupont-Sommer also cited other texts—namely, 1QH and 4QpPs 37—but these were employed to substantiate other alleged aspects of the life of the Righteous Teacher.

8. M. P. Horgan, *Pesharim: Qumran Interpretations of Biblical Books* (CBQ

Monograph Series 8; Washington, D.C., 1979). Brackets circumscribe restorations of text that is not preserved because of holes (lacunae) in the leather. Qumran texts are cited according to column and then line number.

9. See Dupont-Sommer, *Essene Writings*, p. 264; the fourth French edition does not change the restoration.

10. G. Vermes, *The Dead Sea Scrolls in English* (London, 1987 [3d ed.]) p. 287.

11. Elsewhere in the Habakkuk Pesher we learn that the Wicked Priest persecuted the Righteous Teacher, probably at Qumran and during the Qumranites' celebration of the Day of Atonement. Long ago M. Burrows concluded that the Wicked Priest "persecuted" the Righteous Teacher. "The purpose of the persecution was either uncovering of some kind or banishment, probably the latter." Burrows, *The Dead Sea Scrolls* (New York, 1955; repr. 1986) p. 157. Banishment obviously does not entail martyrdom or crucifixion.

12. See, e.g., J. T. Milik, who thinks that the lines refer to the death of Jonathan. Milik, *Ten Years of Discovery in the Wilderness of Judaea*, trans. J. Strugnell (SBT 26; London, 1989) p. 69. F. M. Cross interprets the lines, and a section of 4QTestim, to refer to the murder of Simon and his sons by Ptolemy at Jericho. Cross, *The Ancient Library of Qumran and Modern Biblical Studies* (Garden City, N.Y., 1958) pp. 108–17. Obviously the debate continues into the present, but 1QpHab 9.9–12 is taken to refer not to the Righteous Teacher but to the Wicked Priest.

13. See J. H. Charlesworth's discussion in chapter 5 above. See also the references mentioned in that chapter, especially the seminal work of G. Jeremias, *Der Lehrer der Gerechtigkeit* (SUNT 2; Göttingen, 1963).

14. R. B. Y. Scott, "The Meaning for Biblical Studies of the Qumran Scroll Discoveries," *Transactions of the Royal Society of Canada* 50 (1956) 39–48; quotation from p. 45.

15. Milik wrote his book in French in 1957; see *Ten Years of Discovery*, p. 80.

16. J. Daniélou, *The Dead Sea Scrolls and Primitive Christianity*, trans. S. Attanasio (New York, Toronto, 1958) p. 59.

17. Cross, *Ancient Library*, p. 117.

18. Vermes with P. Vermes, *The Dead Sea Scrolls: Qumran in Perspective* (Cleveland, 1978) p. 154.

19. The leading scholars have repeatedly warned that it is not a valid interpretation. Note the following additional warnings: "Of this crucifixion there is not the slightest mention in any of the texts [Dead Sea Scrolls], and we are nowhere told how the Teacher of Righteousness died." H. H. Rowley, "The 'Crucifixion' of the Teacher of Righteousness," in *The Dead Sea Scrolls and the New Testament* (London, 1957) pp. 6–9; quotation from p. 6. Rowley was the distinguished Professor of Hebrew Language and Literature in the University of Manchester.

20. R. de Vaux, "The Dead Sea Scrolls," *The Bible and the Ancient Near East*, trans. D. McHugh (Garden City, N.Y. 1971) pp. 167–80; quotation from p. 177.

21. See Cross, *Ancient Library*, pp. 106–7.

22. Y. Yadin, *The Temple Scroll: The Hidden Law of the Dead Sea Sect* (London, 1985) pp. 216–17. See L. Díez Merino, "La crucifixión en la antigua literatura judía," *Estudios Eclesiásticos* 51 (1976) 5–27; and F. García Martínez, "4QpNah y la Crucifixión: Nueva hipótesis de reconstrucción de 4Q 169 3–4 i, 4–8," *Estudios Bíblicos* 38 (1979–80) 221–35. All three of these scholars rightly see that 4QpNah refers to Alexander Janneus's crucifixions of Jews.

23. The Hebrew verb *tlh* literally means "to let down" or "hang." The Hebrew *tlh* of Esther 7:9 was understood in Palestine as crucifixion by the Greek translator of Esther, who employed the Greek verb "to nail to the cross," "to crucify" (*stauroō*). As M. O. Wise pointed out, the Greek translator understood that Haman had been executed by crucifixion. Wise, *A Critical Study of the Temple Scroll from Qumran Cave 11* (SAOC 49; Chicago, 1990) p. 125.

24. Y. Yadin, "Pesher Nahum (4QpNahum) Reconsidered," *IEJ* 21 (1971) 1–12. The excellent Semitist J. M. Baumgarten cautions that the roots *tlh* and *ṣlb* do not denote crucifixion but "hanging," as one would expect in light of rabbinic regulations. The Targum on Ruth 1:17 seems to indicate that *ṣlybt qys'*, "hanging on a tree," is aligned with one of the four means of execution—specifically, stoning, burning, decapitation, and strangulation (not crucifixion). Baumgarten, "Does TLH in the Temple Scroll Refer to Crucifixion?" in *Studies in Qumran Law* (SJLA 24; Leiden, 1977) pp. 172–82. Baumgarten's suggestion was developed before the publication of the Temple Scroll. While he wisely urged us not to confuse "hanging while alive" with "hanging up a corpse" for desecration, his interpretation does not now seem as probable as Yadin's understanding. See J. A. Fitzmyer, "Crucifixion in Ancient Palestine, Qumran, and the New Testament," in *To Advance the Gospel: New Testament Studies* (New York, 1981) pp. 125–46, esp. pp. 131–35; and M. Hengel in *Crucifixion in the Ancient World and the Folly of the Message of the Cross*, trans. J. Bowden (London, 1977) p. 84.

25. Y. Yadin, *The Temple Scroll: Text and Commentary* (Jerusalem, 1983) vol. 2, pp. 288–91.

26. As J. Maier states, "Hanging is clearly the cause of death." Maier, *The Temple Scroll*, trans. R. T. White (JSOTSS 34; Sheffield, 1985) p. 133.

27. See especially the New Testament and early Syriac literature. See M. Wilcox, "'Upon the Tree'—Deut 21:22–23 in the New Testament," *JBL* 96 (1977) 85–99; and J. Massyngberde Ford, "'Crucify him, crucify him' and the Temple Scroll," *ExpT* 87 (1976) 275–78.

28. Hengel suggests that these "women," who were charged with sorcery, were actually Sadducees who were victims of the Pharisaic counter-reaction during the reign of Salome. See Hengel, *Crucifixion*, pp. 84–85.

29. The Hebrew and Aramaic verb *ṣlb* means "to hang," "to impale." It can also mean "to crucify." In Syriac *ṣlb* clearly means "to crucify."

30. See m.Sanh 6:4; y.Ḥag 77d–78a; y.Sanh 23. I am indebted to Baumgarten for these references. See Baumgarten, *Studies in Qumran Law,* p. 176.

31. Consult m.Sanh 7:1. In an erudite article D. J. Halperin demonstrates that "Jews borrowed the practice of crucifixion from the Romans, and . . . 'naturalized' it into Jewish law by invoking *Deuteronomy* 21:22–23." Halperin, "Crucifixion, the Nahum Pesher, and the Rabbinic Penalty of Strangulation," *JJS* 32 (1981) 32–46. O. Betz suggests that the rabbis, interpreting Dt 21:22–23, recommended the hanging of a criminal on a tree after he had been stoned or executed by some other acceptable means. See Betz, "The Temple Scroll and the Trial of Jesus," *SWJTh* 30 (1987–88) 5–8.

32. On robbers, recall SyrMen 295: "Stealing is the constructor of a cross." *OTP,* vol. 2, p. 600. Concerning revolutionaries, R. A. Horsley persuasively argues that the Synoptic Gospels reveal, despite their apologetics, that Jesus did threaten the Temple (I would say the Temple cult) and claim that the old order was passing away. See Horsley, *Jesus and the Spiral of Violence: Popular Jewish Resistance in Roman Palestine* (San Francisco, 1987) pp. 160–64. Many scholars would add that how Jesus was perceived is not to be equated with his own intentions. For other crimes punishable by crucifixion, see Hengel, *Crucifixion,* pp. 33–35.

33. See the judicious comments by E. Bammel in *Judaica: Kleine Schriften I* (WUNT 37; Tübingen, 1986) pp. 76–78.

34. For a succinct discussion and bibliography, see H. H. Cohn, "Crucifixion," *EJ* (1971) vol. 5, cols. 1133–35; and Hengel, *Crucifixion.*

35. Cicero, *In Verrem* 2.5.162: *istam pestem.* In Philo's time many found Flaccus's crucifixion to be entertaining. See Philo, *In Flaccum* 72.84–85.

36. See H.-W. Kuhn, "Die Kreuzesstrafe während der frühen Kaiserzeit: Ihre Wirklichkeit und Wertung in der Umwelt des Urchristentums," in *ANRW* II.25.1 (1982) 648–793.

37. See V. Tzaferis, "Jewish Tombs at and near Giv'at ha-Mivtar," *IEJ* 20 (1970) 18–32, esp. 20–27.

38. N. Haas, "Anthropological Observations on the Skeletal Remains from Giv'at ha-Mivtar," *IEJ* 20 (1970) 38–59.

39. J. Zias and E. Sekeles, "The Crucified Man from Giv'at ha-Mivtar: A Reappraisal," *IEJ* 35 (1985) 22–27.

40. W. Edwards, J. Wesley, M. Gabel, F. Hosmer, "On the Physical Death of Jesus Christ," *Journal of the American Medical Association* 255 no. 11 (March 21, 1986) 1455–64.

41. A. A. LeBec, *Catholic Medical Guardian* 3 (1925).

42. P. Barbet, *A Doctor at Calvary: The Passion of Our Lord Jesus Christ as Described by a Surgeon,* trans. Earl of Wickow (New York, 1963).

43. Ibid., p. 208.

44. Ibid., p. 110.

45. F. Zugibe, "Two Questions About Crucifixion," *BR* 5 (1989) 35–43.

46. See especially Hengel, *Crucifixion,* pp. 22–38.

47. See, e.g., J. Hewitt, "The Use of Nails in the Crucifixion," *HTR* 25 (1932) 29–45.

48. Ibid., p. 40.

49. Haas, "Anthropological Observations," 58; and H.-W. Kuhn, "Der Gekreuzigte von Giv'at ha-Mivtar: Bilanz einer Entdeckung," in *Theologia Crucis—Signum Crucis: Festschrift für Erich Dinkler,* ed. C. Andresen and G. Klein (Tübingen, 1979) pp. 303–34.

50. Translated by W. Whiston, *The Works of Josephus* (1734–37; repr. Philadelphia, 1960) p. 823. The archaisms in his translation seem suited to the present excerpt.

51. See chapter 1 above.

CHAPTER 11

Two Ascended to Heaven—
Jesus and the Author of 4Q491

M O R T O N   S M I T H

I write this article with unusual pleasure because it reports new evidence that confirms a conjecture I published in 1973. To make the matter clear, however, I must review rapidly the evidence that led to the conjecture. Hence, readers familiar with my earlier work may find the first section of this chapter somewhat repetitive. The new material begins with section II.

I

Clement of Alexandria says that in his church (175–200 c.e.) a "secret Gospel" believed to have been written by Mark was "carefully guarded" and "read only to those being initiated into the great mysteries."[1] He also quotes a fragment of this gospel, a version of the Lazarus story of John 11:1–44. This version is written in Marcan style and is form-critically more primitive than the Johannine text.[2] Moreover it goes on to report that Jesus and the disciples went to the house of the young man after he had been raised and stayed with him for six days, after which he came to Jesus, "wearing only a linen cloth" and "stayed with him that night, for Jesus taught him the mystery of the Kingdom of God."[3]

Whether or not this report was written by the author of canonical Mark, it was almost certainly revered and read in the "mysteries" celebrated in Clement's church in Alexandria. Clement, to judge from his preserved works, was a model of ascetic propriety. The story, therefore, must have been understood to have an edifying meaning.

The key to this meaning is the linen cloth worn as the sole garment. This was a common costume for ancient religious, especially mystery, ceremonies; it was customary for magically induced visions, and it became the standard costume for Christian baptism, the initiatory mystery of the church.[4]

A quarter of a century before Mark wrote, baptism and the Eucharist had been classed by Paul among the "mysteries of God" which he administered (1Cor 4:1). Therefore, given the characteristic costume, the nocturnal setting (mysteries were commonly celebrated at night), and the concluding explanation (that Jesus "taught him the mystery of the kingdom of God"), it seems the reader was expected to understand that Jesus administered a mystery.[5] If the reader were a Christian, he would also understand that the initiatory rite of this mystery was baptism.[6]

That Jesus should have founded a mystery cult should not be surprising. It was something men of extraordinary religious powers were expected to do. Such cults were generally attributed to great men of the past (including Moses),[7] but some were founded in historical times. There were, for instance, mysteries of Ptolemaic kings and of Roman emperors.[8] Lucian (who classed Christianity as a mystery cult[9]) has left us a full account of the founder and founding of an unusually successful second-century cult well documented by the coinage minted in honor of its peculiar god.[10] The cults founded by Simon of Samaria and by other miscalled "gnostics" would probably be recognized as "mysteries" had not their distinguishing traits been obscured by immersion in Irenaeus's "gnostic" stew.[11] W. Burkert has done well, in his perceptive book *Mystery Cults,* to emphasize that these were *cults* and to "abandon the concept of mystery *religions* from the start" (his italics) because "in the pre-Christian epoch" the mysteries "appear as varying forms, trends, or options within the one disparate yet continuous conglomerate of ancient religion" (pp. 3–4). Here I need add only that the work of Jesus occurred in the pre-Christian epoch.

If we suppose that Jesus founded a mystery cult and that the initiatory rite was some sort of "baptism" (or immersion),[12] we have now to ask, What was the mystery? Mark 4:11 and "Secret Mark" say that it was "the mystery of the kingdom of God." This makes it somewhat different from the other cults. They were "mysteries of" various gods, and the mystery revealed by each was some sort of practice and/or knowledge by which the initiate could gain the god's favor and consequently enjoy, both in this life and hereafter, the blessings that the god might give.

The kingdom of God, however, was impersonal. We should not think about it as a mere metonymy for "God," since one is said to "enter" it. The kingdom of God is commonly spoken of as a place, but a place that could move and "come." The most likely explanation conceives of it as the area of God's rule, which he will soon extend. Therefore, the "mystery" of it—the way to derive benefit from it—might have been by knowing when it would "come," that is, be extended to the earth. However, although the Gospels contain many assurances that it is "near,"[13] the precise time of arrival is never specified. There are likewise many warnings to watch for and expect it, and statements that it will come when least expected, for instance, "as a thief in the night."[14] Besides, Jesus is credited with the statement that even the Son does not know when it is coming; only God knows (Mk 13:32; Mt 24:36; "credited," because this time he was right). If we can trust the Gospels, therefore, the proximity of the kingdom was, for Jesus, not a mystery but a message to be proclaimed.

A different set of sayings either heightens or, depending on the exegete's attitude, contradicts the preceding. These declare that the kingdom is not only near; it is here. By contrast with the preceding, they are usually less clear—so, for instance, the series of parables indicating that the kingdom is already in the world, a treasure to be taken now (Mk 4:26, 30; Lk 13:21; Mt 13:44, 46). These look like fragments of teaching intended—as Jesus said they were—*not* to be understood by outsiders (Mk 4:11–12). To have a mystery is a profitable thing; people will pay to be initiated, as Alexander of Abonuteichos and Sigmund of Vienna demonstrated. Then there are sayings which indicate that the kingdom is now accessible: it is within your grasp (Lk 17:21); it can be had by violence and violent men seize it (Mt 11:12; the parallel in Lk 16:16 says everybody pushes in, a wishful revision); those who *were* entering were hindered (Mt 23:13); a scribe can already be a disciple of the kingdom (Mt 13:52). These are capped by another series promising that what we saw were the common objectives of mystery cults—the benefits the initiates might gain: they are exempt from fasting—or were, while Jesus was with them (Mk 2:19); they need not observe the Sabbath (Mk 2:23–27) or purity laws (Mk 7:2–13); they can exorcize (Mk 3:15; 6:7; Lk 10:17); they can heal the sick and proclaim the coming of the kingdom (Lk 10:9). The least among them is greater than the Baptist (Lk

7:28). They will get whatever they ask (Lk 11:10); or at least they are sure of food, drink, and clothing (12:29–31); and Jesus will give them rest (Mt 11:28). Their names are already written in heaven (Lk 10:20).

With all these promised benefits[15] to be had by entering the kingdom, and the assurance that it can be done now (at least, by violence), we are led directly to the questions, Where is the kingdom? and, How can we get in? These the Gospels do not answer. Presumably the answer was given in "the mystery of the kingdom of God."

This convenient presumption leads to a further question: What could Jesus have done in his mystery rite to persuade his initiates that they had entered the kingdom and would now enjoy these benefits, and to do this so powerfully that they not only left everything to follow him around Palestine but, even after he had been taken and crucified, saw him risen from the dead, watched him ascend into heaven, and reshaped their hopes so as to continue to believe in him? Whatever he did, its effect was dazzlingly different from that of any rabbinic teaching known to us. The nearest Old Testament analogue is Elijah's call of Elisha, but the similarities are minor and the consequences comparatively trivial. Hence, we must conjecture.[16]

The steps of the conjecture are as follows: First, with regard to baptism. Bits of evidence suggesting that Jesus baptized have been touched on above, but what chiefly leads us to conjecture that he did so is the great change from the baptism of the Baptist to that known to Paul. The baptism of John (about 30 C.E.) merely removed impurity and remitted sin, but according to Paul—if we suppose him to have held faithfully to the teaching given him when he was baptized (about 35 C.E.)—in baptism he died, his body was taken over by the spirit of Jesus, and he and his body were raised by this spirit to a new life, a long battle in which the spirit would finally subjugate and remake the body (2Cor 4–5; Rom 6–8). These ideas may reflect the imagery of death and resurrection after the Easter experience, but that is not basic. The basic notion is that of possession by a more powerful spirit, which drives out not only death but also sin and subdues the body to order. This goes back beyond Easter to Jesus' work as an exorcist. Many of his followers are said to have been women from whom evil spirits had been driven out (Lk 8:2–3)—we should say, by the power of his personality, but they said, "by his spirit." We may therefore conjecture that the baptism given in his mystery was a baptism similar to the one that he—unlike the Baptist's other followers—had himself experienced, one in which the initiate was possessed by the spirit. This was what Paul believed and is what the church still officially teaches. It may have been true.

Second, with regard to the entrance to the kingdom. Let us accept the common opinion that the kingdom of God is the area of God's rule, primarily the heavens, where God and his throne are (Mt 6:1, 9, etc.; Rev 4:2, etc.)[17] Thither Jesus was thought to have ascended at or after his resurrection,[18] and Christians hoped to go there immediately after death,[19] a belief that contradicted the prevailing Jewish one. Some claimed even to have gone there while alive.[20] Hence it is not surprising that John 3:12–13 makes Jesus himself claim to have been in heaven (and 3:32 adducces unlikely confirmation of this claim from the Baptist). A lot of secondary evidence—not probative, but not certainly worthless—tends to corroborate the assumption that Jesus claimed during his lifetime to have ascended to heaven.[21]

Such ascent stories were popular in the thought of the time, particularly among the Jews. Half a dozen Old Testament pseudepigrapha credit their heroes with visits to the heavens.[22] So there is no doubt that the idea was well known to Jesus. More important is the fact that there was a method for attaining the experience by self-hypnosis (presented as magic, but involving expectation of the events, recitation of repetitive formulas, gazing at the sun [perhaps], and regulation of breathing; see PGM 4.475–829, esp. 537–40).[23] The same rite includes instructions for "using a fellow initiate so that he alone may hear with you the things spoken . . . and if you wish to show him (the things seen). . . ." Directions follow for preliminaries that would incline him to submit to hypnosis.

If it is in fact true that a man practicing self-hypnosis can communicate his hallucinations to a companion, we have here the sort of means by which Jesus might have introduced his initiates to the kingdom of God and given them experiences, like that of his transfiguration, which prepared them to see him risen from the dead and, by their worship, to make him the "Savior of the world." This conjecture seemed, and seems, to me the most likely explanation of the data.

II

This conjecture was of course rejected at once by most New Testament scholars since they had "never heard of such a thing"—to their minds this was an adequate reason. So I let the matter ride.

Now, to my amazement, the Qumran fragments have provided a little poem by some egomaniac who claimed to have done just what I conjectured Jesus claimed, that is, entered the heavenly kingdom and secured a chair with tenure, while yet commuting to earth and carrying on his teaching here.

The fragment in question is printed as col. 1 of fragment 11 of 4Q491.[24] M. Baillet says that it and the material printed as col. 2 of the same fragment have been pieced together from seventeen scraps and that the small connection between the two columns is "only probable."[25] He might have added, "if that," since the second column is clearly a fragment of the War Scroll text, in which this bit of self-glorification has no apparent place. Baillet's description of the main part of col. 1 as "a song by the archangel Michael" was probably an act of desperation. Since the scraps have been put together mainly on the basis of similarities of hide and handwriting, and since it is likely that the same scribe with the same hand may have written several different texts on different pieces of the same skin, assignment of this text to the War Scroll is not likely. Yet more dubious is its location in the War Scroll. Apparently there was no external evidence for the order of the fragments. Baillet seems to have arranged those that had parallels with the War Scroll in the sequence in which the parallels occurred in that text, and then inserted the unparalleled ones wherever he thought they would go. Consequently, this text can be treated by itself. This material may have come from a collection of poems like the Thanksgiving Hymns, and an oversized *lamed*, which appears on Baillet's printed text, but of which only a vertical line shows on his manuscript—and of which he could not guess the use—may, if correctly conjectured, have been the number of the poem (or book of poems?) that begins beside it.[26]

I discussed Baillet's text in the 1986 New York University conference on the Dead Sea Scrolls.[27] My paper discussed the details of textual criticism and the calculations on which must be based the restorations in the (relatively small) lacunae.

From the corrected and completed text it appears that the preserved remains of col. 1 contain fragments of three poems. The first, which ends with *'ōlāmim* in Baillet's line 11 (p. 26), is the end of a hymn in praise of God; it does not concern us. The third, beginning with Baillet's line 20, is plausibly described by him as a "canticle of the righteous"; neither does it concern us. The nine lines intervening are a brief paean of self-praise, which will be clearer if translated as verse. Differences from Baillet's readings are indicated in the notes to the translation.[28]

[El Elyon gave me a seat among] those perfect forever,
a mighty throne in the congregation of the gods.
None of the kings of the east shall sit in it
and their nobles shall not [come near it].
No Edomite shall be like me in glory,
and none shall be exalted save me, nor shall come against me.
For I have taken my seat in the [congregation] in the heavens
And none [find fault with me].[29]
I shall be reckoned with gods
and established in the holy congregation.
I do not desire [gold,] as would a man of flesh;
everything precious to me is in the glory of [my God].
[The status of a holy temple,] not to be violated,[30]
has been attributed to me, and who can compare with me in glory?
What voyager will return
and tell[31] [of my equivalent]
Who [laughs] at griefs as I do?
And who is like me [in bearing] evil?
Moreover, if I lay down the law in a lecture[32]
[my instruction] is beyond comparison [with any man's].
And who will attack[33] me for my utterances?
And who will contain the flow of my speech?
And who will call me into court and be my equal?
In my legal judgment [none will stand against] me.
I shall be reckoned with gods,
and my glory, with [that of] the king's sons.
Neither refined gold, nor gold of Ophir
[can match my wisdom].

Since Baillet attributed the poem to Michael, that attribution must be briefly discussed.[34]

Michael is never mentioned in this text. In the War Scroll his name is written on some shields (9.15–16); and after the wicked have gained their one permitted victory, the head priest, trying to cheer up the righteous, promises that El will send Michael to help Israel (17.6–7)—hardly the place for the hero to praise his prowess as a lawyer. Would an archangel have stooped to brag that none of the kings of the east can sit in his heavenly throne, nor any of their nobles come near it? When he goes on to say that no Edomite can rival him in glory, the Edomite he has in mind is probably Herod the Great.[35] Consequently, the nobles of the kings of the east, who preceded the Edomite, were probably the Parthian backers of Antigonus, who preceded Herod and was ousted in 37 B.C.E. That the speaker thinks it worthwhile to contrast himself with them probably dates the speech to the early years of Herod's reign. On palaeographic grounds Baillet thought the manuscript late Herodian, or early Herodian.[36]

Michael would not have had to emphasize his indifference to money. The speaker suggests that his got him the status of a temple not to be plundered, an honor much sought in late republican times—but not by archangels, who hardly needed it. The speaker may be contrasting himself with the Temple of Jerusalem. It and the entire city had been granted inviolability in Seleucid times (Josephus, *Ant* 13.51), but had not thereby been saved from looting. As Jesus would say, sixty years later, "A greater one than the Temple is here" (Mt 12:6)—a great claim, but not one likely to be attributed to an archangel.

More anticlimaxes follow. The speaker is unique in glory; no sailor could report having seen the likes of him. Were sailors expected to tell of cruising archangels? This glorious being laughs at sorrows and is uniquely able to bear evil, but the only angels who might have wanted to make such claims were the evil ones. The speaker is unparalleled as a legal teacher, and no one dares call him into court. How often are archangels summoned? He has been "reckoned with the gods"; therefore, he was not originally one of them. In glory he ranks with the king's sons, not even with the king!

In summation, Baillet's attribution of the speech to Michael is useful only because it demonstrates that he has not understood it, and so strengthens the case for immediate photographic publication of all the Dead Sea Scrolls. Baillet's work makes the case clear, but its practical utility does nothing to answer the literary question, Who is this new-made deity with all these human virtues?

One thinks immediately of the author of the Thanksgiving Hymns. There are important similarities: the same insistence on sufferings, though not so much pride in bearing them (1QH 3.7-13; 5.8ff.; etc.); the claim to be purified and free of carnal concerns (4.36ff.; 6.3ff.; 7.16ff.); the pride in his irresistible teaching (2.8ff., 8.16ff.; 10.20ff.; 11.4ff.); the claim to have been admitted to the company of angels (3.22-23), to be united with them (fragment 2.10), to be in the lot (*gôrāl*) of the holy and join the company of heaven (11.11f.) and have glory like that of God (9.26).

However, the angels of the Thanksgiving Hymns and those of the War Scroll usually come down into the assemblies of the saints. This speaker's claim to have been taken up and seated in heaven and counted as one of the gods (*'elîm*) is more direct and explicit than anything I remember in the Thanksgiving Hymns or in any other of the Dead Sea Scrolls hitherto published. To continue the contrast with the Thanksgiving Hymns, there is nothing here of the emphasis on revelation, on the secrets of the heavens, the role of the spirit, and the distinction between the *'elîm* and the one God "with whom there is no other" (12.11). But the silence of the present text on such points cannot be pressed, since a fragment of twenty-eight lines cannot be expected to touch on many themes. Nevertheless, it is probably better to suppose that the Dead Sea group or groups produced more than one preposterous poet with an exaggerated notion of his own sanctity.

Their frequency should perhaps be attributed to the influence of speculation about deification by ascent toward or into the heavens, speculation probably connected with magical practices that produced extraordinary experiences understood as encounters with gods or angels. Ezekiel's attack on the Prince of Tyre, and pseudo-Isaiah's on Lucifer, son of the morning, both seem to have been directed against such practices and consequences in their authors' environments. In the Enoch books and in the legends about the ascension and enthronement of Moses[37] we can see that these ideas (and guess that these practices) have made their way into Judaism. In the fragment discussed here we see that they inspired not only literary fantasies about long-dead heroes but claims by living persons to have made such ascents and to have enjoyed the resultant benefits.

Whether the claims made by the author of 4Q491 ii.1 are completely false, or whether they reflect hallucinations he actually experienced, we have no way of knowing. In either event they prove that fifty or sixty years before Jesus' crucifixion, men in Palestine were actually making claims of the sort that John was to attribute to Jesus. E. R. Goodenough, who argued for years that the Fourth Gospel expressed an early Palestinian theology derived from mystical Judaism, was a voice crying in the stacks of the Yale library. Everybody—and I among them—thought he was riding his hobby too far. Now, I must wonder. As to Philonic philosophy, which he had in mind, I see little sign of it in Palestine, but I must admit that we have no literary remains from the higher priestly circles (I don't trust Josephus' claims). On a more plebeian level, however, it now seems possible and, given the Gospel reports, even likely that Jesus taught a "mystery of the kingdom of God" in which, by means like those known from contemporary magic, initiates were given what they thought was an experience of entering the heavens and they were thus trained to have such visions as those reworked in the transfiguration and resurrection stories. That Jesus ever read 4Q491 ii.1 seems to me utterly unlikely. I doubt that he ever went near Qumran and I think that if he had they would have spat on him—if they hadn't feared a fight with the tough men among his followers. But there is considerable likelihood that both this Qumran document and the mystery material in the Gospels are mushrooms of the same ring, connected not directly but by the ramified root system of popular piety and superstition from which they independently arose.

Notes

1. Letter to Theodore, folio 1, verso, lines 1–5, in M. Smith, *Clement of Alexandria and a Secret Gospel of Mark* (Cambridge, Mass., 1973) pp. 448–53; hereinafter, *Clement*. The Greek text is reprinted in *Clemens Alexandrinus III*², ed. O. Stählin, L. Früchtel, and U. Treu (GCS; Berlin, 1970). Many scholars have accepted the letter as probably authentic (*Clement*, p. 67), and study of the language and style has brought the probability close to certainty (*Clement*, pp. 5–85). Nevertheless, the content of the gospel fragment which the letter quotes has prompted a number of attacks. For the state of the question in the early 1980s see M. Smith, "Clement of Alexandria and Secret Mark, the Score," *HTR* 75 (1982) 449–61. For the present location of the manuscript (the Patriarchal Library in Jerusalem), see. T. J. Talley, "Liturgical Time in the Ancient Church," in *Liturgical Time: Papers read at the 1981 Congress of the* Societas Liturgica, ed. W. Vos and G. Wainright (Rotterdam, 1982) p. 45 (also in *Studia Liturgica* 14 nos. 2–4 [1982]).

2. Smith, *Clement*, 148–58; contra R. E. Brown, "The Relation of 'The Secret Gospel of Mark' to the Fourth Gospel," *CBQ* 36 (1974) 466–85. Brown's examination of the texts prudently stops just before their parallelism becomes close enough to yield probable conclusions.

3. Folio 2, recto, lines 6–10; Smith, *Clement*, p. 452.

4. For pagan usage, see Apuleius, *Metamorphoses* 11.3; W. Dittenberger, *Sylloge Inscriptionum Graecarum*⁴, no. 736 (Andania), sec. 4; W. Burkert, *Ancient Mystery Cults* (Cambridge, Mass., 1987) figs. 6 and 12. For magical visions, see K. Preisendanz and A. Henrichs, eds., *PGM* 3.706, 712; 4.88, 171–75, 3095. For Christian practice, see Smith, *Clement*, pp. 175–77.

5. When writing *Clement*, I supposed that an objection to this theory could be brought from the statement "Jesus taught him the mystery," since mysteries were commonly "given," not "taught" (*Clement*, p. 183). Half a dozen reviewers, no less ignorant than I, appropriated my objection and announced that it refuted my theory. Therefore, I am glad to have found evidence of my error—a good number of passages in which mysteries and/or magical rites are said to have been "taught": Herodotus 2.171; Dionysius of Halicarnassus, *Ant. Rom.* 1.68; Porphyry, *De abstinentia* 4.16; *Orac. Chald.* (ed. des Places) 224.1; *PGM* 4.750, 1372.

6. John's statements that Jesus baptized (3:22; 4:1) are supported by important historical considerations; see Smith, *Clement*, 201–64.

7. Diodorus 3.65.6; 5.64.4, *PGM* 12.92–95.

8. M. Nilsson, "Royal Mysteries in Egypt," *HTR* 50 (1957) 65ff.; H. Pleket, "An Aspect of the Emperor Cult," *HTR* 58 (1966) 331ff.

9. *De morte Peregrini* 11.

10. Glykon. See Lucian, *Alexander;* and *Lexicon Iconographicum* 4.1.279–83; 2.161–62.

11. I.e., *Contra haereses* 1.

12. Ephesians' insistence that its readers should recognize only "one baptism" (4:5) is explained by the reports in Acts that there were several (8:12–17; 18:24–26; 19:3–4).

13. Mk 1:15; 13:28, 29; Mt 3:2; 4:17; 10:7; and parallels.

14. "Watch out" (Mk 13:35, 37 and parallels); "like a thief" (Mt 24:43 and parallels).

15. None of which, by the way, has anything to do with a change of the government of Palestine, much less of the Roman Empire.

16. To this point the argument has followed closely the plain sense of the Gospels. That is why so many commonplace critics have found it unacceptable— the liberal, since it recognized as genuine many elements they gladly dismissed as "unhistorical"; the conservative, because it held to the plain sense of many they disposed of by "exegesis." Both sides exemplify the paradox of the past century's New Testament study: the combination of a "search for the historical Jesus" with a determination not to recognize his historical features.

17. For fuller references, see Smith, *Clement*, pp. 202–4.

18. Col 3:1; Jn 20:17; Acts 1:9; Lk 24:51.

19. 2Cor 5:1–10; Phil 3:20; Mk 10:21; Lk 6:23; 12:23; etc.

20. 2Cor 12:1–5, presumably to match the claims of Paul's rivals; Col 2:18; Rev 4:1–2; 1Pet 1:11.

21. The material is collected in Smith, *Clement*, pp. 240–48.

22. See Smith, *Clement*, 238–40, bibliography in n. 1. LAE 25; 1En passim; TAb 10; ApAb 15; TLevi 6–8; 3Bar 2–4; etc.

23. *PGM* 4 is of the fourth century C.E., about the same date as the *Sinaiticus* and *Vaticanus* manuscripts of the New Testament, the oldest of the New Testament

uncials. It is a collection into which many earlier manuscripts have been copied. The source of lines 475–829 was a manuscript in which a yet earlier text (a rite for a man's immortalization by the sun god) had been reworked as a letter telling a woman how to get a favorable oracle from the god of the pole star. It seems sure that the letter writer did not use the first copy of the original spell, and almost sure that the anthologist of *PGM* did not use the first copy of the letter, and very likely that the text we have is not the first copy of the anthology. Therefore, the text we have is presumably *at least* of the sixth literary generation, if we count the original spell as the first (i.e., spell, copy, letter, copy, anthology, copy). Allowing an average of thirty or forty years to a literary generation (i.e., to the span between the autograph and the *preserved* copy) this would date the original spell to the second half of the first, or the first half of the second, century c.e. The Gospels would seem to be products of about the same time as this spell.

24. M. Baillet, DJD 7 (Oxford, 1982) pp. 26–29; pl. 6.

25. Ibid., p. 27.

26. Ibid., pl. VI.II.11 and p. 28.

27. The papers of that conference are published as *Archaeology and History in the Dead Sea Scrolls: The New York University Conference in Memory of Yigael Yadin,* ed. L. H. Schiffman (JSPS; JSOT/ASOR 2; Sheffield, 1990); my article is pp. 181–88.

28. Professors Shaye Cohen and Burton Visotzky and Dr. Seth Schwartz have made helpful suggestions for restorations in the text and saved me from several errors.

29. Reading *yodh* before *mem,* instead of Baillet's *waw,* which he marked as dubious.

30. *'y* for negation, here with a final aleph, is dubious in Job 22:30, but common in the Mishna. Its use may have increased because of the need to render the Greek *alpha* privative, e.g., *'y 'pšr* for *adynaton, 'y lbwz* for *asylon,* etc.

31. Reading *mem* for Baillet's *kaph,* and a medial *peh* for his final one. He marked both his readings as dubious. Also reading *yodh* for his *waw.*

32. Deleting *nun,* probably due to dittography, and reading *beth* for *waw* before *horayah.*

33. *Gdd,* "attack"; Ps 94.21; CD 1.20. As the dots in the manuscript indicate, the second *waw* should be deleted.

34. These comments follow, with minor changes, my remarks in the conference article.

35. Baillet missed the reference because the aleph of *'edōmi* was separated from the *dalet* by a slight gap. Such gaps within words are fairly frequent in this text; see plate VI.I.

36. Late Herodian: DJD 7, p. 12; early Herodian: DJD 7, p. 45.

37. On these see P. van der Horst, "Moses' Throne Vision in Ezekiel the Dramatist," *JJS* 34 (1983) 21–29; idem, *Mnemosyne* 37 (1984) esp. 363–69.

CHAPTER 12

The Risen Christ
and the Angelic Mediator Figures
in Light of Qumran[1]

ALAN F. SEGAL

ANGELIC CHRISTOLOGIES

Scholarly attention has focused on the relationship between Jesus and the falsely presumed founder of the Dead Sea Scroll community, the Righteous Teacher. Considering the importance of the man Jesus for the Christian religion, there is good reason to pursue the presumed similarities. But the idea that the Righteous Teacher of the Dead Sea Scrolls and Jesus or John the Baptizer might turn out to be the same persons or close associates was misplaced. The demonstrable relationships between them have turned out to be analogies of leadership and "sect" formation but not of provable influence.

In contrast, there has been little study of the relationship between early Christian understandings of the Christ and the angelic mediators at Qumran. Again, there are good reasons why such analogies have not been pursued. Early Christian tradition eschewed the term angel as applied to Jesus, arguing explicitly that the Christ, as son, is higher than the angels and Lord of them (e.g., Heb 1:2b–2:18). Nevertheless, there are important reasons to pursue that analogy today.

L. Hurtado in his important book *One God, One Lord* summarizes the history of this important research question.[2] In 1898, W. Lueken argued that "primitive Christianity," appropriated various aspects of the characterization of the archangel Michael in pre-Christian Judaism.[3] However, Lueken's early study was confined almost entirely to the figure of Michael. Furthermore, his method amounted to arguing that the portrayal of the exalted Jesus had been influenced by Michael speculation because the figures were described in similar terms. Taking the force of the analogy, if not the entire argument, J. Barbel's *Christos Angelos* in 1941 dealt mainly with the patristic evidence.[4]

In the same year, however, M. Werner presented his views that the christology of the earliest church was based on the transformation of the man Jesus into an angelic being as a result of the resurrection.[5] Werner reasoned that the original Christian interpretation of the exalted Jesus was an "angelic christology," even though in later times such a concept was deemed insufficient. Werner recognized that the reverence given the exalted Christ began with the Jewish Christians, far too early to be attributed to the oft-invoked direct influence of pagan cults. Shortly after the appearance of Werner's book, W. Michaelis published a withering refutation of Werner's claims.[6] Michaelis rightly fixed his attention on several weak points in Werner's arguments, but his attack went far beyond the errors of Werner's development. Nevertheless, Michaelis's critique settled the matter for many New Testament scholars.

In spite of Michaelis's strong arguments, a few scholars continued to develop these important ideas. G. Kretschmar argued that Christian trinitarian doctrine was deeply influenced by Jewish speculation about principal angels, though he dealt mainly with the second and third centuries C.E.[7] J. Daniélou wrote an enormously influential volume on Jewish Christianity.[8] Daniélou's main object was to illustrate those Christian doctrines which appeared to reflect the Jewish rather than the Greek or philosophical milieu. H. Odeberg and N. A. Dahl both suggested the importance of Jewish mysticism in the rise of Christianity, stressing the importance of angelic mediation. G. Quispel wrote extensively on the relationship between Jewish mysticism and early christology and Gnosticism. R. Longenecker traced the earliest Christian ideas to the Jewish community. A. Segal, J. Fossum, C. Rowland, and L. Hurtado championed these minority positions by uncovering new and important bodies of evidence illustrating them.[9]

QUMRAN AND ANGELIC TRANSFORMATION

The evidence from Qumran as well as the apocalyptic writings of the Pseudepigrapha have helped uncover the importance of angelology in sectarian Judaism. Josephus tells us that the Essenes "carefully preserved the books of the sect and the names of the angels" (*War* 2.142). Almost all the sectarian writings at Qumran give great attention to angels: 1QS, 1QH, 1QM, and the Enoch literature, all found at Qumran, describe roles for special angels in great detail. Indeed, the Qumran community believed the entire cosmos to be split into opposing camps, led by angelic forces but involving humanity, all of whom were warring in a predestined pattern that would culminate in the eschaton. In the documents of the sect, the captain of the good forces is variously called the "Angel of Light," the "Angel of His Truth," perhaps "Melchizedek," and several other terms. The archangelic villain is "Satan," but more usually is called "Beliar," the "Angel of Darkness," and perhaps even "Malkirasha."

J. A. Fitzmyer clarified another important aspect of angelology by closely analyzing the terminology for "son of God" at Qumran. In his opinion, "son of God" terminology at Qumran has no messianic context. Rather, it is used as a title for angels, as it is throughout the Hebrew Bible.[10] Furthermore, Qumran evidences the use of the term "Lord" (*mr'*) for YHWH, the Tetragrammaton. This suggests that the origin of the church's use of the term "Lord" for "Christ" is not to be found in the Hellenistic environment but in the original Hebrew "church," as it was a feature of Jewish sectarianism before Christianity.

Where Melchizedek appears in the Dead Sea Scrolls, in the document called Melchizedek (11QMelch), he is identified with the "Elohim" of Psalm 82:1, thus giving us yet another variation on the theme of an angel identified with a divine name.[11] As the earlier researchers have seen, typically, the name of the angel varies from tradition to tradition. Thus, Michael is God's "mediator" and general *archistrategos*, 2En 33:10; TDan 6:1–5; TAbr 1:4; cf. LAE 14:1–2). Eremiel appears in the Apocalypse of Zephaniah (6:1–15), in which he is mistaken for God. In the Ascension of Isaiah 7:2–4, an angel appears whose name cannot be given. And Melchizedek is the favored angelic name in 11QMelch.

The Qumran discoveries suggest that the Enoch books were widely known in Early Judaism.[12] Enoch is a primeval hero of the Bible, whose death is not mentioned. Instead, Genesis 5:18–24 twice relates that Enoch "walked with God" and then disappeared, for "God took him." This report became the basis of an enormous literature, which filled in the details left out by the terse biblical report. First, Enoch is known as the primeval hero who was given a tour of the angelic hosts by means of a heavenly journey. Furthermore, in several key portions of the Enoch books, this biblical hero is transformed into the principal angel. Is this transformation because of his heavenly voyage? Is it because he was a mediator figure, pleading mercy for the fallen angels in front of the heavenly throne? All of these are possible. But probably he attains angelic status upon his ascension to heaven at the end of his life because this was the reward of the righteous for their steadfastness. In this respect his reward is similar to the reward allegedly promised to Jesus. The reason for this reward of angelic status is not hard to find. It is the fulfillment of the prophecies in Daniel 7 and 12.

Let us look more closely at these passages. In Daniel 7 the expression "son of man" appears, and this heavenly figure is extremely important for Christian understandings of Jesus. The heavenly son of man appears in the vision in Daniel 7:13 in which an Ancient of Days appoints a human figure ("one like a son of man") to execute justice in the destruction of the evil ones. This human figure is best understood as an angel.[13] Later on in Daniel, resurrection is promised both for the faithful dead and for the most heinous villains, who will be resurrected so that they may be sentenced to eternal perdition. *Hammaskîlîm* ("those who are wise"), apparently the elite of the apocalyptic group, will then shine as the stars in heaven (Dan 12:3). This scripture essentially states that its righteous leaders will be transformed into angels, since the stars were identified with angels in biblical tradition (e.g., Job 38:7).

At the end of the Parables of Enoch (1En 70–71), Enoch is mystically transformed into the figure of the "son of man" on the throne: "My whole body mollified and my spirit transformed" (1En 71:1).[14] This is an extraordinarily important event, as it underlines the importance of mystic transformation between the adept and the angelic vice-regent of God, giving a plausible explanation of how the sectarians that produced the visions in Daniel expected to be transformed into stars. Indeed, it is possible to say that 1 Enoch 71 gives us the experience of an adept undergoing the astral transformation prophesied in Daniel 12:2, albeit in the name of a pseudepigraphical hero.

Because the ascent of the living is supposed to parallel exactly the ascent of the dead after death, 1 Enoch 70–71 may retell Enoch's previous earthly ascent. But it is vastly more probable that it refers to the ascent at the end of his life. The puzzling superscription of chapter 70, the composite nature of the text, and some possible imprecision in chronology prevent complete certainty on this issue: "And it happened after this that his living name was raised up before that Son of Man and to the Lord from among those who dwell upon the earth" (70:1). The journey is taken by Enoch's name, not precisely his soul, again reflecting a level of mystical speculation that predates the importation of the Platonic notion of a soul. It may thus be that the transformation motif is particularly important *because* the notion had not deeply penetrated this level of Jewish society. But, of course, this transformation motif is amenable to an explicit concept of the immortal soul as it develops within Judaism and Christianity.

We immediately run into a difficult problem in interpreting this evidence. Unfortunately, 1 Enoch 71 is *not* evidenced at Qumran and may not have been known by the Qumran covenanters, since they appear to have substituted another group of chapters in place of the Parables of Enoch, of which 1 Enoch 71 is the climax. But the chapters of "1 Enoch" that are extant at Qumran do give us some information. They do show us that the angelic forms of dead heroes, martyrs, and patriarchs were viewed as fulfillments of the prophecies in Daniel, since Enoch quotes that terminology in describing them. The Parables of Enoch contains several references to angelic transformation. In chapter 39, Enoch ascends to heaven while reciting hymns and blessings as do the Merkabah mystics, where he is overcome with the splendor and glory of the throne rooms. His face changes on account of the vision, which evidently reflects the experience of the prophecy that "those who are wise shall shine as the stars" (Dan 11:2), because 1 Enoch 62:15 states that the elect shall shine as stars and be clothed with garments of glory. The Parables of Enoch thus describes the righteous as dwelling with the angels after death: "So there my eyes saw their dwelling places with the holy angels, and their resting places with the holy ones" (1En 39:5). So too in the parts of 1 Enoch attested at Qumran, Enoch promises the righteous that they "will shine like the lights of heaven" (1En 104:2) and "make a great joy like the angels of heaven" (104:4).[15] Thus, it seems safe to assume that when Enoch is transformed into a "son of man" in 1 Enoch 71 he is being rewarded with angelic status, as Daniel 12 predicts. It might also be that much later Jesus "Christ" was viewed as similarly rewarded on account of his martyr's death.

Indeed, the prophet Ezekiel is a central informing passage for the Qumran covenanters.[16] Ezekiel prophesied that the Zadokite priests would be God's chosen ministers in the future era (44:15), possibly giving the

Qumran community its priestly aristocracy (CD 3.20–4.3). But the most interesting material from Ezekiel so far comes from the Angelic Liturgy, which J. Strugnell introduced in 1960. He thought these fragments came from four different manuscripts.[17] The existence of speculation on the heavenly hierarchy has been powerfully suggested in the initial reports of the finds in Cave 4 (4QShirShabb). Strugnell dated the four manuscripts on the basis of their script, assigning the oldest of them to about 50 B.C.E., which becomes the latest possible date for the composition of the document.

Those of us who have championed the importance of this material had been waiting for the publication of the full text of the Angelic Liturgy from Qumran. The long-awaited text has now been published. The new critical edition confirms that various mystical Jewish angelological themes existed at Qumran, themes of Jewish mysticism that we can otherwise date only to the third century C.E. from mystical sources. The Angelic Liturgy is pre-Christian and cannot be later than the first century B.C.E. In it there are many oblique references to the divine hierarchies, the seven heavens inside one another, and the appearance and movements of God's throne chariot familiar to scholars who study Merkabah mysticism. 1 Enoch and Ezekiel 1 seem to be the informing scriptural passages, but the hierarchy of heavens is best known to us from such Merkabah documents as the *Reuyoth Yehezkel* ("The Visions of Ezekiel").[18] The Angelic Liturgy evinces some of the most characteristic aspects of Jewish mysticism in an apocalyptic community of the first century B.C.E. Exactly which parts of Merkabah speculation can be understood as being so early, however, remains uncertain. The setting for such an angelic liturgy must be either earth, to which the angels are invited, or, more likely, heaven, to which the sectarians ascend for their Sabbath service.

Further evidence that humans could ascend to divine status may emerge from the unpublished Qumran Scrolls. Certainly the Qumran covenanters believed that they kept close company with the angels. Josephus reports as much, though we do not know precisely how he meant his comments to be taken. M. Smith points to a text that firmly anchors these experiences in the first century B.C.E. and in Qumran, thus necessarily with a long prehistory.[19] The passage, which was originally more than seventy fragments, has been published in DJD 7.[20] It was identified by Baillet as a psalm of Michael, followed by a psalm of the just. There is no evidence that it is a speech of Michael. Indeed, Michael plays almost no role in 1QM, to which this passage is an addition. Rather, M. Smith suggests that the narrator is human and that the fragments in 4QMa ought to be translated thus:

[El Elyon gave me a seat among] those perfect forever,
a mighty throne in the congregation of the gods.
None of the kings of the east shall sit in it
and their nobles shall not [come near it.]
No Edomite shall be like me in glory,
and none shall be exalted save me, nor shall come against me.
For I have taken my seat in the [congregation] in the heavens,
and none [find fault with me.]
I shall be reckoned with gods
and established in the holy congregation.

Further reflection now will await the reception of Smith's full argument in the preceding chapter of the present book. Smith's translations appear careful and his reconstructions conservative. I am convinced that they are correct and that we have evidence that the mystics at Qumran believed that they were one company with the angels, whom they call the bĕnê ʾĕlōhîm. These mystics must have achieved this unity through some rite of translation and transmutation. If that is so, ought we not to count the Wisdom of Solomon 5:5 ("Why has he been numbered among the sons of God? And why is his lot among the saints?") as another example of "deification" or, as I would prefer to call it, "angelification"?[21] Furthermore, the technical term "glory" is used to describe the splendor of the transformed person, just as Paul uses the term in his description of the transformed Christian.

Thus, in order to understand the implications of Qumran for the Christian understanding of Jesus, we must investigate the confluence of two traditions: the name of God and his principal angelic mediator.

ANGELS IN ANCIENT JEWISH MYSTICISM

How can a monotheistic tradition support such a prominent role for intermediaries? Though it would be impractical here to review all the detailed work currently under way on apocalyptic and Merkabah mysticism, its relationship to these perplexing Qumran traditions and its importance for Christianity should be briefly summarized. In the Bible, God was sometimes described in human form. In other places, such as Exodus 23:21–22, an angel is mentioned who has the form of a human and who carries within him or represents "the name of God." The human figure on the divine throne described in different ways in Ezekiel 1, Daniel 7, and Exodus 24 among other places was blended into a consistent picture of a principal mediator figure who, like the angel of the Lord in Exodus 23, embodied, personified, or carried the name of God, YHWH, the Tetragrammaton. We shall see that this figure, greatly elaborated by Jewish tradition, becomes a central metaphor for the Christ in Christianity. To see how, we must trace its history in Early Judaism.

The preeminence of this angel is due primarily to the description of the angel of the Lord in Exodus. Exodus 23:20–21 states: "Behold, I send an angel before you, to guard you on the way and to bring you to the place which I have prepared. Give heed to him and hearken to his voice, do not rebel against him, for he will not pardon your transgression; for my name is in him." The Bible expresses the unique status of this angel by means of its participation in the divine name.[22] Thereafter in Exodus 33:18–23, Moses asks to see the Glory (*kbwd*) of God. In answer, God makes "his goodness" pass in front of him but he cautions:

> You cannot see my face; for man shall not see me and live. . . . Behold, there is a place by me where you shall stand upon the rock; and while my glory passes by I will put you in a cleft of the rock, and I will cover you with my hand until I have passed by; then I will take away my hand and you shall see my back; but my face shall not be seen."

Yahweh himself, the angel of God, and his Glory (*kbwd*) are melded together in a peculiar way, which suggested to its readers a deep secret about the ways God manifested himself to humanity.

Let us look at the philosophical expression of these issues in more detail. The Septuagint, the second-century B.C.E. translation of the Hebrew Bible into Greek, identifies the figure on the throne in Ezekiel 1:26 with the form (*eidos*) of humanity. This term has a philosophical history starting in Plato's *Parmenides* 130C, in which it refers to the *idea* of humanity. Because of Plato's fortunate use of language, Hellenistic Jews like Philo could reunderstand the term "form of man," describing human resemblance to God in Genesis 1:26 and also occurring in biblical theophanies like Ezekiel 1:26, as referring to the Platonic *eidos* or idea of humanity, which inevitably meant for Platonists the unchanging immortal idea of humanity that survives death. So for Hellenistic Jewish mystics like Philo, the human figure on the divine throne described in Genesis, Exodus, Ezekiel, Daniel, and the Psalms (and which formed the basis of the "son of man" speculation) was also understood as the ideal and immortal man. His immortality and glorious appearance was something Adam possessed in the garden of Eden and lost when he sinned.[23] Paul, as we shall see, uses all these traditions to good advantage. In this form, the traditions are centuries older than Christianity.

In the Hellenistic period many new interpretations of this passage grew up. Foremost among the various names given to this angel in various Jewish groups and conventicles is "Yahoel" in the first century C.E. apocalyptic work the Apocalypse of Abraham. The name Yahoel illustrates one interpretation of carrying the divine name, since it is a combination of the Tetragrammaton and a suffix denoting angelic stature. Yahoel appears in chapters 10–11, where he is described as the one "in whom God's ineffable name dwells." Other titles for this figure included Melchizedek, Metatron, Adoil, Eremiel, and preeminently "the son of man."

Several Jewish traditions discuss the *eikōn* or image of God as Adam's prelapsarian appearance, an especially glorious and splendid form which humanity lost when Adam sinned, since humanity is described as made in "the image and form of God" in Genesis 1:26: *bslmnw bdmwtnw.* The same "image and form of God" is thereafter associated with God's human appearance in the Bible or the description of the principal angel of God who carries God's name. Most significantly, the human figure on the Merkabah which Ezekiel describes is called: "the appearance of the likeness of the glory of the Lord." Thus, God's Glory or *kābôd* can become a technical term for God's human appearances.[24]

Chief angelic mediators appear all through Jewish literature in Early Judaism.[25] The chief angelic mediator, which we may call by a number of terms—God's vice-regent, his Wazir, his gerent, or other terms expressing his status as principal angel—is easily distinguished from the plethora of divine creatures, for the principal angel is not only head of the heavenly hosts but sometimes participates in God's own being or divinity.

The rabbis often call God's principal angel Metatron. The term "Metatron" in rabbinic literature and Jewish mysticism is probably not a proper name but a title adapted from the Greek word *metathronos,* meaning "one who stands *after* or behind the throne." If so, it represents a rabbinic softening of the more normal Hellenistic term *synthronos,* meaning "one who is *with* the throne," sharing enthronement or acting for the properly throned authority. The rabbis would have changed the preposition from one connoting equality (*syn-*, "with") to one connoting inferiority (*meta-*, "after or behind") in order to reduce the heretical implications of calling God's principal helping angel his *synthronos.*[26]

Alongside these traditions lies the stranger but more relevant notion to Christianity in some apocalyptic-mystical groups that certain heroes can be transformed into angels as part of their ascension. This may easily be the most puzzling part of the mystic traditions, but it is the most important to summarize.[27] Amazingly, some patriarchs are exalted as angels. In the Testament of Abraham 11 (Recension A), Adam is pictured with a terrifying appearance and adorned with glory upon a golden throne. In chapters 12–13 Abel is similarly glorified, acting as judge over creation until the final judgment. 2 Enoch 30:8–11 also states that Adam was an angel: "And on earth I assigned him to be a second angel, honored and great and glorious."[28] In the Prayer of Joseph (found in Origen's Commentary on John 2:31, with a further fragment in *Philocalia* 23:15), Jacob describes himself as "an angel of God and a ruling spirit" and claims to be the "firstborn of every living thing," "the first minister before the face of God," "the archangel of the power of the Lord, and "the chief captain among the sons of God.'"[29]

Enoch and Moses, however, are the most important non-Christian figures of divinization or angelic transformation. For instance, Philo describes Moses as divine, based upon the word *God* used of him in Exodus 4:16 and 7:1. Thus, the Greek version of Sirach 45:1–5 compares Moses to God in the Hebrew or "equal in glory to the holy ones." Philo and the Samaritans also expressed Moses' preeminence in Jewish tradition by granting him a kind of deification.[30] In the Testament of Moses, Moses is described as the mediator or "arbiter of his covenant" (1:14), and he is celebrated as "that sacred spirit, worthy of the Lord . . . the Lord of the Word . . . the divine prophet throughout the earth, the most perfect teacher in the world," the "advocate," and "the great messenger" (11:16–19). Indeed, W. A. Meeks concluded that "Moses was the most important figure in all Hellenistic Jewish apologetic."[31]

Another important and rarely mentioned piece of evidence of the antiquity of mystical speculation about the *kābôd* is from the fragment of the tragedy *Moses* written by Ezekiel the Tragedian.[32] There, in a document of the second century B.C.E. or earlier, Moses is depicted as seeing a vision of the throne of God with a figure seated upon it. The figure on the throne is called *phōs gennaios,* "a venerable man," which is a double entendre in Greek, since *phōs* can mean either "light" or "man" depending on the gender of the noun.[33]

The surviving text of Ezekiel the Tragedian also hints at a transformation of an earthly hero into a divine figure when it relates that the venerable man (*phōs gennaios*) handed Moses his scepter and summoned him to sit upon the throne, placing a diadem on his head. Thereafter the stars bow to him and parade for his inspection. Since, as we have seen, throughout the biblical period the stars are thought to be angels (Job 38:7), there can be no doubt that Moses is here depicted as being leader of the angels and hence, above the angels. This enthronement scene with a human figure being exalted as a monarch or divinity in heaven resembles the enthronement of the "son of man"; the enthronement helps us understand some of the traditions that later appear in Jewish mysticism and may have informed Paul's ecstatic ascent. The identification of Jesus with the manlike appearance of God is both the central characteristic of Christianity and understandable within the context of Jewish mysticism and apocalypticism.[34]

Philo speaks of Moses as being made into a divinity (*eis theon*) in several places (e.g., *Sacrifices* 1–10; *Life of Moses* 1.155–58). In interpreting Moses' receiving the Ten Commandments, Philo envisions an ascent not merely up the mountain but to the heavens, possibly describing a mystical identification between this manifestation of God and Moses by suggesting that Moses attained to a divine nature through contact with the *logos*. In *Questions and Answers on Exodus* 1.29 and 40, Philo writes that on Sinai Moses was changed into a divinity. In *Life of Moses* 1.155–58, he says that God placed the entire universe into Moses' hands and that all the elements obeyed him as their master; then God rewarded Moses by appointing him a "partner" (*koinōnon*) of his own possessions and gave into his hand the world as a portion well fitted for his heir (155). In the *Sacrifices of Cain and Abel* 8–10, Philo refers to Deuteronomy 5:31 as proof that certain people are distinguished by God to be stationed "beside himself." Moses is preeminent among these people for his grave is not known, which for Philo apparently means that Moses was transported to heaven.

Many of these themes will surface in Christianity, reapplied to Jesus Christ, but the term "partner" (*šwtp*), describing any of God's helpers, will be understood as heresy by the rabbis. Thus, the sides were set for a great conflict in the first two centuries C.E., all concerned with the existence, nature, status, and meaning of God's primary angelic mediator. Merkabah themes of viewing God may also be witnessed in Philo's allegory. In light of the subsequent battle, it is amazing that such a prominent Jew of the first century c.e. as Philo could suggest so clearly a mystical merging of humans with this divine manifestation.[35] But Philo himself cannot possibly be the author of these traditions. Although he was relying on the Hebrew Bible, he must also have had access to traditions that amplified these texts in a mystical direction, as did the other Hellenistic Jewish writers.

PAUL'S USE OF ASCENSION AND TRANSFORMATION

Paul gives the best evidence for the existence of ecstatic journeys to heaven in first-century Judaism, with his reports in 2 Corinthians 12.[36] His inability to decide whether the voyage took place in the body or out of the body is firm evidence of a mystical ascent and shows that the voyage has not been interiorized as a journey into the self, which later becomes common in Kabbalah. Furthermore, since the rabbis proscribed the discussion of these topics except singly, to mature disciples, and only if they had experienced it on their own (*mbyn md'tw*, m.Hag 2:1), the rabbinic stories interpreting the Merkabah experience often take place during travels through the wilderness from city to city when such doctrines could easily be discussed in private. This is precisely the scene that Luke picks for Paul's conversion.[37]

Paul also reveals much about the mystical religion of transformation as it was experienced in the first century c.e. D. Capes has demonstrated that Paul understands *kyrios* to refer to the Hebrew name of God and that he applies this title to Christ.[38] Paul himself designates Christ as the image of the Lord in a few places (2Cor 4:4; Col 1:15 [if it is Pauline]), and he mentions the *morphē* of God in Philippians 2:6.[39] More often he talks of transforming believers into the image of his son in various ways (Rom 8:29; 2Cor 3:18; Phil 3:21; and 1Cor 15:49; see also Col 3:9), as we have already seen. These passages are critical to comprehending what Paul's experience of conversion was. They must be seen in closer detail to understand the relationship to Jewish apocalypticism and mysticism, from which they derive their most complete significance for Paul. Paul's longest discussion of these themes occurs in an unlikely place in 2 Corinthians 3:18–4:6. Here he assumes the context rather than explaining it completely:

And we all, with unveiled face, beholding the glory of the Lord, are being changed into his likeness from one degree of glory to another; for this comes from the Lord who is the Spirit. Therefore, having his ministry by the mercy of God, we do not lose heart. We have renounced disgraceful, underhanded ways; we refuse to practice cunning or to tamper with God's word, but by the open statement of the truth we would commend ourselves to every man's conscience in the sight of God. And even if our gospel is veiled it is veiled only to those who are perishing. In their case, the god of this world has blinded the minds of the unbelievers to keep them from seeing the light of the gospel of the glory of Christ, who is the likeness of God. For what we preach is not ourselves, but Jesus Christ as Lord, with ourselves as your servants for Jesus' sake. For it is the God who said, "Let light shine out of darkness," who has shone in our hearts to give the light of the knowledge of the glory of the Lord in the face of Christ. (2Cor 3:18–4:6)

The polemical context of this section of Paul's letter (2Cor 3:1–17) should be noted, but I cannot deal with it here. For now, the main point must be the usually unappreciated use of the language of transformation in Paul's works. In 2 Corinthians 3:18, Paul says that believers will be changed into Christ's likeness from one degree of glory to another. He refers to Exodus 33 and 34, where Moses' encounter with the angel of the Lord is narrated. Earlier in that passage, the angel of the Lord is described as carrying the name of God (Ex 23:21). Moses sees the Glory of the Lord, makes a covenant, receives the commandments upon the two tables of the law and, when he comes down from the mount, the skin of his face shines with light, as the Bible states (Ex 34:29–35). Moses thereafter must wear a veil except when he is in the presence of the Lord. Paul assumes that Moses made an ascension to the presence of the Lord, was transformed by that encounter, and that his shining face is a reflection of the encounter.

So far Paul is using significant mystical language. But what is immediately striking is that Paul uses that language to discuss his own and other Christians' experience in Christ. Paul explicitly compares Moses' experience with his own and that of Christian believers. Their transformation is of the same sort, but the Christian transformation is greater and permanent. Once the background of the vocabulary is pointed out, Paul's daring claims for Christian experience become clear. The point, therefore, is that some Christian believers also make such an ascent somehow and that its effects are more enduring than the vision which Moses received. The church has witnessed a theophany as important as the one vouchsafed to Moses, but the Christian theophany is greater still, as Paul himself has experienced. The Corinthians are said to be a message from Christ (2Cor 3:2), who is equated with the Glory of God. The new community of Gentiles is not a letter written on stone (Jer 31:33), but it is delivered by Paul as Moses delivered the Torah to Israel. The new dispensation is more splendid than the last, not needing the veil with which Moses hid his face. Paul's own experience proved to him and for Christianity that all will be transformed.

Thus, Paul's term, "the glory of the Lord," must be taken both as a reference to Christ and as a technical term for the *kābôd* (*kbwd*), the human form of God appearing in biblical visions. In 2 Corinthians 3:18, Paul says that Christians behold the Glory of the Lord (*tēn doxan kyriou*) as in a mirror and are transformed into his image (*tēn autēn eikona*).[40]

Although Paul may be using language taken from his opponents, he characterizes his apostolate as proclaiming that the face of *Christ* is the glory of God. It is very difficult not to read this passage in terms of Paul's description of the ascension of "the man" to the third heaven and conclude that Paul's mystical visions also involved his identification of Jesus as the "image" and "glory of God," as the human figure in heaven, and thereafter as Christ, son, and savior. For Paul, as for the earliest Jewish mystics, to be privileged enough to see the *kābôd* or Glory (*doxa*) of God is a prologue to transformation into his image (*eikōn*). Paul does not say that all Christians have made the journey literally but compares the experience of knowing Christ to being allowed into the intimate presence of the Lord.

The result of the journey is to identify Christ as the "Glory of God." When Paul says that he preaches that Jesus is Lord and that God "has let this light shine out of darkness into our hearts to give the light of knowledge of the glory of God in the face of Christ" (2Cor 4:6), he seems clearly to be describing his own conversion and ministry, just as he described it in Galatians 1, and just as he is explaining the experience to new converts for the purpose of furthering conversion.

Paul's famous description of Christ's experience of humility and obedience in Philippians 2:5-11 also hints that the identification of Jesus with the image of God was reenacted in the church in a liturgical mode:

Have this mind among yourselves, which is yours in Christ Jesus, who though he was in the form of God, did not count equality with God a thing to be grasped, but emptied himself, taking the form of a servant, being born in the likeness of men. And being found in human form he humbled himself and became obedient unto death, even death on a cross. Therefore God has highly exalted him and bestowed on him the name which is above every name that at the name of Jesus every knee should bow, in heaven and on earth and under the earth, and every tongue confess that Jesus Christ is Lord, to the glory of God the Father.

This passage has several hymnic features which lead scholars to believe that Paul is quoting a fragment of primitive liturgy or referring to a liturgical setting.[41] Thus Philippians 2 may easily be the earliest writing in the Pauline corpus as well as the earliest christology in the New Testament. It is not surprising that it is the most exalted christology.[42]

In Philippians 2:6, the identification of Jesus with the form of God implies his preexistence. The Christ is depicted as an eternal aspect of divinity which was not proud of its high station but consented to take on the shape of a human and suffer the fate of humans, "even death on a cross" (though many scholars see this phrase as a Pauline addition to the original hymn).

The transformation from divinity to humanity is followed by the converse, the retransformation into God. Because of this obedience, God exalted him and bestowed on him the "name which is above every name" (Phil 2:9). For a Jew this phrase can only mean that Jesus received the divine name, the Tetragrammaton YHWH, understood as the Greek name *kyrios,* or Lord. We have already seen that sharing in the divine name is a frequent motif of the early Jewish apocalypticism, in which the principal angelic mediator of God is or carries the name Yahweh, as Exodus 23 describes the angel of Yahweh. Indeed the implication of the Greek term *morphē* ("form") is that Christ has the form of a divine body identical with the *kābôd,* the Glory, and equivalent also with the *eikōn,* for humanity is made after the *eikōn* of God and thus has the divine *morphē* (or in Hebrew: *dĕmût*). The climax of Paul's confession is that "Jesus Christ is Lord to the glory of God the Father" (Phil 2:11), meaning that Jesus, the Messiah, has received the name Lord in his glorification, and that this name, not Jesus' private earthly name, is the one that will cause every knee to bend and every tongue to confess.[43]

In paraphrasing this fragment from liturgy, Paul witnesses that the early Christian community directed its prayers to this human figure of divinity along with God (1Cor 16:22; Rom 10:9–12; 1Cor 12:3)—all the more striking since the Christians, like the Jews, refuse to give any other god or hero any veneration at all. When the Hillelite rabbis gained control of the Jewish community, they vociferously argued against the worship of any angel and specifically polemicized against the belief that a heavenly figure other than God can forgive sins (b.Sanh 38b), quoting Exodus 23:21 prominently among other scriptures to prove their point. The heresy itself they call believing that there are "two powers in heaven." By this term the rabbis largely (but not exclusively) referred to Christians who, as Paul says, do exactly what the rabbis warn against: they worship the second power.[44]

Concomitant with Paul's worship of the divine Christ is transformation. Paul says in Philippians 3:10 "that I may know him and the power of his resurrection and may share his sufferings, becoming like him (*synmorphizomenos*) in his death." Later, in Philippians 3:20–21, he says: "But our commonwealth is in heaven, and from it we await a savior, the Lord Jesus Christ, who will change (*metaschēmatisei*) our lowly body to be like (*symmorphon*) his glorious body, by the power which enables him even to subject all things to himself." The body of the believer eventually is to be transformed into the body of Christ.

Paul's depiction of salvation is based on his understanding of Christ's glorification, partaking of early Jewish apocalyptic mysticism for its expression.[45] In Romans 12:2 Paul's listeners are exhorted to "be transformed (*metamorphousthe*) by renewing of your minds." In Galatians 4:19 Paul expresses another transformation: "My little children, with whom I am again in travail until Christ be formed (*morphōthē*) in you! This transformation is to be effected by becoming like him in his death (*symmorphizomenos tō thanatō autou*, Phil 3:10).

1 Corinthians 15:42–51 is one of the most systematic uses of this apocalyptic and mystical tradition, which seems so central to Paul's message of the meaning of Christ:

> So is it with the resurrection of the dead. What is sown is perishable, what is raised is imperishable. It is sown in dishonor, it is raised in glory. It is sown in weakness, it is raised in power. It is sown a physical body, it is raised a spiritual body. If there is a physical body, there is also a spiritual body. Thus it is written. "The first man Adam became a living being"; the last Adam became a life-giving spirit. But it is not the spiritual which is first but the physical, and then the spiritual. The first man was from the earth, a man of dust; the second man is from heaven. As was the man of dust, so are those who are of the dust; and as is the man of heaven, so are those who are of heaven. Just as we have borne

the image of the man of dust, we shall also bear the image of the man of heaven. I tell you this, brethren: flesh and blood cannot inherit the kingdom of God, nor does the perishable inherit the imperishable.

As Paul connects his own conversion with his resurrection in Christ, so it is resurrection which brings the salvation of God and a return to the pristine state of humanity's glory before Adam's fall. He says this explicitly in 1 Corinthians 15:21: "For as by a man came death; so by a man has also come resurrection of the dead." Paul portrays Adam and Christ as contrasting images of fall and salvation respectively. But Paul seems to have more than Jesus' earthly existence in mind, since he uses the term *anthrōpos*, which can also refer to his resurrected nature: "Just as we have borne the image of the man of dust, we shall also bear the image of the man of heaven."[46] The agent that begins and is responsible for this change on earth is the Spirit. The Spirit not only creates the Christ that is within believers; the Spirit itself has taken on the character of Christ. The risen Jesus is to be experienced as a life-giving Spirit, explaining how the transformation starts, just as it is to be experienced as the last Adam, in which, one supposes, is the culmination of the mystic process in the apocalyptic end.[47]

Speaking of the resurrection, Paul describes a reciprocal relationship between Adam and Christ: just as Adam brought death into the world so Christ, the second Adam, will bring resurrection. This depends on an interpretation of Adam's divine likeness as being identical to the glory which "the Christ" had or received. Because of the first human, all humanity is brought to death; but because of Christ's divine image all will be brought to life (1Cor 15:21–22). The first man, Adam, became only a living soul, whereas the last Adam became a life-giving spirit (15:45). The first man was of the earth and therefore earthly; the last man is from heaven, therefore divine. Just as humanity has borne the outward image of the old Adam, those who inherit the kingdom will also bear the inward spiritual *eikōn* of the heavenly man (15:47–49). Paul, however, is not so much talking about the man Jesus as about Christ's exalted nature as *anthrōpos*. Since the imagery is so dependent on the contrast between fallen and raised states, this passage may also imply a baptismal setting. It is also interesting that the alternation is conceived of in bodily terms, not as a transmigration of souls.

When Paul says that Christians shall be raised imperishable, as he does in the famous passage in 1 Corinthians 15:51–52, the best background for his conception is his other descriptions of transformation into the raised Christ. This is exactly the context into which Paul himself puts it. His view of the coming end is merely the culmination of the process that has started with conversion and baptism: "We shall not all sleep, but we shall all be *changed,* in a moment, in the twinkling of an eye, at the last trumpet. For the trumpet will sound, and the dead will be raised imperishable and we shall be changed."

Paul's view of the immortality of believers is parallel to his description of the raised Christ in heaven and depends on it. The believer is to share in Christ's immortality at the last trumpet, just as Paul himself experienced *transformation* by Christ. It appears that Paul considers himself special in that to him has been revealed the whole process of salvation. Others have not had his visions, so his visions give him special powers to speak of the meaning of Christian life. But the process has started within the Christian community, continuing there, whether those who have acknowledged Christ recognize it or not. Although Jesus' humanity is mentioned here and in Romans 5, where a similar theme is voiced, it is not the human life that is the point of the exegesis. Here, it is his resurrection and metamorphosis into the true man that power the analogy. *Christ* is the man *from heaven.* His power on earth is the Spirit.

Of course, the mystical experience of conversion is not only with the *risen Christ* but with the *crucified Christ.* The most obvious relationship between the believer and Christ is suffering and death (Rom 7:24; 8:10, 13). By being transformed by Christ, one is not simply made immortal, given the power to remain deathless. Rather, one still experiences death as Christ did and, like him, survives death for heavenly enthronement. This is a consequence of the Christian's divided state. Although part of the last Adam, living through the Spirit, the Christian also belongs to the world of the flesh. As Dunn noted:

> Suffering was something *all* believers experienced—an unavoidable part of the believer's lot—an aspect of experience as Christians which his converts shared with Paul: Rom. 5:3 ('we'); 8:17f ('we'); 2 Cor. 1:16 ('you endure the same sufferings that we suffer'); 8:2; Phil. 1:29f ('the same conflict which you saw and now hear to be mine'); 1 Thess. 1:6 ('imitators of us and of the Lord'); 2:14 ('imitators of the churches of God in Judea: for you suffered the same things'); 3:3f ('our lot') 2 Thess. 1:4ff.[48]

Thus, the persecution and suffering of the believers is a sign that the transformation process has begun; it is the way to come to be *in* Christ. Paul is convinced that being united with Christ's crucifixion means not immediate *glorification* but *suffering* for the believers in this interim period. The glorification follows upon the final consummation. The connection between suffering and resurrection has been clear in Jewish martyrology; indeed, the connection between death and rebirth was even a prominent part of the mystery religions as well. But the particular way in which Paul makes these connections is explicitly Christian.

In the letters of the Pauline school, some of these themes receive even fuller development. Colossians is a veritable summary of the whole constellation of language describing transformation into the heavenly kābôd, understood as the Christ. In 1:15–20, the Christ is called, "the image of the invisible God," and the "firstborn of all creation" (v. 16). He is the author of creation and the captain of the heavenly hosts and is coeternal with God. As Christ, he is also "firstborn from the dead." He is the head of the body, the church, a remark that hints at possible relationships with Jewish *Shiur Koma* speculation as well as pagan concepts of the *macranthropos*.

In Colossae, important baptismal practices developed that were similar to Jewish mysticism at Qumran.[49] Colossians 3:10 speaks of Christians as having taken off an old nature and put on a new nature in baptism, "which is being renewed in knowledge after the image of its creator." Ephesians 4:24 speaks also of putting on a new nature created after the likeness of God. This language of transformation comes from Jewish apocalyptic mysticism, yet it implies a specifically Christian theology and a baptismal setting. If contemporary scholars are not convinced of the Pauline authorship of these letters, one can nonetheless say that these writings give irrefutable evidence about the popularity of Paul's mystical teaching among his earliest disciples and the direction in which these teachings were interpreted.

THE ANGEL SHAPED LIKE A MAN AND THE GOSPELS

Based on Jewish mystical traditions and Paul's writings, we can speculate about the logical chronology and development of the Gospel traditions. Heavenly man traditions are crucial to the development of the Christian meaning of Jesus' earthly mission.[50] They inform all the studies of the New

Testament Son of Man in ways that have been infrequently discussed by the leading scholars studying the term "Son of Man."[51] While it is quite likely that some of Jesus' followers thought of him as a Messiah during his own lifetime, they were disabused of that idea by his arrest, trial, and death on the cross as "the King of the Jews," for no pre-Christian view of the Messiah conceived of the possibility of his demise at the hands of the Romans.[52] Instead, the disciples' experience of Jesus' resurrection and ascension to the right hand of God confirmed the originally discarded messianic title retrospectively in a new, dynamic, and ironic way. Resurrection and ascension had already entered Jewish thought in the century previous to Jesus, as a reward for the righteous martyrs of the Maccabean wars. Thus, while Christianity represents a pure Jewish reaction to a tragic series of events, the reaction was at the same time impressively novel. The process should be of special interest to Jewish scholars as well as students of christology, because it is the clearest evidence we have from the first century c.e. on how new religious groups were "created" and how Jewish expectations were derived from biblical texts. The events were given meaning by creative interplay between the historical facts and the hermeneutic process.

Since Jesus died as a martyr, expectations of his resurrection would have been normal in some Jewish groups.[53] But the idea of a crucified Messiah was unique. In such a situation, the Christians only did what other believing Jews did in similar circumstances; they turned to biblical prophecy for elucidation. No messianic text suggested itself as appropriate to the situation. But Psalm 110:1 was exactly apposite: "The Lord says to my lord: 'Sit at my right hand, until I make your enemies your footstool.'" Here was a description of the enthronement of a Davidic descendant, now understood as a heavenly enthronement after death and resurrection. Yet nothing in the text makes the death-or-resurrection part of the narrative inevitable. It must have come from the historical circumstances of the early Christian community, after they experienced these events. Thereafter, Psalm 110:1 could be combined easily with Daniel 7:9–13, the description of the enthronement of the "son of man." Daniel 7:9–13 seemed to describe the apposite scene of Christ's exaltation and ascension, because Jesus could be identified with the "Son of Man," the angelic figure. Furthermore Daniel 12:2 promised astral immortality to those who taught wisdom, making plausible while it confirmed the entire set of expectations.

Jesus apparently used the term "Son of Man," though the expression has perplexed modern scholars. Jesus may have predicted the future coming of a human figure, or he may not have referred to the Daniel passage at all.[54]

After his crucifixion and the experience of his resurrection, the Son-of-Man phrases Jesus used were put in the context of the famous statement in Daniel 7:13 about the enthronement of the "son of man." Jesus' disciples understood that his victory over death was followed by his ascension and enthronement in heaven as the gigantic angelic or divine figure who was to bring God's coming justice. Through the imagery of the "Son of Man," the man Jesus was associated with the figure on the throne in Daniel 7:13, and the traditions of Jesus' messianic function were associated with traditions about the "son of man," taking on a uniquely Christian interpretation. Like the description of the venerable fatherly figure in Ezekiel the Tragedian's writing, the scene in Daniel involves the enthronement of an "Ancient of Days" with the "Son of Man" coming to sit next to the "Ancient of Days." The traditions themselves were present in Judaism before Christianity, but it was Jesus' life and mission, together with the post-Easter expectations of his followers, that brought messianism, judgment, and heavenly ascent together in just this particular way.[55]

The Christians identified the "Son of Man," the human or angelic representation of God, with the risen Christ.[56] Christians took the second "Lord" of Psalm 110:1 to refer to Jesus and to signify the divine name Lord. Thereafter, the risen Christ was understood as an aspect of the divinity.[57] Since the angel with the human figure was also divine himself, carrying the name YHWH (Ex 23:21), Jesus can be said to have attained to divinity. For the Gospel of John, Christ also was *logos,* God's intermediary form and *light,* which was Philo's term for God's principal hypostasis as well. Christ as "son" is said to be above the angels, just as Moses is enthroned and worshiped by the stars in Ezekiel the Tragedian's work. This is made explicit in the later document, Hebrews 1:8, where the "son" is identified with the Elohim in Psalm 45:7.

Many of the secrets of Qumran have yet to be unlocked. But it is clear that the Dead Sea Scrolls have an important role to play in understanding the apocalyptic and mystical environment out of which Christianity arose. The best parallels appear to be those of analogy, for both Christianity and the Qumran group represent Jewish movements in the first century C.E. that took a stand against the rulers of that day, looked to heaven for salvation and the destruction of their unrighteous opponents, and envisioned salvation in terms of transformation into angelic creatures as a reward for their steadfastness.

Notes

1. Some of the information in this article has been adapted from my *Paul the Convert* (New Haven, 1990) and is used with permission.

2. L. Hurtado, *One God, One Lord: Early Christian Devotion and Ancient Jewish Monotheism* (Philadelphia, 1988). These paragraphs closely follow his history of scholarship.

3. W. Lueken, *Michael* (Göttingen, 1898).

4. J. Barbel, *Christos Angelos: Die Anschauung von Christus als Bote und Engel in der gelebten und volkstümlichen Literatur der christlichen Altertums* (Bonn, 1941, repr. 1964).

5. M. Werner, *Die Entstehung des christlichen Dogmas* (Bern, 1941; 2d ed., 1954); Eng. trans. by S. G. F. Brandon as *The Formation of Christian Dogma* (New York, 1957; repr. Boston, 1965).

6. W. Michaelis, *Zur Engelchristologie im Urchristentum: Abbau der Konstruction Martin Werners* (Basel, 1942).

7. G. Kretschmar, *Studien zur Frühchristlichen Trinitätstheologie* (Tübingen, 1956).

8. J. Daniélou, *The Theology of Jewish Christianity*, vol. 1 of *The Development of Christian Doctrine Before the Council of Nicaea*, trans. and ed. J. A. Baker (London, 1964; U.S. edition, Chicago, 1964).

9. I am indebted to N. Dahl, *Christology Notes* (unpublished) and G. Quispel, *Gnostic Studies* (Istanbul, 1974); see A. F. Segal, *Two Powers in Heaven: Early Rabbinic Reports about Christianity and Gnosticism* (Leiden, 1977); J. Fossum, *The Name of God and the Angel of the Lord* (WUNT 36; Tübingen, 1985); C. Rowland, *The Open Heaven: A Study of Apocalyptic in Judaism* (New York, 1982); idem, *Christian Origins: From Messianic Movement to Christian Religion* (Minneapolis, 1985); R. Longenecker, *The Theology of Early Jewish Christianity* (Grand Rapids, 1981; from the London, 1970 edition). Also see J. H. Charlesworth, "The Portrayal of the Righteous as an Angel," in *Ideal Figures in Ancient Judaism: Profiles and Paradigms*, ed G. W. E. Nickelsburg and J. J. Collins (SCS 12; Chico, Calif., 1980).

10. J. A. Fitzmyer, "IV Addendum: Implications of the 4Q 'Son of God' Text" in "Qumran Aramaic and the New Testament," reprinted in *A Wandering Aramean: Collected Aramaic Essays* (Missoula, Mont., 1979) pp. 102–7.

11. F. J. Horton, *The Melchizedek Tradition: A Critical Examination of the Sources to the Fifth Century A.D. and in the Epistle to the Hebrews* (Cambridge, 1976); P. J. Kobelski, *Melchizedek and Melchireša'* (Washington, D.C., 1981); S. F. Noll, "Angelology in the Qumran Texts" (Ph.D. diss., Manchester, 1979); G. Quispel, "Gnosticism and the New Testament," in *The Bible and Modern Scholarship*, ed. J. P. Hyatt (Nashville, 1965) pp. 252–71; idem, "The Origins of the Gnostic Demiurge," in *Kyriakon: Festschrift Johannes Quasten*, ed. P. Granfield and J. A. Jungman (Münster, 1970) vol. 1, pp. 272–76.

12.   The Enoch literature is possibly as old as or older than the Daniel "son of man" traditions in which it participates. M. A. Knibb, *The Ethiopic Book of Enoch* (Oxford, 1978).

13.   M. Black, "The Throne-Theophany Prophetic Commission and the 'Son of Man': A Study in Tradition-History," in *Jews, Greeks, and Christians: Religious Cultures in Late Antiquity,* ed. R. Hamerton-Kelly and R. Scroggs (Leiden, 1976) pp. 57–73; C. Rowland, "The Vision of the Risen Christ in Rev. 1:13ff.: The Debt of an Early Christology to an Aspect of Jewish Angelology," *JTS* 31 (1980) 1–11; and J. Fossum, "Jewish Christian Christology and Jewish Mysticism," *VC* 37 (1983) 260–87.

14.   Trans. E. Isaac, in *OTP,* vol. 1, p. 50.

15.   In 2 Baruch the righteous dead are promised equality with the angels and the stars (51:10) and then splendor even greater than that of the angels (51:12).

16.   On the topic of the use of Ezekiel, see D. Halperin, *The Faces of the Chariot: Early Jewish Responses to Ezekiel's Vision* (Tübingen, 1988), esp. pp. 49–55.

17.   J. Strugnell, "The Angelic Liturgy at Qumran—4 Q Serekh Shirot 'Olat ha-shabbat," in *Congress Volume: Oxford 1959* (VTSup 7; Leiden, 1960) pp. 318–45. Y. Yadin, J. M. Baumgarten, N. S. Fujita, and C. Rowland discussed different aspects of the material (see bibliography in Halperin, *Faces of the Chariot,* p. 50 and notes). See also the commentary by L. H. Schiffman, "Merkabah Speculation at Qumran: The 4Q Serekh Shirot 'Olat ha-Shabbat," in *Mystics, Philosophers, and Politicians: Essays in Jewish Intellectual History in Honor of Alexander Altmann,* ed. J. Reinharz and D. Swetchinski (Durham, N.C., 1982) pp. 15–47.

18.   See C. Newsom, *Songs of the Sabbath Sacrifice: A Critical Edition* (HSS 27; Atlanta, 1985) esp. pp. 45–58.

19.   M. Smith, "Ascent to the Heavens and Deification in 4QMª," in *Archaeology and History in the Dead Sea Scrolls: The New York University Conference in Memory of Yigael Yadin,* ed. L. H. Schiffman (JSPS; JSOT/ASOR 2; Sheffield, 1990).

20.   M. Baillet, *Qumran grôtte 4,* DJD 7 (Oxford, 1982) no. 491.

21.   In any event, Smith's translation parallels other hints of ascension in the Qumran texts. See, e.g., 4QAgesCreat 2; 4QpIsa 11.1–4; 1QSb; 1QH 3.3; 3.19; 4.12; 7.22; 18.16; and fragment 2.

22.   See on a related theme, J. H. Charlesworth, "The Jewish Roots of Christology: The Discovery of the Hypostatic Voice," *SJT* 39 (1986) 19–41.

23.   See G. Quispel, "Hermetism and the New Testament, Especially Paul," in *ANRW* II.22 (forthcoming); and Fossum, *Name,* p. 278.

24.   See C. Newman, "'Glory of God in the Face of Jesus': A Tradition-Historical Investigation into the Origin of Paul's Identification of Christ as 'Doxa'" (Diss., Baylor University, 1989) for a sound analysis of the Hebrew Bible references to the *kābôd* or Glory.

25.   See my *Two Powers,* pp. 182–219; P. Schäfer, *Rivalität zwischen Engeln und Menschen: Untersuchungen zur rabbinischen Engelvorstellung* (Berlin, New York, 1975)

pp. 9–74; H. B. Kuhn, "The Angelology of the Non-Canonical Apocalypses," *JBL* 67 (1948) 217–32; F. Stier, *Gott und sein Engel im Alten Testament* (Münster, 1934).

26. See S. Lieberman, "Metatron, the Meaning of his name and his Functions," Appendix in I. Gruenwald's *Apocalyptic and Merkabah Mysticism* (AGJU 14; Leiden, 1980) pp. 235–41, esp. pp. 237–39.

27. For the growing consensus that apocalypticism implies visionary or "mystical" experience as well as secret knowledge of the end of time, see Rowland, *Open Heaven;* Charlesworth, "Portrayal of the Righteous as an Angel," in *Ideal Figures in Ancient Judaism,* ed. Nickelsburg and Collins; and M. Idel, *Kabbalah: New Perspectives* (New Haven, 1988).

28. Trans. M. Pravednoe, in *OTP,* vol. 1, p. 152.

29. J. Z. Smith, "The Prayer of Joseph," in *Religions in Antiquity,* ed. J. Neusner (SHR 14; Leiden, 1968) pp. 253–94. See A. M. Denis, *Fragmenta Pseudepigraphorum quae Supetrunt Graeca Una Cum Historicum et Auctorum Judaeorum Hellenistarum Fragmentis* (Leiden, 1970) pp. 61–62.

30. E. R. Goodenough, *By Light, Light: The Mystic Gospel of Hellenistic Judaism* (New Haven, 1935) pp. 199–234; W. A. Meeks, *The Prophet-King* (NovTSup 14; Leiden, 1967); idem, "Moses as God and King," in *Religions in Antiquity,* ed. J. Neusner (SHR 14; Leiden, 1968) pp. 354–71; idem, "The Divine Agent and His Counterfeit in Philo and the Fourth Gospel," in *Aspects of Religious Propaganda in Judaism and Early Christianity,* ed. E. S. Fiorenza (Notre Dame, 1976) pp. 43–67; C. R. Holladay, *Theios Anēr in Hellenistic Judaism* (SBLDS 40; Missoula, Mont., 1977) pp. 103–69.

31. Meeks, "The Divine Agent," in *Aspects of Religious Propaganda,* ed. Fiorenza, p. 45; see also Hurtado, "Exalted Patriarchs," in *One God, One Lord.*

32. See G. Quispel, "Ezekiel 1:26 in Jewish Mysticism and Gnosis," *VC* 34 (1980) 1–10; his review of J. Frickel, *Hellenistische Erlösung in christlicher Deutung* (Nag Hammadi Studies 19; Leiden, 1984) in *VC* 39 (1985) 196–99; also Quispel, "Gnosis," in *Die orientalischen Religionen im Römerreich,* ed. M. J. Vermaseren (Leiden, 1981) pp. 413–35; see also C. R. Holladay, "The Portrait of Moses in Ezekiel the Tragedian," in *SBL 1976 Seminar Papers* (Missoula, Mont., 1976) pp. 447–52; H. Jacobson, "Mysticism and Apocalyptic in Ezekiel's Exagoge," *Illinois Classical Studies* 6 (1981) 272–93; P. van der Horst, "Moses' Throne Vision in Ezekiel the Dramatist," *JJS* 34 (1983) 21–29; idem, "Some Notes on the *Exagoge* of Ezekiel," *Mnemosyne* 37 (1984) 354–75.

33. See *The Exagoge of Ezekiel,* ed. H. Jacobson (Cambridge, 1983) lines 68–89 (pp. 54–55). Jacobson denies that there is any mystical content to the book. But this is not the best conclusion from these traditions. For one thing, those scholars who most vociferously deny the mystical content of these traditions seem to have an anachronistic idea of mysticism. R. G. Robertson has pointed out, if only in passing, the relevance of this passage to the "son of man" figure. See his translation of EzekTrag in *OTP,* vol. 2, p. 812 and n. b2.

34. See Segal, *Two Powers;* see also Dahl, Quispel, Fossum, and Hurtado, as cited in n. 59.

35. See Segal, *Two Powers,* pp. 159–82; and Fossum, *Name,* pp. 268ff. For the whole picture of Philo's allegory on this topic, see L. K. K. Dey, *The Intermediary World and Patterns of Perfection in Philo and Hebrews* (SBLDS 25; Missoula, Mont., 1975). See especially now Hurtado, *One God, One Lord.*

36. T. Callan, "Prophecy and Ecstasy in Greco-Roman Religion and in 1 Corinthians," *NovT* 27 (1985) 125–40.

37. A. Neher, "Le Voyage mystique de Quatre," *RevHistRel* 140 (1951) 59–82; and N. Sèd, "Les traditions secrètes et les disciples de Rabban Yohanan b. Zakkai," *RevHistRel* 184 (1973) 49–66.

38. D. B. Capes, "Paul's Use of Old Testament Yahweh-Texts and Its Implications for Paul's Christology" (Doctoral diss., South West Baptist Theological Seminary, 1990).

39. In this section, I am particularly indebted to Quispel, "Hermetism and the New Testament."

40. The use of the mirror here is also a magico-mystical theme, which can be traced to the word ʿyn occurring in Ezekiel 1. Although it is sometimes translated otherwise, ʿyn probably refers to a mirror even there, and possibly refers to some unexplained technique for achieving ecstasy. The mystic bowls of the magical papyri and talmudic times were filled with water and oil to reflect light and stimulate trance. The magical papyri describe spells which use a small bowl that serves as the medium for the appearance of a god for divination: e.g., *PGM* 4.154–285 (Betz, pp. 40–43), *PDM* 14.1–92, 295–308, 395–427, 528–53, 627–35, 805–40, 841–50, 851–55 (Betz, pp. 195–200, 213, 218–19, 225–26, 229, 236–39). The participant concentrates on the reflection in the water's surface, often with oil added to the mixture, sometimes with the light of a lamp nearby. Lamps and charms are also used to produce divinations, presumably because they can stimulate trance under the proper conditions. The *Reuyoth Yehezkel,* for instance, mentions that Ezekiel's mystical vision was stimulated by looking into the waters of the River Chebar. It seems to me that Philo appropriates the mystic imagery of the mirror to discuss the allegorical exposition of scripture; see *The Contemplative Life* 78. See also D. Georgi, *Die Gegner des Paulus im 2. Korintherbrief* (Neukirchen-Vluyn, 1964) pp. 272–73; also Schulz, *ZNW* 49 (1958) 1–30. Paul's opponents then look into the mirror and see only the text. But because Paul and those truly in Christ actually behold the Glory of the Lord, they have a clearer vision on the truth. See my *Paul the Convert,* ch. 6, for further discussion of Paul's opponents in Corinthians. My thanks to D. Balch for insisting that I deal with these issues, though he will no doubt dissent from my opinion.

41. R. P. Martin, *Carmen Christi: Philippians 2:5–11 in Recent Interpretation and in the Setting of Early Christian Worship,* (Grand Rapids, 1983 [rev. ed. from

the Cambridge University Press, 1967 edition]). See also J. Sanders, "Dissenting Deities and Phil. 2:1–11," *JBL* 88 (1969) 279–90.

42. The other candidate, Peter's Pentecost discourse in Acts 3, seems to me to have undergone much more editing before reaching written form. See J. A. T. Robinson, "The Most Primitive Christology of All," in *Twelve New Testament Studies* (London, 1962) reprinted from *JTS* 7 (1956) 177–89; R. Zehnle, *Peter's Pentecost Discourse* (Nashville, 1971).

43. The bibliography on the Pauline and post-Pauline hymns in Phil 2:6–11 and Col 1:15–20 appears endless. See E. Schillebeeckx, *Jesus: An Experiment in Christology* (New York, 1979); M. Hengel, "Hymn and Christology," in *Between Jesus and Paul,* ed. E. A. Livingstone (Philadelphia, 1983) pp. 78–96; J. Murphy-O'Connor, "Christological Anthropology in Phil. 2:6–11," *RB* 83 (1976) 25–50; and D. Georgi, "Der vorpaulinische Hymnus Phil. 2:6–11," in *Zeit und Geschichte: Dankesgabe an Rudolf Bultmann,* ed. E. Dinkler (Tübingen, 1964) pp. 263–93, esp. p. 291 for bibliography. As Balch reminds me, Käsemann emphasizes that Paul's metaphorical use of the body and its separate parts is characteristic of parenetic sections, emphasizing the relationship between the believer and the risen Lord. See E. Schweitzer, *TDNT,* vol. 7, s.v. "*sōma,*" p. 1073.

44. See my *Two Powers,* pp. 33–158, esp. pp. 68–73; and now Hurtado, *Binitarian,* pp. 377–91.

45. Scholars (e.g., S. Kim) who want to ground all of Paul's thought in a single ecstatic conversion experience which they identify with Luke's accounts of Paul's conversion, are reticent to accept this passage as a fragment from Christian liturgy because to do so would destroy its value as Paul's personal revelatory experience. But there is no need to decide whether the passage is originally Paul's (hence received directly through the "Damascus revelation"), since ecstatic language normally is derived from traditions current within the religious group. Christian mystics use Christian language; Muslim mystics use the languages developed for mysticism in Islam; and no mystic is ever confused by another religion's mysticism unless it is the conscious and explicit intent of the mystic's vision to do so. See R. C. Zaehner, *Hinduism and Muslim Mysticism* (New York, 1969); S. Katz, "Language, Epistemology, and Mysticism, and other essays," in *Mysticism and Philosophical Analysis,* ed. S. Katz et al. (New York, 1978) In this case the language is not even primarily Christian. The basic language is from Jewish mysticism, though the subsequent exegesis about the identification of Christ with the figure on the throne is Christian; the vision of God enthroned is the goal of Jewish mystical speculation.

46. R. Scroggs, *The Last Adam: A Study in Pauline Anthropology* (Philadelphia, 1966) pp. 75–114.

47. See J. D. G. Dunn, *Jesus and the Spirit* (Philadelphia, 1975) p. 322.

48. Ibid., p. 327.

49. F. O. Francis, "Humility and Angelic Worship in Col. 2:18," *ST* 16 (1962)

109–34; F. O. Francis and W. A. Meeks, *Conflict at Colossae: A Problem in the Interpretation of Early Christianity Illustrated by Selected Modern Studies* (SBLSBS 4; Missoula, Mont., 1975 [rev. ed.]); W. Carr, *Angels and Principalities: The Background, Meaning and Development of the Pauline Phrase: hai archai kai hai exousiai* (Cambridge, 1981); C. A Evans, "The Colossian Mystics," *Bib* 63 (1982) 188–205.

50. See the summary article of M. Smith, "Ascent to the Heavens and the Beginnings of Christianity," *Eranos Jahrbuch* 50 (1981) 403–29, as well as the works of Odeberg, Meeks, and Dahl.

51. See my *Two Powers*, pp. 205–19; also now Hurtado, *Binitarian.*

52. This was one of the consensual statements of the NEH conference on first-century Jewish messianism. The papers and agreements of the conference will be published in *The Messiah*, ed. J. H. Charlesworth, with J. Brownson, S. Kraftchik, and A. Segal (forthcoming).

53. See A. Segal, *Rebecca's Children: Judaism and Christianity in the Roman World* (Cambridge, Mass., 1986) pp. 60–67, 78–95 for a thumbnail sketch of this development.

54. A plausible history of tradition, locating the connection between Dan 7:13 and Jesus in the interpretation of the early church, has been suggested by D. Juel, *Messianic Exegesis* (Philadelphia, 1987).

55. J. J. Collins, "Apocalyptic Eschatology as the Transcendence of Death," *CBQ* 36 (1984) 21–43. See also A. F. Segal, "Heavenly Ascent in Hellenistic Judaism, Early Christianity and Their Environment," *ANRW* II.23.2 (1980) 1334–94; idem, "'He Who Did not Spare his Own Son . . .': Jesus, Paul and the Akedah," in *From Jesus to Paul: Studies in Honour of Francis Wright Beare*, ed. Peter Richardson and John C. Hurd (Waterloo, Ontario, 1984) pp. 169–84.

56. As a summary, see Rowland, *Christian Origins;* idem, "The Influence of the First Chapter of Ezekiel on Jewish and Early Christian Literature" (Diss., Cambridge University, 1974); idem, "The Vision of the Risen Christ," *JTS* 31 (1980) 1–11; Black. "Throne-Theophany," in *Jews, Greeks, and Christians*, ed. Hamerton-Kelly and Scroggs; S. Kim, *The Son of Man as the Son of God* (Tübingen, 1983); Fossum, *Name;* Segal, *Two Powers*, pp. 182–219; in *Binitarian*, Hurtado agrees with my view of the novelty of the Christian interpretation within a general context in which such identifications were possible. Indeed, in *One God* he takes the claim of the uniqueness of worshiping the second power much further than I have done. While Hurtado may have overlooked occasional examples of angelolatry in sectarian Judaism, his point is well taken. Granting to Christ worship as a divinity was characteristic of early Christianity, even in the eyes of its detractors, while other groups with angelic heroes seem more circumspect about offering prayer to them.

57. See now Juel, *Messianic Exegesis.*

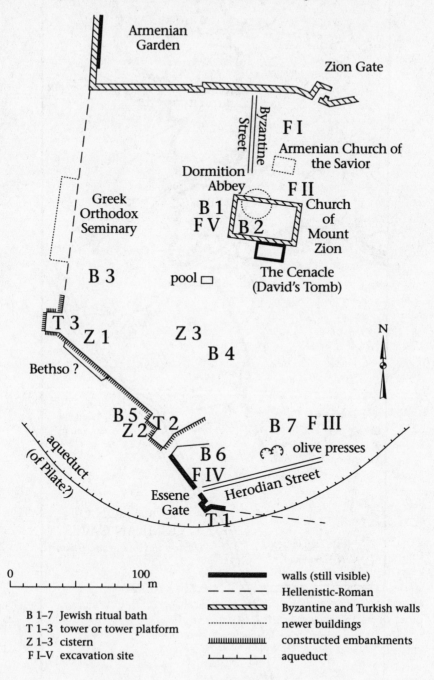

JERUSALEM: ALLEGED ESSENE QUARTER

Armenian Garden

Zion Gate

Byzantine Street

F I

Armenian Church of the Savior

Dormition Abbey

F II

B 1

F V

B 2

Church of Mount Zion

Greek Orthodox Seminary

B 3

pool

The Cenacle (David's Tomb)

T 3

Z 1

Z 3

B 4

Bethso ?

B 5

Z 2

T 2

B 7 F III

olive presses

B 6

F IV

Essene Gate

Herodian Street

T 1

aqueduct (of Pilate?)

N

0   100 m

B 1–7 Jewish ritual bath
T 1–3 tower or tower platform
Z 1–3 cistern
F I–V excavation site

walls (still visible)
Hellenistic-Roman
Byzantine and Turkish walls
newer buildings
constructed embankments
aqueduct

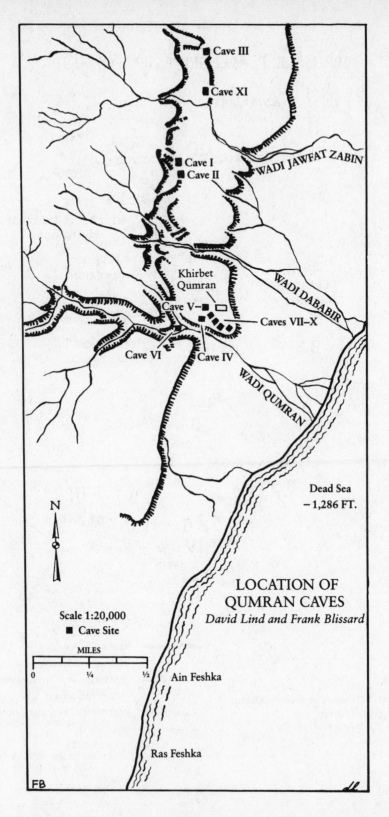

Cave III

Cave XI

WADI JAWFAT ZABIN

Cave I
Cave II

WADI DABABIR

Khirbet
Qumran

Cave V

Caves VII–X

Cave VI

Cave IV

WADI QUMRAN

Dead Sea
− 1,286 FT.

N

LOCATION OF
QUMRAN CAVES
David Lind and Frank Blissard

Scale 1:20,000
■ Cave Site

MILES

0   ¼   ½

Ain Feshka

Ras Feshka

FB

DRAWING OF THE QUMRAN RUINS
David Lind with Frank Blissard

Drawing of the Qumran Ruins (loci numbers from R. de Vaux)

A	Entrance of the aqueduct		
B	Main water canal		
C	Western wall of the settlement		
D	Western retaining wall	71, 91, 117, 118	Large cisterns
E	Eastern wall near cemetery	68, 138	Baths (?)
1-2	Upper rooms	97	Stables (?)
8-11	Tower	64	Potter's kiln
13	Steps leading up to the terrace and the upper rooms of loc. 1, 2, and 30	77	Great Room (for assemblies and meals)
4	Room with low benches (a council chamber?)	86, 89	Pantry for Great Room
		100	Mill (where wheat and barley were ground)
30	Scriptorium (two ink wells and a table were found in the debris on the ground level)	110	Cistern from 8th–6th century B.C.E.
38-41	Kitchen	111	Courtyard
49	Large cistern	120–123	Storerooms (loc. 120 disclosed 561 pieces of silver hidden in three pots)
52	Laundry		
58	Large cistern	125	Workshop
70, 75	Potter's laboratory	132, 137	Decantation basins

331

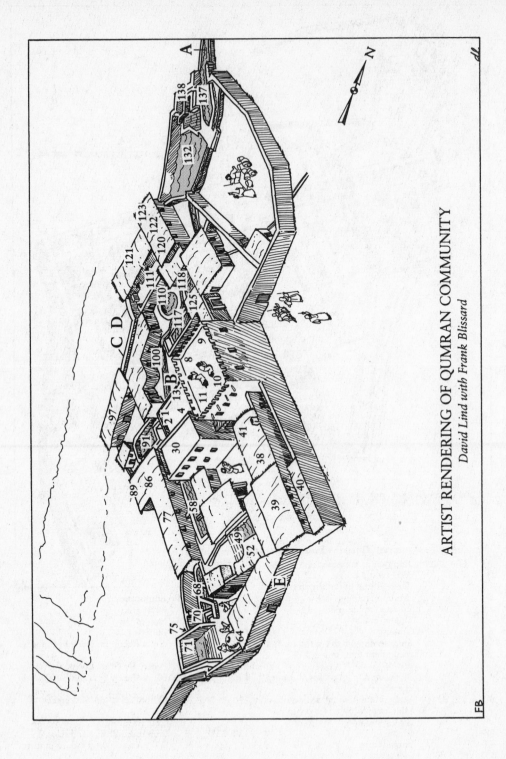

ARTIST RENDERING OF QUMRAN COMMUNITY

David Lind with Frank Blissard

Selected Bibliography

Allegro, J. M. "Jesus and Qumran: The Dead Sea Scrolls." In *Jesus in History and Myth*, ed. R. J. Hoffmann and G. A. Larue. Buffalo, N.Y., 1986. Pp. 89–96.

Ashton, J. "Qumran and Christianity." *Month* 42 (1969) 257–66.

Aune, D. "A Note on Jesus' Messianic Consciousness and 11QMelchizedek." *EvQ* 45 (1973) 161–65.

Barr, J. "Which Language Did Jesus Speak?—Some Remarks of a Semitist." *BJRL* 53 (1970) 9–29.

Barrick, W. B. "The Rich Man from Arimathea (Matt. 27:57–60) and 1QIsa." *JBL* 96 (1977) 235–39.

Baumgarten, J. M. "Does *TLH* in the Temple Scroll Refer to Crucifixion?" *JBL* 91 (1972) 472–81.

———. "The Duodecimal Courts of Qumran, Revelation, and the Sanhedrin." *JBL* 95 (1976) 59–78.

Beckwith, R. T. "St. Luke, the Date of Christmas and the Priestly Courses at Qumran." *RQ* 9 (1977) 73–94.

———. "Daniel 9 and the Date of Messiah's Coming in Essene, Hellenistic, Pharisaic, Zealot and Early Christian Computation." *RQ* 10 (1981) 521–52.

Benoit, P. "Note sur les fragments grecs de la grotte 7 de Qumrân." *RB* 79 (1972) 321–24.

———. "Nouvelle note sur les fragments grecs de la grotte 7 de Qumrân." *RB* 80 (1973) 5–12.

Berger, K. "Hartherzigkeit und Gottes Gesetz: Die Vorgeschichte des antijüdischen Vorwurfs in Mc 10:5." *ZNW* 61 (1970) 1–47.

Bernstein, N. J. "'ky qllt 'lhym tlwy' (Deut. 21:23): A Study in Early Jewish Exegesis." *JQR* 74 (1983) 21–45.

Betz, O. *What Do We Know About Jesus? The Bedrock of Fact Illuminated by the Dead Sea Scrolls.* Trans. M. Kohl. London, 1968.

———. "Die Bedeutung der Qumranschriften für die Evangelien des Neuen Testaments." *BK* 40 (1985) 54–64.

Black, M., ed. *The Scrolls and Christianity.* London, 1969.

Braun, M. "The Significance of Qumran for the Problem of the Historical Jesus." In *The Historical Jesus and the Kerygmatic Christ: Essays on the New Quest of the Historical Jesus,* ed. C. E. Braaten and R. A. Harrisville. New York, 1964. Pp. 69–78.

———. "Jesus und der qumranische Lehrer." In *Qumran und das Neue Testament.* Tübingen, 1966. Vol. 2, pp. 54–74.

Brooke, G. J. "The Amos-Numbers Midrash (CD 7:13b–8:1a) and Messianic Expectation." *ZAW* 92 (1980) 397–404.

Brownlee, W. H. "Jesus and Qumran." In *Jesus and the Historian,* ed. F. T. Trotter. Philadelphia, 1968. Pp. 52–81.

Bruce, F. F. "The Dead Sea Scrolls and Early Christianity." *BJRL* 49 (1966) 69–90.

Buchanan, G. W. "Jesus and Other Monks of New Testament Times." *RelLife* 48 (1979) 136–42.

Burgmann, H. "Antichrist–Antimessias: Das Makkabäer Simon?" *Judaica* 36 (1980) 152–74.

Carmignac, J. *Le docteur de justice et Jésus-Christ.* Paris, 1957.

———. "Les apparitions de Jésus ressuscité et le calendrier biblico-qumrânien." *RQ* 7 (1971) 483–504.

Casciaro Ramírez, J. M. "El tema del 'Misterio' divino en la 'Regla de la Comunidad' de Qumran." *ScrT* 7 (1975) 481–97.

Charlesworth, J. H. "The Historical Jesus in Light of Writings Contemporaneous with Him." In *ANRW* II.25.1, ed. W. E. Haase. Berlin, New York, 1982. Pp. 451–76.

———. "Research on the Historical Jesus Today: Jesus and the Pseudepigrapha, the Dead Sea Scrolls, the Nag Hammadi Codices, Josephus, and Archeology." *PSB* N.S. 6 (1985) 98–115.

———. "Jesus and the Dead Sea Scrolls." In *Jesus Within Judaism,* by J. H. Charlesworth. ABRL 1. Garden City, N.Y., 1988. Pp. 54–76.

———. "The Righteous Teacher and the Historical Jesus: A Study of the Self-Understandings of Two Jewish Charismatics." In *Perspectives on Christology,* ed. W. P. Weaver. Nashville, 1989. Pp. 73–94.

Charlesworth, J. H., ed. *Jesus' Jewishness: Exploring the Place of Jesus in Early Judaism.* New York, 1991.

Daniel, C. "'Faux Prophètes': Surnom des Esséniens dans le Sermon sur la Montagne." *RQ* 7 (1969) 45–79.

——. "Les Esséniens et l'arrière-fond historique de la parabole du Bon Samaritain." *NovT* 11 (1969) 71–104.

David, K. "The Development of the Concept of Salvation in the Qumran Community and its Significance for our Understanding of Salvation in the New Testament." *IJT* 30 (1981) 131–37.

Delcor, H. "Le Targum de Job et l'aramean du temps de Jésus." *RScRel* 47 (1973) 232–61.

Delorme, J. "Lecture de l'Évangile selon saint Marc." *CEv* 54 (1973) 3–123.

Derrett, J. Duncan M. "New Creation: Qumran, Paul, the Church, and Jesus." *RQ* 13 (1988) 597–608.

Díez Merino, L. "El suplicio de la cruz en la literatura judía intertestamenta." *SBFLA* 26 (1976) 31–120.

Drane, J. W. "Some Ideas of Resurrection in the New Testament Period." *TynBul* 24 (1973) 99–110.

Emerton, J. A. "The Problem of Vernacular Hebrew in the First Century A.D. and the Language of Jesus." *JTS* 24 (1973) 1–23.

Fee, G. D. "Some Dissenting Notes on 7Q5=Mark 6:52–53." *JBL* 92 (1973) 109–12.

Feuillet, A. "Les hommes de bonne volonté ou les hommes que Dieu aime: Note sur la traduction de Luc 2, 14B." *BAGu* 91–92.

Fitzmyer, J. A. "The Purpose of Genealogies." *TS* 30 (1969) 700–704.

——. "The Contribution of Qumran Aramaic to the Study of the New Testament." *NTS* 20 (1974) 382–407.

——. "The Matthean Divorce Texts and Some New Palestinian Evidence." *TS* 37 (1976) 197–226. Reprinted in *To Advance the Gospel: New Testament Studies* (New York, 1981).

——. "Crucifixion in Ancient Palestine, Qumran Literature, and the New Testament." *CBQ* 40 (1978) 493–513. Reprinted in *To Advance the Gospel: New Testament Studies* (New York, 1981).

——. "The Dead Sea Scrolls and the New Testament After Thirty Years." *TD* 29 (1981) 351–67.

——. "The Ascension of Christ and Pentecost." *TS* 45 (1984) 409–40.

Flusser, D. "The Last Supper and the Essenes." *Immanuel* 2 (1973) 23–27.

——. "Some Notes to the Beatitudes (Matt. 5:3–12, Luke 6:20–26)." *Immanuel* 8 (1978) 37–47.

——. "The Hubris of the Antichrist in a Fragment from Qumran." *Immanuel* 10 (1980) 31–37.

——. *Die rabbinischen Gleichnisse und der Gleichniserzähler Jesus.* Judaica et Christiana 4. Bern, 1981. Pp. 265–81.

Flusser, D., and S. Safrai. "The Slave of Two Masters." *Immanuel* 6 (1976) 30–33.

Ford, J. M. "Mary's Virginitas Post–Partum and Jewish Law." *Bib* 54 (1973) 269–72.

——. "'Crucify him, crucify him' and the Temple Scroll." *ExpT* 87 (1976) 275–78.

Galot, J. "La motivation évangélique du célibat." *Gregorianum* 53 (1972) 731–58.

García Martínez, F. "4QpNah y la Crucifixión: Nueva hipótesis de reconstrucción de 4Q 169 3–4 i, 4–8." *Estudios Bíblicos* 38 (1979) 221–35.

Garnet, P. "O'Callaghan's Fragments: Our Earliest New Testament Texts?" *EvQ* 45 (1973) 6–12.

Gnilka, J. "Jesus —ein Essener? Jesus und Qumran." *BK* 26 (1971) 2–5.

Groh, J. E. "The Qumran Meal and the Last Supper." *CTM* 41 (1970) 279–95.

Hemer, C. J. "New Testament Fragments at Qumran?" *TynBul* 23 (1972) 125–28.

Higgins, A. G. McL. "A Few Thoughts on the Dead Sea Scrolls." *Modern Church* 23 (1972) 125–28.

Jeremias, G. "Der Lehrer der Gerechtigkeit und der historische Jesus." In *Der Lehrer der Gerechtigkeit*. Göttingen, 1963. Pp. 319–53.

Kee, H. C. "The Bearing of the Dead Sea Scrolls on Understanding Jesus." In *Jesus in History and Myth,* ed. R. J. Hoffmann and G. A. Larue. Buffalo, N.Y., 1986. Pp. 54–75.

Kirchschläger, W. "Exorzismus in Qumran?" *Kairos* 18 (1976) 135–53.

Klein, R. W. "Aspects of Intertestamental Messianism." *CTM* 43 (1972) 507–17.

Lapide, P. "Insights from Qumran into the Languages of Jesus." *RevQ* 8 (1975) 483–501.

Limbeck, M. "Flucht oder Annahme? Das Beispiel Jesu in der Auseinandersetzung mit dem Bösen." *BK* (1975) 41–43.

Lohfink, G. "Der Ursprung der christlichen Taufe." *RQ* 156 (1976) 35–54.

Longenecker, R. N. "The Messianic Secret in the Light of Recent Discoveries." *EvQ* 41 (1969) 207–15.

Maillot, A. "Notules sur Luc 16/8b–9." *ETR* 44 (1969) 127–30.

Manrique, A. "El bautismo en el judaísmo contemporáneo de Jesús." *CD* 189 (1976) 207–20.

Merkel, H. "Auf den Spuren des Urmarkus? Ein neuer Fund und seine Beurteilung." *ZTK* 71 (1974) 123–44.

Murphy, R. E. "The Dead Sea Scrolls and New Testament Comparisons." *CBQ* 18 (1956) 263–72.

Mueller, J. R. "The Temple Scroll and the Gospel Divorce Texts." *RQ* 10 (1980) 247–56.

O'Callaghan, J. "New Testament Papyri in Qumran Cave 7?" *Supplement to JBL* 91 (1972) No. 2.

Parker, P. "7Q5: Enthält das Papyrusfragment 5 aus der Höhle 7 von Qumran einen Markustext?" *EA* 48 (1972) 467–69.

Peretto, E. "Ricerche su Mt 1–2." *Marianum* 31 (1969) 140–247.

Pickering, S. R., and R. R. E. Cook. *Has a Fragment of the Gospel of Mark Been Found at Qumran?* Papyrology and Historical Perspectives 1. Sydney, 1989.

Plessis, P. J. "Love and Perfection in Matt. 5:43–48." *Neot* 1 (1967) 28–34.

Rubinkiewicz, R. "The Parable of the Wedding Garment (Mt. 22:11–13) and 1 Enoch 10:4." [in Polish] *RTK* 27 (1980) 53–69.

Sabugal, S. "1Q Regla de la Comunidad IX, 11: Dos Ungidos, un Mesias." *RQ* 8 (1974) 417–23.

Schuller, E. "The Dead Sea Scrolls and the Bible." *BibToday* 21 (1983) 162–69.

Stegemann, H. "Some Aspects of Eschatology in Texts from the Qumran Community and in the Teachings of Jesus." In *Biblical Archaeology Today: Proceedings of the International Congress on Biblical Archaeology (Jerusalem, April 1984)*, ed. J. Amitai. Jerusalem, 1985. Pp. 408–26.

Stolz, F. "Psalm 22: Alttestamentliches Reden vom Menschen und neutestamentliches Reden von Jesus." *ZTK* 77 (1980) 129–48.

Strecker, G. "Die historische und theologische Problematik der Jesusfrage." *EvT* 29 (1969) 453–76.

———. "Die Makarismen der Bergpredigt." *NTS* 17 (1971) 255–75.

Talmon, S. "Messianic Expectations at the Turn of the Era." *Face to Face* 10 (1983) 4–12.

Thiede, C. P. "7Q—Eine Rückkehr zu den neutestamentlichen Papyrusfragmenten in der siebten Höhle von Qumran." *Bib* 65 (1984) 538–59.

———. *Die älteste Evangelien-Handschrift?: Das Markus-Fragment von Qumran und die Anfänge der schriftlichen Überlieferung des Neuen Testaments.* Wuppertal, 1990 [2nd ed.].

Thiering, B. E. "The Qumran Interpretation of Ezekiel 4, 5–6." *AJBA* 1 (1969) 30–34.

———. "The Teacher of Righteousness and the Messiah in the Damascus Document." *AJBA* 1 (1971) 74–81.

———. *Redating the Teacher of Righteousness.* Australian and New Zealand Studies in Theology and Religion 1. Sydney, 1979.

———. "Inner and Outer Cleansing at Qumran as a Background to New Testament Baptism." *NTS* 26 (1980) 266–77.

———. *The Gospels and Qumran: A New Hypothesis.* Australian and New Zealand Studies in Theology 2. Sydney, 1981.

Vargas-Machuca, A. "Divorcio e indisolubilidad del matrimonio en la Sagrada Escritura." *Estudios Bíblicos* 39 (1981) 19–61.

Vermes, G. "The Impact of the Dead Sea Scrolls on the Study of the New Testament." *JJS* 27 (1976) 107–16.

Villalon, J. R. "Sources vétéro-documentaires de la doctrine qumranienne des deux Messies." *RQ* 8 (1972) 53–63.

Wacholder, B. Z. "Chronomessianism: The Timing of Messianic Movements and the Calendar of Sabbatical Cycles." *HUCA* 46 (1975) 201–18.

Wachter, L. "Jüdischer und christlicher Messianismus." *Kairos* 18 (1976) 119–34.

Wieder, N. "The 'Land of Damascus' and Messianic Redemption." *JJS* 20 (1969) 86–88.

Wolbert, W. "Die Liebe zum Nächsten, zum Feind und zum Sünder." *ThGl* 74 (1984) 262–82.

Yadin, Y. "Militante Herodianer aus Qumran: Die Essener zwingen Christen und Juden zum Umdenken." *LuthMonat* 18 (1979) 355–58.

Zeller, D. "Zu einer jüdischen Vorlage von Mt 13:52." *BZ* 20 (1976) 223–26.

Index of Scriptures Cited

*Indented first entries under a title refer to the complete work. Specific references follow flush left.

Index of Dead Sea Scrolls Cited

*Indented first entries under a title refer to the complete work. Specific references follow flush left.

347

Index of Other Ancient Writings Cited

The following index is organized according to seven major categories: (1) Apocrypha; (2) Old Testament Pseudepigrapha; (3) Graeco-Roman Literature; (4) Josephus and Philo; (5) Additional Early Christian and Gnostic Literature; (6) Other Early Jewish Literature; and (7) Other Ancient Writing. Within these groupings, the organization is either traditional/canonical (as with the Apocrypha) or alphabetical (as with the Old Testament Pseudepigrapha, Graeco-Roman literature, Josephus and Philo, and early Christian and gnostic literature), or a combination of traditional and alphabetical (as with the early Jewish literature).

*Indented first entries under a title refer to the complete work. Specific references follow flush left.

3. GRAECO-ROMAN LITERATURE

5. EARLY CHRISTIAN AND GNOSTIC LITERATURE

6. EARLY JEWISH LITERATURE

7.   OTHER ANCIENT WRITING

Index of Modern Authors

365